PHOTOGRAPHY
IN JAPAN 1853-1912

PHOTOGRAPHY
IN JAPAN 1853-1912

TERRY BENNETT

TUTTLE PUBLISHING
Tokyo • Rutland, Vermont • Singapore

Published by Tuttle Publishing, an imprint of Periplus Editions (HK) Ltd, with editorial offices at 364 Innovation Drive, North Clarendon, Vermont 05759, U.S.A. and 130 Joo Seng Road #06-01, Singapore 368357.

Library of Congress Control Number 2005934848
ISBN 10: 0 8048 3633 7
ISBN 13: 978 0 8048 3633 3

Printed in Singapore

Distributed by:

North America, Latin America and Europe
Tuttle Publishing
364 Innovation Drive
North Clarendon, VT 05759-9436 U.S.A.
Tel: 1 (802) 773-8930
Fax: 1 (802) 773-6993
info@tuttlepublishing.com
www.tuttlepublishing.com

Japan
Tuttle Publishing
Yaekari Building, 3rd Floor
5-4-12 Osaki
Shinagawa-ku
Tokyo 141 0032
Tel: (81) 03 5437-0171
Fax: (81) 03 5437-0755
tuttle-sales@gol.com

Asia Pacific
Berkeley Books Pte. Ltd.
130 Joo Seng Road #06-01
Singapore 368357
Tel: (65) 6280-1330
Fax: (65) 6280-6290
inquiries@periplus.com.sg
www.periplus.com

10 09 08 07 06
6 5 4 3 2 1

Page 1 Fig. 1. Anonymous, "Geisha Looking through a Graphoscope at a Cabinet Photograph," ca. 1910, hand-colored lithographed postcard. Rob Oechsle Collection. Graphoscopes were multipurpose magnifiers and binocular devices, which were also used for viewing *cartes de visite* and stereoviews.

Page 2 Fig. 2. Ueno Hikoma, "Samurai Harada Kiichi," Nagasaki, ca. 1870, large-format albumen print. Old Japan Picture Library.

Page 5 Fig. 3. Charles Leander Weed, "No. 5. River View in Nagasaki," 1867, mammoth-plate albumen print. Canadian Centre for Architecture, Montreal. This is the Nakashima River where Ueno Hikoma's house and studio were situated. Ueno would have been impressed and enthralled to see Weed employ his mammoth-plate technical skills. It is highly likely that Weed would have sought, and Ueno offered, his support and local geographical knowledge.

Pages 6–7 Fig. 4. Nadar (Gaspard Félix Tournachon, 1820–1910), "Members of the 1864 Ikeda Mission to France," Paris, 1864, large-format albumen print. Old Japan Picture Library. The mission leader, Ikeda Nagaoki (1837–79), is shown in the center. One of the key purposes of the mission was to negotiate the closure of Yokohama in order to protect Japan's silk trade. Ikeda failed to achieve this objective, and on his return to Japan was stripped of half of his estates.

Page 8 Fig. 5. Tomishige Rihei, "Suizenji Garden, Kumamoto," ca. 1874, large-format albumen print. Old Japan Picture Library.

Page 9 Fig. 6. Frederick Sutton, "Group of Ainu with Non-Ainu Japanese Official," Hokkaido, 1867, small-format albumen print. Nederlands Scheepvaartmuseum, Amsterdam. The significance of this photograph, taken in July 1867, together with one other similar image, is that they appear to be the only confirmed Bakumatsu-era images of Ainu. It is curious that no earlier Ainu photographs have surfaced since there were at least two commercial Japanese studios in operation in Hokkaido at this time. Sutton had some kind of commercial relationship with Felix Beato, who included the two images in his portfolio and published them from time to time.

Preface

This book was written with four objectives in mind: first, to provide collectors, photo-historians and curators with an up-to-date picture of the state of Japanese photo-history research, both in Japan and in the West; second, to provide biographical details of the early photographers, many of whom led extraordinary lives; third, to argue that the importance of identifying who took the photographs, and their motivations for doing so, is crucial in arriving at a deeper understanding of the subject; fourth, to provide important and practical research tools, in the Appendices, to enable identification of otherwise anonymous images to take place.

With respect to the Appendices, it was decided that it would be better to include the majority of these in a separate publication. A number of the Appendices are very lengthy and likely to appeal, in the main, to photo-historians and researchers. Inclusion here would have severely limited the general text and illustrations. In this book, therefore, the reader will occasionally be referred to the companion volume: Terry Bennett, *Old Japanese Photographs: Collectors' Data Guide*, Purley, Surrey: Old Japan, 2006.

The study of Japanese photo-history is a fast-developing field which is appealing to more and more researchers. Our relative closeness to the nineteenth century makes it possible for any determined and informed individual to make new discoveries. One can still meet, and interview, grandchildren of some of the photographers profiled in this book. In recent years, many books and articles have been written and new discoveries about the photographers and photographs are being made, both inside and outside Japan.

The writer's *Early Japanese Images* (1996) has, in many respects, been superseded and improved upon. For example, some writers have uncovered important new material on certain early photographers, whilst others have focused on a particular region of Japan, say Kanagawa or Kyushu, and the work of these authors has been mentioned elsewhere in this book. But in the last ten years, nothing of a comprehensive nature seems to have appeared which brings together the latest Japanese and Western research developments. Anne Wilkes Tucker et al.'s ground-breaking work, *The History of Japanese Photography* (2003), concentrates on Japanese photographers and says very little about the early Western pioneers. The present book attempts to address that need.

A major difficulty in studying Japanese photography is the language barrier. Getting access to, and then deciphering nineteenth-century Japanese text is beyond more than a handful of Western photo-historians. In fact, surprisingly few Japanese can confidently read a script that has changed a great deal over the last century. It also takes several years' study for a Westerner to gain any degree of competence in reading modern Japanese; a lot of hard work and constant practice are required to maintain any fluency since there are so many characters to remember – and forget. There are many Japanese, of course, who speak and read English very well. But it is tedious for them to absorb lengthy pieces of technical writing, particularly if written in the usual discursive and sometimes opaque style so enamored of our Victorian ancestors.

For more effective progress in this field to be made, a certain polarisation of research methodologies would seem to suggest itself. For example, almost nothing is known about the Japanese photographer Enami Tamotsu, or of the English photographer Charles Parker, and yet we know that both were significant figures. In trying to contact family descendants, success in tracing Enami's genealogical footsteps is more likely to materialize were a Japanese to attempt the task, just as it would be for a Western researcher to trace Parker's. In bringing out this book, the writer will feel satisfied if it is later judged to have succeeded in any one or more of the abovementioned objectives. The writer also apologizes in advance for any errors and would welcome any comments or new information addressed to: info@old-japan.co.uk

Contents

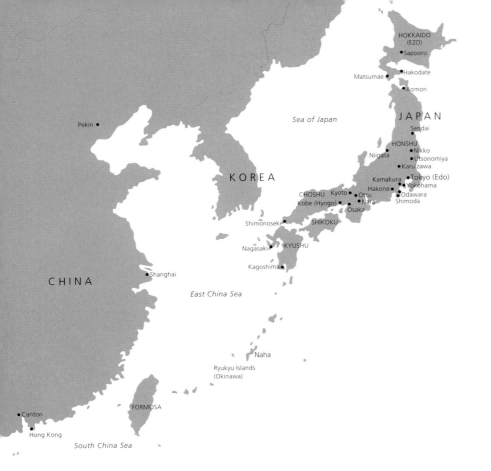

Photography Meets Japan

This book considers the photographers, Japanese and Western, who were involved in the early development of photography in Japan. The photographs that have survived from the late Edo or Bakumatsu period (1853–68) to the end of the Meiji era (1912) tell us much about Japanese photo-history and of Japan itself. Moreover, early photographs of any country and its people are now increasingly appreciated by historians for what they are: precious, sometimes unique visual records which can complement and add value to other contemporary written materials and artifacts. Arguably, though, there is something else that needs to be done before the full value of these old images can be realized. When an historian, for example, is poring over a nineteenth-century manuscript, it is undeniable that knowing the identity of its writer is very helpful, if not vital. The background and personality of the writer will also help in weighing up the significance of what is written, as well as putting it into some kind of historical or social perspective. Photography is no different.

When considering early images, we should try hard to identify the photographers and to learn something about their backgrounds. Doing so can tell us much about a photograph that might otherwise afford little or no information. Just to take one example. In Chapter 1 of this book, "A British Camera in Tokyo," there is a photograph by Jocelyn entitled "Japanese Commissioners." If we did not know the photographer, we would probably conclude that the image was most likely taken in Japan, sometime in the 1860s – and most likely by an amateur because of the poor print condition and the overall rather poor composition. With the discovery that the photographer was William Nassau Jocelyn, we immediately see the photograph in a different light and appreciate its historical importance. Yes, Jocelyn was an amateur; and whilst that might go some way towards explaining the indifferent composition, the reason for the print's poor condition is that the ship in which his equipment and chemicals were being transported suffered greatly in a typhoon off the Japanese coast. Knowing it is by Jocelyn tells us that the photograph is particularly early and we discover that it was taken in Edo (Tokyo) on August 26th, 1858, just after the commissioners had signed the draft treaty between Britain and Japan. Pursuing these revelations, we ascertain that this photograph is also the earliest known photographic paper print of Japan, and the first to be taken in Tokyo. An old and faded photograph, of unknown attribution, now being tied to the man who photographed it, transforms the meaning and value of the image beyond measure.

Although this may appear to be an extreme example, many others could be given. In any case, it serves to illustrate the writer's point. There is much in this book, therefore, about the lives of the photographers – although, of course, there is also a great deal that we do not yet know. Recently, it has been

Below Fig. 9. Felix Beato, "Governor of Nagasaki and Attendants," ca. 1864, hand-colored large-format albumen print. Author's Collection. The Governor, Hattori Tunesumi (1815–75), who held office from May 1863 until January 1865, is shown in the center. The standing foreigner is currently unidentified, as are the other Japanese.

possible to track some of the movements of Pierre Rossier, surely now one of the most significant personalities in early Japanese photography. But it is clear that what we do *not* know is preventing us from accurately dating many of his early photographs of both China and Japan. Given that these were the first published commercial views of these countries, establishing a more precise chronology of his travels is very important to photo-historians.

Because of the perceived importance in being able to attribute the authorship of such early Japanese photographs, this book, and the volume *Old Japanese Photographs: Collectors' Data Guide* (hereafter referred to as *OJP*) part company with others written on the subject. In the extensive Appendices to both books, there are various important sections which will assist historians, curators, collectors, and photo-dealers in identifying their images. For example, Appendix 1 in this work lists all of the known Pierre Rossier photographs taken in China and Japan. Although the backs of these photographs are numbered and captioned, there are no obvious clues to the publisher, least of all the photographer. This list will, for the first time, facilitate the identification of many of

these first commercial photographs of East Asia. William Saunders was one of the finest nineteenth-century photographers in the Far East, more usually known for his work in China, a country in which he lived for many years. In 1862, however, he visited Japan and compiled a portfolio of some ninety photographs, of which only three or four have so far been identified. *OJP* gives the full transcript of a contemporary description of this work which appeared at the time in an English language newspaper published in Japan. This key, difficult-to-access piece of writing should help uncover other images from this rare and important series. Another group of important photographs which is yet to be discovered is the series of lantern slides put together by the English photographer Frederick Sutton, covering the time he spent in Japan in 1866. A complete listing of these important images is given in *OJP*. From the year 1876 almost all Japanese photographs carried an identifying number which is visible today. A list of some 1200 of these, together with their associated photo-studios, was given in the writer's previous publication, *Early Japanese Images* (1996). *OJP*, however, gives a much extended inventory and provides the owner of a particular photograph,

02 CARRYING CHILDREN

Left Fig. 11. Mathew Brady, "Members of the First Japanese Embassy to the United States," 1860, Washington, large-format gelatin silver print, probably printed in the late nineteenth century. Author's Collection. Shown here are the senior members of the 77-strong group of Japanese emissaries who arrived in Washington in May 1860. The two seated central figures from left to right are Muragaki Norimasa (second envoy) and Shimmi Masaoki (chief envoy).

or photograph album, a greater chance of identifying the photo studio. Finally, *OJP* gives an index of Japanese stereoviews with unprecedented information on the subject matter, photographers, and publishers.

Some ten years ago, when the writer was researching for *Early Japanese Images*, it became clear that accessing and interpreting Japanese sources was going to present extraordinary difficulties. Apart from the obvious language barrier, it was quite common a century and more ago for Japanese to change their names, sometimes several times in one lifetime. Except for royalty and some of the aristocracy, registration of births, deaths, and marriages took place at the local temples. However, very little of this data seems to have survived due to frequent fires and World War II. The number of Japanese characters in common usage has fallen dramatically over the last century. Consequently, it is often difficult, even for a specialist, to interpret nineteenth-century documents. All of this must make Japan relatively impervious to the ever-increasing reach of the genealogist. From the photo-historian's point of view, researching the lives of Japanese photographers appears more difficult than doing so for their Western counterparts.

Notwithstanding the comments above, the list of publications by photo-historians in Japan over the last ten years seems to have grown exponentially. We know much more today about the early Japanese photographers thanks largely to the efforts of researchers and historians such as Fukagawa Masafumi, Goto Kazuo, Himeno Junichi, Hiraki Osamu, Iizawa

Kotaro, Ishiguro Keisho, Izakura Naomi, Kaneko Ryuichi, Kinoshita Naoyuki, Kuraishii Shino, Ozawa Takesi, Saito Takio, Takahashi Norihide, and Yokoe Fuminori, to name just a few. Saito Takio from the Yokohama Archives of History has also done much ground-breaking work in uncovering facts about some of the Western and Japanese photographers who worked in Yokohama.

With new discoveries also being made by Western photo-historians, it follows that any work will likely find itself in need of revision before too many years have passed. Nevertheless, one of the purposes of this book is to present the latest consolidated picture of Japan's photo-history, in so far as the subject is currently understood by today's photo-historians.

In carrying out the research for this book, the writer was truly surprised by the number of early photographers who led such interesting and colorful lives. If we were to focus on just a few of the names, we might start with the Japanese and look at Nakahama Manjiro, who is not known as a photographer but rather as a famous castaway. Manjiro, as he is popularly known, was a simple fisherman whose boat drifted out of control in 1841 and who was shipwrecked with several colleagues on a tiny deserted island, which became their home for four months. Rescued by an American whaler, he was taken to America where he led an adventurous life as a whaler and gold prospector. Despite risking summary execution, he returned to Japan ten years later, where he was

imprisoned and interrogated. Released, he was an interpreter when Commodore Perry came in 1853 and again when he accompanied the 1860 Embassy to America. Returning the same year, Manjiro brought with him a daguerreotype camera and was one of the first Japanese to take successful pictures. Furthermore, Manjiro opened a commercial studio in Edo, albeit for a short time, sometime between 1860 and 1862. Certainly he was one of the first Japanese to do so – and subject to further research, it is even possible he was the first. There is, in any case, a suspicion in the writer's mind that Manjiro's role in the development of photography in Japan is not yet fully appreciated or understood.

Ukai Gyokusen, a samurai, has now arrived center stage after being belatedly recognized as probably the first Japanese to open a commercial studio. In later life he unaccountably buried several hundreds of his glass negatives and insured that when he died his body was buried alongside. Before being replaced by Ukai, Shimooka Renjo was known as the first professional Japanese photographer. Also of samurai stock, he left home at thirteen to become an artist but

ended up instead becoming fascinated by photography and desperate to learn its secrets. A talented artist, with claim to being Japan's first oil painter, he exchanged some paintings for an American photographer's camera and equipment and opened his studio in Yokohama. He was later associated with a number of commercial enterprises: the first omnibus service between Yokohama and Tokyo, the introduction of the *jinrikisha*, and possibly the first Japanese lithography business. Ueno Hikoma was the son of a wealthy merchant who had imported the first camera into Japan in 1848. His nineteenth-century Nagasaki studio was very popular with foreign visitors. Uchida Kuichi opened his first studio whilst still a teenager and soon became recognized as Japan's most talented photographer. Still in his mid-twenties, his reputation was sealed when he was requested to take the first official portraits of the Emperor and Empress. Just when he was on the point of gaining international recognition, he caught pneumonia and died at the age of thirty-two. Tamamura Kozaburo was probably the most commercially successful Japanese photographer – once famously receiving an order from America

for one million photographs! Kajima Seibei inherited his family's saké business and was one of the wealthiest men in Japan. He became literally obsessed with photography and managed to lose his business, his wealth, and his wife. Once, he had been known throughout Japan as the "millionaire photographer," but he ended his life in poverty and obscurity. It is not generally known that the famous novelist and poet Koda Rohan was also an enthusiastic amateur photographer and converted one of the rooms in his house to a darkroom.

Western photographers who came to Japan did so for a variety of reasons. Some, like the Austrian aristocrat Baron von Stillfried and the Italian adventurer Adolfo Farsari, took up photography professionally after arriving in the country. Others, like the wealthy Walter Clutterbuck and Francis Guillemard, were amateur photographers who liked to travel. Felix Beato was a world-famous war photographer when he arrived in 1863. He would stay in Japan for twenty years, making and losing his fortune several times over. Julia Brown, the missionary daughter of Samuel Brown, caused a scandal in the Yokohama community by becoming pregnant outside marriage. She was also an amateur photographer and is today recognized as Japan's first female photographer. Adolfo Farsari left Italy to escape his creditors and ended up in America fighting for the North in the civil war. He married a wealthy widow who gave him three children and then, fleeing an unhappy marriage, left his family and settled on a military career. After an eventful few years, he settled in Yokohama and taught himself photography. He opened a studio in 1885 and was very successful until a fire burnt it to the ground and simultaneously destroyed all of his stock and negatives. His wife traveled to Japan from America twice, begging him to return – once taking along one of their children – but was rebuffed on both occasions. Farsari's family in Italy had long given him up for dead when he wrote to them after an

absence of twenty-one years. Two years later he went home on a visit, taking his daughter but not her Japanese mother. He never returned to Japan. The author Jack London traveled to Japan in 1904 as a correspondent to cover the Russo-Japanese War and was already famous before he arrived. He was arrested for taking photographs in a sensitive military area. Karl Lewis was an ordinary American sailor who taught himself photography and opened the last Western studio in Japan in 1902. He was arrested after the attack on Pearl Harbor as a suspected American spy and died shortly afterwards, broken-hearted, when his Japanese wife predeceased him.

At the same time that photography was being introduced to Japan, the country was experiencing a period of fundamental political, social, and economic convulsions to be followed by rapid reform and modernization. The speed with which Japan moved from being a backward, feudal society to a modern, industrial, and military power is astounding. Whilst all of this was taking place, the early photographers, Western and Japanese, were able to record the people, places, and events on camera.

HISTORICAL BACKGROUND

By 1850 the 250-year-old ruling Tokugawa family were showing signs of weakness and vulnerability. The arrival of
Commodore Perry's fleet in 1853 was not helpful, and the
treaty which the shogun's government felt unable to refuse
had the effect of destabilizing its regime further. A complex
internal power struggle was taking place and the shogun's
enemies were circling.

It was back in the twelfth century that the Emperor of
Japan had been encouraged to surrender the day-to-day
management of state affairs to his supreme commander, or
shogun. The Emperor and his court were still the nominal
rulers, but in reality they became increasingly marginalized
and impotent. Shoguns, whose regimes were known as
bakufu or shogunate, were military dictators responsible for
maintaining the peace of the realm and protecting its bor-
ders. There were three such shogunates: the first was based
in Kamakura (1192–1333), the second in Muromachi, Kyoto
(1338–1573), and the last in Edo (now Tokyo) (1603–1867).
During the four centuries covering the first two shogunates,
competing regional warlords (or *daimyo*) often schemed and
fought with each other for the coveted position of shogun.
Intermittent civil wars culminated in the key battle of Sekigahara in 1600, which resulted in a decisive victory for
the Tokugawa clan. Tokugawa Iyeasu, the head of the clan,
accepted the title of shogun and his family ruled for the
next 250 years.

Iyeasu was ruthless and cunning. He eliminated some
of the *daimyo* who had opposed him at Sekigahara and confiscated or reduced the fiefs of others. Those *daimyo* known to
be loyal were given lands strategically positioned to protect
and strengthen the Tokugawa power base. They were called
the *fudai-daimyo* and were expected to keep a watch on the
former enemies known as the *tozama*, or outer lords. Iyeasu
also decreed that all *daimyo* must attend his court in Edo
once a year. When they were not resident in the capital,
they were required to leave their families there as effective
hostages. Many *tozama* were located on the northern and
western peripheries of Japan and the cost of maintaining
suitably impressive estates in Edo, and financing annual
processions to and from the capital, was considerable. While
this no doubt had the effect of weakening their financial
ability to equip and embark upon anti-government military
adventures, it did nothing to lessen their deep-seated resent-
ment and hatred for the ruling Tokugawa regime.

During the sixteenth and seventeenth centuries, Western
Christian missionaries had made some converts amongst
the *daimyo*. By the early 1600s the shogunate was becoming
increasingly concerned and suspicious about the real motives
of the missionaries and foreign traders. The loyalty of some
of the Christian *daimyo* was questioned and the result was a
series of persecutions which saw native converts and foreign
missionaries tortured and executed. A rebellion at Shimabara
was ruthlessly put down and Portuguese and Spanish traders
and missionaries were expelled from the country. The only
foreigners allowed to live in Japan were a handful of Chinese
traders at a small enclave in Nagasaki, and the Dutch. Prior
to the general expulsions, the Dutch and the British enjoyed
the relative freedom of the trading post at Hirado, north of
Nagasaki. The British left of their own accord, in 1623, as the
trading venture had ended in failure. The Dutch were now

moved to Deshima, a tiny three-acre, artificially constructed island in Nagasaki Harbor, connected to the mainland by a carefully guarded bridge. There the Dutch were incarcerated and lived and traded for more than two centuries, comforted only in the knowledge of the monopoly they held over Western trade with Japan (Fig. 12).

From 1639 Japan was effectively isolated from the outside world. But the Japanese were not wholly ignorant of developments in the West as information did reach them through the Dutch at Deshima. A tradition for *rangaku* or Western learning had developed amongst certain Japanese scholars, and intercourse with the Dutch on Deshima was permitted for the study of subjects such as the Dutch language, Western medicine, surveying, and military technology. The shogunate would, therefore, have been well aware of the growing industrial and military might of the Western powers. News about the Opium War of 1839–42, and the British destruction of the Chinese Navy, would have been received in horror and disbelief. What would have really made an impression, however, was the Chinese acquiescence in ceding territory (Hong Kong) to the victors.

By the early nineteenth century, Japan's isolationist policy was becoming untenable. As Hugh Cortazzi in *Victorians in Japan* (1987) explains, the Industrial Revolution had created enormous production facilities in the West, and new markets were necessary. Increased wealth expanded consumers' appetites for foreign products, and the rapid development of the China trade would have encouraged many to look for other Far Eastern markets. The American Pacific coast was opening up and an exponential increase in shipping in the East Asian seas would have been only too evident to the Japanese. The

expansion of whaling in the North Pacific brought increasing numbers of American whalers to the coasts of northern Japan. The refusal of the Japanese to replenish stocks of food and water, or to allow such ships to shelter from storms at sea, was becoming unacceptable to the American and European authorities. The mistreatment of shipwrecked mariners aroused public indignation in the West and had the effect of putting pressure on the policy-makers to take action. Meanwhile, in 1853, having successfully colonized both Siberia and Kamchatka, the Russians were seeking to expand southwards and were preparing for an expedition to Japan.

As we have seen, the Tokugawa shogunate had ruled Japan for some 250 years and the policy of national seclusion had helped in shoring up its power base. Intelligence about the growing numbers of Westerners resident at Hong Kong and in China's treaty ports would nevertheless have filtered through to the authorities, and the occasional sightings of foreign warships sailing around Japan's coastline would not have felt comfortable. It is certain that the Dutch would have warned the Japanese about the proposed American Japan Expedition. Nevertheless, the arrival in Edo Bay of Commodore Perry and his four American warships on July 8th, 1853 would have been nothing short of a political nightmare.

Commodore Matthew Calbraith Perry (1794–1858) was the highest ranking officer in the US navy (Fig. 13). His mission was to make three demands: that future shipwrecked mariners be treated humanely; the opening of one or more ports for provisions and fuel; and the opening of one or more ports for trade by sale or barter. His orders from President Fillmore were to be firm and to only use military force in self-defense. Perry's expedition was a calculated risk. A

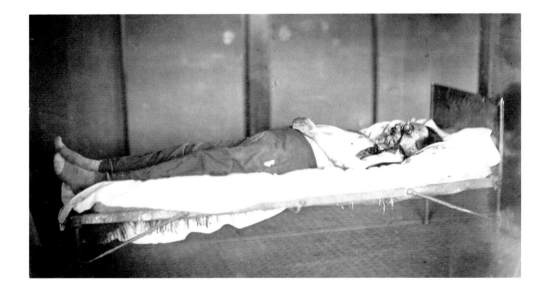

point-blank refusal by the Japanese to negotiate was a distinct possibility. Perry did his homework and read all that was published on Japan. He knew that the Japanese had issued an edict in 1825 which stated that any foreign ships entering Japanese waters would be fired upon and anyone setting foot on shore would be arrested and executed.

There were nine days of tense negotiations, during which time Perry refused to meet with anyone less than an emissary of the Emperor. Finally, Perry landed a force of around 350 men and presented a letter from the President of the United States, which contained the above-mentioned demands. The waiting reception included 4000–5000 Japanese troops. Imperiously, Perry announced that he would return in the spring, with a larger force, to receive an answer. The squadron then sailed to Hong Kong and Macau and waited. Hearing that the Russians were heading for Japan, Perry brought forward

his plans and returned in February 1854. This time he had a fleet of nine warships and 1600 sailors and marines, representing a quarter of the total US navy. The Japanese acceded to most, but not all, of his demands, and the Kanagawa Treaty was signed on March 31st, 1854 and Perry's mission was accomplished. The ports of Shimoda and Hakodate were opened to receive American ships in the case of distress. The Americans secured the right to station a consul at Shimoda from 1856, but did not succeed in convincing the Japanese to trade. Nevertheless, the Japanese now found it difficult to resist similar treaties with other countries. Within a few years, agreement was reached whereby treaty ports would, in fact, be opened for trade and foreign residence on July 1st, 1859. These ports were Nagasaki, Kanagawa (soon to be replaced by Yokohama), and Hakodate (Figs. 15, 18).

When foreigners duly began to arrive and settle, they

were generally unwelcome, reviled, and targets for assassination (Figs. 16, 17). But the foreigners had come to trade, and trade they would. They were tough-minded merchants who were not easily intimidated. Besides, they could always call on their governments for support in upholding their treaty rights. Powerful military assistance from ships on the China Station was never far away. Sometimes it was needed, and sometimes not.

The Chinese had tried several times to resist Western encroachment; but each defeat brought new demands from the Western barbarians, loss of face, and increasing danger of piecemeal colonization. The Japanese wanted to avoid any such fate. They would therefore modernize, acquire the same military power and technology, and then discuss trade on their own terms. But this would take time, and meanwhile there were acute internal political problems to resolve.

By 1867 the anti-Tokugawa forces were in open revolt. They rallied behind the cause of destroying the shogunate and reinstating the full powers of the Emperor. A civil war erupted, the Tokugawas were defeated, and the Emperor Meiji was given full powers and moved into the shogun's palace in Edo – now renamed as Tokyo.

Although it probably would have happened under the Tokugawas in any case, a period of unprecedented reform and modernization began. No one, however, least of all Perry, could have predicted the speed with which Japan would transform its social, political, and military structure. No country before, or since, has ever achieved such a feat. These changes had their own momentum, which would continue beyond the death of the Emperor in 1912 and have unforeseen consequences for Japan, and the world as a whole. But that is, as they say, another story.

CHAPTER 1

1850s
The First Images

In 1839 the Frenchman Louis Daguerre announced his invention of the daguerreotype and practical photography was born. How soon after that was the art practiced in Japan? There is no definite answer to this question, but Japanese scholars now agree that a daguerreotype camera was imported through the Dutch trading settlement on Deshima Island, Nagasaki, in 1848. The importer was the Japanese merchant Ueno Shunnojo, whose son Hikoma would later become one of the first professional Japanese photographers. A year later, the camera, together with chemicals and equipment, was sold to the powerful Shimazu Nariakira, lord of the Satsuma domain, and this *daimyo* began photographic experiments in earnest, as described in Himeno Junichi's "Encounters with Foreign Photographers" (2003).

Japan had been closed to the outside world for over 200 years. It was forbidden on pain of death to leave the country, and foreigners were not allowed to take up residence, with the exception of some Chinese traders confined to a small area of Nagasaki. Ships were turned away – by force, if necessary. Limited trade was conducted through the Okinawan Islands, hundreds of miles south of the mainland; and Okinawa would not officially become part of the Japanese Empire until 1879. The only other place where foreigners lived was Deshima, an artificial three-acre island constructed in Nagasaki Harbor by the Tokugawa shogunate between 1634 and 1636. Originally prepared for the Portuguese, the Dutch were ordered there in 1639 following the expulsion from Japan of all other Westerners. The Dutch were tolerated since they did not propagate Christianity. Deshima was connected to the mainland by a carefully guarded bridge, and the inhabitants were kept under strict and constant surveillance. In these claustrophobic conditions, the Dutch lived and traded for more than two centuries, jealously guarding their monopoly on trade between Japan and the West.

Although serious photographic experiments on the mainland began in 1849, no extant photograph taken by a Japanese can be dated earlier than 1857. The evidence is that the Japanese had great difficulty in mastering the art in those early years. This should not really surprise us. Photography in the 1840s and 1850s was a technically demanding exercise, even for seasoned professionals. Even after 1851, and the invention of wet-plate collodion photography where photographic prints could be produced on albumenized paper, working in the Far East necessitated coping with the general lack of ready chemicals and equipment and a climate which could, and did, play havoc with the chemicals that were available.

The typical camera at that time was a heavy wooden box fitted with a fragile glass lens. A pristine glass plate would need to be evenly coated with a wet-collodion solution and then sensitized in a darkroom with silver nitrate. The glass plate was then carefully inserted into the camera and the lens cap was taken away to expose the plate to the view the lens had been pointing at. Estimating the appropriate exposure time, which could be anything from a few seconds to a few minutes, was largely a matter of lighting conditions, intuition, experience, and luck. The lens cap would then be replaced and the glass plate removed and taken back to the darkroom for further chemical treatment. The aim here was to "fix" the image on the plate, which then became the glass negative. If the process had been successful, then prints could be taken from the negative. But even this printing required a significant degree of skill and dexterity.

Imagine, also, the various accessories which would be an essential part of any photographer's baggage. Apart from the camera and darkroom (a portable tent if traveling), he would need a tripod, various lenses, a large number of fragile glass plates, bottles of chemicals, and fresh water. These hard-to-get and relatively expensive chemicals would need to be mixed in the right proportions. No wonder that early photography in Japan got off to a slow start.

THE CHINA CONNECTION

How does this progress measure up to what was happening in China? There have always been important historical links between these two countries, and Japan has been enriched in the past by the importation of Chinese art, ideas, and culture. This book will refer, from time to time, to Chinese photography and photographers since, as we shall see, Japanese photography benefited from the close proximity of an established foreign community, which included a number of experienced practitioners.

Foreigners had encroached on Chinese territory following that country's defeat in the First Opium War of 1839–42. This resulted in the 1842 Treaty of Nanking, which opened up, for British trade and residence, the five ports of Amoy, Canton, Foochow, Ningpo, and Shanghai. Hong Kong Island was also ceded to Britain and it should be remembered that Portugal had been in de facto control of Macau since the mid-sixteenth century. The earliest recorded reference to photography in China is contained in the journal of Harry Parkes quoted in S. Lane-Poole and F. V. Dickins's *The Life of Sir Harry Parkes* (1894, Vol. 1, p. 31). In his journal entry for July 16th, 1842, the fourteen-year-old Parkes writes: "Major Malcolm and Dr. Woosnam took a sketch of the place to-day on their daguerreotype. I cannot understand it at all: but on exposing a highly

polished steel plate to the sun by the aid of some glass or other it takes the scene before you on to the plate and by some solution it will stay on the plate for years. It is no use me trying to describe it, it is quite a mystery." The photograph taken was of an unnamed town on the banks of the Yang-tse Kiang River, up which the British Expeditionary Force was sailing towards Nanking. Parkes and the daguerreotypists were on board HMS *Queen*. Major Malcolm was private secretary to Sir Henry Pottinger and was tasked with taking the signed 1842 Treaty of Nanking to England.[1]

Another early mention is given in Jules Itier's book *Journal d'un voyage en Chine* (1848). Itier described taking daguerreotypes in Macao and Canton in 1844. The earliest reference to a photo studio in China is that of a Mr West, whose Hong Kong establishment was advertised in the *China Mail* on March 6th, 1845:

MR. WEST BEGS LEAVE TO INFORM THE INHABITANTS OF VICTORIA THAT HE HAS OPENED A PHOTOGRAPHIC OR DAGUERREOTYPE ROOM IN PEEL STREET, NEAR QUEEN'S ROAD. HIS ROOM WILL BE OPEN FROM 10AM UNTIL 4PM. SINGLE MINIATURES $3. $2 CHARGED FOR EACH ADDITIONAL HEAD IN A GROUP.

It is possible that the earliest surviving photographic print of China is of the Five-Story Pagoda, Canton, apparently taken by Dr John McCosh in 1851. This salted paper print, from a calotype negative, is illustrated in Clark Worswick's *Imperial China* (1978, p. 55). The earliest dated photograph taken by a Chinese is a daguerreotype portrait of General Ko-Lin, which was auctioned in Christie's London on October 19th, 1994. The studio's printed label on this 1853 image carries the name of the Shanghai photographer Lai Chong. Another early view is an 1857 photograph of the town of Canton just prior to the allied bombardment (Fig. 21).

By the time that Japan had reluctantly opened the treaty ports of Yokohama, Nagasaki, and Hakodate in July 1859, photography in China had been practiced for around seventeen years. Photographic activity there, however, was limited to only a handful of photo studios, which were invariably adjuncts to their owners' main businesses, which could be anything from watch repairing to running a general store. However, the population of the various China coast settlements was increasing steadily and the demand for photography was consequently rising, albeit slowly (Fig. 20).

How did these photographers assess the opportunities in the newly opened Japan? Based on their experiences in China, they would have been cautious. They would have known that early residents' priorities, like those in China before them, would have to be focused on the scramble to find accommodation and business opportunities. Not many would have the time or inclination to patronize portrait studios. Nevertheless, as we shall see in the next chapter, there were those who were enterprising enough to try. Orrin Freeman and William Saunders would set out from Shanghai, and Charles Parker from Hong Kong. Pierre Rossier, however, was ahead of them all. On instructions from his employers in London, he moved into Japan just as soon as it was opened.

CASTAWAYS: FIRST IMAGES OF JAPANESE

Until just a few years ago, it was thought that the first ever photographs of Japanese subjects were those taken in 1853 by the American photographer Eliphalet M. Brown, who accompanied Commodore Perry on the expedition that opened up Japan to the West. While Brown may well have been the first to obtain successful photographs inside Japan, he was not the first to photograph a Japanese subject.

At a New York auction in April 1996, the writer acquired a daguerreotype of a Japanese man who was described as being one of the members of the 1860 Japanese Embassy to the United States (Fig. 19). Although this was quite late for a daguerreotype, the New York studio of C. D. Fredricks was known to have photographed at least one member of the Embassy using this format (see list of extant Japanese daguerreotypes in the writer's *Old Japanese Photographs – OJP*). However, the shabbiness of the subject's costume was more suggestive of someone of low social rank, and the image seemed earlier than stated. There was also a distinct resemblance to four other daguerreotypes of similar subjects held by the Yokohama Museum of Art and Kawasaki City Museum. These images, which are illustrated and discussed in Ozawa Takesi's *Bakumatsu Shashin no Jidai* (1994, pp. 24–5), were thought by Japanese scholars to be connected, but they were undated and, at that time, unattributed.

They appeared to the writer to be photographs of Japanese fishermen, or cargo boat crew. From as early as 1617, documentary evidence shows that Japanese castaways were being encountered across the Pacific. As the whaling grounds off the coast of Japan were increasingly exploited from the 1840s by American trading vessels, these encounters became more frequent. It was necessary to research those Japanese who had been rescued and taken to the United States between the years 1845 and 1860. Katherine Plummer's work on Japanese castaways, *The Shogun's Reluctant Ambassadors* (1984), was helpful in narrowing the search to two incidents, as detailed in Terry Bennett and Sebastian Dobson's "The Sentaro Daguerreotype" (1997). The first was of an entire seventeen-man crew of the shipwrecked Japanese vessel *Eiriki-Maru*, who had been brought to San Francisco in February 1851, and the second concerned two Japanese castaways who visited Boston and New York in 1854 after having worked on an American whaler.

The two Japanese from the latter incident served for two years on a whaling voyage before reaching America, and it was most unlikely that they would have retained the traditional Japanese hairstyle shown in the daguerreotype. The crew of the *Eiriki-Maru*, however, had drifted for "only" fifty days and, upon being rescued, took another forty-five days to reach San Francisco. So there seemed a definite possibility that the daguerreotype was one of the crew members of the *Eiriki-Maru*, but there was no proof and the research had hit a brick wall: the identities of the Japanese and the photographer were unknown, and it was far from clear when and where the photograph had been taken.

Below Fig. 22. Anonymous, "Anonymous Portrait," ca. 1854, ninth-plate daguerreotype. Author's Collection. This appears to be an American daguerreotype portrait of a Japanese in American sailor's uniform. As the image is clearly from the early 1850s, there is a strong possibility that the subject is a Japanese castaway. On April 15th, 1852, the American whaler Isaac Howland rescued four Japanese on board the *Eikyu-Maru*, who were stranded in the Pacific. Two of these, Yujiro and Sakuzo, signed up for a two-year voyage and returned to New Bedford on April 24th, 1854. This portrait may be of one of these adventurers.

In June 1996, out of the blue, the writer received a fax from the Japanese photo researcher Izakura Naomi, who said she had acquired an issue of the extremely rare New York periodical, the *Illustrated News*. This issue was dated January 22nd, 1853 and contained an article referring to "the first daguerreotypes of Japanese individuals ever taken." Amazingly, the article contained woodblock engravings of the portraits of the captain and crew of the *Eiriki-Maru* taken during their stay in San Francisco! (Actually, the illustrations showed eighteen Japanese but one castaway was engraved twice by mistake).

On the basis of this article, Ms Izakura had solved the riddle and had matched four of the illustrations with the daguerreotypes held by the previously mentioned Japanese museums. It was also clear that the subject of the writer's photograph was the ship's cook, Sentaro. The photographs had been taken in San Francisco by the American photographer Harvey R. Marks (1882–1902) some time between February 17th, 1851 and March 13th, 1852, during their stay in the city.[2] Marks was based in Baltimore, Maryland, where the 1850 census noted he maintained a studio employing three assistants and producing 5000 images a year. Quite why he made the long and hazardous journey west is not known; perhaps he was attracted by the California Gold Rush, either as a prospector or photographer. In any case, following his return he exhibited daguerreotypes of San Francisco and of the seventeen Japanese castaways at the Maryland Institute in 1852 or 1855. The former date is the more likely. After 1855 he moved his studio to Mobile, Alabama.

Sentaro, or Sam Patch as he came to be known, subsequently accompanied Commodore Perry to Japan on the famous 1852–4 expedition. Although he was supposed to

act as an interpreter, his timidity and fear of Japanese officialdom meant he was of little help to the Americans. Fearing for his life, he decided against going ashore and returned to America. Sentaro's story does not end there, but his future adventures are not relevant to the subject matter of this book. But he, and his fellow sailors, unless and until proven otherwise, go down in history as being the first Japanese to be successfully photographed.[3]

ELIPHALET BROWN JR

The official photographer to the Perry expedition, Eliphalet M. Brown Jr (1816–86), was an accomplished daguerreotypist, lithographer, and artist and has the distinction of taking the earliest surviving photographs in Japan. Between 1846 and 1848 he was in business with his younger brother, James Sydney Brown, a daguerreotypist in New York City. He left the partnership in 1848 and joined Charles Severyn, a lithographer. Later, in 1852, whilst successfully working as a lithographer for Currier and Ives, he was chosen as Commodore Perry's expedition photographer. Competition was stiff, despite the low pay, and perhaps Brown was thought more suitable given his additional artistic skills. William Heine was chosen as the official artist, and William Draper as the supervisor of the telegraphic equipment. In practice, all three helped each other throughout the two years' voyage.

According to Samuel Eliot Morison in his book *"Old Bruin": Commodore Matthew Calbraith Perry* (1967), Brown reportedly took more than 400 daguerreotypes during the expedition. Bruce T. Erickson also gives the same number in his article "Eliphalet M. Brown, Jr: An Early Expedition Photographer" (1990). Many of these were given away by Perry to the Japanese who sat for their portraits, and a number were destroyed in an April 1856 fire at a Philadelphia print shop, one of the sites used for reproducing lithographs for the official book of the expedition, *Narrative of the Expedition of an American Squadron to the China Seas and Japan* (1856), by Francis L. Hawks. Although approximately twenty of Brown's Japanese daguerreotypes were illustrated as lithographs and woodcuts in the book, only six have so far been found (Fig. 24).

It is often stated that all of Brown's daguerreotypes were lost in the aforementioned fire at the P. S. Duval Lithographic Company premises. However, Rob Oechsle in his 1987 book *Aoi Me Ga Mita Dai Ryukyu*, was the first to provide convincing evidence that many must have survived. Because the book of the expedition required a large print run and several different editions, various printing establishments were engaged for the work, some in Philadelphia and others in New York. One can see which firms were involved by looking at the book illustrations themselves. In Oechsle's work and Erickson's article, it is clear that the dispersal of the daguerreotypes amongst these firms precluded their all being destroyed. For example, of the ninety lithographs which appeared in the various editions of the book, only twenty-one were produced by P. S. Duval; and, of these, only six were

Drawn from Nature by Heine Figures by Brown   Ackerman Lith. 379 Broadway N.Y.

TEMPLE AT TUMAI LEW CHEW

from Brown's daguerreotypes and again, of these, just two were of Japan. T. Sinclair of Philadelphia also reproduced six lithographs from daguerreotypes, Ackerman of New York four, and Sarony & Company, also of New York, three. A further fifteen daguerreotypes were reproduced as wood engravings by various other New York firms.

An obscure, but tantalizing reference to Brown's photography is given in Perry's own journal in an entry made in August 1853 and described in Roger Pineau's *The Japan Expedition 1852-1854* (1968). Based at the time in Macau, Perry records that "The hospital soon had a good number of inmates sent from the different ships, and at the house hired for the purpose, the several apparatus of the magnetic telegraph, the daguerreotype, and the Talbotype were established and put into full operation." This means that Brown was not confining himself to daguerreotype photography but also experimenting with talbotypes (or calotypes), a process that had been invented by William Henry Fox Talbot in 1844.

Before going to the mainland of Japan, Perry dropped anchor off Naha, the capital of the Okinawan Islands, on May 26th, 1853. These islands were then under nominal Japanese control although this was not recognized by China, which considered them Chinese. The Okinawans, meanwhile, con-

sidered their territory sovereign. When Japan did lay official claim in 1879, it would take another fifteen years for this to be accepted by the Chinese and Okinawans, prompted by Japan's comprehensive victory over China in the 1894-5 Sino-Japanese War. One member of Perry's expedition was the popular writer Bayard Taylor. In his book *A Visit to India, China, and Japan in the Year 1853* (1887), he gives an interesting account of Brown's and Draper's activities on Okinawa where the two of them spent three weeks at a temple which they used as a base for their photography: "They were daily visited by a number of the better class of natives, who watched their operations with the greatest of curiosity. They at once comprehended the properties of the daguerreotype, and willingly sat for their portraits. They understood the necessity of remaining perfectly quiet, and were as rigid as statues, not venturing to move an eyelid. When the impression was good, nothing could exceed their wonder or delight. The excessive moisture in the air of Loo-Choo, and the absence of any fitting location for the instruments, operated unfavorably on the plates, and not more than twenty good pictures were procured. These, however, are of much value, as giving perfect representations of the features and costumes of the Loo-Chooans."

On February 11th, 1854, during the expedition's second

Above Fig. 24. Eliphalet Brown Jr, "Portrait of Namura Gohachiro," 1854, sixth-plate daguerreotype. Bishop Museum, Honolulu, Hawaii. Brown took this photograph, which he signed, at Yokohama between January and March 1854. Namura, usually based in Nagasaki, was the third most senior interpreter assigned to communicate with the Americans. The daguerreotype, which was presented to Namura, was passed on to his descendants who eventually emigrated to Hawaii.

visit to the Japanese mainland, the artist Heine makes a seemingly innocuous entry in his journal: "I had been topside all day to photograph the coastline with Mr. Brown...." The significance of this statement, contained in Frederic Trautman's *With Perry to Japan* (1990), has been overlooked. Brown and Heine must have been trying to take daguerreotypes (or calotypes?) of the coastline from the deck of a ship. It is commonly believed that exposure times of several minutes were required for photography in the early 1850s. However, although this was true when the daguerreotype was first introduced, within two to three years exposure times had been reduced to around one minute. Even these speeds would seem to rule out photography from a ship which would, even if anchored in a sheltered harbor, be rocking gently from side to side. However, in the hands of a skilful operator, and with correct plate preparation, one to three seconds in good weather was possible by the mid-1850s.[4]

It is to be hoped that the six surviving Brown daguerreotypes taken in Japan will be added to over time. In the meantime, daguerreotypes of Japan and Japanese subjects are of the utmost rarity; including the six known Brown images, only sixteen have so far been positively identified.[5] According to Erickson, Brown seemed to give up art and photography following his return from Japan. He did, however, publish large folios of lithographs based on his drawings made in Japan. In 1860, again according to Erickson, he failed in an attempt to secure financial reimbursement from Congress

for the money he spent during the expedition. His contribution of over 400 daguerreotypes was recorded and acknowledged, but compensation was denied on the grounds that the expense had not previously been sanctioned. Earlier, in a short note given in the *New York Times* (March 16th, 1858, p. 4), hopes were high that both Brown and Heine would receive recompense, albeit small. The report stated that Perry had enlisted them both as master's mates at just twenty-five dollars a month each, on the understanding that Congress would make a suitable compensation upon their return. In an obituary, which appeared in the *New York Times* (January 24th, 1886, p. 5), Brown is said to have been attracted to a naval career and spent the next twenty years in service. He served as a master and ensign during the Civil War, and when the conflict was over he switched to clerical duties. For a number of years he was attached to the Mediterranean squadron as admiral's secretary and in that capacity served Admirals Le Roy, Worden, Alden, and Bell.

Brown was very popular with his colleagues and his retirement in 1875 was much regretted. He married the same year and seems to have spent his retirement years peacefully until his death at his home at No. 101 Park Avenue, New York, on January 23rd, 1886, after an illness of some three months.

EDWARD KERN

Edward Meyer Kern (1823–63) was an American topographical artist and daguerreotypist who, in the 1850s, made several official visits to Japan with the US navy (Fig. 25). He took a number of photographs which, with the possible exception of an attributed daguerreotype taken in 1855 in a Shimoda cemetery, have not been found.

Kern, the youngest child of a deputy customs collector, was diagnosed early as an epileptic and the symptoms of this disorder were to recur throughout his life. Born in Philadelphia on October 26th, 1823, he and his two brothers, Richard and John Kern IV, were trained as artists and operated from a studio in the family home, from where they derived some income as instructors.

In March 1845 Kern received a commission to accompany the soldier, explorer, and later politician John Charles Fremont on a government-sponsored expedition to the Far West. The objective was to survey and map what was then largely unknown territory. Kern was soon given the additional task of topographer and acquitted himself well in an expedition that started to take on more of a military nature with skirmishes with Mexican and native Indian forces. After two years, in failing health, Kern signed off in May 1847 and headed back home.

Kern and his two brothers joined Fremont on another expedition to the West in 1848 and Kern's role was that of artist. The expedition ended in failure and his brother John was killed. Edward and Richard moved to Santa Fe, New Mexico, in the summer of 1849 and then served on a number of United States Army Topographical Engineer surveys, which helped locate sites for frontier forts.[6]

Late in 1851 Kern returned to Philadelphia and started experiments with a daguerreotype camera. He tried, and failed, to secure an appointment to Commodore Perry's expedition to Japan, but in early 1853 was employed as an artist, photographer, and taxidermist on Commodore Cadwalader Ringgold's North Pacific Exploring Expedition with which he would remain involved for the next seven years of his life. Prior to departure, Kern worked hard on perfecting his photographic skills. According to P. E. Palmquist and T. R. Kailbourn in *Pioneer Photographers of the Far West* (2000), he made three trips to New York for this purpose, and received lessons from the firm E. Anthony. When he left on the expedition, he took with him no less than 432 plates, together with supplies of the necessary chemicals and two headrests for portrait work.

Kern left on the USS *Vincennes*, one of the five ships of the task force, on June 11th, 1853. The expedition arrived in Hong Kong in March 1854 and stayed there for almost six months whilst repairs were carried out on the ships. Ringgold caught malaria and was replaced by Lieutenant John Rodgers, and by the autumn of 1854 Kern was involved in surveying first the Bonin (Ogisawara) Islands and then the Ryukyu (Okinawa) Islands. The USS *Vincennes* arrived at Okinawa on November 17th, 1854. The Okinawans resisted supplying the ship with provisions, despite this being a condition of Perry's treaty of four months earlier. Rodgers decided on a show of force and landed 100 sailors and marines and a field-piece and marched to the palace at Shuri. Kern apparently took along his camera, but whether he used it on this occasion is not clear. According to Charles O. Paullin's *American Voyages to the Orient* (1971), the Okinawans were in no position to resist and the supply problems fell away.

The *Vincennes* left Okinawa on December 13th and set sail for Kagoshima Bay where they anchored on December 28th. Kagoshima was not one of the ports opened by Perry's treaty, and according to George M. Brooke's *John M. Brooke: Naval Scientist and Educator* (1980), Rodgers was deliberately "pushing the Treaty to its fullest extent." Although the Japanese refused to trade, they offered no real objections to Rodgers making observations for his chronometers and, according to Paullin, were reasonably friendly and supplied the ship with provisions on several occasions. In anticipation of coastal surveys planned for the following year, Rodgers wrote to the Japanese "secretary of state for foreign affairs" explaining the scientific exigencies that compelled him to go ashore to make observations for the purpose of rating his chronometers. Whether Kern had the opportunity to use his camera at Kagoshima is not known, although it should be remembered that the *daimyo* Shimazu Nariakira had been experimenting with his own daguerreotype equipment since 1849. After a few days the *Vincennes* left Kagoshima and surveyed several of the southern Japanese islands before reaching Hong Kong on January 30th, 1855.

In April the *Vincennes* carried out further surveying of the Ryukyu Islands and then headed for Shimoda with the steamer *John Hancock*. They anchored in the bay on May 13th,

1855, fifteen months before the American Consul-General Townsend Harris would take up residence there at the Gyokusen-ji Temple. Rodgers was taken aback to find ten Americans living at the same temple: five men, three women, and two children aged five and nine. As their unexpected presence has an important bearing on the story of the one tentatively attributed Kern daguerreotype, some background to their activities would be appropriate.

Grant Romer explains in his article "Near the Temple at Yokushen" (1986) that the Americans were pioneer traders, led by William Reed and Thomas Dougherty. These entrepreneurs were opportunistically trying to take advantage of Perry's newly negotiated treaty, acting on the assumption that the treaty would permit trade between the two countries. Accordingly, they had chartered a schooner in Honolulu, the *Caroline E. Foote*, with the intention of establishing themselves at Hakodate and supplying the American whaling fleet with ship's chandlery. First of all they called at Shimoda, on March 15th, 1855, and found there the Russian Admiral Count Poutiatine with the crew from the flagship *Diana*, which had been wrecked by an earthquake at the port on December 23rd the previous year, leaving the Russians stranded. Poutiatine made a tempting offer to the Americans to transport him and his men to the Russian port of Petropavlovsk, on the Kamchatka peninsula. The Japanese, at least glad to be rid of a number of the Russians, reluctantly agreed to let the schooner's cargo land and to accommodate the Americans at the Gyokusen-Ji Temple until the schooner returned from Petropavlovsk.

When the *Vincennes* arrived with Edward Kern on board, the Americans had been at Shimoda for two months. According to Howard F. Van Zandt's meticulously researched *Pioneer*

American Merchants in Japan (1981), after the return of the *Caroline E. Foote* on May 27th, the Americans made arrangements to leave for Hakodate, and they finally did so on June 5th, 1855.

Rodgers, meanwhile, had requested permission of the governor to survey the coasts of Japan. The governor passed on the request to Edo and the reply, when it came back, was negative. Rodgers went ahead anyway, and on May 28th dispatched a small launch under the command of Lieutenant John Brooke whose orders were to survey the eastern coast of Japan from Shimoda to Hakodate. On board were Edward Kern and a crew of thirteen well-armed volunteers. Rodgers left in the *Vincennes* the same day, while the *John Hancock* left shortly after.

The subject matter of the daguerreotype, illustrated in Fig. 26, has been shown to be the gravestones of four American sailors who were attached to the Perry expedition. Romer chronicles how this discovery was made in 1986 by the Japanese scholar Matsumura Akira, who found that the cemetery is attached to the Gyokusen-ji Temple in Shimoda. Today, there are actually five monuments because a fifth American sailor was buried there following his death on July 31st, 1858. From the inscriptions on all five graves, Romer has been able to deduce that the photograph had to have been taken between February 1855 and July 1858.

Romer discounts Eliphalet Brown as the photographer since he believes that by February 1855 Brown would have returned to America. The official photographer to Count Poutiatine's expedition was Alexandr Feodorovich Mozhaiskii. One of his daguerreotypes of a "Priest of the Gyokusen-ji Temple at Shimoda," taken in April 1854, still survives. Romer has speculated that Mozhaiskii could have been one of those Russians stranded at Shimoda and, if so, must be a candidate. He also does not rule out the possibility that one of the American passengers on the *Caroline E. Foote* may have had a camera. Will Stapp, writing in the 1992 Tokyo Metropolitan Museum of Photography exhibition catalogue, *Early Works of Photography*, attributes the work to Edward Kern. He states, "It is possible that the image was taken by ... Mozhaiskii, who is known to have been in Shimoda about this time. It is far more likely, however, that it was made by Edward Kern, an American artist aboard the United States naval vessel *Vincennes*.... Kern was a civilian employed to create a visual record of the Expedition."

If Kern did take the photograph, then he would have had to have done so between the 13th and 28th of May, 1855, which was when he was based at Shimoda. The party from the *Caroline E. Foote* are connected, because in the foreground of the view is the figure of what appears to be a Western child. This group of Americans was based at Shimoda from March 15th until June 5th, 1855, and did have with them two young children, as we have seen. If attribution were a choice between Mozhaiskii and Kern, it would seem that the latter, an American, would have been the more likely to photograph American graves than the Russian.

It should be mentioned that Romer notes a faint pencil inscription on the rear of the frame which reads: "June 25th 18−." Although the year is not legible, if the date were to be taken literally as the date the photograph was made, then the June date would exclude Kern. It would also mean that the child in the picture could not be from the party. If not, that would certainly extend the possible dateline to August 1858. Many foreign ships also called at Shimoda between the years 1855 and 1858.

The ship that accompanied the *Vincennes* into the harbor of Shimoda, the *John Hancock*, was commanded by Lieutenant A. W. Habersham who wrote about the expedition in his book *The North Pacific Surveying and Exploring Expedition* (1858, p. 208). Habersham talks of four of Commodore Perry's men and one of his officers (Dr James Hamilton) being buried in the cemetery. This does not tie in with the four monuments seen in the daguerreotype. On the other hand, the fact that Habersham mentions his surprise at seeing American monuments in a Japanese cemetery leads one to suppose that the existence of this novelty might, in itself, have been sufficient motivation for the scene to be photographed – and Kern was certainly on the spot.

Circumstantially, then, Kern would seem to have been the likely photographer of the scene. However, his candidature is severely undermined when it is appreciated that one of the pioneers on board the *Caroline E. Foote*, Edward A. Edgerton (see page 34), was not only a keen photographer but also had with him his own daguerreotype camera and was successful in securing photographs!

As mentioned above, Kern left on May 28th to survey Japan's eastern coastline in the survey boat named the *Vincennes Junior*. Given that the boat, which only measured twenty-eight feet long and seven and a half feet wide, contained a twelve-pounder brass howitzer (in case of trouble), fifteen men, and supplies, it is unlikely that Kern would have taken along the bulky daguerreotype equipment. He did, though, take his sketching materials with him. The cruise of some twenty-one days in an open boat along a treacherous coastline was extremely hazardous. The boat visited ports never before entered by foreigners and landings were made at several places. The reception from the Japanese seems to have varied, depending on the attitude of the local officials. In any case, the whole coastline was mapped and the mission was a success. The boat reached Hakodate on June 17th, 1855.

The expedition's next task was to survey the Sea of Okhotsk and the Aleutian Islands. Kern, as second-in-command to Lieutenant Brooke, was put ashore at Glazenap Harbor, Siberia, where he amassed a collection of ethnographic sketches and daguerreotypes of the local tribes. Unfortunately, the daguerreotypes have not been found. Kern was back in San Francisco on October 13th, 1855. Re-embarking on the *Vincennes* the following February, Kern visited the Sandwich Islands (Hawaii) and South America. After returning to America, he spent some months in completing the maps and sketches of the expedition.

In 1858 the Navy Department authorized the completion of the North Pacific Survey between San Francisco and China and Kern signed on again as artist. Lieutenant Brooke was in command. Kern left on September 26th, 1858 on board the

USS *Fenimore Cooper* and it is not known whether he took his daguerreotype equipment with him on this occasion. After spending time in Honolulu and Hong Kong, as well as surveying islands south of Japan, the ship put in at Kanagawa on August 13th, 1859, just six weeks after the port's opening. The same month Kern rode with Brooke to Edo to confer with Consul-General Townsend Harris, who requested that they survey the port of Niigata the following spring.

Brooke decided to spend the intervening months surveying the treaty port of Kobe and the eastern end of the Inland Sea and agreed with Harris that they would leave on September 1st. However, when he and Kern returned to Kanagawa they received the appalling news that the *Fenimore Cooper* had been beached at Yokohama and was no longer seaworthy. As a result, Kern spent some six months at Yokohama, from August 1859 until February 1860. It is very interesting to speculate whether Kern, the experienced photographer, engaged in any form of photographic activity during this period. More research is required here.

On February 10th, 1860 Kern accompanied Brooke on the Japanese ship *Kanrin Maru*, which crossed the Pacific on its way to America as part of the first Japanese Embassy to that country. Kern would have communicated with Nakamura Manjiro, the senior interpreter on board. When Manjiro returned to Japan later that year, he brought back with him a daguerreotype camera. Could he have received instruction from Kern?

When the ship arrived in America on March 17th, Kern spent some time escorting the Japanese around San Francisco and visited various sites, including the ironworks, gas works, shipyards, and Mint. This was Kern's last involvement with Japan and the Japanese and he next spent some months in Washington, with Brooke, completing the field papers of the expedition. In July 1861 Kern joined the Union Army but had to leave in November having experienced increasing epileptic attacks. Despite failing health, he established an art studio in Philadelphia and taught drawing. He died at home on November 23rd, 1863.

A description of Kern is given in Brooke's *John M. Brooke* (p. 78): " ... a lanky six-foot bachelor from Philadelphia ... brought to the Expedition a number of useful skills.... Under Fremont's tutelage he had developed his talents as a surveyor and topographer ... as a naturalist he had collected and classified specimens for his scientific friends and learned taxidermy. But he is principally remembered as an artist, and the sketches he made with the North Pacific Expedition as with Fremont were of great value. Also, when feasible, he used the extensive daguerreotype equipment he took with him. Brooke and Kern had similar scientific and artistic interests and shared a love of adventure and zest for travel. Although Kern had periods of gloom and seemed to attract bad luck, he was by nature more optimistic than his southern friend. His gloom was leavened by a sense of humor and a love for practical joking...."

Apart from the tentatively attributed daguerreotype of the American cemetery at Shimoda, none of Kern's photographs is known to have survived. Many of his pencil and

Below Fig. 26. Attributed to Edward Meyer Kern, "American Cemetery, Gyokusen-Ji Temple, Shimoda, Japan," ca. 1855, full-plate daguerreotype. George Eastman House. This impressive daguerreotype has been variously attributed to Kern, Eliphalet Brown, and Alexandr Feodorovich Mozhaiskii. However, the writer feels that a stronger case can now be made for the previously unknown Edward A. Edgerton (see page 34). Note the child playing among the gravestones, and that the image, being a daguerreotype, is horizontally reversed.

watercolor sketches, however, can be found at various museums throughout the United States. His personal papers are kept by the Huntington Library, San Marino, California, the same state wherein two rivers, a National Wildlife Refuge, and a huge county north of Los Angeles are named after him. Given the numerous visits that Kern made to Japan, and his proficiency as a photographer, it would seem probable that he took many important daguerreotypes. More research into his life might well yield further information, possibly leading to the whereabouts of his missing photographs.

EDWARD EDGERTON

The virtually unknown Edward A. Edgerton (ca. 1827–?) may well turn out to be the photographer of the famous ca. 1855 daguerreotype of the American gravestones at the cemetery attached to the Gyokusen-ji Temple in Shimoda.[7]

Edgerton, a member of this group, was a young American lawyer from Massachusetts. According to Van Zandt's little-known but excellent book, *Pioneer American Merchants in Japan*, Edgerton had at some stage moved to California and in the 1851 San Francisco Census of July 28th his age was noted as twenty-four. He decided to take a vacation in the Hawaiian Islands and in a letter dated July 31st, 1855, which was published in the *Daily California Chronicle*, San Francisco (September 20th, 1855), he wrote: "Possessed by that roving spirit of adventure peculiar to the universal Yankee nation, I left San Francisco ... last November (1854), for a visit of pleasure to the Sandwich Islands. I had a grand time visiting the different islands of the groupe [sic], especially the Volcano of Pete Kilaued [sic] at Hawaii...."

It was known in Honolulu that a group of merchants had chartered the schooner *Caroline E. Foote*, and were going to leave for Shimoda and Hakodate with the aim of trading with the Japanese as well as selling ship's chandlery to visiting American whalers. Edgerton, whose reasons for making the voyage are unknown, decided to join the group and made up the party of ten passengers, which was augmented by the ship's captain, his wife, and the crew of approximately nineteen. The ship left on February 13th, 1855. Edgerton, who was preparing himself for the trip, writes in the same letter: "On leaving Honolulu for Simoda and Hakodadi, Japan, I purchased a very complete apparatus, and afterwards a very superior instrument and stock of chemicals, &c., from a brother amateur in the U.S. Naval service, for the express purpose of taking views and portraits in Japan, that unknown and hitherto inaccessible country. It was my first attempt at the art, but for an amateur I have been very successful, and would have been more so but for the faithlessness of the Japanese in breaking the treaty to our great prejudice and damage. I was the first American resident in Japan, sleeping ashore a week before my companions left the vessel. We resided at Simoda nearly three months, and then left for Hakodadi, where I slept ashore two nights, after great difficulty, being refused permission to reside even for a single night; no others staid [sic] ashore at Hakodadi over night...."

This is the significant reference which, in the absence of any other information, must make Edgerton the most likely candidate for authorship of the Shimoda daguerreotype: having made a considerable investment in state-of-the-art photographic equipment, with the firm intention of capturing views in Japan, it is clear from the account above that Edgerton used his camera successfully in Shimoda.

The Japanese were finally able to persuade the Americans to leave Shimoda, and the whole party embarked for Hakodate on June 5th, where they arrived on the 14th. However, the Americans were refused permission to reside ashore and although Edgerton, in his letter, states that he himself managed to sleep ashore for two nights, it is unlikely that in the tense circumstances pertaining he would have had time to unload and use his camera. After days of fruitless discussions with the Japanese authorities, the furious Americans decided to head back to San Francisco. But because they could not secure sufficient supplies from the Japanese, they made an involuntary detour and sailed for Guam on June 28th, arriving there on July 15th.

On August 1st the *Caroline E. Foote* did leave for America, but Edgerton was not amongst the passengers. In his letter, which he wrote the day before the ship sailed, he said that he had decided to stay in Guam: "[For] tropical beauty, excellence and abundance of fruit, Guam far surpasses any of the Sandwich Islands.... I have become tired of sea life, and much charmed with the fair promise of a very pleasant tropical life at Guam, having with some difficulty obtained permission to reside here for a few months and take daguerreotypic and photographic portraits and views.... I may next visit Manila, and afterwards China, and hope ere long to find you in San Francisco...."

But the Spanish authorities at Guam soon made life difficult for Edgerton. They made it clear that he could not stay without going to the Philippines and personally seeking permission from the Spanish Governor-General in Manila. Meanwhile, the Governor of Guam had written privately to Manila asking that permission be refused. His stated reason was that foreigners did not give sufficient respect to the Spanish authorities on the island and this served to undermine the Governor's authority. In mid-December, nevertheless, Edgerton embarked on an American ship for Manila to seek permission to reside in Guam as secretary to the US Consul. The request was denied on January 23rd, 1856. On March 17th, 1856 Edgerton returned to Guam on the *E. L. Frost*, but there was an outbreak of smallpox on board after leaving the Philippines and the ship was quarantined. Some of the passengers disobeyed orders and landed in Guam anyway, and Edgerton was apparently amongst them. As a result, a smallpox epidemic arose, lasting nine months, and more than 3500 Guamanians, 40 percent of the population, died.

Edgerton was on shore when the *E. L. Frost* departed at the end of April. On January 14th, 1857 he embarked on the French frigate *Washington*, bound for Hong Kong. It may be that he was unable to leave until the epidemic had run its course. At Hong Kong perhaps Edgerton considered the possibility of a career as a commercial photographer.

At around this time Edgerton found his way to Singapore where he was one of the first to set up a photo studio and, according to John Falconer in *A Vision of the Past* (1995), the first to introduce the wet-collodion process commercially. His studio was advertised in the *Straits Times* on February 13th, 1858 where he advertised "photographic and stereoscopic portraits on glass or paper" which he described as being superior to daguerreotype photography. Intriguingly, he advertises for a colorist and may have been the first to offer colored photographs in East Asia. By May 1858 Edgerton is in partnership as Alfeld & Edgerton but by July 1859 is again trading in his own name. Although still involved in photography, in January 1861 he edits a new monthly periodical, *The Singapore Review and Monthly Magazine*, which only lasted a few months. What he does next is unclear, but in around the 1870s he is running a portrait studio in Gowanda, New York.

FIRST CAMERAS, FIRST STUDENTS

When the powerful Satsuma *daimyo* Shimazu Nariakira purchased the daguerreotype equipment in 1849, he ordered his retainers, the Western scholars Kawamoto Komin and Matsuki Koan, to study and learn the art of photography at the Satsuma mansion in Edo (Tokyo). It was not until 1857, however, before any tangible results were attained, the equipment and operating manuals proving exceptionally difficult to master. In September of that year, Ichiki Shiro and Ujuku Hikoemon successfully took a portrait of their Lord and this

daguerreotype is kept today in the Shimazu family museum in Kagoshima and is illustrated here (Fig. 27).

However, evidence is growing that other Japanese *daimyo* were importing cameras and chemicals and carrying out experiments throughout the 1850s. Specifically, the Lords of Saga, Fukuoka, Fukui, Kaga, Mito, and Matsushiro were active. Research by the Leiden-based photo-historian Professor Herman J. Moeshart, outlined in his article "Nihon Shashinshi" (1986), has shown that cameras were ordered from Dutch merchants at Deshima in the years 1850 and 1852. By 1855 at least five cameras had reached Japan. The fact that "physician's collodion" had been included in the list of imported chemicals suggests strongly that the wet-plate collodion process was also being used, following its invention in 1851 by F. S. Archer. Whether the intermediate process of calotyping was ever employed is not clear, but if it were, attention very quickly shifted to wet-plate technology. It is also worth recording that daguerreotype equipment was one of the presents left at Kanagawa by Commodore Perry's expedition, just before it departed in June 1854.

Although the treaty ports of Yokohama (nearby Kanagawa had officially been stipulated in the treaty, but Yokohama was more practical), Nagasaki, and Hakodate did not open to foreigners until July 1859, it should not be imagined that up until that time Deshima was the only contact point between the outside world and Japan. The Kanagawa Treaty, which Commodore Perry signed in 1854, provided for an American Consul to reside at the port of Shimoda. In 1856 Townsend Harris arrived with his assistant and interpreter, the Dutchman Henry Heusken. Since 1855, moreover, the Dutch on Deshima were able to roam freely around the town of Nagasaki as a naval academy had been set up there at the request of the shogunate. Many students arrived and were taught naval sciences, medicine, chemistry, and Dutch.

A very early example of photography in Nagasaki concerned ships of the Russian fleet, which arrived on June 13th, 1859 and stayed for some twenty days. On board was the Englishman Henry Arthur Tilley, who wrote about his experiences in *Japan, the Amoor, and the Pacific* (1861). In that book he recounts an amusing and interesting photographic episode which involved Russian officers and local Japanese: "In one of these tea-houses of which the Russian officers of the squadron took almost exclusive possession, several mornings were passed in photographing Japanese of both sexes decked out in full costume, dancing and singing girls, with now and then some curious beauty from the neighbourhood; also musical instruments, swords, gongs, teapots, &c. − in fact, everything that was characteristic of the country and the scene, or could help to fill up the picture. Group after group was taken of figures sitting, dancing, attitudinizing, eating, drinking, or smoking, and glass after glass spoiled, owing to the laughing and frolic-some behaviour of the highly amused moosoome. After several well-portrayed scenes were taken, though not without great trouble in keeping the subjects in a state of repose for a few seconds, the hilarity of the whole party was increased by the changing of the costume. Moosoome came out in uniform, with pantaloons and swords girded on;

Below Fig. 28. Dr J. L. J. Pompe van Meerdervoort, "Self-portrait," Nagasaki, 1862, small-format albumen print. Bauduin Collection, The Netherlands.

towards the end of 1859 considerable progress had been made and students were able to understand the basic elements of photography and produce images, albeit of indifferent quality. What was required was instruction from a seasoned professional. That professional was on his way from China. He would show the students how to build on the foundations put in place by Pompe van Meerdervoort and his predecessors and convert their theoretical knowledge into practical results. He would also prove to be the catalyst that brought real momentum to photographic studies in Japan. The tipping point had been reached, and now photography would quickly spread throughout the country. The name of this professional was Pierre Rossier.

THE NORWEGIAN

One of the enduring mysteries of nineteenth-century Japanese photography is the identity of the Westerner who allegedly traveled and photographed in and around the Nagasaki region before it was legally permissible to do so. That is, of course, if the event took place at all.

The only evidence we have is an extensive article in the well-regarded nineteenth-century periodical, *The Photographic News*. The article in question ran for several issues, from October 1859 to February 1860. The unnamed author, who states his nationality as Norwegian, describes an illicit trip in the summer of 1857, inland from Nagasaki, and outside the prescribed traveling area. Discovery of either himself or his Japanese traveling companion would have had serious consequences. To understand the importance of this apparent photographic event, one has to consider the historical context in regard to Japan's then isolationist policy, which meant that contact with the outside world was minimal.

It is generally thought that the Dutch, and any other foreigners at Deshima, were not allowed to move around the port town of Nagasaki until it had been officially opened for trade in July 1859. However, in the Norwegian's journal he states that he was in the town of Nagasaki photographing a group of Japanese and Dutch when he first met a Japanese who would become his subsequent traveling companion.

In a little-known episode in the history of Japanese–Western relations, the Dutch had achieved something of a diplomatic coup by encouraging the authorities to seek their help in setting up a naval military school in Nagasaki from November 1855. This involved the employment of Dutch naval officers, sailors, and engineers. The Deshima-based J. Donker Curtius, who as well as being head of the Dutch trading post also doubled as the Dutch Commissioner for Japan, used these circumstances to full advantage. In the November 1855 "Preliminary Convention of Commerce," as explained in J. H. Gubbins' *The Progress of Japan* (1911), he obtained full freedom of movement in the town of Nagasaki for naval school employees and the Dutch residents on Deshima. The actual town area is not defined in this particular treaty and so one imagines that there may have been disagreements, from time to time, when travel outside the central area was attempted.

officers in Keremon and Obee, their hair dressed out *a là Japonaise* with coloured crape, and flowers. Each played the part of his or her assumed character, the moosoome strutting up and down, and the men prostrating themselves like the Japanese women, till the scene became so ridiculous that the most serious could not hold out. The people around roared with laughter; tears were running down the cheeks of a fat old bonze, as his ponderous sides shook, whilst two caustic-looking, two-sworded gentlemen, putting their noses in at the garden gate, shook their heads, and, no doubt, vowed to themselves that the barbarians were spoiling the people."

Jan Karel Van den Broek (1814–65), a Dutch physician at Deshima from 1853 to 1857, was asked in 1856 to give some students lessons in photography and he set up a photographic teaching room next to his house on Deshima. His first students were the physician Furukawa Shumpei and Yoshio Keisai. No doubt Van den Broek was able to teach photographic theory adequately, but the well-meaning amateur's practical experiments ended in failure. His medical successor, Jonkheer J. L. C. Pompe van Meerdervoort (1829–1908), was also unable to satisfy the Japanese students, although by December 1859 Himeno (2003) confirms that he was able to take photographs – albeit with some difficulty (Fig. 28). At this time the samurai Matsumoto Ryojun (1832–1907) was employed as supervisor in Pompe van Meerdervoort's chemical laboratory and seems to have acquired some proficiency in photography (Fig. 159, page 126).

Amongst his students, as we shall see, were Ueno Hikoma and Uchida Kuichi. We can imagine, therefore, that

From December 1855, communication with the Japanese in the town was no longer prohibited. This was a major liberalization of the laws as hitherto applying to foreigners in Japan, and it enabled the Dutch to steal a march on their Western counterparts who would have to wait almost four years longer to obtain the same privileges. This would partly, but not wholly, explain why our Norwegian, who said he spoke fluent Dutch, was able to gain access to the town.

At this stage it would perhaps be sensible to give a quick synopsis of the Norwegian's story: Whilst taking the above-mentioned photograph in Nagasaki, he is approached by an elderly Japanese who spoke excellent Dutch with little or no accent. The Japanese asks some questions about the process, simultaneously revealing some rudimentary understanding of the subject. In later conversation the Japanese, whose name is Dsetjuma, shows himself to be a local official and merchant. The two strike a deal: The Norwegian will stay at the home of the wealthy Dsetjuma and teach him photography and, in return, the Norwegian would be allowed to freely practice photography. In order to square this with the Japanese authorities, the Norwegian would have to become an employee of Dsetjuma, helping him in his merchandising. After spending a few weeks at his friend's home, the Norwegian talks Dsetjuma into traveling with him outside the permitted treaty limits, in order to secure photographs of the interior. Dsetjuma points out the dangers of this to both himself and the Norwegian. The latter convinces him by stating that he will disguise himself as a Japanese (this to be accomplished by cutting his hair in Japanese style, donning the appropriate costume, and darkening his "already dark complexion" with photographic chemicals). Dsetjuma reluctantly agrees and they set off in mid-summer on horses, with four servants carrying their luggage and photographic equipment in a palanquin. Their eventful journey, during which they secure numerous photographs, appears to take several weeks, after which they return by ship to Nagasaki.

What can we know of the Norwegian from the journal he presents us with? If we take it at face value, we learn that he arrived in Nagasaki around April 1857, and was still there until at least July 6th, 1859, since that was the date of his letter to the journal. He also claims to have lived in *other places* during that time, although it is not clear whether he is referring to Japan. We understand that he had attended a London photographic society meeting in 1854 or 1855 and met there the employee of *The Photographic News* to whom he writes and sends the journal for publication. From the text we further understand that he speaks English, Norwegian, and Dutch. We also infer he understands French and German since he refers to seeing articles in those countries' newspapers. Judging from the text of the journal, he writes excellent English, unless it has been edited for publication.

The Norwegian speaks no Japanese when he arrives but, at the time of writing, his conversational Japanese is quite good. He also states that despite being Norwegian he has "habitually spoken Dutch for years." We learn that he is assumed to be Dutch by the Japanese, and he has clearly brought his own camera equipment to Nagasaki in order to capture photographs of the local scenery and people. This is a cultured and intelligent man who has traveled extensively, certainly in Europe. Throughout his journey, on several occasions, he compares things he sees to those in Holland, and only once or twice makes reference to Norway. We learn that he has a dark complexion, made darker when he disguises himself by putting certain photographic chemicals on his face and hands.

Finally, we note that he and Dsetjuma both needed to seek permission from their respective seniors before employment by the Japanese could be effected. It is, of course, possible that the Norwegian has changed the names of Dsetjuma and the places visited in order that they are not readily recognizable. The letter and journal are apparently sent through a contact known as F. Van Hoogen, Rue du Marche oux Pouleta (aux Poulets), Brussels.

His journey was certainly eventful, perhaps too eventful. He witnesses the arrest and punishment of a young Japanese woman accused of stealing. He is also arrested himself, and subsequently released, due to a misunderstanding with an innkeeper. Whilst staying at another inn, he witnesses a ritual suicide. Finally, he sees some unfortunate shipwrecked sailors being murdered by Japanese as they struggle to the shore where the survivors are then robbed of whatever possessions they still had on them.

Can we believe this story or not? Crucially, the evidence by way of the photographs themselves does not seem to have materialized. *The Photographic News* at the end of the article raises its readers' expectations by quoting Van Hoogen's short letter, which states he has just received a parcel of photographs from Japan and will bring them to London shortly.

The story is extremely well written, detailed, and interesting. But, all in all, the Norwegian's account does not quite ring true. He certainly does not seem to have been associated with the naval school. Why would the Dutch, knowing him to be Norwegian, take him on in a trading capacity? What was he doing there? He makes a number of references to Holland in his journal and it would be easier to believe that he was, in fact, Dutch. He may have said he was Norwegian and used pseudonyms for Dsetjuma and the places he passed through in order to avoid any possible repercussions from the Dutch or Japanese authorities. After all, if he really had witnessed sailors being murdered...?

His journey, lasting only a few weeks, seems to have had more than its fair share of incidents. This is all very well if you are writing a fictional account, but we are led to believe that this is not the case here. He met and communicated with many Japanese during his journey. He seems to switch from avoiding conversation by feigning deafness, to conversing enthusiastically with others along the way. It is not credible that his appearance, mannerisms, or accent would have failed to have aroused suspicions and encouraged the people he met to report him to the local authorities. Any unusual activity in what was then an extremely regimented society, should have been reported. Carrying and using photographic equipment is not conducive to maintaining a low profile! Crowds would have gathered whenever the camera was used.

Dsetjuma seems to have been taking incredible risks. Having taken the novel step of employing a foreigner, and having him stay at his house, did he expect his neighbors and the local officials to be unaware of a subsequent trip into the interior? If the Norwegian has produced a work of fiction, then the question arises: is there any truth at all in the story? It is possible that an amateur photographer, working in another capacity on Deshima, could have taken pictures in and around the town. Back in Europe there would have been a considerable demand for these alone. It is most unlikely, however, that he would have been able to go, undetected, into the interior. If Van Hoogen in Belgium did receive a parcel of photographs from Japan, were they prints or the glass plates themselves? What condition were they in? Were they exhibited? There is no record of their being exhibited.

There are many unanswered questions and some lines of enquiry to follow up. Attempts could be made in Norway to look through the contemporary newspapers and journals to see whether any mention is made of this extraordinary story. Dutch scholars of Japan would know more about the personnel attached to Deshima and the Naval School, whether Dutch or foreign. They would also know how the Japanese were interpreting the Japanese/Dutch Treaty of Commerce (signed in January 1856) in so far as the Article on "personal freedom" within the town of Nagasaki was concerned. For example, Pompe Van Meerdervoort, a Dutch physician who arrived in Deshima in September 1857, mentions that the 1855 treaty gave the Dutch personal freedom in Nagasaki and its environs. However, the wording of the actual treaty talks of the town of Nagasaki only.[8] How much physical freedom did foreigners have in practice? Japanese scholars might well have something to add, particularly in relation to the observations the Norwegian makes regarding Japanese manners and customs. Were these valid? But unless and until any new information comes to light, it is probably appropriate to treat the story as an interesting but elaborate hoax.

A BRITISH CAMERA IN TOKYO

Some ten years ago the writer came across a group of twenty-two original letters written by William Nassau Jocelyn (1832–92) during the period when he was attached to Lord Elgin's Suite during the latter's 1857–9 diplomatic mission to China and Japan (Fig. 29). The letters, addressed to his father, were written between March 1858 and May 1859. Arriving in Shanghai on July 28th, 1858, Jocelyn immediately joined the mission as an assistant secretary and official photographer. The discovery of the letters, outlined in Terry Bennett and Sebastian Dobson's article "The First British Photographer in Japan" (1998), was particularly exciting since some of them carried descriptions about his photographic work in both China and Japan. Laurence Oliphant's well-known book on the mission, *Narrative of the Earl of Elgin's Mission to China and Japan* (1859), acknowledges Jocelyn's photographic work in the preface, but only includes engravings of four of his photographs taken in China: "I am indebted to Mr. Jocelyn for several admirable photographs of the principal Chinese officials with whom we came in contact" (Fig. 31). Lord Elgin records in his own journal, published in Theodore Waldron's *Letters and Journals of James, Eighth Earl of Elgin* (1872, p. 281): "This morning at ten, I went to a temple which lies exactly between the foreign settlement and the Chinese town of Shanghae, to meet there the Imperial Commissioners, and to sign the tariff. We took with us the photographs which Jocelyn had done for them, and which we had framed. They were greatly delighted, and altogether my poor friends seemed in better spirits than I had before seen them in."[9]

It had been thought that if Jocelyn did photograph in Japan, then the photographs had been lost, otherwise Oliphant would surely have used them in his book. Adding a little to the confusion was a report in the *The Photographic News* (January 14th, 1859), which talked of a Mr R. Morrison's being attached to Elgin's mission in China and having had damaged all of the negatives he took there. This report has served to confuse Jocelyn's status as official photographer and to suggest that whatever photographs were taken were unusable. The Foreign Office List records that a Robert Morrison was temporarily attached to Elgin's staff in China on April 17th, 1857 until 1858. Why he was replaced by Jocelyn is not known. *The Photographic News*, when talking of Morrison's negatives, said: " ... all of these negatives, together with many others, were destroyed by an accident that befell a part of the ambassadorial baggage." This suggests that "the many others" is a probable indication that the same fate was met

Below Fig. 30. William Jocelyn, "Japanese Commissioners after Signing the Treaty of Edo," August 26th, 1858, large-format albumen print. V&A Images/Victoria and Albert Museum. This important historical photograph is currently the earliest known to have been taken in Tokyo. It is also the oldest extant photographic paper print of Japan. The Treaty meant that with effect from July 1st, 1859, the ports of Kanagawa (later switched to Yokohama), Nagasaki, and Hakodate would be opened for trade. Foreigners were also permitted to take up residence at the ports but within strictly prescribed geographic limits.

Left Fig. 31. Anonymous, "William Nassau Jocelyn," ca. 1850s, small-format albumen print. V&A Images/Victoria and Albert Museum.

Above Fig. 32. "HMS Steam Frigates *Furious* and *Retribution* (the latter towing the *Emperor* Yacht) Caught in a Cyclone off the Southern Coast of Japan," 1858, woodcut engraving. Author's Collection. Elgin and his suite were on their way to Edo when a three-day storm hit them from August 6th. Jocelyn, on board the *Furious* with Elgin, later reported that his photographic equipment and chemicals took a heavy pounding. This is a possible reason for the poor condition of the surviving prints. The engraving appeared in *The Illustrated London News*, November 27th, 1858, p. 498.

Below Fig. 33. Pierre Rossier, "Nagasaki Harbor," October 1860, large-format albumen print. The National Archives, Kew. This three-part panorama was one of a series of photographs commissioned by the British Consul at Nagasaki. Shown here is Oura, the proposed site for the foreign settlement, and the British consulate with its flagpole. This series represents the earliest known large-format topographical photography in Japan. See also Rossier's stereoviews, some of which could well have been taken in Nagasaki in June or July 1859.

by most, if not all, of Jocelyn's negatives (Fig. 32). It is important to note that *The Photographic News goes* on to say: "It is possible that by a little manoeuvring pictures may still be obtained from some of these negatives...." and " ... we have seen one, the Imperial commissioners, Kweiliang and Hwashana, which, though it shows signs of having been 'touched' ... is a photograph of great merit...." Attempts to identify Morrison have so far been unsuccessful. This is a pity since he is also a prime suspect for authorship of a group of important early Shanghai photographs which are known to researchers of early Chinese photography.

What Jocelyn's letters did prove, beyond any doubt, was that he did take photographs in Japan during the mission's stay there in August 1858. In one letter (Jocelyn, leaf 75) he writes: "I have taken some very valuable photographs of some of the Commissioners and Japanese who came to our house.... The chief object was to get the dress which is so very characteristic and I think very beautiful from its usefulness and plainness. The crape wings are especially beautiful which they wear on their shoulders and which stick out at each side."

In another (leaf 113): "I send you a photograph of the [Japanese Commissioners] by the way, as they appeared just after signing our Treaty. The man on the left with wings is Moriyama, our interpreter and a very nice fellow, only unfortunately he popped down rather suddenly and the poor man was out of health so that he did not sit quite still and that makes him look so old and wizen. The other six are our six Commissioners – they are all in their riding dresses without wings, and made of silk and silver poplin and trousers large & wide of the same. The Imperial Cypher you may observe on most of their dresses. They are as follows arranged as in the picture...." (Fig. 30).

Jocelyn gives an accompanying sketch which tantalizingly shows how the Commissioners were posed for the photograph. But where were the actual photographs? In view of the comment in *The Photographic News* about the state of Morrison's negatives, and the non-appearance of any Japanese images in Oliphant's book, photo-historians had simply assumed that Jocelyn's Japan images, like most of Brown's daguerreotypes, were lost to posterity. A few years later this proved to be unduly pessimistic.

Professor John Clark of the University of Sydney had researched extensively into the history of artistic exchanges between Japan and the West. In his "A Revised Chronology of Felice Beato" (2001), which he co-authored with John Fraser and Colin Osman, an entry for 1858 appears which referred to an album of photographs in the Victoria and Albert Museum. This album purported to contain photographs of Elgin's visits to China and Japan. Clark had not viewed the album but suggested in correspondence with the writer that this might be an interesting line of enquiry. Furthermore, he understood that the present Lord Elgin had some photographs from that period. Clark's chronology was well known to photo-historians, and the album's museum reference had even been given. It seemed most unlikely that photo-historians would have missed anything this significant.

On further investigation it was found that the album had belonged to an amateur photographer who had included pages and pages of unexceptional views of England and Europe and numerous family portraits. It seemed a red herring. But right at the back were a few pages of Chinese and Japanese photographs. One of the latter, captioned "Japanese Commissioners," showed a group of seven men in formal dress. Although none of the photographs was dated, two portraits featured Lord Elgin. These were Jocelyn's missing photographs! The album belonged to a Lewis Strange Wingfield, and genealogical research soon established that Wingfield was Jocelyn's nephew. On closer examination, several of the photographs bore the blind-stamped impression of a family crest, and further research established this as the armorial of the Jocelyn family. The photograph of the Commissioners, which was incidentally taken in Edo, matched the description and sketch in one of the letters above. It also turned out that the present Lord Elgin's album contained almost the same Chinese and Japanese photographs, although they had been cropped, presumably for aesthetic reasons.

There are approximately ten photos in all, of which only three can be said to have definitely been taken in Japan. The condition of the wet-plate collodion photographs is very poor. Most show significant fading and/or other defects and it is very likely that they were not considered suitable for publication. Nevertheless, their historical importance is unquestioned. They represent the earliest extant examples of wet-plate collodion photography in Japan, and are the first photographs known to have been taken in Tokyo.

PIERRE ROSSIER

The identity of the nineteenth-century photographer known only as P. Rossier had always eluded photo-historians. Rossier was known to have had some involvement with the London firm of Negretti and Zambra, who published in stereographic form the first commercial views of China and Japan between the years 1859 and 1861. Furthermore, Japanese sources all agree that in 1860, whilst in Nagasaki for a few weeks, Rossier taught wet-plate photography to Ueno Hikoma, Horie Kuwa-jiro, Maeda Genzo, and others. The collection at the Siebold Museum, Nagasaki, also contains a photograph of Alexander Siebold, with a contemporary inscription on the back which identified the photographer and said it had been taken in the summer of 1859 (Fig. 34).

The British National Archives have panoramic photographs of Nagasaki taken by Rossier in 1860, and these are referred to in the official correspondence between the British Consul at Nagasaki and the British Minister at Edo. They represent the earliest dated wet-plate collodion photographs of Japanese landscape so far discovered (Fig. 33). Two contemporary references to the photographer referred to him as M. Rossier. This can obviously be interpreted as Monsieur Rossier and lead to the conclusion that his nationality was French, particularly as "Rossier" is a French name. These scattered pieces of information, when pieced together, told us very little indeed about Rossier. However, the discovery of his true identity, together with other biographical details, prove that he was a very significant figure indeed when it comes

Above Fig. 34. Pierre Rossier, "Portrait of Alexander Von Siebold," Nagasaki, 1859, large-format albumen print. Siebold Museum, Nagasaki. On the reverse, a contemporary Japanese inscription explains that Siebold was photographed by Rossier at Nagasaki with members of the Saga clan, in the summer of 1859.

to assessing the history of photography in the Far East.

Pierre Joseph Rossier was born on July 16th, 1829 in Grandsivaz, a small village in the canton of Freiburg, Switzerland. That Rossier's nationality turned out to be Swiss was not a huge surprise. Some time ago, the writer noticed references to a photographer, "P. Rossier," having produced 1860s or 1870s stereoview photographs of Freiburg and Einsiedeln in Switzerland.[10] Given the stereo format of the Negretti and Zambra series, this seemed at the time to be too much of a coincidence. On the other hand, Rossier was not an uncommon name and Freiburg was, and is, a French-speaking region of Switzerland.

Checking the Swiss museums to see what holdings, if any, they might have of Rossier's photographs was a task made infinitely easier when the writer was introduced to the Swiss photo-curator Sylvie Henguely. With her specialist knowledge, Henguely uncovered a number of stereos and *cartes de visite* of Swiss scenes and portraits scattered across various Swiss museums. From the printed captions on either the front or the back of the mounts, it was clear that P. Rossier was a photographer who at some stage had a studio in Freiburg. Other photographs produced by the Swiss photograph collector Gerard Bourgarel indicated that Rossier also had a studio in Einsiedeln. However, none of the museums had anything other than Swiss photographs, and no other information, including Rossier's first name, came to light. Henguely and the writer visited the Freiburg Town Archives. The head archivist, Hubert Foerster, helped tremendously; he produced trade directories which included a photographer named Pierre Rossier, copy passports issued to him in 1855 and 1872, and other information. Despite Rossier's being a common name in Freiburg, after some hours it was possible to build up a family tree.

Rossier was born into a Catholic farming family of modest means, the fourth eldest of ten children. Unlike his brothers and sisters, Pierre was not destined to follow a farming career. He must have shown early intelligence because at the age of sixteen he was given a teaching post at a school in the nearby village of Mannens-Grandsivaz.[11] On October 19th, 1855 a passport was issued to Rossier, whose occupation was shown as "photographer," for a period of three years. Countries noted to be visited were France and England, and the purpose of travel was to practice his profession as a photographer. Rossier was aged twenty-six and described as five feet three inches tall (1.6 meters) with brown hair and grey eyes.[12]

It appears that Rossier was away from Switzerland for seven years and did not return until some time in 1862.[13] In October 1865, in the nearby town of Aarau, Rossier married Catharine Barbe Kaelin (1843–67) who came from Einsiedeln.[14] Less than a year later, on July 30th, 1866, Christophe Marie Pierre Joseph was born. Perhaps Catharine failed to recover from giving birth, because on April 4th, 1867 she died at the tragically young age of twenty-three.

Pierre continued to work in his studio in Freiburg and on May 24th, 1872 applied for a one-year passport to travel to France. The link between Pierre Rossier and the Far East was contained in a key nineteenth-century Swiss book on the history of Freiburg canton's notables and personalities – Alfred Raemy's *Livre D'or du Canton de Freiburg* (1898). This book mentions that Rossier died in Paris, but does not give the date, and that he was the first photographer to traverse the Far East taking photographs: "Rossier Pierre, Ier photographe ayant parcouru les Indes, decede à Paris."[15]

The Freiburg trade directories also show that Rossier's photo studio, based in 211 Place du College, was in operation there until at least 1876. Sometime between 1871 and 1884

Rossier married for the second time. His wife, Marie Virginie Overney, was a domestic working for the landlords of 211, according to the Freiburg Census held in the Freiburg State Archives. On March 16th, 1884, Joseph Louis, Rossier's second son, was born in Paris. Joseph would own a café in Vevey, in the canton de Vaud, Switzerland, and would die there in 1927.[16] We can therefore deduce that Rossier died in Paris between 1883 and 1898. We now need to turn to non-Swiss sources to fill in some of the gaps in his life between the years 1855 and 1862.

Negretti and Zambra was a very successful London operation which specialized in the manufacture and sale of photographic and scientific equipment. The firm, which also managed its own photo studios, received a considerable boost when it was appointed as official photographer to the Crystal Palace Company in Sydenham, which opened in 1854. Partly because of this, Negretti and Zambra became one of the most successful photographic businesses in the country. In addition to their manufacturing concerns, Negretti and Zambra was a large retailer of stereoscopic views, issuing a significant number of collections from the early 1850s onwards. Albeit from a position of financial strength, the firm took on the heavy expense, and uncertainty, of sending Rossier to China to photograph the Second Opium War of 1857–60.

These China views were published by Negretti and Zambra in a set of fifty in November 1859.[17] Taken almost exclusively in and around Canton, they were favorably reviewed by the photographic periodicals of the time.[18] Interestingly, one of these reviews in *The Photographic News* (November 4th, 1859) makes clear that Rossier's instructions were not just to restrict himself to China on his "... roving commission to the East in search of novelties.... The time seems rapidly approaching ... [to] be able to see the most distant corners of the world in miniature in the stereoscope ... and the pictures we have received of Chinese people, costumes, and buildings, will, before long, be followed by others of Japan.... The photographer, a portion of whose work we have before us, left Canton, according to his instructions, and proceeded to the Philippine Islands...."

Rossier's detour to the Philippines – likely to have taken place in June 1859 since the *Overland China Mail* for June 22nd, 1859 records Rossier arriving at Hong Kong from Manila on June 18th on the ship *Chusan* – is also reported in *The Illustrated London News* (February 4th, 1860, p. 109): "Some time since Messrs. Negretti and Zambra, with an amount of enterprise for which they deserve the thanks of the public, dispatched a representative of their firm to China and Japan.... Having accomplished a considerable part of this interesting and difficult mission, he was directed to make his way to the Philippine Islands, and visit the Taal Volcano."

What then follows is a report from Rossier, in his own words, describing the difficulties encountered in securing these photographs. Neither *The Photographic News* nor *The Illustrated London News* mentions the "representative" by name. Unfortunately, Negretti and Zambra's early records were destroyed in the bombing of London during World War II, but it seems quite possible that Rossier was taken onto the Negretti and Zambra staff after he left Switzerland in 1855. Negretti and Zambra, when appointing him for the task, may have calculated that the neutrality implied by his Swiss nationality would have been useful in helping him secure passage on British or French warships in the Far East – a huge advantage for a photographer trying to obtain images in far-off and otherwise inaccessible places.

Below Fig. 37. Pierre Rossier, "Nagasaki Harbor," October 1860, large-format albumen print. The National Archives, Kew. A five-part panorama showing the harbor and its entrance. One of a series of views commissioned by the British Consul at Nagasaki, which represents the earliest known large-format topographical photography in Japan. This view, together with Fig. 35, appears to be a 360-degree eight-part panorama with one plate, Deshima and its vicinity, missing. Rossier probably took the photograph from the residence of the British merchant Thomas Glover.

We get our first official "sighting" of Rossier when the *North China Herald*, on July 17th, 1858, records Rossier as a passenger arriving at Hong Kong from England on the *Pottinger* on July 7th. It seems likely that this is the date that Rossier first arrives in China. The English author Albert Smith, writing in *To China and Back* (1974), describes meeting him in Hong Kong on August 25th, 1858: "Paid a visit to Messrs. Negretti and Zambra's photographer, M. Rossier, who lived at the Commercial Hotel, belonging, I believe, to Messrs. Lane and Crawford. He complained much of the effect of the climate on his chemicals."

It had been thought that Negretti and Zambra's China and Japan photographs might have been taken by somebody other than Rossier, perhaps Walter Woodbury or the British consular secretary Abel Gower. The writer speculated on the authorship of these photographs in *Early Japanese Images* and concluded that either Rossier or Woodbury was the likely artist. It is now clear that Pierre Rossier was the photographer: there is absolutely no evidence that Woodbury went to Japan and Gower was only an amateur, occupied full time with consular duties.

There are other sources which confirm Rossier as being Negretti and Zambra's photographer. The first is particularly significant and comes from a private journal which the writer acquired a while ago written by one of the officers of the British ship HMS *Sampson* – the ship charged with the task of escorting the British Minister Rutherford Alcock, together with the other Consuls, to Japan, where they would take up their positions ahead of the official opening of the country on July 1st, 1859.[19] The journal entry for July 8th, 1859 reads: "I was included in a photographic view taken by Mr. Rossier,

a gentleman we brought from Nagasaki, employed by the Crystal Palace Company."

Negretti and Zambra was almost synonymous at that time with the actual Crystal Palace, and from the journal it is clear that the photograph was taken in Edo on the same day that a party of officers inspected Alcock's legation and residence-to-be, Tozenji Temple. As the ship also visited Kanagawa and Yokohama, Rossier would also have had ample opportunities to photograph in those places.

The above excerpt suggests that Rossier did not travel to Nagasaki on the *Sampson* but secured passage on another ship, which must have arrived by June 20th. Rossier had embarked on the ship *Formosa* at Hong Kong on May 23rd, 1859. It arrived at Shanghai on the 27th (*North China Herald*, May 28th, 1859) and it looks as though Rossier moved on to

the Philippines to photograph the Taal Volcano. He was back in Hong Kong on June 18th (*Overland China Mail*, June 22nd, 1859) and must have rushed to Nagasaki. HMS *Sampson* and the Consuls had arrived in Nagasaki on June 4th, having left Shanghai on May 30th. The ship had lost its bearings.

HMS *Sampson* left Nagasaki for Edo with Rossier and the Consuls at 5pm on June 20th, 1859, so Rossier must have made the crossing from Hong Kong in the quick time of just under three days. It is worth noting that Abel Gower was one of those on board and he may well have become friendly with Rossier. There is an undated portrait, supposedly of Gower, signed "P. Rossier," in the Leiden University photograph collection (Fig. 141).

Rossier's Japan movements around this time are, to say the least, sketchy. It is reasonable to assume that he secured

Below Fig. 40. Pierre Rossier, "Yakuama. General View of Yakuama," No. 72, from Negretti and Zambra's *Views in Japan*, first series, albumen-print stereoview, published 1861. Author's Collection. This is the earliest known photograph of Yokohama. The caption on the reverse reads: "Yakuama [*sic*] is a city built only during the last twelve months." Serious building work by the Japanese commenced at the end of 1858 or the beginning of 1859. The photograph was probably taken in June or July 1859.

Above Fig. 41. Pierre Rossier, "Kanagawa. Port of Kanagawa, with Japanese Shipping," No. 70, from Negretti and Zambra's *Views in Japan*, first series, albumen-print stereoview, published 1861. Author's Collection. The first known view of Kanagawa Port.

a good number of negatives at this time, which he would have been anxious to get back to London as quickly as possible. If he returned to Nagasaki with the *Sampson*, he would have left Kanagawa on July 22nd and arrived at Nagasaki on July 28th, 1859. His destination would have been Shanghai or Hong Kong in order to ship his negatives to London, a tried and tested sea route. But at this stage we cannot be sure what his movements actually were.

Our next sighting of Rossier is on February 27th, 1860 when the *North China Herald* (March 15th, 1860) reports Rossier as having left Kanagawa on that day for Shanghai via Nagasaki. In fact, he arrived at Nagasaki on March 2nd, left the next day, and arrived at Shanghai on the *Azof* on March 6th. It is of course possible he had been in Japan since June

Below Fig. 42. Pierre Rossier, "Jeda. Group of Japanese Officers, with Messrs Macdonald, Gower, and Fletcher, Attachés to the British Legation, at Jeda," No. 60, from Negretti and Zambra's *Views in Japan*, first series, albumen-print stereoview, published 1861. Author's Collection. Abel Gower, second from the left and a lifelong diplomat and amateur photographer, had previously been wrongly credited with authorship of this series. The photograph was probably taken in June or July 1859.

of the previous year, but it seems more likely that he was on his second trip to the country.

We know from the *North China Herald* (June 30th, 1860, p. 102), that he was in Shanghai on June 27th, 1860. The July 14th edition (p. 110) of the same newspaper has him staying at the exclusive Astor House Hotel and that prior to that he had been in Hong Kong.[20] He may have gone to Shanghai for photographic chemicals but it is far more likely, however, that he was there primarily to try to convince the British and/or French military authorities to allow him to accompany them to the scene of the imminent conflict in North China. If so, it seems that he was singularly unsuccessful. The British already had Felix Beato and John Papillon, and the French had Du Pin, Fauchery, and possibly Legrand. Rossier would have been devastated. His employers, Negretti and Zambra, would have expected an explanation from the thirty-year-old Rossier. That is why he had been sent to China in the first place.

We know that Rossier was not in Peking during the sacking of the Summer Palace on October 18th because he was in Nagasaki, on presumably his third visit to Japan, taking photographs of the harbor on behalf of the British Consul, George Morrison. In a letter of October 13th, 1860 to Minister Alcock in Edo, enclosing the photos, Morrison reports that he has "taken advantage of the presence of a professional photographer ... here for the moment, Mr. Rossier, an employee of the firm of Negretti & Zambra of London ... the cost ... namely seventy Dollars ... but considering that M. Rossier's time is specifically devoted to other purposes, and that he was occupied with them for several days ... as he is not a tradesman here for the sale of photographs, was not in a position to bargain ... and have seen very fair photographs taken, unassisted, by a pupil of M. Rossier..." (possibly Ueno Hikoma)[21] (Figs. 33, 35, 37).

The publication by Negretti and Zambra of Rossier's group of Japan photos was not until October or November 1861 and is reported in the November 1861 edition of *The Art Journal* (p. 351). Given the fact that Rossier was taking photographs in Japan more than two years earlier, why would Negretti and Zambra not want to publish them when public interest was at its height? The only explanation that suggests itself is that the negatives were damaged on their way to London or that Rossier, as he mentioned to Albert Smith, was finding difficulty in securing satisfactory chemical supplies. This seems distinctly possible when we see that Negretti and Zambra placed the following advertisement in *The Times* (May 28th, 1860, p. 3):

JAPANESE LADIES IN FULL DRESS – A STEREOGRAPH (FULL COLOURED) OF THE ABOVE INTERESTING SUBJECT, TAKEN BY MESSRS. NEGRETTI AND ZAMBRA'S ARTIST, NOW IN JAPAN, FORWARDED ON RECEIPT OF 24 STAMPS – 1, HATTON GARDEN, AND 59, CORNHILL.

This advertisement illustrates the earliest known example of a hand-colored Japanese photograph (Fig. 45). (An identical advertisement was published a few days earlier, on

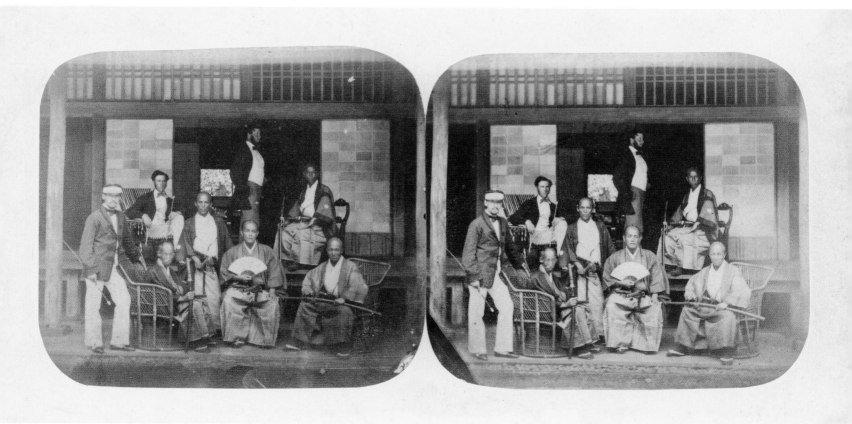

May 23rd, p. 5, but without the words "full coloured.") It also suggests that Rossier sent back to London a batch of Japanese negatives which must have been taken some three or so months earlier, bearing in mind that in those days the journey by sea could take ten to twelve weeks. There really must have been a serious problem with the quality of those negatives. A second (?) batch of negatives arrived four months later, as announced in *The Times* (October 3rd, 1860, p. 11):

PHOTOGRAPHS FROM JAPAN –A CASE OF RARE AND CURIOUS PHOTOGRAPHS OF THE SCENERY OF THIS INTERESTING COUNTRY, AND ILLUSTRATIVE OF THE MANNERS AND CUSTOMS OF THE JAPANESE TRIBES, WHICH HAVE BEEN EXECUTED BY A SPECIAL ARTIST SENT OUT FOR THE PURPOSE BY THE ENTERPRISING FIRM OF NEGRETTI AND ZAMBRA OF LONDON, ARE EXPECTED BY THE PENINSULAR AND ORIENTAL COMPANY'S STEAMSHIP CEYLON, WHICH WILL PROBABLY ARRIVE AT SOUTHAMPTON ON WEDNESDAY.

Even then, Negretti and Zambra must have been unhappy with what they saw, since they would not publish them for another year! Ironically, the first time we see some of these views in published form is in George Smith's *Ten Weeks in Japan*, which included five from the series, including the one advertised in June 1860. This book appeared on April 9th,

1861, still six months before Negretti and Zambra would eventually publish. In July 1861 Henry Arthur Tilley published *Japan, the Amoor, and the Pacific* in which eight of Rossier's Japanese photographs were lithographed. Whatever the real reason for the inordinate delay, it must have put a further strain on the relationship between employer and employee.

Rossier is again in Shanghai on October 20th, 1860 because the *North China Herald* (October 26th) reports his arrival from Hong Kong where he left on October 15th on the *Aden*. His activities for the next few months are not known, but at some stage he put together a second series of some forty Japanese stereoviews. He also managed to increase the original fifty Chinese views up to more than a hundred.[22] The next mention of Rossier is not until a year later when the October 15th, 1861 issue of the *Overland China Mail* lists him as arriving in Hong Kong on the 1st from Bangkok on board the SS *Viscount Canning*. At around this time he met the French zoologist Firmin Bocourt and assisted him by taking, or providing, ethnographical portraits of Siamese subjects which were required for a French museum.[23] Whether Rossier traveled to Bangkok with Bocourt or had already returned to the capital is not clear. But in any case, his involvement with Thailand must have been over by early 1862 at the latest. In 1863 Negretti and Zambra issued a series of thirty stereoviews of portraits and scenes of Siam. These were undoubtedly produced by Rossier and may have been his final assignment for the company. Certainly his next movements would seem to suggest so.

Rossier now seems to be preparing to leave for home. The *North China Herald* issues of March 8th and 15th, 1862 record him embarking on the *Ly-ee-Moon* on March 7th at Shanghai, bound for Hong Kong. At the same time, an advertisement appeared in the March 1st and 8th issues of the *North China Herald*:

FOR SALE A BARGAIN A NEW AND COMPLETE SET OF PHOTOGRAPHIC APPARATUS COMPRISING: A PATENT MAHOGANY FOLDING CAMERA, WITH ALL IMPROVEMENTS, FIRST CLASS IN EVERY RESPECT. A ROSS PORTRAIT LENS, VERY SUPERIOR. A ROSS LANDSCAPE LENS, DO. ALL IN SMALL PORTABLE CASE. ALSO, A PORTABLE MAHOGANY TRIPOD STAND, WITH BALL AND ROCKET JOINT AND PATENT SCREW ADJUSTMENT. ALSO, A TRAVELLING CASE COMPLETELY FITTED UP, CONTAINING ALL THE NECESSARY APPARATUS, TOGETHER WITH A LARGE FRESH SUPPLY OF CHEMICALS JUST RECEIVED FROM LONDON, AND TWO PRACTICAL WORKS ON PHOTOGRAPHY. THE WHOLE QUITE NEW AND IN PERFECT ORDER. THE ABOVE IS TO BE SOLD A BARGAIN, IN CONSEQUENCE OF THE OWNER'S LEAVING SHANGHAI. FOR FURTHER PARTICULARS APPLY AT THE "SHANGHAI DISPENSARY", BRIDGE STREET. SHANGHAI, 27TH FEBRUARY, 1862.

Rossier had probably received instructions from Negretti and Zambra to dispose of his chemicals and equipment in Shanghai, before leaving China for home.

Rossier's views of China and Japan represent the first commercially published photographs taken in those countries.[24] For this reason alone, Pierre Rossier's place in Far Eastern photo-history is assured. He also produced a series of views in Siam and possibly in India, too. He also photographed the Taal Volcano in the Philippines. Until he arrived in Nagasaki, in 1859, Japanese students of photography had struggled to master the subject, this despite the unstinting assistance from the capable Dutch medical instructors. A seasoned professional photographer like Rossier, equipped with the right chemicals and equipment, was able to give the necessary impetus to Japanese self-sufficiency. But we still know too little about Rossier's activities during his seven years' absence from his homeland. Further research may reveal a number of other surprises.

Above left Fig. 46. Pierre Rossier, "Jeda. Houses by the Sea, in the Bay of Jeda," No. 66, from Negretti and Zambra's *Views in Japan*, first series, albumen-print stereoview, published 1861. Author's Collection.

Center left Fig. 47. Pierre Rossier, "Jeda. General View of Jeda, from the Gardens of Yatoan," No. 67, from Negretti and Zambra's *Views in Japan*, first series, albumen-print stereoview, published 1861. Author's Collection. The main street, in the center of the picture, leads to Kanagawa.

Below left Fig. 48. Pierre Rossier, "Yakuama. View in the Vicinity of Yakuama," No. 73, from Negretti and Zambra's *Views in Japan*, first series, albumen-print stereoview, published 1861. JCII Camera Museum, Tokyo. Another first view of Yokohama, probably taken in June or July 1859.

Top Fig. 49. Pierre Rossier, "Jeda. Group of Japanese, and General Construction of a Japanese Dwelling," No. 61, from Negretti and Zambra's *Views in Japan*, first series, albumen-print stereoview, published 1861. Author's Collection.

Above Fig. 50. Pierre Rossier, "Panorama of Nagazaki," No. 1387, from Negretti and Zambra's *Views in Japan*, second series, albumen-print stereoview, ca. 1863. Author's Collection. It is not clear exactly when Rossier photographed this second series of forty views, which is listed in a November 1863 Negretti and Zambra catalogue. The labeling and numbering on the backs of this second series, of which fifteen refer to Nagasaki, are inconsistent and often absent, making identification difficult. Despite the handwritten number here, the official number in the series, judging from the Negretti catalogue, is likely to be between 1 and 5. In other words, this view may be one of a five-part panorama. Note the spelling of Nagazaki. See also the Negretti and Zambra Appendix 1 (page 305) for more information.

CHAPTER 2

1860s
Western Studios Dominate

SAMUEL BROWN
FRANCIS HALL
ORRIN FREEMAN
UKAI GYOKUSEN
JOHN WILSON
OVERSEAS MISSIONS
SHIMOOKA RENJO
UENO HIKOMA
UCHIDA KUICHI
YOKOYAMA MATSUSABURO
TOMISHIGE RIHEI
FELIX BEATO
WILLIAM SAUNDERS
CHARLES PARKER
ANTOINE FAUCHERY
FREDERICK SUTTON
WILHELM BURGER
MILTON MILLER
CHARLES WEED
OTHER WESTERN PHOTOGRAPHERS
OTHER JAPANESE PHOTOGRAPHERS

Although the treaty ports of Kanagawa, Nagasaki, and Hakodate opened for foreign trade on July 1st, 1859 on schedule, the Japanese were determined to substitute Yokohama for Kanagawa. Why they wanted to do this, and how they succeeded, is of no relevance to this book, but by the beginning of 1860 Kanagawa was all but ignored except for some American missionaries and foreign legation staff who continued to live there. The British and American Ministers initially resisted what they saw as a direct contravention of the Treaty provisions. They were worried about the dangerous precedent being set and were anxious not to encourage future acts of non-compliance on behalf of the Japanese authorities and appealed to the foreign merchant community for support. However, several ships had arrived with merchants from Shanghai and Hong Kong and these traders wanted immediate accommodation and facilities and were not overly concerned with the implications for long-range national interests or policy. They saw that Yokohama had a better harbor and that the Japanese had erected jetties and a customs house there, together with housing and other facilities. The "diplomatic stand-off" ended when William Keswick, of the prominent trading house Jardine Matheson, took a house in the new settlement. That was the signal for the other Western traders to follow suit. The Japanese had won.

Early residents of the three new ports knew what kind of infrastructure was required to provide for the basic amenities and luxuries of life. The foreign communities in Hong Kong, and the treaty ports of China, had been established for over fifteen years. Residents there had their own houses, shops, restaurants, newspapers, clubs, hotels, cemeteries, municipal councils, chambers of commerce, prisons, and courts.

But these models could not be replicated overnight. It is worth noting that at the end of 1859 there were only forty foreign residents of Yokohama and the first foreign language newspaper was not established in Japan until the *Nagasaki Shipping List and Advertiser* came out in 1861. Early hotel owners could not afford to be too selective when taking in their guests. In October 1862, the British diplomat Ernest Satow confided to his diary that he was determined to leave the Yokohama hotel where he was staying because of nightly fights and quarrels and guns being fired "without caring where the bullets go."[25]

In the early months and years, the treaty ports were frontier towns where the niceties of life were not always observed in the scramble for property, business connections, and trade. Against this background, it is not too surprising that the pursuit of photography, either for recreational or commercial purposes, was not considered a priority. That is not to say there was no photographic activity.

SAMUEL BROWN

The role of Samuel Robbins Brown (1810–80) in early Japanese photography has been underestimated and needs to be reassessed (Fig. 53). He did not introduce photography to Japan, as William Elliot Griffis claimed in his biography of Brown, *A Maker of the New Orient* (1902), but his influence, as we shall see, was not insignificant.

Born in Connecticut, Brown graduated from Yale University and ended up in China as a teacher and missionary from 1839 to 1847. After returning to America, he accepted the post of principal at a private teaching college in New York State. The school proved to be an uneconomic venture and he resigned in the spring of 1851 before accepting the role of pastor at the Reformed Dutch Church in Owasco, New York. In early 1859 his church decided to send three missionaries to Japan. Brown was appointed senior missionary, and on May 7th sailed from New York with the Reverend Guido F. Verbeck and Dr Duane B. Simmons. All three men were accompanied by their wives, and Brown's two daughters were also in the party. They reached Hong Kong in August, and then moved on to Shanghai where they rested a few days. The party then split up, with Verbeck deciding to go to Nagasaki. Brown and Simmons settled on Kanagawa and arrived on November 1st, 1859, four months after the port had been officially opened.

The Reformed Dutch Church had provided the missionaries with camera equipment and this seems to have been entrusted to Simmons, who set up a photographic room or studio at the temple where he stayed. The American merchant Frank Hall had traveled to Japan with the three missionaries

and kept a diary, which was later edited by F. G. Notehelfer and published as *Japan through American Eyes* (1992). From his journal we learn that Hall visited Simmons' temple on May 3rd, 1860 in order to use the equipment. However, we do not know how long the studio had been functioning.

The following month, Simmons' wife, disenchanted with missionary life, left her husband and returned to America. The Reform Church then voted to recall Simmons, but he resigned from the Church, returned the photographic equipment to Brown, and established a private medical practice in Yokohama. According to F. Calvin Parker in his book *The Japanese Sam Patch* (2001), for the next twenty years Simmons enjoyed a distinguished medical career serving at the Juzen Hospital in Yokohama, the Tokyo Eye Infirmary, and

the noted educationalist Fukuzawa Yukichi's Keio School.

The contemporary passenger lists record several visits back and forth to America by Simmons and/or his wife. It is not clear how long his marriage lasted. In 1882, in ill-health, he made the decision to return to America. However, according to the brief death notice in a February issue of the *Japan Weekly Mail*, he returned to Japan in 1886, together with his aged mother, and died there on February 19th, 1889 at the age of fifty-three.[26]

Brown was already approaching fifty when he reached Japan, and were it not for Simmons' sudden separation from the Church he would probably not have got involved with photography. According to Griffis, it was not until the commencement of the American Civil War (1861–5) that Brown, with the consequent dearth of missionary funds curtailing his activities, occupied some of his increased leisure hours in "mastering the fascinating art of photography." Griffis goes on to state that "He was thus one of the very first to photograph Japanese costumes, works of art, and varied human characters. One result was the instruction of Renjio Shimooka, still living at the age of over four score years, the first native of Japan to learn the fascinating art of photography, in which so many of his countrymen now excel." Shimooka was thought, until recently, to have been the first Japanese professional photographer when he set up his studio in

Below Fig. 54. Anonymous, "American Protestant Mission, Kanagawa," ca. 1860–1, albumen-print stereoview. Author's Collection. This photograph seems to be taken outside Jobutsuji Temple, Kanagawa, Dr J. C. Hepburn's home. From left to right: Reverend S. R. Brown's younger daughter; Reverend S. R. Brown, Mrs Brown, Dr D. B. Simmons (possibly), Dr Hepburn, Mrs Hepburn, Miss Caroline Adrian (possibly), Dr Hepburn's son, and Julia Brown (probably).

Yokohama in 1862 (see page 69). Griffis is wrong to assert that Shimooka was the first native to learn photography, as this would deny the activities of earlier Nagasaki-based students, and others. Nevertheless, it is extremely interesting to note that Brown was instrumental in teaching Japan's most famous photographer.

Griffis went on to record: "On the 5th October, 1862, Mr. Brown sent forty-three large photographs of Japanese scenes, with proper notes and explanations, to be delivered to the Reformed Churches at Owasco Outlet, Utica, Syracuse, Geneva, Farmer, and Ithaca, the people of which had contributed to purchase apparatus and chemicals for his use. He had promised these when in America, expecting that Dr. Simmons would make them." These, or indeed any of Brown's photographs, have so far failed to surface.

On October 14th Brown accompanied the United States Minister Robert Pruyn on a diplomatic visit to Edo Castle. In one of his letters home, dated November 8th, 1862, he says: "American Minister receives trust and respect of government very much. Recently I have been to Edo castle, with a minister, to meet Roju, ministers of the cabinet. We had a pleasant 4 hours. Whilst we were there, the ministers let an English photographer take their portraits. They went out of the building 4 times in the fine rain. Mr. Pruyn kindly had permission for Mr. Gulick, Mr. Saunders and for me to take photos in Edo, where it was completely prohibited 2 years ago." This intriguing reference is mentioned in Saito Takio's article, "The First Photography in Yokohama and William Saunders" (1989). Saunders had arrived in Yokohama on August 30th for a short stay and it is more than possible that Brown would have been receiving some technical advice from this fine photographer.

Sometime in 1864, Griffis says that Brown sent home another package of photographs and books valued at some $500. However, these were destined to become a casualty of the Civil War since the ship carrying them was sunk by the predatory Confederate ship, the *Alabama*. According to the

London and China Telegraph (July 8th, 1867, p. 354), Brown suffered a serious fire at his home on the previous 26th April. He lost his entire library, including a great many valuable Japanese books and translations, and it is quite possible he lost photographic prints and negatives as well. After twenty years in Japan, Brown's health broke down and he returned home to America and died there in 1880.

An interesting footnote, mentioned in Notehelfer, is that Brown's eldest daughter, Julia Maria Brown (1840–1919), became a competent photographer at around the same time (or perhaps earlier) as her father. Accordingly, she has the distinction of being the first recorded female photographer in Japan (Figs. 52, 54). As Parker noted in *Jonathan Goble of Japan* (1990), she caused a considerable scandal in the foreign community, and acute embarrassment to her father, when sometime in 1860 it was discovered she had become pregnant by a seventeen-year-old language student at the British Legation, John Frederick Lowder. Brown was devastated; and Lowder's mother, who was to marry the British Minister Rutherford Alcock, was against her son's "marrying an American and into an unaristocratic circle." But they did marry – albeit just forty-eight hours before their baby was born. Julia died in Japan and is buried with her husband in the Gaijin Bochi (the Foreigners' Cemetery, Yokohama). Sir Henry F. Woods in *Spunyarn* (1924, Vol. 1, p. 217) describes meeting her in Nagasaki in March 1866 where she was living with Lowder, who was Assistant Consul at the time. Although wrongly identifying her as Alcock's daughter, he referred to her as "a very nice little woman, chatty and agreeable."

Aside from Samuel and Julia Brown, it is interesting to reflect on how many missionaries working in the Far East in the nineteenth century had their own photographic equipment. A number are mentioned in this book, but it is highly probable that others were involved. As missionary archives – one of the great untapped resources – become accessible to scholars, new images and information are likely to emerge.

FRANCIS HALL

Until the publication of his diaries in *Japan through American Eyes*, edited by F. G. Notehelfer (1992), Francis Hall (1822–1902) was virtually unknown amongst historians of nineteenth-century Japan (Fig. 56). And yet the records show that Hall was a long way from being a nonentity. For a start, he was a partner and leading light in Walsh, Hall & Co., which would become the foremost American trading house in Japan, and looking through the early records of life at Yokohama, we see that Hall was a regular and prominent spokesman for his fellow Americans and acted, occasionally, as temporary US Consul. More than that, he was an intelligent and perceptive observer of life in the treaty port and, fortunately for us, recorded his impressions in his diaries which covered the crucial period 1859–66.

Francis Hall arrived in Japan on 1st November, 1859, on the same ship as the missionaries Samuel Brown and Duane Simmons with whom, significantly, he maintained a close friendship throughout his time in Japan. He had not traveled to Japan as a merchant, but rather to collect material for a book and to act as correspondent for the *New York Tribune*. It was for these reasons that he kept a diary, which ran to nearly 900 pages. Notehelfer believes that Hall probably only intended to stay for one or two years, but that successful business ventures in Yokohama extended his stay. Interesting as it is, we will not consider his life before or after his residency in Japan since what is of concern to us here are his photographic activities as an enthusiastic amateur during his stay. It is very likely that he intended to use his photographs to provide illustrations for any future book, and perhaps to supplement his articles for the *Tribune*. In any case, from his diaries we know that he was active as an amateur photographer between May 1860 and April 1861.

However, we know of only one extant photograph of Hall's. It is illustrated on page 162 of Notehelfer and is now in the Griffis' archives at Rutgers (Fig. 55). It was sent to

William Elliot Griffis with a letter in 1901 when the latter was in the process of writing his biography of Samuel Brown. Griffis had asked Hall for any photographs of the period and Hall replied that what photographs he had of the early days were "in book," but that he would be able to provide Griffis with a photograph of the temple they lived in. This was the Jobutsuji, occupied by the Hepburns and where Hall and Simmons stayed. Although not identified, the Japanese standing by the front gates bears some resemblance to the castaway Sam Patch, who worked there as a servant for a while. Hall went on to say in his letter that Brown's daughter, Mrs Lowder, was an amateur photographer who might also be able to assist him in finding photographs to illustrate his book.

It is a pity that Hall's photographs have not surfaced. Despite the very welcome references to photography in his diary, it is regretful that Hall did not once talk about the general state of photography in Yokohama. His significance for us is that he is connected directly with Simmons' studio, has produced at least one surviving photograph from that period, and rubbed shoulders with at least two other early amateurs – Brown and his daughter Julia with whom he was friendly. It is also Hall who tells us that the famous Japanese Manjiro had, and used, a daguerreotype camera.[27]

Hall's references to photography actually raise more questions than answers. It is not clear, for example, whether he continued to photograph beyond April 1861, the last time he mentions the subject. Perhaps he became too involved with his growing business interests to do so. Did Hall give lessons to Shimooka Renjo, as his friends the Browns did? When did Simmons first open his photographic room? Was it before Orrin Freeman established his ambrotype studio? And did Hall meet with his fellow American, Orrin Freeman, and discuss photography? It almost seems inconceivable he would not do so. He would also have had opportunities to meet with other American photographers living at Yokohama, for example Edward Kern and John Wilson. Unless an undiscovered archive of Hall's letters exists, it is possible we will never know the answers to these questions.

ORRIN FREEMAN

Until recently, very little was known about the American merchant Orrin Erastus Freeman (1830–66), who moved to Yokohama from Shanghai in late 1859 or early 1860. Freeman's significance is that his was almost certainly the first commercial photo studio to open in Japan and that he taught the first Japanese professional photographer.

We can start by looking at the reminiscences of an old-time Yokohama resident, G. W. Rogers, contained in an article, "Early Recollections of Yokohama," published in the *Japan Weekly Mail* (December 5th, 1903): "The first general store was opened by O. E. Freeman somewhere about the spot where now stands the Chartered Bank. Mr. Freeman brought the first photographic camera and accessories used for the purpose of trade, and he carried on business as a photographer for some months, taking portraits only, unfortunately, and then sold the whole turn-out to a Japanese, taught him the business, and thus took the first step in that line. With the proceeds of this profitable transaction, and with the assistance of his brother in China, he had sent over a large assortment of goods and stocked a general store where he amassed a nice fortune" (Fig. 57).

Elsewhere in the article, Rogers, who himself arrived in Yokohama on December 27th, 1859, talks of the property he first stayed in being a place where new arrivals were offered accommodation until they found their feet. The context implies that Rogers arrived before Freeman, so we can infer the latter's arrival in Japan as being early 1860. However, some small doubt arises from a reading of Saito Takio's book *Bakumatsu Meiji: Yokohama Shashinkan Monogatari* (2004), where we learn that Freeman gave evidence in a British Consular court case in July 1865 (*Japan Herald*, July 22nd, 1865) stating he had been running his general store in Yokohama for five and a half years. If, as Rogers says, Freeman had previously been practicing photography for several months, then this suggests he arrived in Japan in late 1859. Or Perhaps Freeman was involved in trading goods at the same time as he opened his studio. He was still listed in the 1860 *China Directory* as a merchant in Shanghai, but this may not be significant since it is not known exactly when the directory was printed.

Rogers' mention of Orrin's brother in China refers to Albert Lamper Freeman (1833–70), a respected Shanghai merchant since April 1855 and, for a period of several months from January 1858, a reluctant US Consul at that port. At the age of fifteen, Albert had joined the American trading house W. H. Fogg Brothers, and in 1855 was sent to Shanghai to help run their operations in China. Since leaving America, Albert had been writing to his friend in Boston, Dr Charles Cullis.[28] The letters throw much light on Orrin Freeman's activities, but it should be mentioned that on several occasions Albert refers to letters from Orrin himself being enclosed and addressed to Dr Cullis. These letters are missing and undoubtedly would give important additional information regarding Orrin's photographic operations both in China and Japan.

September 3rd, 1858 (Shanghai) "Mother I see in her letters is fully determined upon coming to China and so I shall look for her early next year...."

November 6th, 1858 (Shanghai) "Orrin I see has a notion of coming. I hardly know what he will do unless he shows a little more pluck than he has in his previous life...."

Clearly Albert, who is three years younger, is not impressed with Orrin's career to date. A recent check of the *Boston City Directories* for 1856 and 1857, at the New York Public Library, listed Orrin E. Freeman as a saloon keeper in Boston.

March 22nd, 1859 (Shanghai) "Mother is here having arrived safely with her two big boys on the 9th March. She came in the steamer from Hong Kong. The *Charmen* arrived in Hong Kong after a passage of 125 days, [According to the passenger list in the *Overland China Mail*, February 26th, 1859, the family arrived in Hong Kong on February 21st having departed Boston on October 24th the previous year.] Orrin has written you a letter to send with this so I must refer you to him for particulars as to the voyage.... Orrin is about starting his daguerreotype establishment and will do well I think. The Chinese appreciate them, and he will find plenty to do."

Orrin's other brother, Melvin Palmer Freeman, would stay in China for a number of years, initially working with Albert but then operating on his own. Albert undoubtedly confused daguerreotype with ambrotype since it is the latter format with which Orrin would work.

April 4th, 1859 (Shanghai) "Orrin has just been up to Soochow the place where I went when playing the part of despatch bearer and he thinks of settling down and starting a 'Daguerreotype Room' next week, he is delighted with the country – and no doubt will do well, Melvin went with him and was pleased with all he saw. He is to be in the office with me. I shall look out for him and hope to make a smarter man of him than his brother."

Although from the letters it is possible to infer a reasonable relationship between Albert and Orrin, again we see that the younger brother remains unimpressed with his elder brother's achievements. It is also possible that Orrin resented his brother's success; certainly the large sums of money made by Albert would have been a key driver in persuading him to come to China. The apparent choice of Soochow (present-day Suzhou and known as the Venice of the Far East) for Orrin's first studio is fascinating. At that time Soochow was a very large city, fifty miles inland from Shanghai, where few foreigners lived. Orrin would therefore have been relying upon the native Chinese to walk into his portrait studio. He also perhaps calculated that he could charge well for giving photography lessons to aspiring Chinese photographers.

April 20th, 1859 (Shanghai) "Shanghai is a very quiet place and might easily pass for another 'Sleepy Hollow!'... Orrin is at Soochow where he has gone to establish himself as an Ambrotypist in which business I doubt not he will be quite successful as it is something the Chinese fancy. He has written you a letter by this mail in which he gives you a list of sundries which he requires for his business. For the payment of the amount I have written to Mr. W. H. Fogg in New York by this mail to honour your draft."

This missing letter of Orrin's would be extremely interesting.

May 8th, 1859 (Shanghai) "Orrin is settled down in the interior at Soochow, he will doubtless do well at his business, as it takes with the Chinese."

September 3rd, 1859 (Shanghai) "Mother is well as are Orrin & Melvin – they all like Shanghai and are very much contented with it. Orrin is taking pictures and is doing fair to middling at it."

This is the first indication that the studio in Soochow did not succeed. Orrin has been back in Shanghai for some weeks and the following advertisement was placed in the *North China Herald* on July 23rd, 1859. It continued to feature until the last insert on August 20th, 1859. Albert's comment suggests that Orrin's Shanghai studio is not a blazing success:

AMBROTYPES-AMBROTYPES. THE UNDERSIGNED RESPECT-FULLY BEGS TO INTIMATE TO THE COMMUNITY THAT HE IS PRE-PARED TO TAKE THE AMBROTYPE LIKENESS IN A STYLE SUPERIOR TO ANYTHING HITHERTO OFFERED IN SHANGHAI. CHARGES LOW AND SATISFACTION GUARANTEED. YANG-KING PANG ROAD, NEXT DOOR TO MESSRS. H. FOGG & CO. ORRIN E. FREEMAN. SHANGHAI, 21ST JULY, 1859.

On August 27th, 1859 the same newspaper advertised a change of studio address. Significantly, this advertisement ran until its last insert on November 26th, 1859. We therefore know that if Freeman did reach Japan in 1859, it would have been December. Unless any firm information to the contrary comes to light, it does seem safe to assume that Freeman moved to Yokohama in early 1860.

REMOVAL

THE UNDERSIGNED HAS REMOVED HIS AMBROTYPE ROOM TO THE FRENCH BUND, NEXT DOOR TO KIN-TE-YUEN'S SILK SHOP. ORRIN E. FREEMAN   SHANGHAI, 26TH AUGUST 1859

April 17th, 1860 (Shanghai) "The Barque *Onward* arrived a few days ago from California bringing my father who is now with us.... Orrin is in Kanagawa – Japan. He has written to you to go with this, he has just built him a house and hopes to do well."[29]

Simon B. Freeman, the father, appears in the *Boston City Directories* for 1839–51 and is listed as a housewright (house builder). His father had been a surgeon, and his grandfather a colonial governor and chief judge of the Supreme Court of New Hampshire. Simon Freeman spent some years in the Far East with his wife and sons and died in San Francisco on October 30th, 1867 at the age of sixty-three, according to the *London and China Telegraph* (November 27th, 1867, p. 615).

May 15th, 1860 "Orrin is still in Kanagawa." *June 30th, 1860* "Orrin is still in Kanagawa and I believe is doing well." *July 16th, 1860* "Orrin is still in Kanagawa and I think is doing well." *September 3rd, 1860* "I enclose a letter from Orrin." *November 21st, 1860* "Orrin is in Japan. Melvin has just returned from Japan. He doesn't like the people." *December 21st, 1860* "Orrin sends a letter with mine."

April 6th, 1861 "Orrin has written you a letter which I enclose." *April 23rd, 1861* "... greet her as I would my own sister (were I the happy possessor of such a treasure) ... Mother is well – father and Melvin also.... Orrin was well at last accounts." In February 1862 Albert is back in America. *April 10th, 1862 (New York)* "By the way if you find any orders for goods in Orrin's letters you need not take any notice of them until you hear from me respecting them. *June 27th, 1862 (San Francisco)* "I am off tomorrow morning early in the Schooner *Storm Cloud*, a vessel of 300 tons bound for Kanagawa, Japan.... I shall meet Orrin.... I learn through a friend who came in here that Orrin had left for Shanghai a day or two previous to his sailing, it will be a benefit to know from him when I arrive in Kanagawa just how my affairs stand in Shanghai ... the vessel is called the *Rival* ... she came over from Kanagawa in 29 days ... father will come on to Shanghai first opportunity [he appears to be working in Canada on a trading deal in which Albert is involved].... I may require his services there...." *August 26th, 1862 (Kanagawa)* "I arrived ... 22nd inst. ... after passage of 55 days [the journey was a very rough one and at one time the ship and passengers were in mortal peril] ... found Orrin well and pleased to see me.... A steamer leaves [for Shanghai] on the 1st September." *October 2nd, 1862 (Shanghai)* "Melvin is here and seems to be doing a good business. I am living with him, he is engaged in the River Trade, he owns quite a fine craft and I have just furnished him with money to buy another. He will make more money in business for himself than he would working for others.... Write Orrin occasionally as it will please him. He is a little jealous – He says that he sent you some Japanese coin with those pictures – you will probably find them between the picture and the case that contains them...."

Albert's last letter is dated November 6th, 1862 when this important resource ends.

According to Patricia McCabe's *Gaijin Bochi* (1994, p. 480), Orrin Freeman died in Yokohama and is buried at the Gaijin Bochi (Foreigners' Cemetery) where the inscription on his gravestone reads: "Orrin E. Freeman of Boston, Mass., U.S. of A. Born Sept. 3rd. 1820. Died August 16th, 1866,

Yokohama." Although the date of death is correct, Freeman was born in 1830. Saito Takio's *Bakumatsu Meiji* gives 1830, and at the time of Freeman's death in 1866 US Consul Fisher, and a contemporary newspaper reference state his age at death as thirty-six. It should also be mentioned that Saito gives the 9th as Freeman's birth date, not the 3rd.[30] The only other scrap of information we have is that until October 1861, Freeman acted as the Kanagawa agent for the *Nagasaki Shipping List and Advertiser* (see September 21st, 1861 issue); after that the paper was produced from Yokohama as the *Japan Herald*. In fact, the first issue of November 23rd carries an advertisement which shows Freeman trading as a "Ship Chandler and General Store Keeper, Yokohama."

It is highly probable that Freeman's studio predated Simmons'. When Freeman arrived in early 1860, with the intention of practicing photography, he would have lost no time in locating premises and opening for business. Although Dr Simmons' studio is not mentioned by Frank Hall in his diary until May 1860, it is possible that the facilities had been available for some time before that date. But there would not have been the same urgency on Simmons' part who, in any case, spent the first few months in Japan looking for suitable accommodation.

We know that Freeman sold his camera and equipment to a Japanese and that the purchaser was Japan's first professional photographer, Ukai Gyokusen. We can only speculate on why Freeman agreed to the transaction, which included lessons on photography. Rogers implies that a high price was paid, and perhaps it was as simple as that. Freeman may well have calculated that reinvesting the proceeds into setting up his general store would be more rewarding. There is also the possibility that he sold his ambrotype equipment to Ukai but continued his studio using glass plates.

Saito Takio's *Bakumatsu Meiji* contains a photograph of

Otsuki Takayuki taken by Freeman (Fig. 58). Otsuki was a scholar of Western studies who spent time in Yokohama shortly after the port was opened. The photograph was presented by Otsuki's grandson to the Numazu City Archives of Meiji History and has an inscription which translated reads "Portrait of Otsuki Yasutaro (Takayuki's alias) aged twenty-six taken by a camera by an American photographer Freeman in Yokohama on June 15th 1860." A piece of board accompanying the photograph is inscribed "This American photographer Freeman is a person who recently started a photography business in Japan for the first time in Yokohama. He has recently switched to using a camera with glass plates but this method costs money and people say that it is expensive." Saito also mentions two other photographs that may well have been taken by Freeman although there is no definite proof.

Orrin Erastus Freeman died in Yokohama of paralysis on August 16th, 1866. The writer has not been able to discover any obituaries, but a copy of his last Will and Testament was sent by George S. Fisher, the United States Consul for Kanagawa, to Washington together with Freeman's death notification in Consular Despatch No. 214 (August 22nd, 1866, FM 135, US National Archives). In his Will, signed on September 30th, 1865, just under a year before his death, Freeman bequeaths the annual sum of $1,000 each to his mother Ann Freeman and his father Simon B. Freeman for the rest of their lives. The balance of his estate he leaves to be shared equally between his brothers, Albert Lamper Freeman and Melvin Palmer Freeman. The estate includes properties at No. 57 Main Street, Yokohama, No. 125 Swamp Concession, Yokohama, and a home in Russell Street, Charlestown, Middlesex County, Massachusetts, United States. A boat, the American barque *Philip 1st*, is also left.

Freeman's executors are noted to be Thomas Hogg of Yokohama and his brother Albert Lamper Freeman or, "should my brother Albert Lamper Freeman be absent from Japan then my brother Melvin Palmer Freeman." Consul Fisher estimated Freeman's estate as approximately $130,000, a significant sum in those days and proof that Freeman's merchant career in Japan had been successful. Albert would finally have been impressed. Orrin Freeman is rightly celebrated as the first to open a commercial photo studio in Japan and for teaching Japan's first professional photographer, Ukai Gyokusen.

UKAI GYOKUSEN

Ukai Gyokusen (1807–87) was Japan's first professional photographer, opening a studio in Edo in 1860 or 1861 (Fig. 59). Until recently, his reputation has been overshadowed by both Shimooka Renjo and Ueno Hikoma. We will look at the careers of these two shortly, but it is significant to note that their own studios did not open until 1862. That Ukai has languished in the backwaters of Japanese photo-history for so long, barely meriting a mention by either Japanese or Western scholars, is quite extraordinary.

In 1883, four years before his death, Ukai buried several hundred glass negatives in the Yanaka Cemetery, Tokyo, underneath a monument on which was carved some biographical details. When he died, in 1887, he was buried next to the monument and his gravestone carries more detailed biographical information.

A key passage mentions that Ukai wanted to learn about photographic technique and realized he would need to consult a foreigner. He therefore went to Yokohama in the year that the port was opened. He states that he learnt from an American called Freeman who was teaching the subject. Soon afterwards he returned to Edo, moved to Yagenbori, and set up a photographic studio called Eishin-do. What this passage suggests is that Freeman was teaching other aspiring photographers at the same time. Ukai does not say that he purchased Freeman's equipment, and this leaves open the possibility that he sold it to another Japanese who may, or may not, have subsequently opened a studio.

The glass plates under the monument were excavated on September 30th, 1956 by the *Sun Shashin Shimbun* (Sun Photo Journal), which then wrote about the findings on October 20th. In 1969 Nishina Matasuke wrote two articles on the life of Ukai, which reaffirms Ukai's status as the first professional photographer. Ichikawa Ninzo also wrote about Ukai's career in the March 1989 *Rissei University Bulletin*, No. 22. The Yokohama photo-historian Saito Takio wrote about Ukai in *Saishoku arubamu – Meiji no Nihon – "Yokohama shashi" no sekai* (1990). But full recognition of the significance of Ukai's career has only recently emerged following the publication of Saito's *Bakumatsu Meiji* (2004) and Mitsui Keishi's "The Relationship between Two Portraits of Yokoi Shonan" (2003).[31]

According to Mitsui, Ukai came from a financially secure background; his father was a finance commissioner for the *daimyo* Matsudaira Jiju Yorisaki and also carried the title of grand chamberlain. Ukai was born in Ishioka-shi, Ibaraki Prefecture, the youngest of four brothers, and at the age of thirteen he was adopted by the saké supplier to another *daimyo*, Mikawaya, and as a consequence took up merchant status. However, after making the acquaintance of the painter Tani Buncho, he developed an all-consuming interest in art and antiques. In 1831, at the age of twenty-four, he left the saké business and became a full-time artist.

Left Fig. 59. Anonymous, "Portrait of Ukai Gyokusen," ca. 1880s. Courtesy of Boyd and Izakura. This image appeared in the *Asahi Gurafu Rinjizokan Shashin Hyakunen-sai Kinengo* (Asahi Graph Special Photographic Centenary Number), *Asahi Shimbunsha Hakko*, December 1925, p. 18.

We then lose track of Ukai until he decides to move to the newly opened port of Yokohama where he meets Orrin Freeman. If Ukai did, in fact, purchase Freeman's camera, equipment, and a series of lessons he must have had access to considerable capital because we have to assume that Freeman would have struck a hard bargain in making the "profitable transaction" referred to by Rogers.

In any case, by the autumn of 1861 an Edo publication, *O-edo tosei hanakurabe shohen* (First Compilation of Great Edo Contemporaries), makes mention of Ukai's photographic studio.[32] It is interesting that he took up his new profession at the late age of fifty-four, and that he also chose Edo to establish his ambrotype studio. It could be argued that his contemporaries, Shimooka Renjo in Yokohama and Ueno Hikoma in Nagasaki, took the "safer" options when opening their studios in 1862 in the treaty ports frequented by their likely customers – foreigners. Ukai, on the other hand, would be operating in a town from which foreigners were excluded. In a curious way, this mirrors the decision of his teacher Freeman to open his first studio in Soochow (Suzhou), China, where few foreigners were resident. The local Japanese would have barely heard of photography, and not many of them would have had the money to spend on a sitting. But perhaps Ukai had a different form of clientele in mind: on the monument above his buried glass plates he said that within a few years he had photographed over 200 members of the aristocracy.

The studio name was Eishin-do and it was based at Ryogoku Yagenbori, Tokyo, until 1867 when Ukai says he closed it for good. In 1879 (presumably having already retired), he is employed as a temporary worker at the Treasury Printing Office, traveling for five months with the director inspecting and photographing antiquities in western Japan. The results of these researches were published by the

Below Fig. 61. Attributed to John Wilson, "Body of Henry Heusken," 1861, large-format albumen print. Nederlands Scheepvaartmuseum, Amsterdam. On the night of January 15th, 1861, Heusken, the universally popular interpreter at the US Legation, was attacked by seven assassins whilst riding back from the Prussian envoy's residence. Mortally wounded, he managed to get back to the Legation but died several hours later, conscious throughout. John Wilson was known to have been at his bedside and is therefore attributed as the likely photographer.

Treasury Printing Office between 1880 and 1881 as *Kokka Yoho* (Remaining National Glory). This publication contained lithographs of the works studied, and these seem to have been produced from photographs taken by Ukai.

There are numerous unattributed ambrotype portraits from the 1860s in existence, and some of these may well have been taken by Ukai. Saito Takio, in his abovementioned book, discusses one or two surviving photographs that could well have been taken by Ukai; but he also illustrates one portrait that can definitely be attributed. In 2002 the Yokohama Archives of History was presented with a portrait of Miura Shushin by a family descendant. The presentation case has an imprint on the back which reads "Toto Ryogoku Yakkenbori – Eishindo Ukai Gyokusen." The inside of the case lid has an inscription in black sumi ink: "Portrait of Miura Shushin aged 21, taken on 9th March 1863" (Fig. 60).

Now that Ukai Gyokusen's pioneering role in Japanese photography has been fully recognized, it is likely that further research will take place and more details on his life and career will hopefully emerge.

JOHN WILSON

Thanks to the research done by Japanese photo-historian Saito Takio, we now know much more about the American photographer John Wilson (ca. 1816–?) and his role in Japanese photo-history. From what we currently understand, his significance stems from his having taken early photographs in Edo, and for selling his photo equipment to Shimooka Renjo and enabling that famous Japanese photographer to start out on his career.

It is not clear when the American first went to Yokohama, nor whether he had practiced photography in America or elsewhere before arriving. We do know that he was in Yokohama in 1860 because the Prussian Embassy hired him for a few days in December 1860 as their official photographer. He then went with them to Edo and was able to take a number of photographs in and around the city. Four of these photographs were engraved for the May 25th, 1861 issue of the German periodical *Illustrirte Zeitung*.[33] An interesting reference appeared in *The Far East* journal (February 4th, 1873, p. 200), which mentioned that in 1861 Count Eulenberg's Prussian Embassy gave "a fine series of photographic views" as a gift to the Shogun. These may well have been of Germany, but if they were of Japan they would most likely have been taken by Wilson. Assuming these photographs have survived, they will now probably be in the Tokugawa family photographic collection or with the archives of the Imperial Household.

On the night of January 15th, 1861 the US Legation's interpreter, Henry Heusken, was attacked by seven sword-wielding assassins whilst riding back from a visit to the Prussian Embassy's temporary residence in Edo. Mortally wounded, he managed to ride back to the US Legation where he died some three hours later. It is clear from the dispatch sent to Washington by Consul-General Townsend Harris, on January 22nd, 1861 (FM 133), that John Wilson was at

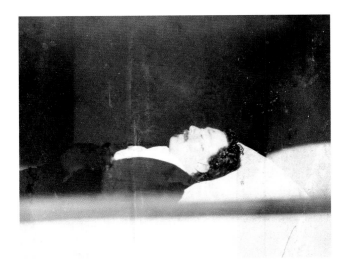

Heusken's bedside having himself been with him and the Prussians that evening. Consequently, it seems likely that the photograph of Heusken's body, which was sent to the murdered man's mother, together with the indemnity, was taken by Wilson (Fig. 61).

Wilson was now settled in Yokohama but saw an opportunity to market his photographs in Europe and America. Either on his own initiative or on a suggestion of Raphael Schoyer, an American merchant with whom he was staying, Shimooka Renjo was commissioned, with other artists, to produce a giant scroll containing paintings of the photographs taken by Wilson. In a financial transaction whose terms are not clear, Wilson apparently acquired the scroll from Shimooka in return for his photographic equipment.

Wilson was now anxious to take the scroll to Europe and America to exhibit it together with his photographs and hopefully make a considerable profit. He applied for a passport on December 16th, 1861 and this was issued on the 30th. From Wilson's passport information, we learn that he was forty-five years old, born in Albany, New York, and was five feet six and a half inches tall.

Wilson went to London and exhibited the photographs and scroll. According to the art journal *The Athenaeum*, Wilson promoted the paintings on the scroll as showing "with scrupulous fidelity the costumes, temples, streets, bridges, scenery and rivers of the Japanese Empire."[34] Consul Fisher, as we will learn, wrote in 1865 that the enterprise ended in failure and consequently Wilson did not return to Japan. We currently know nothing more about him other than what emerged from a curious property row now outlined.

By 1865 there had been a long-running property dispute between the Japanese government and the American merchant Schoyer, mentioned above. The details of the dispute are covered in Saito's *Bakumatsu Meiji* and in Jack L. Hammersmith's *Spoilsmen in a "Flowery Fairyland"* (1998). Exhaustive background and primary source material are contained in the US National Archives, Diplomatic Despatches, FM135. In summary, Schoyer claimed that John Wilson purchased land in Yokohama for 265 Mexican dollars on August 16th, 1861 and sold it to him for 1350 dollars on December 27th, 1861. By 1865 the land was worth substantially more and the Japanese claimed that the paperwork had not been dealt with correctly and that consequently the property belonged to the government. Remarkably, the US Yokohama Consul, George Fisher, and the US Legation's Acting Minister in Edo, Anton Portman, took opposite sides in the dispute and great antipathy developed between them as a result. Washington was brought into this embarrassing affair and Fisher, who was already out of favor in Washington, was dismissed. Because of the acrimonious and long-running nature of the dispute, some additional light is thrown on Wilson's activities.

In a letter to Fisher dated June 5th, 1865, Acting Minister Portman writes: "I was well acquainted with Mr. Wilson, having met him both at Yedo and Yokohama. I also know that Mr. Wilson was anxious to leave Japan, and had not only stated this on more than one occasion that he applied through the Consul Mr. Dorr to this Legation for a passport which was ultimately granted him. He was not a bonafide resident and could not comply with the property qualifications required of applicants for ground, and as such his application could not have met with Mr. Dorr's approval." Fisher replied on June 6th, 1865: "Mr. W. was an applicant for land, he was an American, he was a photographer & trader & he was for a few days in Count Eulenburgh's [*sic*] employ...." And a further letter on June 8th: "Mr. Wilson came here to reside and he left here intending to return but owing to his failure in exhibiting his Panorama of Japan in Europe and the United States he has not as yet returned."

What happened to Wilson, his photographs, and the giant panoramic scroll are all mysteries waiting to be solved.

OVERSEAS MISSIONS

In this section we are concerned with those Japanese who traveled abroad on official duties in the 1860s and were photographed for posterity. The first such event was the 1860 Japanese Embassy to the United States (Figs. 62–64, 66, 67). Contained in Article xiv of the 1858 Japan/US trade treaty was a clause stipulating that ratifications of the treaty would be exchanged in Washington. W. G. Beasley, in his book *Japan Encounters the Barbarian* (1995), records that the Japanese delegation that left for America consisted of seventy-seven persons. These included eleven officials, two interpreters, an apprentice interpreter (Tateishi Onojiro, a young sixteen-year-old who was to become popular with the American ladies), and three doctors. The rest were attendants to the officials, drawn from various Japanese domains.

The party left Yokohama on February 13th, 1860 on the USS *Powhatan*, arriving in San Francisco on March 29th after a brief stop at Honolulu for supplies. From there they traveled south to Panama and crossed the isthmus by train and finally by ship up to Washington. Some 5000 Americans witnessed their arrival on May 14th, and another 20,000 lined the streets along the route to their hotel, the Willards. A sense of the excitement at the time is captured in a number of stereoview photographs executed by several different studios. During their stay in America, many studio portraits were taken of the ambassadors, and a number of these have survived, mainly in stereoviews or *cartes de visite*.

Whilst the Japanese were heading to America in the *Powhatan*, a support group was on its way to San Francisco in the Japanese ship, the *Kanrin Maru*. One purpose of this

mission was to provide a replacement envoy in the event of anything happening to any one of those who had traveled on the American ship. There were ninety-six Japanese on the voyage, which had a secondary purpose of demonstrating Japanese naval skill in crossing the Pacific. The party consisted of naval trainees, doctors, a number of volunteer samurai and attendants, and an interpreter, Nakahama Manjiro, the former castaway. A reference in Francis Hall's diary, transcribed in *OJP*, shows that Manjiro became a competent daguerreotypist shortly after his return from America, and certainly by October 1860. Also on the ship, as one of the American naval advisers was Edward Kern, about whom we read earlier. It would not be surprising if Manjiro received some photographic training from Kern during their time together. Alternatively, Manjiro could have taken lessons when the ship reached San Francisco.

Other official missions were sent to Europe in 1862 (Fig. 68), France in 1864 (Figs. 51, 65, 71), France and England in 1865, and the United States in 1867. The Shogun's younger brother, Tokugawa Akitake, also visited Europe in 1867 (Fig. 70). Some selected students were also allowed to travel to the West for study purposes. There were also unofficial and therefore illegal journeys made by individuals and groups. These were few in number, however, not least because participants were aware that they were committing an offence, which theoretically risked the death penalty.

During the first European mission in 1862, an amusing incident occurred at Nadar's (Gaspard-Felix Tournachon) photographic studio in Paris. The ambassadors had come to have their portraits taken and showed great interest in the workings of the establishment. One of the officers produced from his pocket a brush and ink and asked Nadar to sit for

Below Fig. 66. C. D. Fredricks & Co., "Members of the First Japanese Mission to the United States with a New York Lady," New York, 1860, Japanese Embassy series, No. 15760, hand-colored albumen-print stereoview. Old Japan Picture Library.

Bottom Fig. 67. C. D. Fredricks & Co., "Portrait of Tateishi Onojiro (Tommy)," New York, 1860, albumen-print *carte de visite*. Old Japan

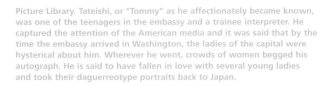

Picture Library. Tateishi, or "Tommy" as he affectionately became known, was one of the teenagers in the embassy and a trainee interpreter. He captured the attention of the American media and it was said that by the time the embassy arrived in Washington, the ladies of the capital were hysterical about him. Wherever he went, crowds of women begged his autograph. He is said to have fallen in love with several young ladies and took their daguerreotype portraits back to Japan.

London Stereoscopic and Photographic Company.

No. 74. View in the Japanese Court.

Below Fig. 70. Disderi & Co., "Tokugawa Akitake," Paris, 1867, albumen-print *carte de visite*. Old Japan Picture Library. The Shogun's younger brother was only fourteen when he visited Paris to represent Japan at the Paris International Exposition. The original plan was to spend five years studying and traveling around Europe, but when news came through of the fall of the shogunate, he and his party immediately returned to Japan.

Below Fig. 71. L. De Lucy, "Japanese Ambassadors at the Jardin d'acclim-atation, Paris," 1864, large-format albumen print. Christian Polak Collection. The Jardin d'acclimatation opened as a zoological garden in 1860. The display of plant specimens and live animals, collected from all over the world, must have startled the visiting Japanese.

DISDÉRI & Cᵒ (Limited)

Below Fig. 72. William England, "The Japanese Court," No. 24, stereoview, published by the London Stereoscopic and Photographic Company, 1862. Author's Collection. Here we see another view of the Japanese articles on display.

The International Exhibition of 1862.

London Stereofcopic and Photographic Company.   24.   The Japanefe Court.

his portrait. The Frenchman, not to be outdone, called for his own pencil and paper and the two artists proceeded to draw one another. According to the *British Journal of Photography* (May 1st, 1862, p. 178), Nadar's work was by far the superior.

These overseas missions played a major part in shaping Japan's future policy towards the treaty powers. In traveling around Europe and America, it would have been all too clear to the Japanese that their country was in no position to compete militarily. Consequently, in order to resist excessive Western trading demands and latent imperialist ambitions, compromise in its dealings with foreigners would be necessary – at least for the time being. Suffering the same fate as China was not an option, and Japan's survival rested on its ability to learn from the West, modernize, and build up its own industrial and military strength as quickly as possible. These missions were therefore a major turning point in Japan's history. Surviving photographs of these overseas envoys bear witness to this change – a change that was to have important consequences not only for Japan, but for the world as a whole.

SHIMOOKA RENJO

Shimooka Renjo (1823–1914) is probably the name that most Japanese would mention in relation to the history of photography in their country (Fig. 73). Until the recent revelations concerning Ukai Gyokusen, Shimooka was thought to have operated the first professional studio in Japan when he opened it in Yokohama in 1862.

There is still some uncertainty about the details of Shimooka's life, in particular how and when he came to learn the techniques of photography. The best research on this photographer has been carried out by Saito Takio, the photohistorian at the Yokohama Kaiko Shiryokan (Yokohama

Archives of History Museum). He quotes a number of sources in his article "Shimooka Renjo (1823–1914)" (1997), some of which he admits are contradictory. In the circumstances, Saito's preference is to place more reliability on sources closest to the time that the supposed events took place. For this reason, an article published in 1891 by Shimooka's friend Yamaguchi Saiichiro, entitled "Shashin Jireki," is the work from which much of the following information has been taken. This work was also translated and summarized in the photographic journal *The Practical Photographer*, September 1896 and appears in full in *OJP*. This article was supplied by Izawa Shuji, who at the time was the editor of the *Sashin Sowa* photographic magazine. Moreover, this article, and others submitted for publication at the same time, was vetted by the British engineer and co-founder of the Nihon Shashin Kyokai (Photographic Society of Japan), William K. Burton, professor of engineering at the University of Tokyo and a lifelong photographic enthusiast. Burton, always a reliable commentator on "things Japanese," and a particular expert on all matters to do with photography, was obviously satisfied with the substance of the article. Yamaguchi had based his article, incidentally, on interviews he had conducted with Shimooka himself. It is also reassuring to note that Shimooka, who was still living at the time, had sent his congratulations to *The Practical Photographer* (p. 243) and was presumably aware of the content.

Born in Shimoda, the son of an official shipping agent to the ruling Tokugawa family, Shimooka, being the third son, followed the not uncommon Japanese tradition of being adopted into another family. Showing artistic promise, he attempted to become an artist at the age of thirteen and went to Edo to study, whilst also being employed as an apprentice to a local merchant. He was not successful in his artistic studies and in 1843 served as a samurai at the Shimoda artillery battery. Whilst there, he was introduced to the

famous artist Kano Tosen, and became a student. In 1844 Shimooka's time at the battery expired and he returned to Edo with the intention of making another attempt to succeed as an artist. It was there that he apparently saw a Dutch daguerreotype in the house of one of the members of the Tokugawa clan. Fascinated, he resolved to find a way of making photographs. Knowing that in order to do this he would need to talk to foreigners, he managed to get employment as a draughtsman, employed by the coast guard office at Uraga. Whenever the occasional foreign vessel came into the port, he would attempt to find out something about photography. In this he was unsuccessful, and it was not until Henry Heusken arrived in 1856 that he made any progress at all.

Heusken was employed as Dutch translator and secretary to the first American Consul, Townsend Harris. Although nothing is mentioned in Heusken's diaries, Shimooka apparently obtained the rudiments of photography from Heusken who, without the advantage of readily available equipment, simply described the main principles and improvised by substituting some twigs for a tripod, folded paper in the shape of a box for a camera, and a piece of glass in lieu of a lens.

When the government decided to open the port of Yokohama in 1859, Shimooka decided to move there to enhance his chances of studying photography. He met with an American merchant, Raphael Schoyer, whose wife, a talented artist, taught him Western-style painting. Shimooka also met around this time an American, John Wilson, who had been hired as the official photographer to the 1860 Prussian Embassy. Following the conclusion of the treaty, Wilson decided to stay

on in Japan. He had taken many photographs in and around Edo and these were used by Shimooka and other Japanese artists who were commissioned by Wilson (with the possible financial involvement of Schoyer) to create a colossal panoramic oil-painted scroll of some 8858 feet (2700 meters).

At the end of 1861 Wilson decided to take the scroll to America and Europe in the hope of selling it at a profit. Apparently, in exchange for the scroll, he gave Shimooka his camera, photographic equipment, and chemicals. However, it seems that Wilson did not spend enough time explaining the techniques of photography, and Shimooka struggled to master the art. This is independently confirmed by a travel notebook compiled by a visiting American missionary, Thomas C. Pitkin: "The arrival of a photographer caused no slight excitement in Yokohama. The result of his efforts appears in many beautiful views of the country including some of the finest in Yedo, which are for sale in London and perhaps also in New York. He left his instrument and chemicals behind which an enterprising native whose gallery I visited was endeavouring to use with no very good success."[35]

Pitkin, who was in Japan for four months from the end of 1861 to the beginning of 1862, is undoubtedly referring to both Wilson and Shimooka. This reference, discovered by Luke Gartlan and mentioned in his "Chronology of Baron Raimund von Stillfried-Ratenicz" (2001), appears to confirm that Wilson was a professional photographer. It is hard to imagine the Yokohama community being "excited" by the arrival of an amateur, and the Prussian mission would surely have been much more likely to hire a professional. If Pitkin is referring to Shimooka's *photographic* gallery, then the perennial question of exactly when Shimooka opened his first studio is answered – early 1862. However, it is more than possible that Shimooka was running his own *art* gallery and was perhaps some weeks or months away from being able to operate a photographic studio (Fig. 76).

At about this time Shimooka had become friendly with the American missionary Samuel Brown and his daughter Julia. We know that Brown taught Shimooka and Japanese sources record that he also received help from a missionary girl called "Rauda." This is obviously Julia Brown (1840–1919) who, at this time, was married to John Lowder.

Shimooka and the Reverend Brown would remain friends throughout the missionary's tenure in Japan. There was an incident that occurred in 1902 in Yokohama, more than twenty years after Brown's death, which attested to Shimooka's enduring respect for his old friend. The eighty-year-old Shimooka, a committed Christian who, according to Yamaguchi, had been baptized in 1872 by the American missionary James Ballagh, was attending a special anniversary commemorating the setting up of the first Reformed Church in Japan. In front of a very distinguished audience, and in response to a chance remark made which recalled some controversy which arose during Brown's time in Japan, Shimooka spoke out in defense of Brown saying how the missionary had been falsely accused of using Church funds to improve his own residence. A reference to Shimooka's interest in Christianity appears in a letter written by a friend, Samuel Cocking.[36]

Sometime in 1862 Shimooka felt confident enough to open his own studio in Yokohama. He struggled commercially during the first few years, but by 1865 his business had prospered and he had moved into larger premises. A number of students were taken on, some of whom would later become well-known photographers in their own right. These included Yokoyama Matsusaburo, Usui Shusaburo, Esaki Reiji, and Suzuki Shin-ichi I and II.

Within a few years Shimooka felt secure enough to diversify into other businesses. He invested money in a dairy and also operated a horse-drawn carriage service between Tokyo and Yokohama. However, these businesses were not successful. The restless Shimooka also seems to have learnt the principles of lithography, and to have had some involvement in the controversy surrounding the invention of the *jinrikisha*. Another American missionary and friend of Shimooka's, Jonathan Goble, is credited by some authorities as having invented this two-wheeled, man-drawn carriage which was to become omnipresent from around 1869 onwards. Others credit Shimooka himself, although this is unlikely.[37]

Shimooka can be credited, however, with opening the first Japanese commercial photo studio in Yokohama. He also has a strong claim to being the first Japanese oil painter and lithographer. As far as his photographic work is concerned, more than a hundred *cartes de visite* have now been positively attributed to his studio. However, his larger format work

Above Fig. 76. Shimooka Renjo, "Shimooka's Yokohama Branch Studio," ca. 1870, small-format albumen print. Ozawa Takesi Collection, Tokyo.

remains elusive, with just a handful of images having so far been identified. As such, it is still too early to provide a reliable critique and assessment of his work. He seems to have ceased being active in photography from around the early to mid-1870s, leaving his studios in the hands of his assistants. Increasingly, he returned to his old love of painting. It seems that his various business activities did not make him particularly wealthy. However, he lived a long and interesting life, finally passing away at the age of ninety-one.

In Japan, Shimooka is still thought of as the "Father of Japanese Photography." It is also believed that he was the first native professional. With the re-emergence of Ukai Gyokusen and his prior claim to that mantle, Shimooka's role in Japanese photo-history needs redefining, particularly so if it turns out that Nakahama Manjiro also preceded him. What endears him to the Japanese is the fact that he struggled for many years before being able to open his studio. However, there seems to be no suggestion that his photography was anything other than adequate, and his contemporary in Nagasaki, Ueno Hikoma, seems to have produced work of higher quality. However, we should be cautious here given the relative paucity of surviving examples. In any event, Shimooka did open the first commercial Japanese studio in Yokohama.

Below Fig. 77. Shimooka Renjo, "Yokohama," ca. 1870, small-format albumen print. Old Japan Picture Library.

Below Fig. 78. Shimooka Renjo, "Unknown Location," ca. 1870, small-format albumen print. Old Japan Picture Library.

Above Fig. 79. Shimooka Renjo, "Unknown Location," ca. 1870, small-format albumen print. Old Japan Picture Library.

Above Fig. 80. Shimooka Renjo, "Unknown Landscape," ca. 1870, small-format albumen print. Old Japan Picture Library.

UENO HIKOMA

No history of Japanese photography would be complete without considering one of its most famous pioneers, Ueno Hikoma (1838–1904), who operated one of the earliest and most successful studios in Japan (Fig. 82). Unlike his contemporary Shimooka Renjo, whose tortuous road to photographic mastery is well documented, Ueno's approach was far more direct and straightforward. In fact, as we have seen, his merchant father, Ueno Shunnojo, was handling the import of photographic equipment from the 1840s.

There are other major differences between the two pioneers: unlike Shimooka's samurai status, Ueno was from the merchant class and much the younger when their respective studios were opened in 1862. Ueno was twenty-four when he opened what was probably Nagasaki's first commercial studio, while Shimooka in Yokohama was thirty-nine. Whereas the older man pursued a number of business enterprises unrelated to photography, Ueno seems to have been utterly consistent in following his chosen career. He seems, possibly as a direct result, to have been far more financially successful than his Yokohama-based counterpart. Whereas Shimooka was a trained artist, there is no evidence that Ueno indulged in any such activities.

Born in Nagasaki in 1838, Ueno's early schooling centered on studying the Chinese classics, but following the death of his father in 1851, he decided to switch to the study of chemistry in order to continue the family business, which had evolved into chemical manufacturing. Himeno Junichi, in his article "Encounters with Foreign Photographers" (2003), goes on to explain that a chemistry school had been attached

Above Fig. 81. Attributed to Ueno Hikoma, "Nagasaki River Scene," ca. 1874, large-format albumen print. Old Japan Picture Library.

Left Fig. 82. Anonymous, "Ueno Hikoma," ca. 1864, small-format albumen print. Old Japan Picture Library.

to the Dutch-run medical training establishment at Nagasaki, and Ueno subsequently enrolled in around 1858 and received lessons there from the principal, Pompe Van Meerdervoort. Almost immediately Ueno developed an interest in photography but, as we have seen, Pompe's attempts to teach this subject were limited by his personal lack of practical experience in the field. As H. J. Moeshart explained in his article "Nihon Shashinshi" (1986, p. 227), it was not until December 1859 that Pompe succeeded in creating a wet-plate photographic image.

Although progress by the students at the school was slow and unsteady, by 1860 experiments were occasionally yielding satisfactory results, and it is likely that an adequate understanding of the theory of the subject had been reached. But

Above Fig. 83. Ueno Hikoma, "Japanese Cemetery, Nagasaki," ca. 1874, large-format albumen print. Old Japan Picture Library. Very similar photographs by Felix Beato and Charles Weed have caused attribution problems in the past.

the arrival of Pierre Rossier was the necessary catalyst, which enabled Ueno and others to accelerate their understanding by putting theory into practice under the instruction and encouragement of a seasoned professional.

In 1860 Ueno traveled with fellow student Horie Kuwajiro to Edo where they stayed at the Tsu domain estate owned by Lord Todo. This *daimyo* had provided the money for Horie and Ueno to purchase a camera in Nagasaki, and the pair of them continued with their experiments in Edo. It is not known whether they met there the former castaway Nakahama Manjiro, who was about that time succeeding in taking his own daguerreotypes. In any case, progress was being made in Edo, as is demonstrated by the existence of an early glass-plate portrait of the 23-year-old Ueno taken in 1861 by Horie, and illustrated in Fig. 86. Further evidence of Ueno's technical mastery of the subject is the *Shamitsu-kyoku hikkei* (Manual of Chemistry), which he co-wrote in 1862 with Horie, and which subsequently became a textbook at the clan school.

Returning to Nagasaki in 1862, Ueno found that his previous teacher, Pompe, had left Japan and he therefore decided to leave the school and open his own photographic studio beside the Nakashima River. The first few years were hard, but gradually the studio's fame grew and his business started to prosper. Ueno took on a number of students, including Tomishige Rihei. Branch studios were also opened in Vladivostok in 1890 and Shanghai and Hong Kong in 1891. Ueno's brother Sachima had studios in Kobe in 1870 and

Tokyo in 1876, according to Boyd and Izakura's *Portraits in Sepia* (2000) and Tucker et al.'s *The History of Japanese Photography* (2003).

Always at the forefront of the latest technology, Ueno was one of the first photographers in Japan to embrace the new improved gelatin dry-plate photography and started experimenting with it in 1881. The first Japanese to succeed with the process, however, appears to have been Esaki Reiji in 1883, or possibly Usui Shusaburo a year earlier. Ueno had always been willing to learn from foreign photographers, and he seems to have struck up a friendship with Felix Beato following on from the Yokohama-based photographer's frequent visits to Nagasaki, and it is clear that they assisted one another. There are a number of extant Beato photographs which show members of Ueno's family and acquaintances, and Himeno's "Encounters" (2003) cites other examples of co-operation. Beato's technical ability was unquestioned, and Ueno would no doubt have benefited from discussions with this already famous Western photographer. Moreover, if Ueno's technique needed any further refinement, then the passing through in 1869 of the fine Austrian photographer,

Below Fig. 84. Anonymous,"Ueno Hikoma and Family," ca. 1870, large-format albumen print. Bauduin Collection, The Netherlands.

Bottom Fig. 85. Ueno Hikoma, "Portrait of Rodney H. Powers and Daughter Iida Masa Powers," Nagasaki, ca. 1906, cabinet-size albumen print. Old Japan Picture Library. Rodney H. Powers (1836–1909) left the United States navy in 1868 and settled in Nagasaki where he ended up operating the most successful American firm in town. With his common-law wife Iida Naka, he had two children, a son John (1870–1907) and a daughter Iida Masa (1891–1976). Masa married the politician Nakayama Fukuzo, and went on to become the first woman to hold a cabinet post when she was appointed Welfare Minister in 1960. Both Powers and Iida Naka died in 1909.

Wilhelm Burger, would have provided just such an opportunity. As mentioned in the writer's *Early Japanese Images* (1996), it is obvious from the studio props used in Burger's Nagasaki portraits that he is using Ueno's studio.

Ueno's work was exhibited at the 1873 Exposition in Vienna and reference to this and his reputation were referred to in the December 21st, 1872 issue of the *Nagasaki Express* when that newspaper reviewed the exhibits being sent from Nagasaki: "... photographs of the town of Nagasaki and the villages adjacent taken by Uyeno-hikoma of Nakasima, an artist not unknown to fame, as most foreign visitors to this place have taken away specimens of his talent." Ueno also received a number of special commissions during his career. For example, in 1874 he was asked to assist the American Venus Transit Expedition, and in 1877 the Nagasaki prefectural government commissioned him to photograph the battlegrounds of the recently concluded Seinan War (Satsuma Rebellion).

It is relatively easy to find examples of Ueno's studio portrait work in *carte de visite* and *cabinet* formats. However, it is exceptionally rare to come across albums of costumes and views (portraits and scenery). Although he encouraged foreign patronage of his studio, he does not appear to have pandered to the general demand for the typical souvenir album of hand-colored photographs. As far as rarity is concerned, the writer knows of no more than four albums that have been attributed to this artist. From these, however, it

is clear that Ueno was extremely talented as both a portrait and landscape artist. Some of his Nagasaki river and landscape views display great artistry and are sublime examples of pre-Meiji era Japanese scenery and compare favorably with similar work executed by Felix Beato and Uchida Kuichi. The best reference source for identifying Ueno's images is the rare 1975 work by his descendant, Ueno Ichiro (et al.) entitled *Shashin no Kaiso: Ueno Hikoma* (1975). Another detailed and much more recent work is Claude Estebe's dissertation "Ueno Hikoma (1838–1904) Un pionnier de la photographie japonaise" (1998).

According to Kinoshita Naoyuki in his article "The Early Years of Japanese Photography" (2003), Ueno's fame amongst visiting foreigners to the port of Nagasaki was such that over half his income came from taking their portraits. An interesting and evocative account of a visit by unidentified foreigners to what must undoubtedly be his studio appeared on page 40 of the February 1877 edition of *The Far East* periodical under the heading "Rambling Notes, Adrift at Anchor: First Visit to Nagasaki." It reads: "A few yards up from the bridge, on the banks of the stream, stands the house of a Japanese photographer. He told us he had studied the art from Dutch books, and he had certainly made considerable progress in its practice. My friends and I had ourselves taken in a group, and a capital picture he made. He had all his bottles labeled in ordinary Italian characters, with the proper chemical signs. His English, like that of very many of his countrymen who are occasionally, but not often, brought into contact with foreigners, consisted principally of 'es' for 'yes' and 'No 1' for 'very good.' The rooms of his house were all open to our inspection, as we passed through to his studio; and his wife, and other members of his family, old and young, were quite familiar

and easy with us…. In the family of this photographer, the natural unconstrainedness [*sic*] of their manners was very pleasant. There were many pictures of Japanese, carte de visite size, in a drawer, for sale. Some were already mounted – and some not; but as we required some of the latter, the little wife handed the baby to a servant, and at once set to work to trim the rough ones and stick them on the cards in the most business-like manner possible, while the husband went to prepare the materials for the picture he was about to take. On leaving the photographers, we took another good look at the pretty stream, and then trudged back to the settlement…."

Another visit to Ueno's studio is described by the French traveler Edmond Cotteau in his travel reminiscences *Une Touriste dans L'Extreme Orient* (1899, pp. 23–4).[38] He was most impressed with the quality and low prices and bought seventy-eight "large photographs, mostly coloured." This is an interesting reference to Ueno's apparently succumbing to the Western tourists' taste for colored works. Curiously, Cotteau also stated that Ueno had spent two years in Holland perfecting his art. Ueno Ichiro, a descendant of Hikoma's, told the writer that this was a mistake as he had never traveled to the West. It is likely that Cotteau has confused Ueno with one of the other photographers he visited in Nagasaki.

Ueno Hikoma has iconic status in Japan, especially in Nagasaki. His knowledge of chemistry, combined with intelligence and a willingness to learn from foreigners, were key factors in insuring his early success. The fact that his studio was in operation for more than forty years also underlines Ueno's commercial credentials. He was an early pioneer, but also a great photographer.

UCHIDA KUICHI

In the writer's 1996 work, *Early Japanese Images*, it was only possible to say, "No real evaluation can be made of Uchida's photographic ability, since only a few images have so far been attributed to him…." Three years earlier, Clark Worswick, the Asian photo-historian, had written "The Disappearance of Uchida Kyuchi," and bemoaned the dearth of attributed work for this artist. However, the last ten years have seen a great increase in the amount of research into early Japanese photography and many new books and articles have appeared inside Japan. One result of this has been the emergence of a clearer picture of the life and work of Uchida Kuichi (ca. 1844–75). Although scholars continue to disagree over a number of dates and events, there is now general consensus on several key elements. More of Uchida's photographs, particularly landscapes, have now been identified. In looking at these images, and comparing them to the work of other nineteenth-century Japanese masters, it is easy to see why he enjoyed such a high reputation.

A few years ago, the writer acquired from a Japanese antiquarian book dealer what turned out to be an unpublished and undated nineteenth-century manuscript biography of Uchida's life, written by one of his apprentices, Iioka Sennosuke, and titled "Ko Uchida Kuichi Tanreki" (ca. 1876). The information it contained has helped to fill in some of the missing details of Uchida's life. Nevertheless, Uchida's year of birth in Nagasaki is disputed: Boyd and Izakura give 1843; Tucker as well as Koizumi Kinshi (ed.) in *Nihon Rekishi Jinbutsu Jiten* (1994) cite 1844; Ozawa Takesi in "The History of Early Photography in Japan" (1981), Himeno in "Encounters," Worswick in "The Disappearance of Uchida Kyuichi," and Iioka above give 1846.

Following the early death of his father, Uchida was cared for by his uncle Yoshio Keisai (1822–94), who was a student at the Dutch medical school and studying photography with Van den Broek. It is very likely that Uchida's future career was influenced by his uncle's activities. Most scholars say that Uchida was an apprentice to Ueno Hikoma, but Iioka states that the relationship was rather one of "friendly rivalry" and that Uchida's teacher was Pompe van Meerdervoort (Fig. 93). According to Himeno, by 1863 Uchida had set up a successful photographic equipment import business and in 1865 moved to Kobe and opened his first studio with Ueno Sachima,[39] a younger brother of Ueno Hikoma.

Later that year he moved his studio to Osaka and it is there that he began to build his reputation. Echoing the success obtained by early Yokohama-based Western photographers who promoted their businesses to the military, Uchida took numerous portraits of samurai from various clans loyal to the ruling Tokugawa shogunate, who were undergoing military training at Osaka Castle due to the conflict with the insurgents from Choshu. At this time Uchida apparently obtained samurai status by assisting a local magistrate by the name of Okubo. In 1868 he moved to Yokohama and opened a studio there, again taking many military portraits. A branch studio was established at Asakusa, Tokyo, in 1869.

With his fame growing, Uchida was commissioned by the Imperial Household Agency to photograph Edo Castle. What sealed his reputation, however, was being asked in 1872 to photograph the Emperor and Empress Meiji and the Empress Dowager. The same year he was instructed to accompany the Emperor on visits to central Japan and Kyushu in order to make a photographic record of the tours (Figs. 87, 91). Although he was not permitted to photograph the Emperor

Below Fig. 88. Uchida Kuichi, "Benten-dori, Yokohama," ca. 1870, large-format hand-colored albumen print. Old Japan Picture Library. This image often appears in the albums of Kusakabe Kimbei.

Bottom Fig. 89. Uchida Kuichi, "Yokohama Railway Station," ca. 1873, large-format albumen print. Old Japan Picture Library. Kusakabe Kimbei recaptioned and continued to print this image into the 1880s. Leaving

copyright questions aside (and which are anyway discussed elsewhere in this book), further research is needed before determining how Kusakabe obtained the image. Possibilities include contracting with Uchida's heirs (he died in 1875) to obtain a supply of prints from the original negative(s); obtaining the original negative, or a copy negative made by Uchida at the time; or making a new negative by rephotographing an original print.

on tour, he was able to take another official portrait the following year (Fig. 92). Less than two years later, however, Uchida suffered a sudden bout of pneumonia and died on February 17th, 1875. A short obituary notice, referred to by Gartlan in his "Stillfried Chronology," appeared in the *Japan Gazette Mail Summary* on February 25th, 1875 (p. 38):

UCHIDA KUICHI, THE WELL-KNOWN PHOTOGRAPHER, WHO HAD TWO LARGE ESTABLISHMENTS IN TOKIO AND ONE IN YOKOHAMA, DIED OF CONSUMPTION ON THE MORNING OF THE 17TH INST., AGED 32. HE HELD THE APPOINTMENT OF PHOTOGRAPHER TO KUNAICHO, AND HAD THE HONOUR OF TAKING THE PORTRAITS OF THE EMPRESS AND HIS MAJESTY THE MIKADO.

As a measure of Uchida's growing celebrity during his lifetime, we can draw on testimonials from those who witnessed his work at first hand. The Henry Smith Munroe Papers contain a fascinating anecdote: Henry Smith Munroe was an American engineer who wrote to his parents on April 6th, 1874, mentioning Uchida's Tokyo studio: "The photographer here who takes the best landscapes is Uchida – a Japanese – I have looked over his magnificent collection of 500 pictures!! – & want to buy them all – but the price is $250 – '50 cents for one picture, $250 for 500 – I have but one price.' The execution is perfect – & the landscape subjects are admirably well chosen – real artistic pictures!!"[40]

An early 1874 tourist guidebook by F. R. Wetmore & Co., entitled *Guide Book of Yedo*, exhorted its readers "To buy Photographs of celebrated places in Tokio, go to Uchida's, on the road to Asakusa...." Worswick in "The Disappearance of Uchida" cites the inscription on the back of a *carte de visite* portrait of a young samurai, Nakayama Kawarokuro. The photograph was presented to an American lady and Nakayama wrote in English: "This picture was taken by an apprentice under Mr. Uchida the best photographer in Japan – 3rd September 1873."

The American missionary William Elliot Griffis mentions Uchida in the preface to his book *The Mikado's Empire* (1876): "The photographs of the living, and the renowned dead, from temples, statues, or old pictures, from the collections of daimios and nobles, are chiefly by Uchida, a native photographer of rare ability, skill, and enthusiasm, who unfortunately died in 1875."[41] The editor of *The Far East*, J. R. Black, refers to Uchida in the May 1st, 1873 edition (p. 272), when commenting on the inclusion of some photos of Nikko: "Those we now give are copies from some very excellent views taken by Mr. Uchida, a Japanese photographer of singular ability, who has a great variety of views of all parts of the country most interesting to foreigners. His studio is to be found at Asakusa, Yedo, and is quite worth a visit."

Until recently, problems over attribution have been an obstacle in making an assessment of Uchido's work. More of his landscape work is known, but only a handful of portraits have been identified – apart, that is, from his *carte de visite* work. After his death, Uchida's negatives appear to have been sold to several different studios: Kusakabe Kimbei, in particular, certainly acquired a number and continued to print from them for many years. Uchida's prints were not in copyright, and in the years following his death, many have been copied and passed off as the work of other studios. This has certainly created confusion for photo-historians who will need to work hard to track down the 500-image portfolio referred to by Munroe. Judging by the selection of tributes above, if Uchida had not died suddenly at such a young age, his reputation today might well have rivaled the great Felix Beato's. Whether it now will, remains to be seen.

YOKOYAMA MATSUSABURO

Although Yokoyama Matsusaburo (1838–84) is considered one of the leading figures amongst Japanese photographers, his work is quite hard to attribute and a fuller assessment of his contribution awaits further research (Fig. 95). He was born on Etorofu Island, which is now claimed and occupied by Russia, and in early life he moved with his family to the port city of Hakodate. At the age of fifteen he was apprenticed to a kimono dealer, and it is about this time that he developed an interest in painting. When Commodore Perry's ships visited Hakodate in 1854, Yokoyama was intrigued by the photographs taken by the photographer Eliphalet Brown. This interest was reinforced when, later that year, the Russian ship *Diana* arrived and the photographer Mozhaiskii took daguerreotypes of the streets of Hakodate.

A few years later, Yokoyama met the Russian painter Lehman, who was based at the port and looking for an assistant. Yokoyama started to help the Russian, and in this way became exposed to Western-style painting. His latent interest in photography was simultaneously revived since he thought, like many artists before and since, that mastery of the subject would enable him to more truthfully render the landscapes he wished to capture on canvas. Accordingly, he traveled to Yokohama and managed to persuade Shimooka Renjo to take him on as an assistant. Returning to Hakodate, soon after learning the basics, his technique was further refined by the Russian Consul Goshkevich, an amateur photographer.

Yokoyama's life between 1865 and 1868 is not well recorded, but he apparently opened his first studio in 1868 in Tokyo, according to Boyd and Izakura and Tucker, but in Yokohama according to Yokoe Fuminori in his article "Yokoyama Matsusaburo" (1997). Later that year he moved to his (second?) studio in Ikenohata, Tokyo, which at the time was the most modern and well-equipped studio in Japan.

Yokoyama's reputation was growing and in 1870, at the request of his old teacher Shimooka, the two of them photographed Nikko and presented the jointly signed work to the Tokugawa family. A year later he photographed the partially destroyed Edo Castle, and in 1873 a number of his photographs of Japanese art works were sent to the Vienna Exposition. In the same year he added an art school to his studio and instructed a number of art and photography students, amongst them photographers Nakajima Matsuchi, Azukizawa Ryoichi, and Suzuki Shinichi (although it is not clear whether this was Suzuki I or II). A number of the studio souvenir albums which he spent the next few years marketing to foreign residents and tourists, have survived to this day.

It is possible that he tired of being a photography practitioner, because in 1876 Yokoe writes that he passed over operational control to his assistant, Oda Nobumasa, and taught both photography and photolithography at the Japan Military Academy until 1881. There he experimented with a number of printing techniques and also developed a form of photographic oil painting (*shashin abura-e*). This involved peeling off the emulsion covering the face of a photograph and then painting the rear side with oil paints. In 1882 he contracted tuberculosis and his health began to deteriorate. He spent the last two years of his life in painting (particularly photographic oil painting) and immersing himself in a photolithography company which he had founded.

TOMISHIGE RIHEI

Tomishige Rihei (1837–1922) was an important Kyushu-based photographer and one of the pioneers in Japan of the wet-plate process. In 1854 he moved from Yanagawa in the north to Nagasaki and became a general merchant in the town but was not successful. In 1862 he became an apprentice to a little-known but early Nagasaki photographer, Kameya Tokujiro. When Kameya moved to Kyoto, Tomishige continued his training with Ueno Hikoma, with whom he developed a life-long friendship. In 1866 he opened his own studio back in his home town of Yanagawa. This was not a commercial success, and during the years 1868 and 1869 he again apprenticed to Kameya who by this time had moved back to Nagasaki. In 1870 Tomishige decided to continue his career in Tokyo, but according to Tucker et al.'s *The History of Japanese Photography* (2003), he somehow became involved with an army garrison stationed in Kumamoto and opened his studio there instead in 1871. Himeno Junichi in "Encounters with Foreign Photographers," however, gives the date as 1870. In either case, it is likely that this was the first studio to open in the city. One of the military commissions he received was to photograph Kumamoto Castle and these photographs have become important historical documents because the castle was burnt to the ground in the 1877 Seinan War (Satsuma Rebellion), along with Tomishige's studio (Fig. 98). However, his studio was rebuilt the following year and is still operating in the city today and run by his descendants. In celebration of its 130 years of existence, in 1993 the studio, collaborated in putting together an exhibition at the Kumamoto Prefectural Museum of Art. That museum issued a catalogue entitled *Tomishige Shashinjo no 130 nen*. Tomishige enjoys a very high reputation in Japan, particularly in Kyushu (see also Fig. 5).

Below Fig. 99. Felix Beato, "View on the Tokkaido," ca. 1867–8, large-format hand-colored albumen print. Author's Collection. It is often said that Beato left his landscapes uncolored, but the writer has seen many colored examples, such as this one. On a separate matter, no Beato stereoviews have so far been discovered, but the composition of this

picture seems deliberately designed to increase its depth and perspective – thereby enhancing any stereoscopic effect.

FELIX BEATO

When Felix Beato (1834/5–ca. 1907) set foot in Japan in 1863, he was already famous (Fig. 100). During the following five years he produced, intermittently, a body of work that enhanced his reputation even further. Then, apart from a few "cameo" photographic appearances in 1871 Korea, photographing the opening in 1872 of Japan's first railway and hiring himself out to the odd camera-wielding wealthy tourist, he retired. That is to say, he spent progressively less time behind the camera.

As soon as he arrived in Japan, Beato enjoyed considerable commercial success, and it was not very long before he was able to delegate management of his studio to others whilst he went off to pursue other business activities. However, throughout his life, he was never quite able to make a complete break from photography since these various enterprises invariably ended in failure. Whenever they did, he was always able to return to the studio and rebuild his fortune. He could do this for two reasons: he was an extraordinarily

Above Fig. 100. Anonymous, "Portrait of Felix Beato," ca. 1864, small-format albumen print. Old Japan Picture Library.

Below Fig. 102. "A Young Photographer." In the June 1869 issue of *Japan Punch*, the editor Charles Wirgman parodies Felix Beato's marketing techniques. One detects more than a grain of truth, however.

Below Fig. 103. "Album Price Barometer." In the same issue of *Japan Punch*, Wirgman suggests how Beato classifies his various customers.

Right Fig. 104. Felix Beato, "Atango-Yama, Edo," ca. 1867, large-format albumen print. Author's Collection.

gifted photographer and he had superb connections with the British military.

Beato had accompanied the British armed forces on several campaigns prior to arriving in Japan. Affable, and something of an extrovert, he was a big favorite with the officers and made many friends. These connections, which also extended to members of the diplomatic corps, were assiduously cultivated by Beato and were the key factor behind his photographic success. Not only did they increase his chances of securing transportation to any scene of conflict, they also insured he was in with a fighting chance of getting the front-line images which would command high prices on subsequent sale. In addition, getting access to warships as they came into port was something to which resident photographers always aspired. Taking group portraits of officers and crew on board their ships was an effective way of eliciting multiple sales and Beato, with his extensive range of connections, took full advantage when he was living in Yokohama. Following these on-board photo sessions, Beato would extend invitations to the officers to visit his studio in order to tempt further purchases from his Japanese portfolio. His friend Charles Wirgman, founder and editor of the satirical *Japan Punch*, gave an amusing insight into the marketing activities of "Count Collodion" in the June 1869 edition (Fig. 102).

A clear example of the cordial relations that Beato enjoyed with the British military establishment is seen in Captain S. H. Jones-Parry's book *My Journey Round the World* (1881), in which he records his pleasure in his reunion with Beato in Yokohama in 1879: "I met my old friend Signor Beato here … in the streets of Yokohama…. I am sure scores of my old comrades will be glad to hear he is doing well…. Beato is as well known to the British army as any private individual…."

There were other commercial benefits attaching to Beato's association with military and diplomatic personnel. In the early 1860s the only areas of Japan open to foreigners were the treaty ports of Yokohama, Nagasaki, and Hakodate. Visitors looking for photographic souvenirs of other parts of Japan would be disappointed to find that the Western photo studios were only able to offer a geographically limited range of views. Even the few Japanese studios that were operating at that time had very little to offer since it was expensive to transport cumbersome wet-plate photographic equipment across predominantly mountainous terrain, and permission to travel, even for Japanese, would not be readily granted by the authorities. However, the resident consular officials of those countries that had formal treaties with Japan were automatically afforded greater freedom of movement. For example, the first British Minister, Rutherford Alcock, was based in Edo and able to extend invitations, which were eagerly sought, to those of his fellow countrymen who were on official business. Undue preference given to one resident or visitor over another would not have gone unnoticed and so visits to the capital by non-consular staff were still uncommon.

Beato, like other residents, did not have easy access to

Instructions to a young photographer.

My dear Partners

Necessary I teach you a few things about the photograph. I been very excessfuls and it been all the photographys. What is the photography? The photography comprising itself in two parts. The pictures the chemicals and the glass make it on part. The second part making sherry, brandy, soda-water bitters and a few dozens Bourbon whiskey for our American peoples. Supposing you wanting sell photographs very important you keep plenty liquor, being very hearty welcome any peoples coming. Photography is very beautiful arts. Sherry & Bitters is better. Everybody he saying Count Collodion very good claret. Count Collodion sublime cigars necessary you been to know Count Collodion, so you given sprats and catching whales. All strangers coming Japan he going to see Count Collodion.

Necessary you keep pony. Sup...ing any traveller coming you say not seen Oyama with the moonlight! not the trouts playing under the water. not seen Miagasé with the sunstroke? Gregorio go and order seventeen horses for his gentlemans. To-morrow you start before the sun put at his nightcap and show the country - so you sell picture Oyama with the moonlight and the trouts and the sunstroke falling on the valleys.

You give dinner parties strangers he like dinners. I been to sell very handsome album with a dinner and bottle champagne.

You been to patronize the Artist of Punch. Everybody read Punch but you been particular to call it the artist of Punch "that poor devils" by calling him so you been to keep it up your positions. Never mind his.

You remember this partners and you forcing to sell plenty albums I give my Solomon oath this the way doing business you amen teacher Count Collodion di Policastro

The more sublime fellows I never sun — $500
Very gentlemans fellows — 400
He been to be very distinguished travellers — 300
Very clever mans — 200
Very jolly fellows — 100
Very good fellows he got rich fathers in New York — 50
I been to ask him to dinner — 25
Necessary I been civels — 20
He been to be friend mines. — 15
maffs — 10
A maffs like that devil Vorkmans — 0

N.B. the figures represent the price of albums purchased

Albumen Thermometer of Ct. Collodion's affection for his friends being the 2nd Course of study to which his partners attention is directed

the capital and was only too happy, therefore, to travel there vicariously. For an illuminating description of how this could happen, it is instructive to read an extract from the rather obscure memoirs of Sir Henry Woods' *Spunyarn: Strands from a Sailor's Life* (1924), which the writer came across about ten years ago. The extract also throws light on some aspects of Beato's early life and career, as well as underlining his popularity amongst the military in the early 1860s. As an additional point of interest, we are given a fascinating insight into the difficulties of taking photographs using wet-plate technology in those times.

In the relevant section of these memoirs, we find that Woods, a British naval officer, had arrived in Yokohama as commanding officer of the gunboat HMS *Kestrel*. In July 1865 he was ordered to take the newly arrived British Minister, Sir Harry Parkes, to Edo for a conference with members of the Shogun's council. As an amateur photographer, and keen to take photographs in the capital during the forthcoming visit, he approached his friend Beato: "There was at the time, residing in Yokohama, a photographer who had attained a high reputation for the excellence of his work in respect of both portraiture views and landscapes. He was quite a character in a way and a general favourite for his openhandedness and the good temper with which he met his reverses. He had taken up photography in the Crimean War, and going off to India in the Mutiny, worked there for some time, and went on to China. He followed our Army, and was at the sack of the Summer Palace, and made a nice little sum by the purchase and subsequent sale of loot with which he returned to Constantinople. Thinking to make a fortune in a short time he took to the Bourse, and soon lost it all. Off he went to the Far East again, moving on from China to Japan. The gambling fever, however, was ever upon him. He was well paid for his portraits and albums of views, but the work was a 'side-line,' and whenever he had been able to put by sufficient money, off he went into speculation. Not long before I reached Japan he had made what some would have considered a little fortune, but lost it again in the endeavour to enlarge it. His name was Beat [*sic*]. No one knew his real origin, and no one troubled themselves about it. He spoke funny English, and it was an amusement to draw him into a long argument. His most usual expression of welcome was: 'I am delight!' He used it on every occasion.

"We had become great friends, and when I heard of our approaching trip to Yedo I went to him and told him what I wanted to do, and he willingly fitted me out with a portable dark-room and all the necessary gear and chemicals on condition that I handed over to him the plates of any photos I might be able to take. We left soon enough in the morning for His Excellency to land at Yedo in ample time to settle down before his tiffin, to which he invited the Captain and myself. I spoke to him about my desire to do a bit of photography, and he was kind enough to arrange that I should have a 'Yakonin Guard' to meet me when I landed the next day with my outfit, so that I might start work at once. Photography in the open was no easy matter in those days, and my friend Beat's success in that line was due to his wonderful skill in manipulating his plates. There was nothing but the wet process as yet to the fore. It was still in the full vigour of employment as the dry plate had not passed beyond a very elementary stage of experimental success, and the gelatin film had not even entered the realm of thought."[42]

Although nothing is known of Felix Beato's childhood, we do now know he was from the island of Corfu, part then of the British-owned Ionian Islands. Research by John Clark, John Fraser, and Colin Osman, as outlined in Clark's *Japanese Exchanges in Art* (2001), had been pointing in that direction for some years. Fraser had received a letter dated December 5th, 1975 from I. L. McKenzie, the British Vice-Consul in Istanbul, which stated that a Felice Beato, aged ten, had been registered at the consulate by his father in 1844 and that their "birthplace appears to be Corfu." Further evidence of this

Below Fig. 107. "Caricature of Felix Beato." *Japan Punch*, April 1881. Here the artist Charles Wirgman is parodying the photographer's uncertain origins with the operatic assistance of Gilbert & Sullivan, and suggesting that although Beato is a British citizen, he could well have chosen other national identities.

Right Fig. 108. Felix Beato, "Warrior," ca. 1867, hand-colored large-format albumen print. Old Japan Picture Library.

has now been received thanks to the discovery, outlined in Sebastian Dobson's "Felice Beato in Japan" (2004), of Beato's passport application, which was made to the British authorities in Fort William, Calcutta, in March 1858.[43] The application states Beato's age as twenty-four and this fits broadly with the earlier discovery mentioned by Neil Pedlar in his work "Freemasons of Yokohama 1866–1896" (1993), where he gives Beato's year of birth as 1835. On checking this with the Library and Museum of Freemasonry in London, the writer received a letter stating that the only records they have show that Beato was aged thirty-three when he enrolled as a mason at the Yokohama Freemasons' Lodge No. 1092 on July 16th, 1867. Taking account of all this information, we can say that Beato was born sometime between July 1834 and March 1835.

Beato's nationality has also caused problems for photohistorians. Having apparently been born on British territory, Beato would have been a British subject which would, as a result, have made it easier for him to gain passage on British warships. Indeed, when Beato appeared as the plaintiff in a Yokohama consular court case on July 29th, 1878, he claimed, according to John Clark's *Japanese Exchanges in Art* (2001, p. 109): "I am a British citizen." Due to his name (his brother, a photographer who settled in Egypt, was called Antonio) and the constant references by his contemporaries to "Signor Beato," we can assume that he was of Italian ancestry. Corfu had been Venetian territory prior to the British taking control in 1814, and a number of Italians had migrated to the islands. Beato seemed happy to acknowledge his Italian roots and at a lecture he gave in London in 1886 at the London and Provincial Photographic Society, which was reported in the February 26th, 1886 issue of the *British Journal of Photography*, he was introduced to the audience as being of Venetian birth (see transcript in *OJP*). This throws up the possibility that he may not have been born on Corfu but simply moved there with his family at an early age. Nevertheless, he was not above playing the nationality card to his advantage, and following Britain's ceding of Corfu to the Greeks in 1864, he was content to take on the part-time role of Consul-General for Greece in Japan in 1873 (Fig. 107).

In 1870 the anonymous "Yokohama correspondent" for the *Hiogo News* made some interesting, albeit cryptic, comments which emphasized Beato's Italian pedigree. In the issue of April 13th he wrote satirically about his friend's attempt to involve himself in the finances of Yokohama's Bluff Gardens: "Another benefactor has arisen in Yokohama … a native of that flowery land where the Capuan hills look down upon a blue sea that mirrors back a bluer sky. And need I say that we have but one such that could be a benefactor, and 'his name which it is' Collodion. With five thousand dollars and the poetic imagination of his native land, Collodion, with a magnanimity which is truly refreshing, leaves cameras, acids, paste, the society of daimios' daughters and Japanese scenes and proposes to engineer the garden. – Beati giardino!" The same correspondent emphasized Beato's popularity with the local expatriate community in his report published in the August 23rd, 1871 issue. "A dinner is to be given to Mr. Beato this evening [August 19th], and will no doubt be a success.

If his speech is as characteristic as usual I will endeavour to retail [*sic*] the cream of his remarks in my next." Unfortunately, probably distracted by the need to report on the typhoon a few days later, no subsequent mention was made of the dinner – a pity. The dinner was probably convened due to Beato's "going home" with the next mail (*Hiogo News*, August 9th, 1871).

Beato's first name has also been a bone of contention. It is almost certain that he was born "Felice" but he seems to have preferred to use "Felix." This is evidenced in all of his studio advertisements and, significantly, in the passport application in 1858 when he was traveling in India. When enrolled as a freemason at the Yokohama Lodge in 1867, he again used the name Felix, according to the records of the Library and Museum of Freemasonry. Nevertheless, there are a number of examples where "Felice" has been used: Felice was used in the account of the 1886 talk given in London by Beato; the June 28th, 1871 issue of the *North China Daily News* which was referring to the photographer's return from the United States Expedition to Korea; the *Japan Weekly Mail* of November 11th, 1871 reporting a presentation of the Corea Cup at the Yokohama Autumn Meeting, and the transcript of Beato's testimony in a 1874 court case in Yokohama (see *Japan Weekly Mail*, October 17th, 1874, p. 847). It is probable that Beato would not have objected to either name and writers today will no doubt continue to exercise their own preference.

The very best source for tracking Beato's movements

before, during, and after his time in Japan is Clark's carefully compiled "Revised Chronology of Felice (Felix) Beato," put together with the help of John Fraser and Colin Osman, and contained in *Japanese Exchanges in Art* (2001). But even that work, comprehensive as it is, of necessity contains many gaps. We know very little about Beato's private life; he did not appear to marry and no written documents by him have been discovered, apart from two short letters addressed to, and published by, local Japanese newspapers, one in English, the other in French. His sister Maria Matilda married Beato's Crimean War photographic partner, the Englishman James Robertson.

His photographic career, however, is quite well chronicled. We first come across him in reference to his photographing the Crimean War in 1855. His next major assignment is photographing the aftermath of the Indian Mutiny in 1857, followed by his acclaimed work in China during the Anglo-French Military Expedition, which succeeded in occupying Peking and destroying the Summer Palace in 1860.

Beato's movements for the subsequent two or three years are very sketchy. We know he came to England towards the end of 1861 to publicize his China campaign photographs, and exhibitions of his India and China work were held in London between May and July of that year. They were also advertised in *The Times* on October 18th, 1861 (p. 1) prefaced with: "Signor F. Beato has just arrived from China...." Assuming Woods to be correct, he was also busy speculating on the Stock Exchange, losing the money he had made from trading in some artifacts looted from the Summer Palace. The next definite sighting appears in the May 21st, 1863 *China Mail* which shows him as a passenger on the ship *Emeu* bound for Hong Kong from Bombay, accompanied by his friend and *Illustrated London News* artist Charles Wirgman. The next stop is Shanghai and then, by July 1863, we hear from Wirgman himself, in a report published in the September 12th,

1863 edition of *The Illustrated London News*, that Beato is staying at his house in Yokohama and receiving many interested visitors who came to look at his photographs. The earliest recorded mention of Beato in the English language newspapers published in Japan appears to be in the *Japan Herald* for October 10th, 1863. The editor, in discussing the scenery of Yokohama, included the following words: "... add to this a beautiful, bold and picturesque scenery celebrated by many a pen and depicted by Parker and Beatto [*sic*]."

By 1864 Beato was settled in Japan, and in that year he was attached to the British naval forces that joined with the French, Dutch, and Americans in mounting a punitive expedition to Shimonoseki. This was in response to the firing on allied ships in the Shimonoseki Strait by anti-foreign members of the Choshu domain. Between September 5th and 8th the allies bombarded the Choshu military installations and then successfully seized and destroyed the onshore fortifications. Beato recorded the campaign with a memorable series of photographs (Fig. 110). On his return to Yokohama, he was called as a witness at the inquest into the murders of the English officers Lieutenant Bird and Major Baldwin. The report of the inquest in the *Daily Japan Herald*, November 24th, 1864 (p. 626) gives a transcript of Beato's testimony. In April 1865 he traveled to Nagasaki and photographed the area and arrived back in Yokohama in early July. Nagasaki University Library has dated images taken by Beato at that time. In November 1866 his flourishing photographic business was temporarily halted when a devastating fire in Yokohama destroyed his studio. It is generally thought that he lost all of his stock and negatives, but a report of the fire in the *Japan Times Overland Mail* on December 1st, 1866 (p. 347) casts doubt on this: "We have spoken in terms of praise of one detachment of men which came under our immediate notice, we can mention with the same commendation another, which under Captain Cardew, saved a great deal of Mr. Beato's property." He might well have suffered some loss of his negatives since he spent the next few months in putting together a new series of views and costumes culminating in two core volumes of work of approximately a hundred portraits and a hundred views of Japan. Fine examples of these are held by the Victoria and Albert Museum, London.

According to the report of the 1886 London lecture above, Beato stated that he retired from photography in 1867. It is true that after this date there are reports of his becoming more involved in non-photographic ventures. By 1870, for example, Beato owned several Yokohama properties which he rented out, and these were first advertised in the February 12th, 1870 issue of the *Japan Weekly Mail*. He also acted as a general import merchant and by 1873 was part of a business consortium which owned the Grand Hotel. In fact, the May 1876 edition of the *Japan Punch* published a cartoon which lampooned Beato as being involved in too many different activities.

It is sometimes suggested that his "retirement" date of 1867 was a misprint for 1877, the date he finally sold his stock and negatives to the Austrian photographer Baron Raimund von Stillfried. This must be right. During this ten-year period, he appears to have increasingly delegated the running of his studio to others whilst he involved himself in his other enterprises, but he did continue to take photographs from time to time. We know he was in Shanghai in November 1867 photo-

graphing Chinese scenes, and in the February 24th, 1870 issue of the *Japan Weekly Mail*, this advertisement appeared:

SIGNOR F. BEATO, BEGS TO ANNOUNCE TO THE PUBLIC OF YOKOHAMA AND TRAVELLERS VISITING THE EAST GENERALLY, THAT HE HAS JUST COMPLETED A HANDSOME COLLECTION OF ALBUMS OF VARIOUS SIZES, CONTAINING VIEWS &C., OF JAPAN, WITH DESCRIPTIONS OF THE SCENES, MANNERS AND CUSTOMS OF THE PEOPLE; COMPILED AFTER VISITING ALL THE MOST INTERESTING LOCALITIES IN THE COUNTRY DURING SIX YEARS RESIDENCE NO. 17 ON THE BUND

It is possible that this advertisement was placed in earlier issues of the newspaper, and it continued to appear, intermittently, until at least October 8th, 1870. In 1871 he managed to get permission to embark on one of the American warships setting off with the fleet on its punitive mission to Korea, and Beato, together with his assistant Woollett, appear to have been the only civilians taken on. The subsequent photographs of the conflict were actively marketed and sold in China, Japan, Europe, and of course America (see the author's *Korea: Caught In Time*, 1997) (Figs. 111, 112). "Mr. Felice Beato the well-known Japan Photographer arrived here [Shanghai] by the *Millet* and from him we have gathered the above particulars. Mr. Beato, who was in the Crimea with the British

army, says that the fighting on both sides was admirable. The Coreans were standing in their trenches, singing patriotic songs while being cut to pieces" (*North China Daily News*, June 28th, 1871). An illustration of how active Beato could be behind a camera is given in the following advertisement which appeared in the *Hiogo News*, July 29th, 1871:

PHOTOGRAPHIC VIEWS OF THE DISASTERS IN KOBE AFTER THE LATE TYPHOON, AND LANDSCAPE VIEWS OF VARIOUS PLACES OF INTEREST IN THE NEIGHBOURHOOD OF OSAKA AND HIOGO, TAKEN BY MR. BEATO, CAN BE HAD, AFTER THE 6TH AUGUST, AT J.D. CARROL & CO.'S   HIOGO JULY 28TH, 1871

Beato and Woollett were returning to Yokohama from Korea via Shanghai. Leaving China on July 5th, they arrived at Nagasaki on the 7th and Kobe on the 10th. Kobe had experienced, on July 5th, a severe typhoon which had destroyed many homes and buildings. Beato was able, fortuitously, to photograph the aftermath and still find time to secure other views in the area and in Osaka before leaving for Yokohama on the 12th. Back in Yokohama, Woollett worked frantically on the Korean negatives and returned to Kobe two weeks later to market them, together with the typhoon images.

In 1872 the Japanese government allowed foreigners to visit the closed city of Kyoto during an exhibition held there from April to June. Beato, along with a number of other photographers, took the opportunity to secure views in and around the city and advertised them in the June 22nd issue of the *Hiogo News*:

MESSRS. BEATO & CO. OF YOKOHAMA, SOLICIT THE INSPEC-
TION, BY THE RESIDENTS OF KOBE AND OSAKA AND TRAVELLERS,
OF A SERIES OF PHOTOGRAPHIC VIEWS THEY HAVE RECENTLY
TAKEN OF KIOTO, BIWA LAKE AND THE NEIGHBOURHOOD.
SAMPLES MAY BE SEEN AND INFORMATION RECEIVED AT MESSRS.
J.D. CARROLL & CO'S. HIOGO, JUNE 20TH, 1872.

Later that year he photographed the opening of the first Japanese railway, and the Grand Duke Alexis who was visiting Japan. But after that his photographic activities took second place to his pursuit of property and speculations on the Yokohama Bourse. His studio continued to operate, with Beato pulling the strings behind the scenes, but he formally retired in 1877 when he sold out to Stillfried and Andersen.

Following his various speculations, Beato was penniless when he left Japan in 1884 for apparently the last time. He had been resident in the country for twenty years. The *Japan Punch* carried numerous affectionate cartoons and references to "Count Collodion," and he and the editor, Charles Wirgman, were close friends. It is strange, therefore, that no reference in the magazine is made to Beato's leaving (departing residents were invariably drawn with their suitcases in hand and being waved goodbye by tearful friends). In fact, the last *Punch* reference to Beato seems to be in the November 1882 edition. It seems very likely that he and Wirgman must have fallen out over something. After traveling to London (his fare was met by friends), he moved on to the Sudan where he photographed

the British Campaign, and his photographs from that conflict were advertised for sale in the October 7th, 1885 edition of *The Times* (p. 1). He then moved to Burma where he opened photographic studios and a curio store. Noel F. Singer's article "Felice Beato's Burmese Days" (1998) covers in detail Beato's activities in that country. Neither Beato nor his business is mentioned in any of the local trade directories after 1907. His year and place of death have yet to be recorded, and although Beato at this time seems to disappear completely, the writer did recently find a late echo of his business activities in the Guildhall Library, London.[44]

Felix Beato is rightly considered to be the most accomplished nineteenth-century Western photographer to visit Japan. We can see from the extensive body of work he left behind that he excelled in both portrait and landscape photography. The quality of his work was consistently high and the photographs were often attractively presented in albums which contained printed descriptive captions. These albums usually contained a mixture of views and costumes with the latter being exquisitely hand colored by competent (usually Japanese) artists. This coloring was, at the time, a radical departure from the customary sepia-monochrome look, although William Saunders in Shanghai beat him to it. Felix Beato's contribution to Japanese photography was truly outstanding. His experiences and career as a war photographer were no doubt factors in shaping his documentative, non-interpretive approach to portraiture. His landscape work captured, with great sensitivity, the Japanese countryside during the last few years of Japan's feudal period. The sweeping away, in 1868, of 250 years of Tokugawa rule would be followed by rapid modernization and no subsequent photographer would be able to photograph the "Old Japan." By doing so, and doing it so magnificently, Felix Beato, and his contribution to Japanese photography, will always be remembered.

WILLIAM SAUNDERS

We know that William Thomas Saunders (1832–92) was a particularly fine photographer because many of his Chinese views and costumes have survived and his talent is self-evident. In fact, Clark Worswick in *Japan Photographs 1854–1905* (1980) suggests that Saunders may be the most under-rated nineteenth-century photographer of the Far East. He is of interest to us here because in 1862 he spent some ten weeks in Japan and accumulated a portfolio of around ninety photographs. But with the exception of several photographs which appear in the Worswick Collection (one of the most important compilations of early Japanese photography) and a two-plate panorama of Yokohama from the Nagasaki University Library Collection, no other Japanese images have to date been identified. Even these can be confirmed only after a careful comparison with the descriptions given in the *Japan Herald* October 25th, 1862 article referred to later. The panorama was attributed to Saunders by Saito Takio in *Bakumatsu Meiji* (2004). Saito noticed that the panorama matched two of the six plates of the Saunders' Yokohama panorama engraved in the September 12th, 1863 issue of *The Illustrated London News*. But what has happened to the rest of Saunders' photographs?

Very little is known about Saunders' life and career, although we can get some information from the following obituary notice which appeared in the *Japan Weekly Mail* on January 14th, 1893 (quoting an earlier undated edition of the *Shanghai Mercury* which was probably published some time in December 1892): "The only photographer in Shanghai and North China, who had broad respect and high evaluation, William Saunders died last night. He had come to Shanghai in 1860 on the old paddle steamer 'Lea Moon'. He went back to the UK to study photography and brought back a set of 'wet plate' photographs which were called 'black magic' at the time. In a few years he had taken many pictures of Pekin for the first time. He travelled in Japan also, in its Emperor and Samurai period. Nowadays one can find, almost all over the world, many scenic photos of Japan. But he must have been the first person to set the camera to it. He retired a few years ago and travelled to the UK, he came back a few weeks ago. He had a cold when he arrived and this developed into bronchitis which brought him to his death. He was a merry man and left many friends to sorrow for him."

In attempting some genealogical research on Saunders, the writer had the greatest difficulty because of the subject's relatively common name. The discovery of Saunders' last Will and Testament at the National Archives (FO 917/587) gave important leads, but there was much work still to do before being able to piece together the following:

Saunders was born on August 27th, 1832 in the naval town of Woolwich, London, to parents Jane and William Charles Saunders who had married in 1829.[45] Saunders had three younger sisters – Mary Jane (1834–?), Ellen (1837–74), and Ann (1840–1902). Mary Jane married a Charles Green in 1853, but her two sisters remained spinsters. Saunders' father was a shipwright and the 1841 UK Census shows the 30-year-old living with his 25-year-old wife and four children at Coleman Street, Woolwich. Although the three daughters can be traced in subsequent census returns, it has not so far been possible to find references to William or his parents. The suspicion is that they may have gone overseas.

Saunders set foot in Japan, probably for the first time, on August 30th, 1862, when he arrived in Yokohama from

Left Fig. 114. William Saunders, "American Legation, Edo," 1862, large-format albumen print. Worswick Collection.

Below Fig. 115. William Saunders, "Yokohama Panorama," 1862, large-format albumen print. Nagasaki University Library. This photograph consists of only two plates of a five-plate panorama.

Shanghai and left after ten weeks on November 13th. This information comes from the lists of passengers and ships in the *Japan Herald* issues of August 30th, 1862 and November 15th. His activities during those few short weeks will now be considered.

On September 20th, 1862 the *Japan Herald* carried the following advertisement:

PHOTOGRAPHY   W. SAUNDERS BEGS TO INFORM THE COMMUNITY OF YOKOHAMA THAT ON MONDAY NEXT AND FIVE FOLLOWING DAYS HE WILL BE PREPARED TO TAKE PORTRAITS, &C., IN THE NEWEST AND MOST APPROVED STYLES. ALSO FOR SALE AND ON VIEW A COLLECTION OF PHOTOGRAPHS TO WHICH INSPECTION IS INVITED. 51 ENGLISH YOKOHAMA, 18TH SEPTEMBER, 1862.

Saunders had lost no time in setting up his studio and in creating a Japanese portfolio. Interestingly, this advertisement would have appeared just four days after the grisly murder of the British merchant Charles Richardson, who had been set upon by sword-wielding assassins. Richardson's badly mutilated body was photographed, quite possibly by Saunders.

On October 14th, 1862 Saunders accompanied the US Minister Robert Pruyn and the American missionaries Samuel R. Brown (see page 56) and Orramel Gulick on a diplomatic visit to Edo Castle. There he was permitted to photograph the Shogun's senior councilors, and an engraving of this image appeared in the September 12th, 1863 issue of *The Illustrated London News*, together with one of a six-plate panorama of Yokohama, as mentioned earlier. Saunders was also permitted to take photographs around Edo itself (Figs, 114, 116).

The *Japan Herald*, on October 25th, 1862, then published a lengthy critique of some ninety of Saunders' Japanese photographs and ended by lamenting the photographer's imminent return to Shanghai. The article (reproduced in *OJP*) is titled "Mr. Saunders' Photographic Views in Japan" and refers to Saunders being on "a professional visit." This article, and the tone of the advertisement above, gives the distinct impression that Saunders had not intended to stay in Japan and was always destined to return to Shanghai (Figs. 115, 118).

Saunders left Yokohama on November 13th and arrived back in Shanghai on the 18th (*North China Herald*, November 22nd, 1862, pp. 183, 188). Evidence that he sold his Japanese photographs from China is provided by the following advertisement in the December 13th, 1862 issue of the Shanghai newspaper *Daily Shipping and Commercial News*:

PHOTOGRAPHS FROM JAPAN W. SAUNDERS BEGS TO INFORM THE COMMUNITY OF SHANGHAI THAT HE HAS NOW FOR SALE AND ON VIEW A COLLECTION OF PHOTOGRAPHS TAKEN IN JAPAN.... ADJOINING THE ASTOR HOUSE, SHANGHAI 2ND DECEMBER 1862.

In this advertisement, which appeared up until January 2nd, 1863, Saunders also mentioned taking miniature portraits for brooches and lockets, between the hours of 10 a.m. and 3 p.m. A fresh advertisement (alongside the old one) also appeared in the same newspaper on January 2nd:

W. SAUNDERS RESPECTFULLY BEGS TO INFORM THE PUBLIC THAT IN ADDITION TO HIS LARGE VIEWS, HE HAS NOW READY A FEW HANDSOME CARTE DE VISITE ALBUMS FILLED WITH SUBJECTS FROM JAPAN ILLUSTRATING THE DRESS, DWELLINGS ETC. OF THE PEOPLE AND AMONGST WHICH WILL BE FOUND PORTRAITS FROM LIFE OF OFFICERS OF STATE, CELEBRATED CHARACTERS, MOOS-SUMIS, ETC., ETC., VERY SUITABLE FOR PRESENTS. SHANGHAI, 23RD DECEMBER 1862.

Then a later, very interesting advertisement appeared in the May 26th, 1863 issue of the *Daily Shipping and Commercial News* which suggests that Saunders may have been the first Far Eastern photographer to hand color photographs.[46]

TINTED PHOTOGRAPHS W. SAUNDERS BEGS TO INFORM THE COMMUNITY OF SHANGHAI, THAT HE IS NOW PREPARED TO TAKE THE TINTED PHOTOGRAPHS WHICH GIVE A LIFE LIKE APPEARANCE AND THE LATEST NOVELTY IN THE ART. ALSO NOW READY, A COLLECTION OF INSTANTANEOUS AND OTHER PHOTOGRAPHS OF SHANGHAI AND JAPAN CONSISTING OF PANORAMAS, FIGURES FROM LIFE, &C., &C. W. SAUNDERS RESPECTFULLY INVITES INSPECTION OF HIS SPECIMEN SOME HUNDREDS OF WHICH ARE NOW ON VIEW. ROOMS ADJOINING THE ASTOR HOUSE. SHANGHAI, 17TH MAY, 1863.

The *North China Daily News* for September 13th, 1866 carried an advertisement that makes it clear that Saunders had built a photographic portfolio of Peking:

PHOTOGRAPHY MR. W. SAUNDERS HAVING RETURNED TO SHANGHAI, WILL RE-OPEN HIS ROOMS ON MONDAY NEXT, THE 3RD SEPTEMBER, WHEN HE BEGS TO INVITE INSPECTION OF HIS VIEWS OF PEKIN, THE MING TOMBS, NANKOW PASS, YUEN MING YUEN, EMPEROR'S PALACE, TEMPLE OF HEAVEN, ALTAR OF HEAVEN &C., &C., &C SHANGHAI, AUGUST 31ST, 1866.

We also know that Saunders made at least three further trips to Japan. The *Hiogo News* of August 27th, 1868 carried an advertisement on page 93:

VIEWS OF KOBE & OSAKA ON VIEW AND FOR SALE (FOR A FEW DAYS) AT MESSRS. LLEWELLYN & CO'S PHOTOGRAPHS OF THE ABOVE NAMED PLACES TAKEN BY MR. SAUNDERS.

Llewellyn & Co. were chemists and had set up their business in Kobe soon after the port's opening on January 1st, 1868. The *Hiogo News* of September 3rd, 1868 also reported

Below Fig. 116. "Ministers of State, Japan," woodcut engraving. *The Illustrated London News*, September 12th, 1863, p. 256. The engraving is from a photograph taken by William Saunders at Edo Castle on October 14th, 1862. Although Tokyo was outside the treaty limits for non-diplomatic personnel, Saunders had come as the guest of the

American Minister Robert Pruyn, and was able to take a rare picture of the Shogun's highest officers. Unfortunately, the original photograph has not been found.

Above Fig. 117. William Saunders, "Portrait of Mori Arinori," 1876, cabinet-size albumen print. *The Far East*, November 1876. Mori Arinori (1848–88) was a diplomat and statesman of the Meiji period. At the time this photograph was taken, Mori was the Japanese Minister to China. In 1888 he was assassinated by a religious fanatic.

Saunders traveling to Nagasaki on the steamer *Costa Rica*. It seems very likely that he had visited the recently opened port, taken a number of photographs, and then offered them for sale at Llewellyn's, leaving a few days later. These would be amongst the very first photographs taken of Kobe. Saunders continued to use Llewellyn & Co. as his Kobe agent throughout 1869. The following advertisement ran from May 6th to 27th in the *Hiogo News*:

PHOTOGRAPHS OF KOBE AND OSACA, MOUNTED AND UNMOUNTED. BY W. SAUNDERS, SHANGHAI. AT MESSRS. LLEWELLYN & CO. DRUGGISTS, MAIN STREET, KOBE.

Another advertisement in the rival paper *Hiogo and Osaka Herald* ran from June 26th until at least July 31st, 1869. It almost certainly refers to Saunders' combination albums of China and Japan:

A FEW ALBUMS OF PHOTOGRAPHS OF PEKING, SHANGHAI, NINGPO, FOOCHOW, YOKOHAMA, YEDO, NAGASAKI, OSAKA AND KOBE FOR SALE AT J. LLEWELLYN & CO.'S DRUGGISTS, 99 MAIN STREET, KOBE.

As Saito Takio points out in *Bakumatsu Meij*, Saunders was in Kobe again in June 1871. The June 10th, 1871 issue of the *Hiogo News* carried an announcement that Saunders was to auction his photographic equipment:

PUBLIC AUCTION. JOHNSON & CO. AUCTIONEERS. HAVE RECEIVED INSTRUCTIONS FROM MR. SAUNDERS TO SELL BY PUBLIC AUCTION, ON LOT 49, CONCESSION, AT FOUR P.M. ON THURSDAY NEXT JUNE 15TH, 1871, WITHOUT ANY RESERVE, THE WHOLE OF HIS PHOTOGRAPHIC APPARATUS AND MATERIALS: *CONSISTING OF*: SIX FIRST-CLASS CAMERAS,

AND LENSES, FOR TAKING PICTURES FROM CARD SIZE TO 18 INCHES, *INCLUDING*: AN INSTANTANEOUS STEREOSCOPIC CAMERA LENS, BY DALLMEYER, ALSO, THE WHOLE OF HIS MAGNIFICENT SPECIMEN ALBUMS, LOOSE PHOTOGRAPHS, &C. JOHNSON & CO. AUCTIONEERS. HIOGO, JUNE 8TH, 1871.

The same newspaper carried the following advertisement:

NOTICE. MR. SAUNDERS BEGS TO INFORM THE COMMUNITY OF KOBE THAT HE WILL BE PREPARED (WEATHER PERMITTING) TO TAKE PHOTOGRAPHIC PORTRAITS FROM TO-DAY, JUNE 8TH, UNTIL WEDNESDAY, THE 14TH, INCLUSIVE, BETWEEN THE HOURS OF 1 AND 4 P.M, ON THE LOT KNOWN AS NO. 49, CONCESSION. HIOGO, JUNE 8TH. 1871.

On the face of it, Saunders was selling off everything and giving up photography, although he could have been simply disposing of old equipment, perhaps expecting to secure replacements from Europe, though mention of the disposal of the "whole of his magnificent specimen albums" has the ring of finality. Although he may not have completely burnt all of his Shanghai bridges, we now know that he was returning to London to marry and may well have intended to settle down in England, at least for a time.

Whilst waiting for the auction of his equipment in Kobe, Saunders was busy working with a local artist as the following editorial from the June 14th *Hiogo News* makes clear: "Writing of boating reminds us that Mr. Saunders is engaged in printing photographic copies of Mr. Smedley's water colour sketch of the Kobe Regatta of the 24th December last. Those who wish to possess a memento of the occasion cannot do better than secure one of these photographs. Mr. Smedley's sketch is a faithful representation of the view presented from the harbour, and shews the Bund, from Messrs. Kniffler & Co's to the native town, with the hills, from the Moon Temple westwards, in the background. If the artist had laid on his blues and greys with a somewhat lighter hand, the sketch would have been more in accordance with the general appearance that Kobe presents, but those who remember how exceptionally gloomy the weather was on the day on which the Regatta was held, will give Mr. Smedley credit for the fidelity of his representation."

Saunders left Kobe and arrived in Yokohama on June 20th (*Japan Weekly Mail*, June 24th) and took passage to England, probably via America. In London, on December 2nd, 1871, he married Clara Withers (1846–87), a widow. Saunders inherited a stepson from Clara's previous marriage, William Thomas Withers (1867–?). Saunders' father was present at the wedding. Perhaps his marriage failed, because by the following year Saunders is back working in Shanghai.

The Far East periodical, having moved from Yokohama to Shanghai, published some of Saunders' Chinese photographs between November 1876 and June 1878 (Fig. 117) (see John Reddie Black and *The Far East*, page 146). It also made reference to Saunders' studio and implied that photographs of Japan were still available. In September 26th, 1874, the *North China Herald* carried a report of a court case at

Shanghai where one of Saunders' servants had charged him with assault. The judge found in favor of the servant who was awarded $10 plus costs. Saunders was allowed, however, to deduct the cost of the damage inflicted to his trousers "through the biting propensities of the complainant." Another case in 1881, at the Shanghai Civil Summary Court, found in favor of Saunders who was chasing an unpaid bill of $12 from a Mr A. Silverstone in respect of twelve photographs (*North China Daily News*, September 14th, 1881). One other glimpse of Saunders is in the *Rising Sun and Nagasaki Express*, where he is listed as a passenger on the *Hiroshima Maru*, which arrived in Kobe from Shanghai on August 9th, 1878.

Clara Saunders died of cirrhosis of the liver on 20th September, 1887 at the age of forty-one.[47] On hearing the news in Shanghai, where he was still operating as a photographer from No. 2, Whangpoo Road, Saunders was prompted to make his Will which he signed on December 29th, 1887. He appointed a cousin, William Saunders, and his stepson William Withers as joint executors. "I desire in case I die in China … all my personal property in Shanghai such as furniture clothing photographic apparatus and material to be sold as soon after my death as convenient…."

Saunders died in Shanghai five years later, on December 30th, 1892. He left £500 to his stepson and the net estate was to be divided between his two surviving sisters, Ann and Mary. His total assets in China and England then amounted to £6,491 (approximately US$900,000 in today's terms). It is to be hoped that more of Saunders' Japanese work will surface over time so that a proper evaluation of his contribution can be made. If, and when it does, the writer is confident that Saunders' talents will be fully recognized and enable him to take his rightful place alongside the greats of Japanese photo-history.

CHARLES PARKER

Locating Saunders' Japanese photographs is, as we have seen, extremely difficult, and yet, given that he was in the country for less than three months, somewhat understandable. There appear to be no extenuating circumstances, however, surrounding the non-appearance of the work of the Yokohama-based English photographer Charles Parker. It is true that a handful of *carte de visite* photographs have been identified, but that was only because they had the Parker studio imprint on the reverse. The Worswick Collection has several photographs which have been tentatively attributed to this artist, but nothing else seems to have appeared. It would be tempting, therefore, to believe that Parker's photographic activities were confined to operating a portrait studio. However, the facts do not bear this out.

It was probably Parker who arrived in Hong Kong on February 27th, 1861 on board the *Pekin*, which started its journey in Southampton, England, since the *North China Herald* of March 9th, 1861 (p. 38) records a certain Mr Parker among the list of passengers. The date seems to tie in. The 1862 *China Directory* definitely lists him as a photographer, based at Staunton Street, Hong Kong, and the following year has him moved to the Parade Ground. He is probably the Parker recorded as departing Hong Kong for Shanghai on May 16th, 1863 (*North China Herald*, May 20th). If so, he could have been on his way to Yokohama via Naga-saki because by July of 1863 he is in Yokohama issuing the following advertisement in the July 18th, 1863 edition of the *Japan Herald*:

Mr. C. Parker (of "The Photograph Gallery" Hong Kong, and formerly with Messrs. Weed & Howard in China) has fitted up a convenient establishment nearly opposite the Yokohama Hotel. Orders for Views, Portraits &c., &c. received daily 10 to 4. N.B. Ladies and Gentlemen having their portraits taken may rest assured that no copies will be struck off except to their order. Mr. Parker has on sale Panoramas of the Settlement of Yokohama and the neighbourhood. Views showing the Cemetery, Hatoba and Main Street, "The Ly......", The Cricket Field And a large assortment of characters

Parker is clearly a seasoned professional, bursting onto the Yokohama scene. His next advertisement, carried in the *Japan Herald* on September 12th, 1863, promises even more:

Photography Mr. C. Parker, begs to acquaint the Public that he has now (amongst others) On Sale the following interesting Photographic Pictures, View of the Battle of Kagosima. Plan of the Battle of Kagosima. A new View of the Bund and Hatoba. A new Panoramic view of Yokohama. A Panoramic View of the Fleet. A number of new Street Views. Having now secured the assistance of a First-rate London Artist, and received a large stock of new chemicals, Mr. C. Parker is now prepared to execute all orders with promptitude. Address. – 51 Main Street, (nearly opposite the Yokohama Hotel.)

The London "artist" must be William Parke Andrew. More-over, the reference to "views" of the battle of Kagoshima, which took place on August 15th and 16th, 1863, is mislead-ing: the British fleet pounded the town from the sea and the stormy weather conditions made the landing of troops imprac-ticable. Parker, even if he were with the fleet, would not have been able to take photographs. He must instead be referring to photographs of sketches – a number of these were done by Charles Wirgman. The references to panoramas as well as the street scenes mean that Parker was not just a studio portrait photographer (Fig. 121). In the same *Japan Herald* issue, the editor included the following testimonial: "Tempted by the promising Bill of Fare published in our Advertising columns by Mr. C. Parker, we paid a visit to his Gallery; we were amply repaid for the trouble by the gratification we derived, and would recommend all residents and visitors to do likewise."

In the October 10th issue, and in the context of talking about the regatta being held in the beautiful surroundings of Yokohama Harbour, the editor remarked: "... add to this a beautiful, bold and picturesque scenery celebrated by many a pen and depicted by Parker and Beatto [*sic*]." This indicates that Parker and Beato were considered to be the key photogra-phers of Yokohama, and clearly would by now have been com-petitors. The next two advertisements (beginning with the *Japan Herald*, May 28th,1864) show that Andrew has been taken on as a partner, and that an important part of their cus-tomer base is the English fleet anchored in Yokohama Harbor:

MESSRS.C.PARKER & CO., PHOTOGRAPHERS HAVE THE HONOUR TO INFORM THEIR NUMEROUS PATRONS THAT THEY HAVE NOW REMOVED TO MORE COMMODIOUS PREMISES, AND WILL BE IN A POSITION TO RESUME BUSINESS ON MONDAY NEXT THE 30TH MAY, 51 MAIN STREET, YOKOHAMA

And in the *Japan Herald* of September 10th, 1864:

PHOTOGRAPHY MESSRS. C. PARKER & CO. HAVE THE HONOUR TO INFORM THEIR FRIENDS AND THE PUBLIC GENERALLY THAT IN CONSEQUENCE OF THE DEPARTURE OF THE FLEET, IT IS THEIR INTENTION TO LEAVE YOKOHAMA FOR AN ARTISTIC EX-CURSION ABOUT THE 30TH SEPTEMBER NEXT AND WILL BE HAPPY TO EXECUTE ANY ORDERS INTRUSTED [*SIC*] TO THEIR CARE IN THE MEANTIME. N.B. AN ENTIRELY NEW SET OF JAPANESE VIEWS NOW READY

But the partnership is short-lived, as the following notice in the *Japan Herald*, July 22nd, 1865 (p. 688) makes clear:

DISSOLUTION OF PARTNERSHIP WHEREAS CHARLES PARKER AND WILLIAM PARKE ANDREW, DOING BUSINESS AS PHOTOG-RAPHERS, UNDER THE STYLE OF C. PARKER & CO. HAVE THIS DAY DISSOLVED PARTNERSHIP BY MUTUAL CONSENT: ALL PERSONS INDEBTED TO THE SAID CO-PARTNERSHIP ARE REQUESTED TO PAY THE SAME WITHOUT DELAY AND ALL PERSONS HAVING CLAIMS AGAINST THE SAID FIRM WILL PLEASE SEND THEM IN ON THE 1ST OF THE ENSUING MONTH. W.P. ANDREW   C.PARKER YOKOHAMA, JULY 18TH 1865

The editors of the *Japan Herald* in the July 29th,1865 sup-plement commented: "Amongst the changes constantly taking place in Yokohama, we observe that Messrs. Parker & Andrews [*sic*], the Photographers have dissolved [their] partnership. We believe, each intents [*sic*] to establish himself here, and find that Mr. Parker has already taken No. 108, the house opposite to the Parsonage on one side and facing the creek on the other where he will recommence his artistic labors, as soon as the workmen who are employed in the necessary alterations will allow him. Mr. Parker was the first to arrive of the Photographers at present in Yokohama, and is well known, requiring therefore from us no words of recommen-dation, but only the notification of his whereabouts and intentions." Clearly, Parker and his work are held in high regard by the *Herald*. The confirmation that Parker's studio predated Beato's arrival in Japan is also interesting.

A few days later, on August 5th, Parker places his own advertisement which appeared in the *Japan Herald Supple-ment* (p. 697c):

CHARLES PARKER PHOTOGRAPHER NO. 108 MR. PARKER BEGS RESPECTFULLY TO THANK HIS PATRONS FOR THEIR SUPPORT DUR-ING THE TIME HE HAS BEEN AT YOKOHAMA, AND TO ANNOUNCE THAT HE HAS RECOMMENCED HIS PROFESSIONAL AVOCATIONS AT THE ABOVE ADDRESS, WHERE HE TRUSTS HE MAY RECEIVE THE SAME AMOUNT OF APPRECIATION THAT HAS HITHERTO ATTENDED HIM. A LARGE QUANTITY OF JAPANESE VIEWS ALWAYS ON HAND.

It is likely that No. 108 was only a temporary studio, because the October 21st, 1865 *Japan Herald* carried the following advertisement:

CHARLES PARKER, PHOTOGRAPHER BEGS TO INFORM THE
OFFICERS OF THE ARMY AND NAVY AND THE RESIDENTS OF
YOKOHAMA THAT HIS GALLERY IS NOW FINISHED AND READY
FOR THE RECEPTION OF VISITORS. HE WOULD ALSO INFORM THEM
THAT HE IS NOW PREPARED TO TAKE LIFE SIZE PORTRAITS FOR
THOSE WISHING THEM. HE HAS A LARGE NUMBER OF JAPANESE
VIEWS ALWAYS ON HAND, ALSO ALBUMS MADE EXPRESSLY FOR
THEIR RECEPTION.

Parker, alone again, addresses his core audience: the
military stationed at the Port. The impression one has from
the advertisements and editorials above is that, by this time,
Parker was well known, well connected (especially amongst
the military), and established. Beato's arrival at Yokohama
must therefore have been a crushing commercial blow to
Parker: the English military were very important customers,
and Felix Beato was better known amongst them than any
other photographer alive. Beato had great charm, charisma,
and prodigious talent. By now he had been established
at Yokohama for over two years and was consolidating his
position. Parker would now find it harder to survive. With
probably the last throw of the dice, the *Japan Times* (the
Daily Advertiser) of December 7th, 1865 announced that
Parker had taken on a new partner:

NOTICE. I HAVE ADMITTED MR. W.A.CRANE AS PARTNER IN MY
BUSINESS FROM AND AFTER THE 1ST NOVEMBER 1865. THE FIRM
WILL IN FUTURE BE CARRIED ON UNDER THE STYLE OF PARKER
CRANE & CO.   C.PARKER, YOKOHAMA 6TH DECEMBER 1865

The same issue carried this additional information:

PHOTOGRAPHIC NOTICE MESSRS. PARKER, CRANE & CO. RE-
SPECTFULLY INTIMATE TO THE LADIES AND GENTLEMEN OF YOKO-
HAMA THAT THEY ARE NOW FITTING UP A NEW PHOTOGRAPHIC
GALLERY. NOTICE WILL BE GIVEN WHEN IT IS COMPLETED, IN
ORDER THAT THE GALLERY MAY BE VISITED AND INSPECTION MADE
OF THE PHOTOGRAPHS IN COLLECTION. MESSRS. PARKER, CRANE
& CO FURTHER INTIMATE THAT THEY HAVE A FEW VIEWS FROM
THE VICINITY OF OSAKA AND HIOGO   DEC. 6TH 1865

The final advertisement appeared in the *Japan Times*
on December 29th, 1865:

PHOTOGRAPHIC NOTICE MESSRS. PARKER CRANE & CO
ARE NOW READY TO TAKE LIKENESSES ON CARDS OR OTHERWISE.
VIEWS FROM YEDO, ALSO FROM VICINITY OF HIOGO AND OSAKA.
YOKOHAMA 29TH DECEMBER 1865

The reference to photographs of Hiogo and Osaka is
particularly interesting. Parker most likely accompanied the
combined naval squadron of British, French, Dutch, and
American ships to Hiogo in November 1865 when the ministers of those countries co-operated and put on a show of force
to demand the ratification of treaties by the Emperor. Parker
no doubt took the opportunity to get some rare views of the
surrounding countryside.

Nevertheless, this second partnership was also short-
lived. It has not been possible to trace any of the firm's
advertisements after December 1865 and by June 1866 Crane
was announcing the formation of his own studio. In fact, by
the beginning of 1866 Parker had disappeared without trace,
apart from his being listed as an English resident of Yokohama in the 1867 *China Directory*. (It is possible he is the
Parker recorded in the *North China Herald* (December 23rd,
1865) as embarking on the *Granada* on December 18th, 1865
on his way from Yokohama to Shanghai.) Which brings us
back to the question: what has happened to Parker's work? It
has been suggested that Felix Beato acquired Parker's stock
and studio in 1868, or earlier. This is because of a reference
in M. Paske-Smith's *Western Barbarians in Japan and Formosa*
(1968) (Appendix 13b, p. 362), which refers to "C. Parker
(photographer) (later Beato & Co)." However, no corroborating
evidence of this has so far appeared.

Another possibility is that Parker continued his business
for a few more months after the break-up of his partnership
with Crane and then lost his stock and negatives in the Great
Fire of Yokohama in November 1866. If so, we may never be
able to judge the work of this early pioneer. Given the contemporary acclaim he received, this is regrettable. Although we
know next to nothing about this photographic artist, remarkably, and somewhat poignantly, we do have a conversation of
his that the editor of *The Far East* reported when reminiscing
in his periodical about some key events in early Yokohama.
This is contained in *OJP*.

ANTOINE FAUCHERY

Painter, writer, journalist, adventurer, and photographer,
Antoine Julien Fauchery (1823–61) was undoubtedly one
of the more interesting characters who traveled to the Far
East (Fig. 123). He spent only three months in Japan, during
1861, and it is possible he was too unwell to use his camera.
Becoming ill in China, he sailed over to Japan in an attempt
to recover his health but unfortunately died there three
months later. Remembered for his pioneering photography
in 1850s Australia, his contribution to early Chinese and
Japanese photography is, as yet, far from clear.

Born in Paris in 1823, Fauchery studied painting, architecture, and literature. Attracted in his youth to a Bohemian
lifestyle, he was unable to settle down and his restless spirit
was always seeking new adventures. Sometime around 1848,
he and his friend Nadar, the famous Parisian photographer,
attempted to travel to Poland to fight with the nationalists
who were trying to secure the country's independence. However, before reaching their destination they were arrested in
Germany and sent back home.

By 1852 he had shown considerable talent as a writer.
He was becoming well known in Parisian artistic and literary
circles and his career looked promising. However, attracted
by the stories of fortunes being made in the Australian gold-
mines, Fauchery decided to try his luck there. He had never
been financially secure and the move to Australia did not

improve matters. Not finding any gold, he opened a French café in Melbourne and when that enterprise failed he became a grocer. Still unsuccessful, he returned to Paris in 1856 and studied photography. A year later, he somehow secured a commission from the French Societe des Gens de Lettres to travel to the East and "... study and reproduce by pen and camera the most interesting places in China, Australia and India." He left for Australia in 1857.

Fauchery is famous for taking a series of evocative photographs of the 1850s gold rush in Melbourne. Despite the city's newspapers, the *Argus* and *The Illustrated Melbourne News*, advertising his albums for sale in 1858, his Australian photography is extremely rare, although the La Trobe Library in Melbourne does have one album. Fauchery also penned a series of letters about his life amongst the gold miners. These formed the basis of a book, *Lettres d'un Mineur en Australie*, published in 1857. In January 1857 he married Louise Josephine Gatineau who had accompanied him to Australia.

According to Thiriez in *Barbarian Lens* (1998), in February 1859 he moved on to the Philippines and based himself in Manila. However, the May 21st, 1859 issue of the *Overland China Mail* records a Mr. & Mrs. Fouchery [sic] leaving Melbourne on March 13th and arriving in Hong Kong on May 13th. In any case, in 1860 the French authorities advanced him 1000 francs and encouraged him to follow the French Military Expedition to China as a photographer and journalist (Fig. 122). From July to November 1860 Fauchery wrote a series of "Lettres de Chine," which were published in fifteen instalments in *Le Moniteur* between October 12th, 1860 and February 3rd, 1861.

Above Fig. 123. Anonymous, "Portrait of Antoine Fauchery," ca. 1858, large-format albumen print. La Trobe Picture Collection, State Library of Victoria. Possibly taken by Fauchery's friend Richard Daintree.

Coinciding with the ending of hostilities, Fauchery was taken ill but nevertheless decided to fulfil a long-held wish and traveled to Japan; perhaps he also hoped that the climate would be more conducive to a quick recovery. In any case, he left Shanghai with his friend and fellow photographer Colonel Du Pin, and arrived in Nagasaki in mid-January 1861. The *North China Herald* issue of January 19th, 1861 records both Du Pin and Fauchery leaving Shanghai on January 12th on the steamer *Cadiz*, bound for Nagasaki and Kanagawa. Colonel Du Pin also wrote about their journey to Japan in his book *Le Japon* (1868).[48] Moving on a few days later, they arrived in Yokohama on January 24th. Fauchery was attached to the French Legation there and although the current state of research into his activities leaves room for doubt, it is possible he resumed some photography. However, despite the "iron constitution" referred to by his friend de Banville in the introduction to *Lettres d'un Mineur en Australie*, Fauchery did not recover from his illness and died three months later, on April 27th, of the combined effects of dysentery and gastritis.

The French priest Father Mounicou recorded in his diary that Fauchery, on his deathbed, "refused the consolations of the church" and was therefore denied a Christian burial. This caused something of an uproar amongst the French community and some accommodation was reached with Fauchery's being laid to rest in the Yokohama Foreigners' Cemetery.[49]

On a final point of detail, it seems to be far from clear what became of Fauchery's wife after she accompanied him on the voyage to China from Australia.[50]

Fauchery's Australian efforts signaled an impressive photographic talent. However, too little of his other work has been identified and his photography in China and Japan (if any) has only been tentatively attributed by Regine Thiriez in her book *Barbarian Lens* (1998) and then only in stereo form. Sadly, Fauchery's early death prevented his leaving us with any significant portfolio of Japanese work. His close friend, the French poet Theodore de Banville, wrote fondly of Fauchery and has left us some biographical details without which almost nothing would be known about his pre-Australian period. De Banville also makes much of Fauchery's friendship with Nadar, from whom it is highly probable that Fauchery received photographic training and advice.

FREDERICK SUTTON

Of all the amateur Western photographers operating in Japan in the 1860s, Frederick William Sutton (1832–83) is the most significant, not least because he is remembered for being the first Westerner to take photographs of a reigning shogun (Figs. 125, 126). These photographs of Tokugawa Yoshinobu were secured in May 1867 when Minister Parkes traveled to Osaka for an audience. The *Daily Japan Herald* on May 16th, 1867 (p. 2616), reported: "Captain Sutton of H.M. surveying ship 'Serpent' had the honour of a sitting from the Tycoon, and has taken a capital photographic likeness of him. It is small, for unfortunately the boat in which the larger lenses and some of the chemicals were, was upset, and they were lost." Later that year, on a survey of the northern coast, Sutton visited Hokkaido and managed to secure possibly the earliest portraits of Ainu, Japan's aboriginal inhabitants. Sutton must have had some friendly or commercial arrangement with Felix Beato because these portraits found their way into the latter's portfolio and were issued in his albums of Native Types. In March 1868 Sutton accompanied Parkes to Kyoto on an official visit to the Emperor. As Parkes' suite set off towards the Imperial Palace, they were attacked by two sword-wielding would-be assassins. One was killed and the other, Saegusa Shigeru, captured. Sutton photographed the defiant Saegusa just hours before his execution (Fig. 128).

Sutton joined the engineering branch of the Royal Navy in 1854 and made steady progress. By April 1865 he had reached the rank of chief engineer and was assigned to HMS *Serpent*, a steam-powered warship, which was about to join the *China Station* on a four-year tour as a surveying vessel. During the tour, Sutton would visit many countries in the Far East, and in a number of them he used his camera to capture important images.

Sutton returned to England in August 1869 and was re-assigned to the Naval Reserve. He was happy to return to Japan in July 1873, however, as a member of the newly formed British naval training mission, based at the Imperial Naval College at Tsukiji, Tokyo. Sutton and his family enjoyed the next six years of expatriate life in Japan. He became fluent in the language and toured the countryside taking photographs.

In early 1879 his health broke down and he returned to England and retired.

With time on his hands, Sutton converted over 400 of his photographs to lantern slides which, in turn, provided the illustrations for eight separate travel lectures he gave to local audiences. The text and lists of the photographs used make up an obscure publication which is housed in the British Library (without the slides) entitled *First Reading for Lantern Exhibitions of Travels in the Eastern Island World, China, Loo-Choo, and Japan* (1882).

These readings and photo lists make clear that Sutton's Japanese portfolio is more extensive, and earlier, than had previously been recognized. In the summer of 1866, HMS *Serpent* visited Okinawa (Loo-Choo) for a few days and Sutton photographed the scenery and natives. Nineteen of his photographs formed part one of his fourth lecture and show views in and around Naha and Shuri. He also managed to photograph the governors of both towns and one unnamed member of the royal family. The accompanying text is detailed and a delight to read. Sutton found the people courteous and friendly and enjoyed the food and warm climate; he found the landscape "in all directions charming and romantic, the terrace cultivation adding considerably to the beauties of nature." Sutton and his colleagues also enjoyed the hospitality shown to them during a banquet held in their honor on their last night in the country. "I never enjoyed a more delightful evening out of England." Sutton also expressed his fond sentiments on leaving Okinawa: "I never left any place with so much regret as I did Loo-Choo.... Going north for Japan, this delightful island was soon lost to our view; but we shall always cherish in our memories the gentle, hospitable, and esteemed inhabitants of this beautiful island."

HMS *Serpent* continued northwards to meet up with Admiral King's flagship, HMS *Princess Royal*, in Nagasaki Harbor. King was escorting the British Minister Harry Parkes, who had accepted unofficial invitations to visit the western domains of Satsuma and Uwajima. During July and August 1866 Sutton photographed in and around the towns of Nagasaki, Kagoshima, and Uwajima. Thirty-five lantern slides of southern Japan made up the second part of Sutton's fourth lecture. Portraits included the wives and children of the princes of Satsuma, a group of Koreans at Nagasaki, and some boy acrobats and actors in Uwajima.

Sutton's fifth reading is centered on Harry Parkes' official visit to the Emperor in Kyoto, in March 1868. Sutton lists fifty slides, which are mostly of Kyoto and its vicinity. A sixth reading is based around Parkes' earlier visit to Osaka in April and May of 1867. It was here that Sutton photographed the

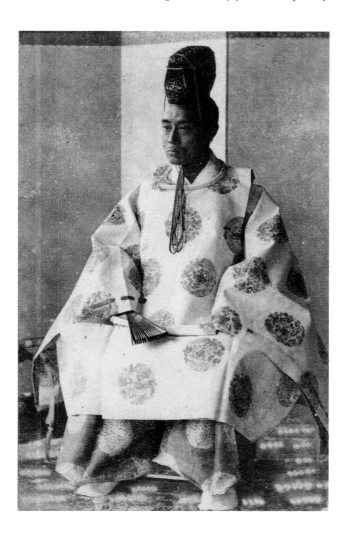

Below Fig. 127. Possibly Frederick Sutton, "Group of Japanese Medical Officers," Yokohama, ca. 1869, large-format albumen print. Courtesy of Mrs J. Brooke-Smith. This photograph was taken at the Yokohama Naval Hospital and also shows Dr Dunwoodie as the central figure and the heavily bearded Dr William Willis to his left. A descendant of Dr Dunwoodie has tentatively suggested the photographer as Sutton.

Although Dunwoodie, the original owner of this photograph, may well have known his Royal Navy colleague, it is not certain that Sutton was the photographer.

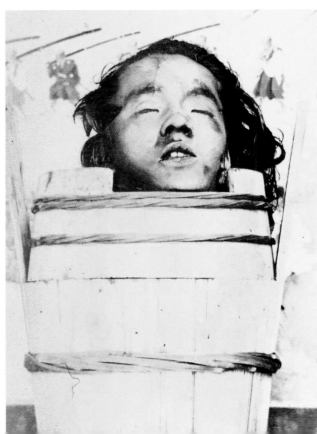

Below Fig. 130. Anonymous, "Portrait of Wilhelm Burger," 1869, small-format albumen print. Old Japan Picture Library. This view was taken in the British Consul's residence in Osaka.

Shogun, and two of his portraits are amongst the fifty-eight lantern slides listed. The seventh reading, entitled "Old and New Japan," is accompanied by a list of no less than fifty-five slides whose subject matter is extremely varied and which attempt to capture images before and after the Meiji Restoration. The other readings concern China, Formosa, and other countries in the Far East.

Including Okinawa, there are some 216 glass lantern slides of Japan which represent an important and early body of work which has yet to be discovered. Judging from the titles, the group does include those few images currently known to be Sutton's. If and when the lantern slides do surface, photo-historians might well be able to attribute many currently unidentified, or indeed wrongly identified, early photographs of Japan.

Sutton died just one year after the publication of the readings and it is doubtful, therefore, whether he was able to give many lectures. Unless the slides are found, it will not be possible to fully appreciate Sutton's overall contribution to early photography in Japan.[51]

WILHELM BURGER

Wilhelm Burger (1844–1920) was appointed as the official photographer to the Austria-Hungary mission, which was dispatched to the Far East in October 1868 in order to initiate diplomatic and commercial relations with Siam, China, and Japan (Fig. 130). Burger arrived in Nagasaki in September 1869, where the mission stayed for just two weeks. During that time he took advantage of a number of photographic portrait opportunities using, as the props suggest, Ueno Hikoma's studio. The props again provide strong evidence that Shimooka Renjo's studio in Yokohama was used when the expedition arrived there on October 2nd. A month later the expedition left Japan, but Burger was prevailed upon to stay behind to produce a detailed photograph record of Japanese works of art. Having accomplished this task, he returned to Austria in March 1870.

Born into a comfortable Viennese middle-class family, Burger received a classic education but early on in his schooling displayed strong artistic tendencies and his parents arranged for private tuition in both painting and drawing. Showing exceptional talent, he was enrolled in the Akademie

der bildenden Kunste and studied there between 1855 and 1860. He then moved to Munich to continue his studies, but he was becoming fascinated by photography, thanks to the influence of his uncle who was a keen photographer. Immersing himself in his new passion, he returned to Vienna in 1863 and studied photography at Vienna University. Gert Rosenberg, in his *Wilhelm Burger: Ein Welt-und Forschungs-reisender mit der Kamera, 1844–1920* (1984), mentions that Burger demonstrated a remarkable ability in the subject and was already lecturing and publishing articles when he received the appointment to the mission.

On his return from Japan, his precocious talent was rewarded by his appointment as court photographer. In 1872 he became the official photographer to the Austria-Hungary Arctic Expedition and he subsequently participated in other expeditions to Asia Minor. Constantly experimenting with new technology and refining his technique, Burger became the most celebrated photographer in Austria.

In many ways Burger was the complete photographer: he combined supreme technical competence with an artist's instinctive understanding of form and composition. His series of Japanese art objects is exceptional, and his published portfolio of fifty-six Japanese views, *Bilder Aus Japan* (1871), contains examples of outstanding landscape photographs, many of which would rival the best work produced by Beato or Uchida (Figs. 131, 132, 134).

WILH. BURGER, PH.

EIN HINRICHTUNGSPLATZ IN YEDO.   AN EXECUTION-PLACE IN YEDO.

Une place d'exécution à Yedo.

Am Fort Suzaki in Jedo.

Above Fig. 131. Wilhelm Burger, "An Execution Place in Yedo," No. 32, large-format albumen print. British Library (ref: Maps 8.d.24).

Left Fig. 132. Wilhelm Burger, "At Fort Suzaki in Jedo," 1869, No. 19, large-format albumen print. British Library (ref: Maps 8.d.24).

Jede Art Vervielfältigung vorbehalten

WILH. BURGER, PH.

JAPANESISCHES DORF BEI YOKOHAMA.   JAPANESE VILLAGE AT YOKOHAMA.

Village japonais près Yokohama.

MILTON MILLER

The American Milton M. Miller operated out of Hong Kong and Nagasaki for a short time in the early 1860s. Unfortunately, nothing much is known about his life although P. E. Palmquist and T. R. Kailbourn in *Pioneer Photographers of the Far West* (2000) tell us that in 1856 he was working as a photographer at the San Francisco gallery of R. J. Vance, California's foremost daguerrean during the 1850s. On May 30th, 1860, Miller embarked on the *Alfred Hill* at San Francisco, which reached Hong Kong on July 19th (*Overland China Mail*, July 26th, 1860). He was almost certainly there at the request of Charles Weed and his partner, someone known only as Howard, who had reached Hong Kong some six months earlier. Weed and Howard, who seem to have come to China on an exploratory tour with a view to determining the viability of establishing operations at one or more of the coastal ports, were presumably keen to continue the experiment, having established a promising base in Hong Kong. Needing a reliable operator to manage the studio whilst they were away, a call had gone out to Miller, someone whom they had probably known in San Francisco. Following Miller's arrival, and judging by the wording in the advertisement below, it is possible that Howard initially managed the studio with Miller as his assistant, releasing Weed to move on to Shanghai. In any case, a few months later Miller seems to have taken control of the studio with Howard having left. The *China Directory* of 1862 lists the following advertisement:"

NOTICE. MR. M. MILLER, LATE OPERATOR AND SUCCESSOR TO MESSRS. WEED & HOWARD, BEGS TO INFORM RESIDENTS AND VISITORS OF HONG KONG, THAT HE HAS FITTED UP THE ROOM LATELY OCCUPIED BY MR. HOWARD, ON THE PARADE GROUND, AND IS NOW PREPARED TO TAKE PHOTOGRAPHIC PICTURES OF ALL KINDS. LIKENESSES FROM MINIATURE TO LIFE SIZE, VIEWS OF HOUSES EXECUTED AT SHORT NOTICE.... AS HIS STAY AT THE ABOVE PLACE IS LIMITED, THOSE WISHING HIS SERVICE WILL PLEASE CALL EARLY.... A COLLECTION OF VIEWS OF VARIOUS PLACES FOR SALE. JAN 1ST, 1861.

Miller's movements are hard to track around this time. He is probably the Miller who traveled from Nagasaki towards the end of May 1861, arriving at Shanghai on May 25th, according to the *North China Herald* of that date. His first views of Japan may date from around this time.

Weed and Howard had moved temporarily to Shanghai, and it is likely that all three expected to return to the US after a few months. However, perhaps because the Hong Kong venture was more successful than expected, Miller stayed on until 1864 and started to produce some exceptional portraits of Chinese subjects, a number of which he signed.[52] He also photographed members of the 1862 Japanese Embassy to Europe, during its stopover in Hong Kong.

The New York stereo producers E. & H. T. Anthony commissioned him for a series on China and Japan and it would appear that all of the six Japanese views were taken in Nagasaki. According to Palmquist and Kailbourn, Miller occasionally visited Macau and Canton where he made panoramic studies. He also took over the Weed & Howard gallery in Canton in September 1861. It was in this latter city that Miller got into trouble when he fired a warning shot at one of the coolies who was working for him at the time. The bullet struck the coolie on his thigh and Miller was arrested. Fortunately,

Below Fig. 137. Milton M. Miller, "Samurai Armor," Hong Kong, 1862, large-format albumen print. Old Japan Picture Library. One of the 1862 Japanese ambassadors to Europe dressed in ceremonial armor.

Right Fig. 138. Charles Leander Weed, "Entrance to the American Legation, Yedo," No. 13, 1867, mammoth-plate albumen print. Canadian Centre for Architecture, Montreal. The great American photographer Charles Weed appears to have been the first to carry out the Herculean task of transporting and using a mammoth-plate camera in Bakumatsu Japan. The actual image size here is 15 x 20 inches (395 x 517 mm).

no serious damage was done and he got off with a fine of seventy-five dollars.

Miller's work is fairly well represented in China collections. His portrait work is quite stunning, imbued with a psychological intensity that is in complete contrast to Beato's non-interpretive style discussed earlier. Both show empathy with their subjects, and yet, we seem to *know* Beato's sitters, but *understand* Miller's. The absence of a sufficient number of attributed landscapes, however, makes it difficult to assess Miller's work in this field.

CHARLES WEED

Charles Leander Weed (1824–1903) was born in New York State, but moved with his family to Wisconsin before later settling in California. He is increasingly recognized as one of the finest landscape photographers in the history of the medium, and is particularly famous for taking the first views of Yosemite Valley in 1859 and subsequent mammoth plates of the same region in 1864. These latter images won an award at the 1867 International Exposition at Paris.

Weed, energetic and restless, traveled extensively and created a large portfolio of geographically diverse views. At the end of 1859, Weed and a companion called Howard left San Francisco for Hong Kong where they temporarily set up a studio known as Messrs. Weed & Howard.[53] The *Overland China Mail* of February 28th, 1860 (p. 821) carried the following interesting note:

PHOTOGRAPHIC ESTABLISHMENT WE HAVE MUCH PLEASURE IN BEARING TESTIMONY TO THE CLEARNESS AND BEAUTY OF THE PHO-TOGRAPHS EXHIBITED BY MESSRS. HOWARD AND WEED, WHO HAVE COME HERE FROM CALIFORNIA, AND OPENED, FOR A SHORT TIME, A PHOTOGRAPHIC ESTABLISHMENT ON THE WEST SIDE OF THE PARADE GROUND. THE VIEWS OF HONG KONG THEY HAVE ALREADY TAKEN ARE A GUARANTEE OF THEIR SURPRISING SKILL, AND THEIR PORTRAITS ARE ALMOST MORE DISTINCT THAN LIFE ITSELF. THOSE WHO DESIRE IT MAY HAVE THEIR HEADS TAKEN OFF LIFESIZE, AND SENT HOME TO THEIR ABSENT FRIENDS.

Weed and Howard then summoned help from Milton Miller who left San Francisco on May 30th, 1860 and arrived in Hong Kong on July 19th. According to the *China Mail* of October 3rd, 1860 and the *North China Herald* of September 29th, they then left Miller behind in Hong Kong, leaving on September 21st and arriving in Shanghai on the 25th. The following year, the *North China Herald* of December 14th, 1861, reported Mr Llewellyn announcing he had purchased the negatives of portraits taken by "Messrs. Weed & Howard during their stay in Shanghai." Weed and Howard had opened a studio in Canton in April 1861 but this was taken over by Miller in September. Weed then returned to America.

In February 1865 Weed left for Honolulu with his brother James and a sister. On arrival they met another brother, Frederick, and established the Weed Brothers Gallery in April of that year. Charles Weed then produced the first mammoth-plate photographs of the Hawaiian Islands. In December Charles, James, and their sister left for China and arrived in Hong Kong on January 26th, 1866. By March the Weed Brothers Gallery had opened and Charles is listed in the *China Directory* for 1866 and 1867. The *Japan Times Overland Mail* for June 13th, 1868 then lists Weed as a passenger leaving Yokohama on June 5th for San Francisco on board the PMSS *China*. He reappears in the 1869 directory as being resident in Shanghai.

According to Palmquist and Kailbourn, Weed returned to California in 1870 where he settled down and married in the mid-1870s. He certainly traveled to San Francisco from

Shanghai on the *Golden Age*, stopping off at Nagasaki, Kobe, and Yokohama on the way, because the *Hiogo News* issue of May 18th, 1870 mentions him as one of the passengers arriving at Kobe on the same day. In 1886 his voter registration described him as six feet tall with gray eyes and hair and a fair complexion. He died aged seventy-nine.[54]

According to Palmquist's "California's Peripatetic Photographer," Weed had a business relationship with the photographic publisher Thomas Houseworth of San Francisco. In 1869 this firm produced a series of mammoth-plate and stereoscopic views of China and Japan entitled *Oriental Scenery*. The mammoth-plate views were almost certainly the first of Japan (Figs. 3, 138). One of the stereos includes the US Minister General Robert Bruce Van Valkenburgh, who held the post between January 1866 and November 1869. It is now possible to date this particular stereoview following recent work by the photo-researcher Izakura Naomi. The view including the US Minister was taken on September 22nd, 1867 according to the personal diary of Katsu Kaishu, one of those also in the photograph. Another in the group, Ozeki Masuhiro, died on December 9th, 1867. It is very likely that all the views in this series are from 1867, making them the last Bakumatsu stereoviews to be published (Figs. 139, 140).

OTHER WESTERN PHOTOGRAPHERS

It will probably never be possible to compile a complete list of all the Western photographers, amateur and professional, who used their cameras in Japan during the 1860s. New discoveries continue to be made, and the following notes should be considered very much a "work-in-progress."

We will start with **Abel Anthony James Gower** (ca. 1836–ca. 1898) (Fig. 141). Despite coming from a banking family background, Gower chose the foreign service and started his career in Hong Kong in 1856. He arrived in Japan in June 1859 as one of the consular assistants to the British Minister Rutherford Alcock at the legation in Edo. It had been previously supposed he was a possible candidate for authorship of the Negretti and Zambra Japan stereo photographs, published in 1861. Although he was known as an amateur photographer, we now know he was not the "special artist sent out for the purpose by the enterprising firm of Negretti and Zambra" (see Pierre Rossier advertisement, page 48). What we do know is that Gower accompanied Alcock and others on an overland excursion from Nagasaki to Edo between June 1st and July 4th, 1861. He took some photographs along the way, one of which is engraved in Sir Rutherford Alcock's *The Capital of the Tycoon* (1863). Whilst describing the journey, Alcock makes the occasional reference to Gower's photographic efforts, but it may well be a reflection on the quality of the end product that only one view was apparently deemed good enough to reproduce.[55]

Because of the false association with the aforementioned Negretti and Zambra stereo series, it was thought that Gower used a stereo camera. However, a related reference to Gower's photographic work on this journey throws doubt on the theory. It appears in a private letter from Rutherford Alcock (at the Edo consulate), dated September 22nd, 1861, to Earl Russell

129. "The Gororgio," or Tycoon's Cabinet, with the American Minister and his Secretary, Yedo. Japan.

which, in places, is very hard to decipher: "My Lord, Mr. Gower who accompanied me overland from Nagasaki made a series of photographic views & a panorama of Osaca from the river which are of some interest as giving with unquestionable accuracy scenes never before even sketched. Mr. Gower had all sorts of difficulties to contend with – no one to aid & he particularly begs me to explain he is (...?) of all their defects viewed as Photographic (...?). Still as I expressed a wish that the Whole (...?) should be sent to your Lordship for acceptance, believing that with all their imperfections they would still prove interesting, he having gladly placed a set at my disposal for that purpose...." (National Archives, PRO/32/22/50). According to Coates in *The China Consuls* (1988), Gower died at the age of sixty-two in Leghorn (presumably Italy).

Whilst on the subject of the Negretti and Zambra stereos, we can mention here another past candidate for their authorship, the British photographer **Walter B. Woodbury** (1834–85). Confusion has arisen due to a reference made to Woodbury in the obituary of the founder of Negretti and Zambra, Henry Negretti, given in the *British Journal of Photography*, October 3rd, 1879 (p. 472). It there states that Woodbury was sent by Negretti and Zambra to Far Eastern countries to secure photographs for publication and that he stayed for several years in China, Japan, and other countries of eastern Asia.

In fact, according to the 1975 *Dictionary of National Biography*, Woodbury moved from England to Australia in 1852, at the age of eighteen, where he subsequently concentrated on photography. In 1858 he emigrated to Java with a partner, James Page. Views were taken of that country and submitted to Negretti and Zambra who published a number of them in stereo form. Woodbury returned to England in 1863 where he settled. He wrote a number of learned articles on photography whilst developing and patenting his famous "Woodbury-type" carbon-printing photographic process in 1866. There is no evidence that he visited China or Japan and no mention of these countries appears to be made in his various writings; the *British Journal of Photography* is very likely mistaking Woodbury for Rossier.

The history of early Russian photography in the Far East has so far been inadequately researched and documented, and this remains an interesting area for future research. Apart from Mozhaiskii's daguerreotype work in 1854 (see page 31), **Iosif Antonovich Goshkevich** (1814–75), the Russian Consul at Hakodate from 1858 to 1865, was an amateur photographer who taught Kizu Kokichi, Yokoyama Matsusaburo, and Yanagawa Shunzo. Henry Arthur Tilley, in *Japan, the Amoor, and the Pacific* (1861), tells us that he met Goshkevich at Hakodate on July 14th, 1859. The Russian had apparently lived in Peking for ten years and spoke Chinese, Japanese, and most European languages fluently. He had been born and raised in a priest's family and later studied at the St. Petersburg Theological Academy. Goshkevich had accompanied the 1853 Russian expedition to Japan and had been on board the *Diana* which had been damaged by the earthquake at Shimoda the following year. Effectively marooned at Shimoda, he was taken prisoner by an English

Below Fig. 141. Pierre Rossier, "Unidentified Portrait," ca. 1860, large-format albumen print. Nederlands Scheepvaartmuseum, Amsterdam. Across the face of the photograph is the signature "P. Rossier." Said to be of Abel A. J. Gower, the portrait is more likely to be of John MacDonald of the British Legation. See Fig. 42.

Below Fig. 142. Abel A. J. Gower, "English Consulate and Nagasaki Harbor", ca. 1860, large-format albumen print, Yokohama Archives of History. This is the only identified photograph by Abel Gower and is signed on the reverse. Professor Himeno Junichi of Nagasaki University has estimated the date from the outline of the harbor and early stages of land reclamation shown in the foreign settlement area. Curiously, Wilhelm Burger seems to have acquired this image during his 1869 visit and subsequently published it as his own work in *Bilder Aus Japan*, Wein (1871).

ship, due to the state of war between the two nations at that time. Vainly protesting that, as a civilian, he should be freed, he was taken to Hong Kong and was held for several months before being liberated. Goshkevich gave an interesting account of his enforced stay in the *China Mail* issue of June 3rd, 1858. Tilley states that Goshkevich had produced much scholarly work on Japan and China and had published a dictionary of both languages.

If Goshkevich did indeed keep any prints or negatives of his photographs at his home or consulate in Hakodate, then these were destroyed in the devastating fire that swept away both properties on March 13th, 1865 and which was reported in the *Japan Herald Supplement* on the 25th of that month (p. 622a).[56] Goshkevich left Japan later that year. The Russian naval medical officer attached to the consulate, **Dr Zalesky**, employed Tamoto Kenzo as his photography assistant and thereby passed on his knowledge.

Antonius Franciscus Bauduin (1820–85) replaced Pompe van Meerdervoort in 1862 as the chief medical officer attached to the Yoseiji Hospital in Nagasaki (Figs. 143, 144). His younger brother, **Albert Johannes** (1829–90), had come to Japan in 1859 as a merchant with the Dutch Trading Society at Deshima and, from 1863 would be the Dutch Consul at Nagasaki. Both were enthusiastic amateurs, particularly Antonius, and took numerous photographs in and around Nagasaki. **Dr Koenraad Wolter Gratama** (1831–88), Antonius's successor-, was also keen and carried on the tradition. He was in Japan from 1866 to 1871 and is venerated there as the founding father of chemistry[57] (Figs. 144, 146).

Charles Parker's first partner in Japan was the Englishman **William Parke Andrew**, and their business relationship lasted, as we saw, from September 1863 to July 1865. After this we find Andrew taking an advertisement in the October 14th, 1865 issue of the *Japan Herald*:

NOTICE OF REMOVAL. W.P. ANDREW, PHOTOGRAPHER (LATE C.PARKER & CO) BEGS TO INFORM THE COMMUNITY OF YOKOHAMA THAT PENDING THE BUILDING OF HIS NEW HOUSE, HE HAS REMOVED FROM NO. 51, MAIN ST. TO NO. 123 HOMURA ROAD., CORNER OF FUSIYAMA AVENUE. SO SOON AS HIS PHOTOGRAPHIC ROOM IS READY, DUE NOTICE WILL BE GIVEN. IN THE MEANTIME, MR. A. HAS ON HAND A LARGE QUANTITY OF JAPANESE VIEWS AND FIGURES LARGE AND SMALL, ALSO LARGE VIEWS OF DAIBUTZ, KAMAKURA AND THE NEIGHBOURHOOD. P.S. – MR. A. IS CONSTANTLY TAKING FURTHER PHOTOGRAPHS OF VIEWS AND OTHER OBJECTS OF INTEREST IN THE NEIGHBOURHOOD.

This advertisement appeared for a few weeks, and then nothing else was heard. Andrew's photo studio, if it ever got started, was clearly not a success, and as his name is absent from later directories, he must have left Japan.

Andrew's successor fared no better. **William Almeida Crane** (1833–1903), also an Englishman, was born in Singapore and came to Yokohama in 1861 in order to join the Bank of Central India as an accountant. When the bank closed, he decided on a change of career and on November 1st, 1865 entered into partnership with Parker. However, by June of the following year he was advertising his own studio in the *Daily Japan Herald* of October 1st, 1866:

NOTICE. THE UNDERSIGNED HAS THE HONOUR TO INTIMATE TO THE RESIDENTS IN AND VISITORS TO YOKOHAMA, THAT HE HAS TEMPORARILY ERECTED – A PHOTOGRAPHIC GALLERY AT NO. 36, WHERE HE IS NOW READY TO TAKE PORTRAITS, AND SHORTLY WILL HAVE A NEW COLLECTION OF VIEWS W.A.CRANE, YOKOHAMA, JUNE 1ST, 1866.

These adverts continued up to and including December 8th, 1866. Either the Yokohama Great Fire of November 1866 destroyed his stock and studio, or he quickly realized that he would not make a success as a photographer because we hear nothing more about Crane's photographic activities. In the July 24th, 1867 issue of the *Japan Herald*, he offered his services as a public accountant. This led to a number of diverse roles over the next thirty years. He was, for a time, employed by the auctioneers Hansard & Black, the Blackiston trading company in Hakodate, and Messrs. Bowden Bros. & Co. in Yokohama. At some stage he was in partnership with a Mr Keil in a piano import and tuning business, and he also sold musical instruments from Chefoo, China. After 1899 he and his wife and three daughters no longer appear in the directories. According to his obituary, Crane was an ardent Freemason who had received the highest degree from the Rising Sun Lodge in Yokohama. Long an invalid, he succumbed to cancer of the stomach and died on October 22nd, 1903.[58]

The French naval lieutenant **Jules Apollinaire Felix Le Bas** (1834–75) was on board the warship *la Semiramis* in 1863–4 during the hostilities at Shimonoseki between the Choshu clan and the Western powers. Le Bas, a more than competent photographer, was charged with making a pictorial record of the campaign. These photographs are extremely rare, and to the writer's knowledge only exist in two collections.[59] A number of them were reproduced as engravings in the December 31st, 1864 issue of *Le Monde Illustre*. Apart from those by Felix Beato, Le Bas's are the only known photographs of the Shimonoseki conflict (Figs. 147–154).

Le Bas entered the navy on October 1st, 1854 and rose to the rank of lieutenant in 1863. The following year he became Chevalier de la Legion d'Honneur and was a commandant in 1868. His distinguished naval career was cut short in May 1874 when it was discovered he had contracted chronic bronchitis. Additional complications set in and he died on March 12th, 1875. The only other reference to Le Bas the writer has found is a mention of his photographs of China and Japan being produced as stereos on pygmalion tissue.[60]

Another French photographer, **Paul Champion** (1838–?), was sent on a mission to China and Japan during 1865–6. The following report in the *London and China Telegraph* of June 11th, 1866 (p. 324) explains: "The French Society of Acclimatization sent M. Paul Champion, a distinguished chemist, on a mission to China and Japan some time since; that gentleman has just returned with an important collection of pheasants and other birds for the gardens of the society. It is said that in addition to the notes that he has made for the society he has brought home valuable information respecting the Chinese and Japanese industries, and that he succeeded in obtaining admission to the famous porcelain factories of Keu-ti-Chin. M. Champion has also brought home a large

Top Fig. 148. Jules Le Bas, "French Horse 'Instantneite' outside the French Legation, Yokohama," 1864, large-format albumen print. Dr Joseph Dubois Collection.

Above Fig. 149. Jules Le Bas, "Residence of the French Minister, Yokohama," 1864, large-format albumen print. Dr Joseph Dubois Collection. This is more likely to be the French Legation (see Fig. 148).

Far left Fig. 150. Jules Le Bas, "Ancient Warrior," Yokohama, 1864, large-format albumen print. Dr Joseph Dubois Collection.

Left Fig. 151. Jules Le Bas, "Ancient Warrior," 1864, large-format albumen print. Dr Joseph Dubois Collection.

Below left Fig. 152. Jules Le Bas, "Attachés at the French Legation, Yokohama," 1864, large-format albumen print. Dr Joseph Dubois Collection.

Right Fig. 153. Jules Le Bas, "French Warship *Semiramis*, Woosun," 1864, large-format albumen print. Dr Joseph Dubois Collection.

Below Fig. 154. Jules Le Bas, "Yokohama Yakonin," 1864, large-format albumen print. Dr Joseph Dubois Collection.

Bottom Fig. 155. Paul Champion, "Habitation de Yokohama," 1866, albumen-print stereoview. Old Japan Picture Library.

Below Fig. 156. Anonymous, "Paul Champion with Camera", ca. 1865–66, detail from albumen-print stereoview from "Chine & Japon" B. K. series. Serge Kakou Collection, Paris.

collection of photographs of some of the most remarkable buildings and views both in China and Japan" (Fig. 155).

Champion was a chemistry engineer by profession and an amateur photographer. However, according to Thiriez in *Barbarian Lens*, he was a respected member of the Societé Francaise de Photographie and published a number of papers in its *Bulletin*, becoming editor in 1872.

During his time in Japan, Champion took both views and portraits of very high quality. Unfortunately, many of them lack contrast and reflect the difficulties Champion experienced with his chemicals. Serge Kakou, the French photo-dealer and collector, has pointed out that a number of these were reproduced as stereoviews in the series published by B. K. Editeur, Paris (A. Block) entitled *Chine & Japon*. Champion's exact dates in Japan do not appear to have previously been researched, but he was there in September 1865 because the *Japan Times Daily Advertiser* for September 13th, 1865 records in its passenger list that he embarked on the *Dupleix* the previous day at Yokohama, bound for Shanghai. Various issues of the *North China Herald* for 1865–6 record in passenger lists that Champion arrived in Hong Kong around March 1865 (presumably from Europe) and moved on to Shanghai the same month. It looks as though he then went to Japan, returning to Shanghai in September after which he traveled to Peking. By March 1866 he has finished his assignment and returns to France. His Japan sojourn, therefore, is very likely to have been between March and September 1865. Champion also gave a talk in Paris on the difficulties of taking photographs in China and Japan, on January 11th, 1867 at a meeting of the Societé Francaise de Photographie. This important and illuminating talk is recorded in the society's *Bulletin de la Société française de photographie* (procès-verbal de la Séance du 11 janvier 1867, pp. 13–18), and a translation appears here in Appendix 3.

An English amateur photographer, **Angus C. Fairweather**, was first mentioned in Worswick's *Japan Photographs* as having taken a collection of views and portraits in Japan during the 1860s. According to the *British Journal of Photography* (June 7th, 1867, p. 270), he apparently used "dry collodion plates, as the artist could not be cumbered with much luggage." Nothing further has emerged on this photographer.

We saw earlier that **Sir Henry F. Woods** (1842–1929), whilst accompanying the British Minister Sir Harry Parkes to Edo in 1865, took the opportunity to borrow some of Beato's equipment in order to take photographs. Woods, in his book *Spunyarn* provides a fascinating account of the difficulties experienced by photographers in those days and his account is given in full in Appendix 3.

Woods was not the only amateur photographer amongst the naval officers serving on the British *China Station* at that time. We have already considered the contribution made by Frederick Sutton, but **Hugo Lewis Pearson** (1843–1912) and **Lord Walter Talbot Kerr** (1839–1927) are examples of others who merit some recognition, and Sebastian Dobson has referred to their activities in his article "Frederick William Sutton" (2002). A number of Kerr's (and Sutton's) photographs are illustrated as engravings in R. M. Jephson and E. P. Elmhirst's *Our Life in Japan* (1869).

The American missionary **Orramel Hinckley Gulick** (1830–1923), who spent a total of sixty years in Japan and Honolulu, took photographs in Edo in October 1862, having been invited by the US Minister Robert Pruyn. (The party also included William Saunders and Samuel Robbins Brown.) Gulick possibly took many photographs in Japan but none has so far been identified.

Above Fig. 158. Lord Walter Talbot Kerr, "Admiral King with Choshu Daimyo and Heir, Mori Takachika and Mori Motonori," 1867, small-format albumen print. Nederlands Scheepvaartmuseum, Amsterdam.

Charles Miller Collins (1820–1909) was an amateur photographer and fleet engineer in the Royal Navy. Using his stereo camera, he recorded life on land and sea at the time of the Anglo-French attack on the Taku Forts in 1860 and in 1862 he was taking stereoviews in Yokohama, including the site of Charles Richardson's grave. The photographs do not seem to have been distributed commercially, and seventy-six of his China and Japan stereoviews were sold at a Phillip's photography auction in London on October 30th, 1985, together with other Collins' family photographs and papers.

August Sachtler operated a commercial studio in 1860s Singapore, according to John Falconer's *A Vision of the Past* (1995). Sebastian Dobson points out that Sachtler, like John Wilson, assisted the Prussian 1860 Mission to Japan and five of his photographs are engraved in the German periodical *Illustrirte Zeitung* (May 25th; June 1st; September 14th, 1861).

OTHER JAPANESE PHOTOGRAPHERS

Apart from the famous Japanese photographers above, and those to be mentioned below, it is worth remembering that Japanese photo-history is a fast-evolving field of study which, in the particular case of Japanese studios, is likely to continue to throw up surprises. A case in point is the amateur photographer and scientific writer **Ono Benkichi** (1801–70). Born in Kyoto, he moved to Nagasaki at around the age of twenty to study Western medicine and science. After an interlude on Tsushima Island, where he studied weaponry and mathematics, he returned to Kyoto and married. Shortly afterwards, Ono and his wife moved to her home prefecture, Ishikawa, where he remained until his death. Research by Motoyasu Hiroshi in "Ono Benkichi and Photography in the Kaga Domain" (1997), strongly suggests that Ono was one of the first Japanese to experiment with photography and that extant work by him may yet prove to predate the 1857 daguerreotype

of Shimazu Nariakira. Although this has not yet been generally accepted, it will be interesting to see any further research emerging in the coming years.[61]

Kizu Kokichi (1830–95) was a tailor by trade, based in Hakodate, a city in the northern island of Hokkaido. One day the Russian Consul Goshkevich visited his shop and asked him to make a suit out of some Western cloth he had bought. Never having tailored Western clothing, Kizu borrowed one of the Consul's suits as a sample. The finished product was the first Western suit made in Japan and Kizu began to specialize in this area. According to Yokoe Fuminori in *The Advent of Photography in Japan* (1997), his business prospered as a result. Some time after, he decided to visit his home town of Echigo, Niigata. Traveling by ship he saw a camera, which he decided to exchange for a bear skin which he had brought along as a souvenir from Hakodate. However, according to George Alexander Lensen in *Report from Hokkaido* (1954), he was unable to develop any of the pictures. On returning to Hakodate, he asked Goshkevich to teach him how to use the camera. As his clothing business had gone badly during his absence, Kizu decided, in around 1864, to open a photography studio and thereby became Hokkaido's first professional photographer.

In 1865 **Hori Masumi (Yohei)** (1826–80) opened a commercial studio in Kyoto which was to remain in existence throughout the Meiji period. Before his involvement in photography, Hori had a shop in the Marutamachi district of Kyoto selling glassware, which he also manufactured. He later switched to learning photochemistry and in 1863 moved into paper printing. Two years later, he opened his photo studio and was one of the first practitioners to experiment with the wet-plate process. Despite his death in 1880, the Hori family continued operating the studio until 1942.

Tamato Kenzo (1832–1912) was born in Kumano, central Honshu, but actually became another one of Hokkaido's successful early pioneers. At the age of twenty-three, Tamato

Above Fig. 160. Tamato Kenzo, "Portrait of Two Ainu Women," Hokkaido, ca. 1890, cabinet-size albumen print. Old Japan Picture Library.

Right Fig. 161. Tamato Kenzo, "Portrait of Young Girl," Hokkaido, ca. 1890, cabinet-size albumen print. Old Japan Picture Library.

Below Fig. 162. Wooden Victorian Graphoscope for Viewing Stereos, Cabinet Photographs, and *Cartes de Visite*. Author's Collection. Although rare these days, at one time these devices would have been considered an indispensable tool for entertainment and education and would have been found in virtually all middle- and upper-income American and European homes.

JAPANESE GEISHAS—SINGING GIRLS.

moved to Nagasaki in order to study Western sciences, where he worked closely with the Western-style physician Yoshio Keisai. According to Tucker et al.'s *The History of Japanese Photography* (2003), in 1859 he moved to Hakodate and served as an assistant to the Russian Dr Zalesky who, as we saw earlier, was an amateur photographer. Fascinated, Tamato decided to make a career for himself in this field. Working as a photographer from 1866, he collaborated with Kizu Kokichi in photographing the construction of Fukuyama Castle, which would become the last Japanese castle to be built. During the civil war in 1868–9, Tamato photographed the rebel leaders Enomoto Takeaki and Hijikata Toshizo. He opened his studio in Hakodate some time between 1867 and 1869 and is particularly famous for documenting, in 1871, the rapid development of Hokkaido as a settlement area and the construction of its roads and buildings and farmland reclamation. A portfolio of some 158 photographs was created as an official document. The views and panoramas, considered to be important historical documents, are now held by the library at Hokkaido University (Figs. 160, 161).

Kameya Tokujiro (1825–84), mentioned above, is an unsung early Nagasaki commercial photographer who was

taught by the Dutch at Deshima. As we have seen, he passed this knowledge on to Tomishige before moving to Kyoto and opening a studio there in 1862, the first commercial studio to open in that city. Japanese sources disagree on whether Kyoto was Kameya's first studio, or whether, in fact, he had opened in Nagasaki before then. In any case, he returned to Nagasaki in 1868 and opened a studio there at Kinoshita-cho, which was in existence until his death in Vladivostok in 1884, in which town Kameya had opened a branch studio. According to Himeno in "Encounters," **Kameya Toyo** (1852–85) had assisted her father in the Nagasaki studio, thereby becoming one of Japan's first female photographers. She died in 1885. The Kameya family had adopted Yoshii Teijiro in 1871. Yoshii took the name **Kameya Teijiro** and was immediately involved at the Nagasaki studio. In around 1880 he opened a Kameya branch studio in Korea but, tragically, he too died in 1885. Insufficient recognition seems to have been given to Kameya Tokujiro who may, conceivably, have started his Nagasaki studio before Ueno Hikoma (Fig. 163).

Morita Reizo (1830–89) opened Osaka's first studio, according to Tucker et al.'s *The History of Japanese Photography* (2003), with Uchida Kuichi in 1865. Himeno Junichi in

"Encounters," however, states that it was Ueno Sachima who worked with Uchida. Morita certainly was operating a studio in Kobe in 1869 since he placed the following advertisement in the *Hiogo and Osaka Herald* which ran from June 18th, 1869 until at least March 26th, 1870: "Morita, Kobe-No-Ftats Chia, will take photographs in Japanese or European style." His address, according to Boyd and Izakura, was Futatsuya Nishi Honmachi, Kobe.

Shima Kakoku (1827–70) was born in present-day Tochigi Prefecture and, in 1847, no doubt influenced by his father who was a keen painter, enrolled in an art school in Edo where he excelled. He married another artist, **Ryu** (1823–1900) in 1855 and the couple seem to have drifted around the Kanto region, moving house on a number of occasions, perhaps showing their work in exhibitions. From Kinoshita Naoyuki's article "Shima Kakoku" (1997), we learn that Shima, during this period, had some pictures accepted as illustrations for books. It is not clear how, or when, the couple learned photography. However, in the Shima family archives there is a wet-plate photographic print portrait of Shima taken by his wife and dated spring 1864. This is the earliest known photograph taken by a Japanese woman. According to Boyd and Izakura in *Portraits in Sepia*, the couple appear to have operated a photo studio in Edo from around 1865 to 1867. Shima then accepted a prestigious position at the Kaiseijo, the shogunate's school in Edo, for the study of Western science, which would later become part of Tokyo University. Shima later worked at the Daigaku Toko, a government medical school, where he was involved in drawing medical charts and inventing the first movable lead type by which medical textbooks were printed. Shima died in 1870 and his wife returned to her native town of Kiryu, Gunma Prefecture, where she opened a photo studio.

Setsu Shinichi (1844–1909) opened a studio in 1869 at Shin-machi, Nagasaki, and it was still in operation in 1903. Setsu initially followed the family tradition of embarking on a career as a Chinese interpreter. Japan's rapid modernization, brought about by the Meiji Restoration, meant that this particular skill was no longer highly valued, so he moved to Tokyo in an attempt to secure a civil service role. According to Himeno in "Encounters," his new career came to an end following the diagnosis of an eye disease. This disability did not, apparently, seriously damage his chances of switching to his new chosen occupation of photography, and after a six months' apprenticeship with Shimizu Tokoku in Yokohama, he opened a studio in Nagasaki. He is known to have accompanied Ueno Hikoma on his 1877 mission to photograph the Satsuma battlefields, but other than that little is known. His studio in Nagasaki was advertised in the *Murray's Hand-Book* between the years 1893 and 1901. It is not known whether the studio just offered portrait work or whether he also supplied souvenir albums.

It is not generally known that the famous castaway **Nakahama Manjiro** (1827–98) was an accomplished amateur photographer (Fig. 164). Manjiro, as he is popularly known, was a fisherman from what is now Kochi Prefecture. In 1841 he was shipwrecked with others on a deserted island, thought now to have been Torishima. This tiny island would

be their home for four months before they were rescued by an American whaler. Manjiro accepted an invitation from the captain to go to America, where he went to school before embarking on an adventurous life that included whaling and prospecting for gold in California in 1849.

Manjiro did manage to find enough gold to finance a return to Japan. His longing to return to his native country had become stronger than the fear he felt about what could happen to him when he got back. Arriving in Okinawa in 1851, he was immediately arrested and interrogated for seven months. Sentence of death was delayed pending a decision from the de facto ruler of Okinawa, Shimazu Nariakira, the Satsuma *daimyo*. Reprieved, Manjiro was allowed to return home. When Commodore Perry arrived in 1853, Manjiro was called into service as an advisor. In 1855 he was an instructor at the Nagasaki Naval Training Center, while in 1860 he acted as chief interpreter for the group of Japanese that traveled to the US on board the Japanese ship *Kanrin Maru*. One of the American advisers on that same ship was the artist and daguerreotypist Edward Kern. In 1868 he was appointed to the post of instructor at the Kasei Gakko, which is now Tokyo University.

It is not known when he first became interested in photography, but the entry for October 29th, 1860 in Francis Hall's diary, edited by Notehelfer in *Japan through American Eyes* (1992) is significant: "Sadajiro reports that Manjiro, the interpreter, has been confined to his home since his return from America. He has been taking daguerreotypes at Yedo with considerable success." This means that Manjiro was one of the first Japanese to master photography. According to Warriner's *Voyager* (1956, p. 186), when Manjiro returned from America in 1860 he brought back with him a camera, a sewing machine, and an accordion. Some time between his return and 1862 he opened a commercial studio in Tokyo. Although successful, he did not enjoy the work and shortly sold the enterprise to a friend. Is it possible Manjiro was the first Japanese to open a commercial studio? Manjiro may have been more influential in the development of early photography in Japan than we yet know. Perhaps he received some instruction from Edward Kern whom he would have met on the *Kanrin Maru*. An 1860 wet-plate portrait by Manjiro of his wife Tetsuko is illustrated in John D. Dower's *A Century of Japanese Photography* (1981, p. 26).

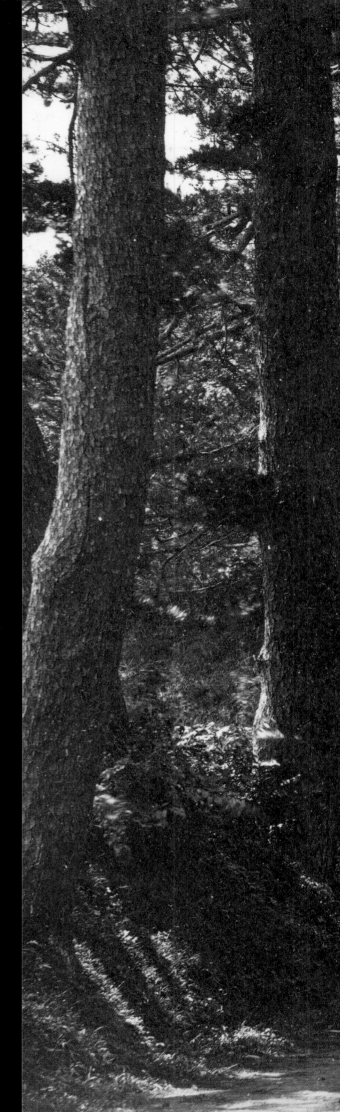

TOKAIDO NEAR **ODAWARRA.**

Below Fig. 166. P. B. Greene, "Iwakura Tomomi in Chicago," 1872, albumen-print stereoview. Author's Collection. Iwakura Tomomi (1825–83) headed a mission to the United States and Europe in 1872–3. On his return he became Acting Prime Minister when the incumbent was taken ill. He survived an assassination attempt in 1874 and died in 1883 when he was given a state funeral.

Views in Chicago & Vicinity
Before and after the Fire.

P. B. Greene, Photographer,
315 West Jackson Street.

By the beginning of the decade, Japan was beginning to modernize at an alarming pace. The telegraph between Tokyo and Yokohama was opened in 1870, and a railway connecting the two cities was under construction. The following year the Japanese Mint opened in Osaka and post offices were established. The early 1870s also saw an influx of foreign employees recruited for their specialist skills in areas as diverse as law, medicine, education, naval training, commerce, and engineering. In 1871 a mission headed by Iwakura Tomomi was despatched to Europe and the United States with one of its aims being the study of Western governmental systems (Fig. 166). The traditional hairstyle where men shaved the top of their heads was prohibited in 1872, although the old style did not die out completely for a number of years. In the same year the Japanese army adopted the conscript system and membership was no longer the exclusive preserve of the samurai. The Western calendar was adopted in 1873 and the wearing of swords was forbidden in 1876. The feudal system, which had been in operation for so many centuries, was being dismantled and the *daimyo* were no longer in control of their local fiefdoms, nor did they have the income to provide for their samurai retainers. Many of the latter group put away their lethal swords and entered the worlds of farming and commerce.

Previous page Fig. 165. Baron Raimund von Stillfried-Ratenicz, "Tokaido near Odawarra," 1871, large-format albumen print. Author's Collection. This is from the first group of topographical studies made by Stillfried in the year he opened his Yokohama studio. (See pages 134–5 for a contemporary review by John Reddie Black.) In later Stillfried albums, the distinctive captioning was removed by trimming. Although no doubt done for aesthetic reasons, the balance of the image is often disturbed.

Some of these changes were opposed by those groups in society who had much to lose. Foremost amongst these were the disenfranchised samurai. The Saga Rebellion in 1874 was a relatively minor disturbance, which was quickly suppressed by the government who executed the ringleaders. The Satsuma Rebellion in 1874, led by the commander-in-chief of the army, Saigo Takamori, was a far more serious challenge to the government. The insurrection was put down, with difficulty, and Saigo committed suicide. This defeat enabled the government to push ahead with little or no resistance.

Photography was no longer something of a mystery and portrait studios began to open in the towns and cities as more and more Japanese overcame their prejudices and sat before the camera. Although some Japanese photographers opened studios in the treaty ports in order to secure patronage from foreigners, increasingly studios were able to position themselves away from these areas and rely upon local custom. Many samurai decided to be photographed wearing their distinctive hairstyles or swords prior to their prohibition. The 1877 Rebellion gave studios another business opportunity as many samurai, anticipating a possible death on the battlefield, wished to leave their families something by which to be remembered. Studio success was far from guaranteed,

however, and many enterprises folded. A regular and reliable supply of chemicals was still a major problem and photographers still required considerable skill and patience in working with the universal wet-plate process. There were tentative signs, however, that the Western dominance in photography was coming to an end.

BARON RAIMUND VON STILLFRIED-RATENICZ

Baron Raimund von Stillfried-Ratenicz (1839–1911) is one of the more interesting figures to emerge from the world of nineteenth-century Japanese photography: aristocrat, soldier, painter, entrepreneur, world traveler, diplomat, and photographer – how could it have been otherwise? (Fig. 167)

Until recently, it has been difficult to untangle the complex web of dates and events surrounding the life of this nomadic Austrian. Thanks largely to the work of Luke Gartlan in his "Chronology of Baron Raimund von Stillfried-Ratenicz" (2001), we now know much more about the man.

Raimund and his two brothers, Franz and Karl, were born into an aristocratic Austrian family in Komotau (now

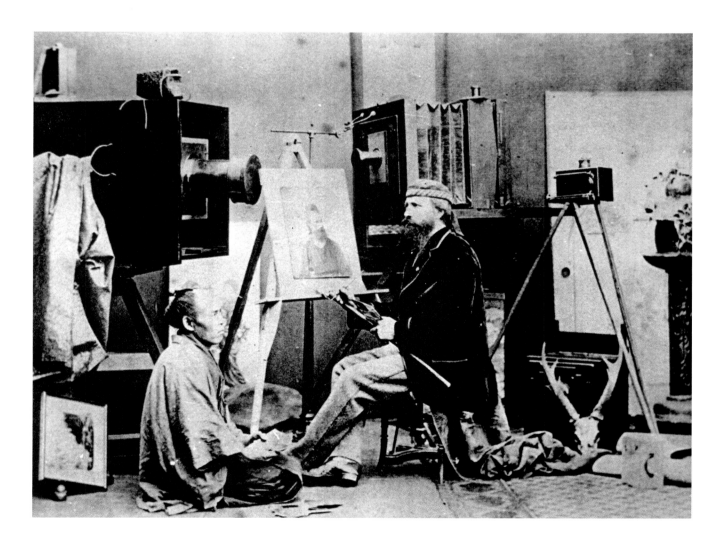

Chomutov, part of the Czech Republic). Destined for a military career, Raimund was enrolled as a boy in the Imperial Naval College at Trieste. He also showed an early interest and ability in painting and therefore also received training in this area. Retiring from the college in 1863 with the rank of Oberlieutenant, he began a series of travels which took him to North and South America, China, and Japan. While staying at Nagasaki, he received further artistic instruction from the well-known landscapist at the time, Eduard Hildebrandt.

Stillfried stayed in Japan for at least a year and is mentioned in the 1865 *China Directory* as working in Nagasaki for the merchants Textor & Co. We also know he visited Yokohama at least once in 1865 since the *Japan Herald* passenger list for April 29th (p. 641) mentions his arrival, three days earlier, on the Prussian schooner *Berlin* from Nagasaki. Some time between 1865 and 1867, Stillfried moved on to the US and Mexico where he joined the ill-fated Emperor Maximilian's campaign, serving as an officer until August 1867 when he returned briefly to Austria before ending up again in Japan. Gert Rosenburg in his book *Wilhelm Burger* (1984) claimed that Stillfried was resident in Yokohama by August 1868, and this is confirmed by the list of arrivals given in the *Japan Times Overland Mail* of August 22nd, 1868, which reports Baron Stedfred [*sic*] arriving at Yokohama three days earlier on the *Isles of the South*.

His movements for the next three years are a bit sketchy, but he is listed in the *China Directory* as working for Textor & Co. in Nagasaki during 1868. He also spent time in Tokyo where he was a secretary and student interpreter at the North German Legation. His involvement as a diplomat, albeit in a modest way, continued until early 1870 and included duties such as assistant at the Prussian Consulate. It was during this time that Stillfried met Margaretha Weppner who was in Japan from December 1869 until February 1870. In her book *The North Star and the Southern Cross* (1876), she was particularly scathing about the manners and character of the foreign residents in Japan and quite vitriolic when discussing her fellow Germans: "Of the so-called German noblemen in Yokohama and Jeddo, Baron Stilfried [*sic*] was the only one who spoke to me without insulting me. He was not only an Austrian baron, but, what is more, a respectable man." According to Luke Gartlan in his article "Changing Views" (2004), Stillfried did not find the diplomatic work stimulating enough and resigned in early 1870. For a short time he then opened a shop in Tokyo, importing photographic equipment.

Stillfried did have some photographic knowledge before arriving in Japan, but only as an amateur. At some stage he must have decided to make photography his profession and in order to facilitate this it seems he sought help from Felix Beato: "A new photographer has started in Yokohama, Baron Stillfried was once a pupil of Mr. Beato and is now trying to undersell him. I rather anticipate a failure...." (*Hiogo News*, August 9th, 1871).

The Yokohama-based correspondent went on, incidentally, to praise Beato's work in Korea. Despite the suggestion of antipathy, it seems that the two photographers maintained good relations during their time in Yokohama. Stillfried appeared as a witness or expert on behalf of Beato in at least two court cases and Beato did, after all, sell his business to him in 1877 (Fig. 168).

In any case, Stillfried opened for business in August 1871 and traded as Messrs. Stillfried & Co. from 61 Main Street, Yokohama, with a William Willmann as his assistant. Within a couple of months of its opening, the editor of *The Far East*, John Black, paid the studio a visit and his review appears in the October 16th, 1871 edition, (p. 120). As a competent photographer himself, and the then proprietor of a fortnightly periodical with its own tipped-in original photographs as illustrations, Black's comments are illuminating:

PHOTOGRAPHIC VIEWS BY MESSRS. STILLFRIED & CO. "WE HAVE BEEN MOST AGREEABLY OCCUPIED IN LOOKING OVER THE NEW PHOTOGRAPHIC ALBUM OF MESSRS. STILLFRIED & CO. AS YET THE RANGE OF COUNTRY OVER WHICH THEY HAVE BEEN TAKEN, IS CONFINED TO TWO ROUTES, NOW COMMONLY TAKEN BY FOREIGNERS:– BY KANASAWA, KAMAKURA, KATASEH, FUJISAWA AND ODAWARA TO MAIANOSHTA AND HAKONE; AND THE YEDO ROAD, THE CITY AND SUBURBS. MANY OF THE PICTURES ARE PARTICULARLY NICE; AND THE POINTS OF VIEW WELL AND TASTEFULLY CHOSEN. THE SUBJECTS ARE BY NO MEANS HACKNIED EITHER; FOR ALTHOUGH AS A MATTER OF COURSE, THE OLD STANDARDS – KAMAKURA, THE SHIBA TEMPLES AND SOME EQUALLY FAMILIAR VIEWS, ARE AMONGST THEM, THERE ARE SOME, WHICH TO THOSE WHO HAVE ANY KNOWLEDGE OF THE HISTORY OF THE COUNTRY ARE FULLY AS INTERESTING. SUCH IS ODAWARRA CASTLE; A FORTRESS NOW FAST SUCCUMBING TO THE INROADS OF TIME.... THE VIEWS TOO AMONGST THE MOUNTAINS ARE EXCELLENT,

The collodion case

Baron Collodion in re Ex-Count Collodion retired

IMOTO BRIDGE.

SHIBA.

TONASAWA.

AND NUMEROUS. WE DO NOT PRETEND TO SAY THAT ALL THE VIEWS HAVE EQUAL MERIT. THIS WOULD BE ABSURD. ALLOWANCES WILL BE MADE BY ALL WHO HAVE ANY ACQUAINTANCE WITH PHOTOGRAPHY FOR THE CIRCUMSTANCES UNDER WHICH PICTURES ARE TAKEN.... WE THEREFORE RECOMMEND ALL WHO WOULD LIKE TO POSSESS SOME GOOD VIEWS OF THE SURROUNDING COUNTRY, TO PAY A VISIT TO MESSRS. STILLFRIED & CO.'S STUDIO – LOOK THROUGH HIS ALBUM, AND SELECT FOR THEMSELVES. THERE ARE PICTURES TO SUIT THE TASTE OF ALL; AND AS WE HAVE SAID, MANY OF GREAT EXCELLENCE."

At this early stage we can see that Stillfried's portfolio, although expanding, is geographically limited and restricted to topographical scenes. A number of the photographs described by Black have recently been identified by Gartlan in "Changing Views." The article goes on to argue that Stillfried's reputation as a landscapist has been underrated, and this does seem to be the case.

Stillfried lost no time in marketing his work beyond the local confines of Yokohama. The November 22nd issue of the *Hiogo News* carried the following advertisement:

FOR SALE PHOTOGRAPHIC VIEWS OF JAPAN, TAKEN BY STILLFRIED & CO. YOKOHAMA. SPECIMENS MAY BE SEEN AT THE PREMISES OF R. RITCHER. HIOGO, NOV. 22ND, 1871.

Just a few months later, Stillfried became embroiled in an incident which threatened his reputation and, potentially, his

residency in Japan. He made the extremely risky decision to clandestinely photograph the Emperor Meiji. No Japanese emperor had ever been photographed, and hearing that His Majesty was to visit the Yokosuka workshops and foundries on New Year's Day, January 1872, Stillfried duly requested permission to take his portrait. This, like all previous requests, was peremptorily refused. Undeterred, Stillfried managed to get on board a ship moored in the harbor, which was close to the Emperor and his suite when they stopped to rest by the jetty. By aiming his camera lens through one of the ship's portholes, Stillfried was able to take two negatives of the group without being detected. Because of the camera speed in those days, only a blurred image of the Emperor's face was produced (Fig. 173).

Nevertheless, he lost no time in making prints from his negatives and offering them for sale. The authorities got to hear of this almost immediately and, exerting considerable diplomatic pressure (the Austrian Minister was in the process of finalizing a treaty between Austria and Japan), they managed to get what they thought was the only photographic negative confiscated from a furious Stillfried. Arguments between him, the Japanese authorities, and the Austrian Minister continued, the latter at one stage threatening Stillfried with deportation. The exchanges became very heated indeed when Stillfried announced the existence of a second negative "held in a safe place."

Despite the event's being reported and debated at length in the contemporary press, by the middle of February nothing

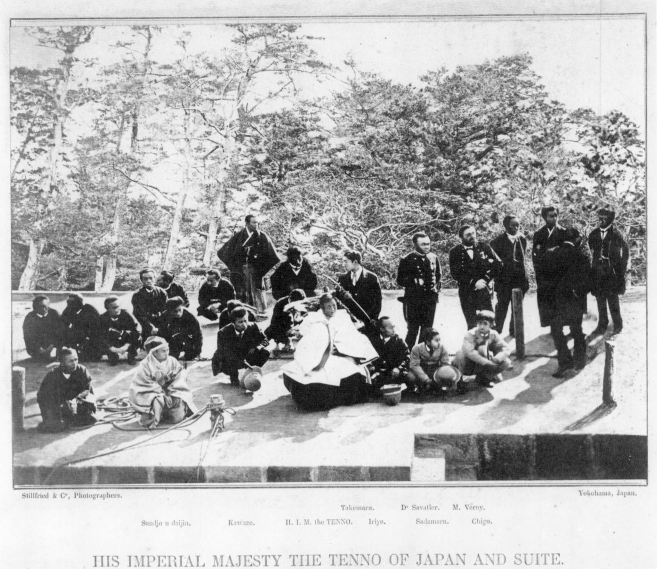

Stillfried & Cᵒ, Photographers.   Yokohama, Japan.

Takemaru.   Dʳ Savatier.   M. Vérny.

Sandjo u daijin.   Kawaze.   H. I. M. the TENNO.   Iriye.   Sadamaru.   Chigo.

HIS IMPERIAL MAJESTY THE TENNO OF JAPAN AND SUITE.

more was heard.[62] Some kind of agreement must have been reached, but its terms are not known. Moreover, within just two weeks of the illicit photograph, the Emperor arranged to have his own official portrait taken, as well as those of the Empress and the Empress Dowager, by the Japanese photographer Uchida Kuichi.

Stillfried's photograph is of exceptional historical importance – the first ever taken of a Japanese emperor. It was not thought likely, given the circumstances, that any examples of this print would ever appear. The incident had also been long forgotten by all but a handful of photo-historians. A few years ago, at a London auction, the image reappeared virtually unnoticed. One of the rarest Japanese photographs of the nineteenth century had been loosely inserted in an album of Stillfried photographs of scenes and portraits. How many of these prints left Japan? We will never know, but it is quite remarkable that this image has survived.

In May 1872 Stillfried embarked on a six weeks' tour of Kobe and Nagasaki in order to extend the geographical boundaries of his photographic portfolio. This included a visit to the closed city of Kyoto, which was temporarily opened to foreigners during the exhibition being held there. The *Hiogo News* carried this advertisement in its May 11th, 15th, and 18th, 1872 issues:

NOTICE. Baron Stillfried, of the firm Stillfried & Co., Photographers, of Yokohama, having arrived for the purpose of taking Photographic Views of the various places of interest at Kobe, Osaka, Kioto and their neighbourhoods, begs to draw the attention of the Community to his SUBSCRIPTION ALBUM. Terms of Subscription: For an album containing 100 views $7; for an Album of 50 views $4; for an Album of 25 Views $2.50, per month for one year. A specimen Album can be seen at the office of this paper. Further notice will be given on Baron Stillfried's return from Kioto. Hiogo, May 10th, 1872

True to his word, the newspaper's May 22nd issue, through until June 26th, carried the following:

NOTICE. BARON STILLFRIED having been very successful in obtaining magnificent views of all the prominent places of interest at Kioto and its neighborhood, begs to announce that the same will be printed and sent to this port for inspection at an early date, to the care of Messrs. JOHNSON & CO. Parties subscribing to the Albums can select from these views as they may desire. The monthly subscriptions, as per previous advertisement, will be collected by Messrs. E.C. KIRBY & CO. Hiogo, May 20th, 1872.

The newspaper's May 25th issue:

BARON STILLFRIED, PHOTOGRAPHIC ARTIST WILL REMAIN IN KOBE TIL THE 27TH INSTANT, AND ANY ORDERS ADDRESSED TO HIM, LEFT AT THE OFFICE OF THIS PAPER, WILL RECEIVE HIS CAREFUL ATTENTION. HIOGO, 24TH MAY, 1872

Stillfried arrived in Nagasaki on the 29th and spent a few days adding Nagasaki scenes to his portfolio. He was back in Yokohama on June 16th, but his portfolio was further augmented when he left for Hokkaido in October, on a government-sponsored two months' tour, incidentally demonstrating that the "illicit photo" incident had done no real damage to his burgeoning reputation and relationship with the Japanese authorities.

At the beginning of 1873, the energetic photographer set out for Austria with five Japanese: three ladies and two male carpenters. Stillfried, the opportunistic businessman, had decided that the Vienna Exposition should be graced with the appearance of an authentic Japanese house, containing authentic Japanese "tea house girls" who would dispense tea and sell Japanese curiosities and their master's photographs. The venture was a commercial failure, and at the beginning of February the following year Stillfried returned to Yokohama after an absence of thirteen months. As he was accompanied by only one servant, it would be interesting to know what had happened to the other four Japanese.

In May 1873, during Stillfried's absence, his company launched a new initiative. In the May 3rd issue of the *Japan Weekly Mail*, Stillfried & Co. advertised a "Circulating Library" of some 4000 books, available on subscription. The enterprise was short-lived, however, since it was destroyed by a fire in March 1874. Stillfried & Co. had also diversified into running an import–export business. Despite all of this commercial activity, Stillfried still found time to indulge in his first love of painting. In March 1875 he spent some six weeks in Shanghai, and in April of the following year he was there again securing photographic portraits of Chinese subjects for his expanding portfolio. These were favorably reviewed in *L'Echo du Japan* (July 10th, 1876). By the start of 1876 Hermann Andersen had joined the firm, which was now known as Messrs. Stillfried and Andersen. Baron Stillfried is listed as a passenger returning from Shanghai on the *Orissa*, arriving at Yokohama on the 22nd or 23rd of May, 1876 (*Japan Weekly Mail*, May 27th, 1876).

The year 1877 started disastrously when a fire destroyed Stillfried's studio. Fortunately, most if not all of the negatives were rescued, but Stillfried's cameras and photographic apparatus were gone. One assumes that some insurance recovery was made, but it is a measure of how successful Stillfried's business had been that within a couple of weeks the local press was reporting that on January 23rd Stillfried and Andersen had acquired Felix Beato's photographic business and moved into that studio's address at No. 17, Bund. From this time on, in an attempt to recoup the investment, Stillfried and Andersen would freely print from Beato's negatives (some of which would have been ten years old) and mix them with

Stillfried's own. This sometimes makes attribution difficult, particularly with landscape views and architectural studies.[63]

On June 1st, 1877 Stillfried auctioned all of his household furniture and effects and left for San Francisco. He then traveled to Philadelphia where he met his brother Franz, whom he had not seen for several years. Stillfried spent the next year traveling, mainly in Europe, where he exhibited the firm's photography in a number of European capitals. For reasons which are unclear, the termination of the Stillfried and Andersen partnership was announced in the local press almost immediately upon his return to Yokohama, in June 1878. A key clause in the separation agreement was that during the following ten years Andersen could not conduct a photographic business in China, whilst Stillfried could not do likewise in Japan. It was also agreed that Andersen could capitalize on the inherent goodwill in the business by retaining the name Stillfried and Andersen. Significantly, Andersen decided at this point that he would himself become an active photographer.

In November 1878 Stillfried received from the Japanese government a lucrative six-month assignment to teach Finance Ministry staff various printing processes, such as lithography and copper-plate printing. Refusing to accept a significant reduction in ongoing earnings, Stillfried resigned his post in April 1879. Then, in direct contravention to his partnership separation agreement, he opened and operated a Tokyo-based photographic studio for approximately one month. Andersen took Stillfried to court and won an easy victory, despite Stillfried's citing an unpaid partnership dissolution amount of $5200.

Based on future events, there is every reason to believe that Stillfried bitterly resented this defeat. At some stage he devised an incredible scheme whereby he could indirectly circumvent the prohibition on his working in Japan, and at the same time damage Andersen's business. What happened next must have shocked his former partner but perhaps amused a good percentage of the residents of Yokohama. But Andersen would not have seen the joke, the immediate effect of which was to confuse his customers and undermine his business. On November 17th the local press announced the

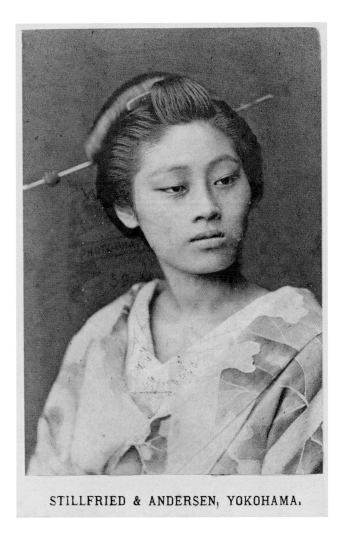

STILLFRIED & ANDERSEN, YOKOHAMA.

STILLFRIED & ANDERSEN, YOKOHAMA.

establishment in Yokohama of a new photographic studio to be called Baron Stillfried. The business would be owned and run by Stillfried's brother Franz!

NOTICE. I HAVE TO-DAY ESTABLISHED MYSELF AS A PHOTO-GRAPHIC ARTIST, UNDER THE FIRM OF BARON STILL-FRIED. THE STUDIO, NOW IN COURSE OF ERECTION, IS SITUATED AT No. 80, MAIN STREET, AND DUE NOTICE WILL BE GIVEN OF ITS COMPLETION. BARON FRANCIS STILLFRIED, OF PHILADELPHIA. YOKOHAMA. *JAPAN DAILY HERALD*, 17TH NOVEMBER 1879.

Naturally, a legal challenge arose. Andersen accused Stillfried of passing his stock and negatives to his brother, knowing that the latter would then sell his Japanese photographs, thereby contravening the dissolution agreement. Stillfried, who at this time was living with his brother, said that the negatives and photographic prints sold to Franz were non-Japanese; the Japanese negatives and prints had been gifted to his brother several weeks earlier. Andersen lost the case.

One result of all this has been to further complicate the identification of Stillfried's work: photo-historians now need to separate out the work of not only Stillfried and Beato, but also Franz Stillfried and Hermann Andersen. It may be worth noting the chronological guide on page 141.

The final 1884–5 year is confusing to say the least. The directories indicate that Franz Stillfried joined Stillfried and Andersen before everything was sold to Adolfo Farsari in 1885. After this date neither Andersen nor Franz Stillfried is listed as a Yokohama resident.

Raimund Stillfried had left Japan for good in May 1881 and embarked on a series of extensive travels. Such was his reputation that he had no trouble in finding work. He spent time in Siberia and operated temporary studios in Vladivo-stok, Hong Kong, and Thailand before returning to Vienna in 1883 where he finally settled and married the twenty-year-old Helene Tankovich de Jeszenicze, who gave him a son and daughter. Whilst in Japan, Stillfried had three daughters by a Japanese woman, who continued to write to him back in Austria. These unpublished letters are held in the Stillfried family archive. We do not know what happened to his daughters, except that they traveled to Singapore in July 1883. Stillfried spent his last years painting, combined with lectur-ing, and the odd photographic tour to Greece and Bosnia. He died in Vienna in 1911 at the age of seventy-two.

Below Fig. 177. Baron Raimund von Stillfried-Ratenicz, "Portrait of a Japanese Woman with Western Clothing and Hairstyle," ca. 1874, cabinet-size hand-colored albumen print. Author's Collection. The studio imprint on the back reads "Japan Photographic Association Yokohama Main Street No. 59B."

Below Fig. 178. Baron Raimund von Stillfried-Ratenicz, "Portrait of a Japanese Woman," early 1870s, large-format hand-colored albumen print. Tom Burnett Collection.

Date	Studio Name	Address	Photographer(s)
1871 & 72	Stillfried & Co.	61	R. Stillfried
1873	Stillfried & Co.	59 and 59c	R. Stillfried
1874	Japan Photographic Association[64]	59, 59b, and 59c	R. Stillfried
1875 & 76	Stillfried & Andersen; Japan Photographic Association	59 and 59c	R. Stillfried
1877	Stillfried & Andersen; Japan Photographic Association	17	R. Stillfried, F. Beato
1878 (July) to 1883	Stillfried & Andersen; Japan Photographic Association	17	R. Stillfried, F. Beato, H. Andersen
1879 (Nov) to 1883	Baron Stillfried	80	F. Stillfried, R. Stillfried
1884	Stillfried & Andersen; Japan Photographic Association	17	R. Stillfried, F. Beato, H. Andersen, F. Stillfried
1885 (ca. Feb)	A. Farsari & Co. (late Stillfried & Andersen)	17[65]	A. Farsari, R. Stillfried, F. Beato, H. Andersen, F. Stillfried
1886 (Feb)	Fire destroys studio and all Farsari's negatives; takes 5 months to replace		
1886 (ca. July) to 1890 (Apr)	A. Farsari & Co.	16	A. Farsari

To say that Stillfried lived a full and interesting life would be an understatement. There seems to be very little he did not try or experience. The three central passions that seem to have driven him, however, were travel, painting, and photography. Above all else, Stillfried is remembered as a great photographer. Now that the confusion regarding the various studio names has been largely resolved, a proper assessment of his photographic contribution can begin to be made. The table at left illustrates the difficulty in identifying Stillfried's work, however. We first need to catalogue the pre-1877 albums which still exist. Beato's work can usually be recognized, so the focus now should be on searching for Andersen and Franz Stillfried's photographs. Until now Stillfried has been under the shadow of his mentor and predecessor, Felix Beato. How posterity will judge the comparative merits of each artist's work, remains to be seen. But the contemporary and knowledgeable observer John Black sounded a note of warning for supporters of the current relative status of these two masters when he wrote in the May 1877 advertisement for his journal, *The Far East*: "... Baron Stillfried in Japan, whose artistic productions admittedly surpass any that have ever been taken of the natives and scenery of that country, and are justly celebrated over Europe and America."

THE GORDES BROTHERS

There seems to have been no serious research done on the French photographers Gordes & Co., who ran photo studios in Osaka, Kobe, and Nagasaki at various times from 1871 (or possibly earlier) to 1888. The partners were actually brothers, Henri and Auguste (Figs. 179, 180). Both long-term residents in Japan, they are buried at the Sakamoto International Cemetery in Nagasaki (Fig. 185). At this point in time, little of their work can be identified. However, there are many albums of Japanese photographs still awaiting attribution, and given the longevity of the Gordes' studios, it is almost certain that matches will be made before too long. Important clues to their work are contained in advertisements placed in Kobe newspapers in the early 1870s, and a *carte de visite* which carries their Nagasaki studio name and illustrates a montage of photographs from their portfolio. One of the photographs depicts a second *carte de visite*, this time of their Kobe studio, whilst the two brothers' portraits also seem to be depicted (Fig. 181).

At least one of the images included in the montage is the work of von Stillfried. This suggests that the firm acted as distributors in Nagasaki for Stillfried's studio, and perhaps also in Kobe and Osaka. As well as producing their own material and providing portrait studio facilities, the firm may also have operated as photographic dealers, selling the work produced by other studios. Also illustrated on the *carte de visite* is a selection of Japanese bronze sculptures. It seems likely that the Gordes brothers were exporting these to the West and were not, therefore, totally reliant upon photography for

Above left Fig. 179. "Portrait of Auguste Gordes," ca. 1872. Boyd and Izakura Collection. Shown here is an indistinct detail from the Gordes studio *carte de visite* illustrated as Fig. 181, where both Auguste and his brother Henri appear to be pictured. There is a possibility that the two portraits are not the Gordes brothers, but the size and positioning of the portraits are strongly suggestive. Auguste looks the younger of the two, and there seems to be a clear family resemblance.

Above right Fig. 180. "Portrait of Henri Gordes," ca. 1872. Boyd and Izakura Collection. Detail from the Gordes studio *carte de visite* in Fig. 181.

Below Fig. 181. "Gordes & Co. Carte de Visite," ca. 1872, albumen print. Boyd and Izakura Collection. This rare promotional Gordes Nagasaki studio card contains useful detail. At least one Stillfried photograph is reproduced, suggesting that the firm acted as the Baron's Nagasaki agent. The image, fourth from the right at the top shows a full-length Oiran portrait with her kimono slightly lifted and is a pre-1876 Stillfried print. The two brothers' oval portraits apparently appear at the bottom of the card, and the Japanese bronzes suggest that the firm exported these to the West. Note also the reproduction, center top, of a companion Kobe studio *carte de visite*.

Below Fig. 182. Auguste Gordes, "Kobe Scenery," ca. 1874, albumen-print *carte de visite*. Boyd and Izakura Collection.

Bottom Fig. 183. Reverse of Fig. 182.

their livelihood. It should be mentioned that the *Japan Directory* of 1887 listed the two brothers as Portuguese. This turns out to have been a mistake, since their names are clearly French. The word *photographie*, just visible on the center top section of the studio card illustrated, is a French rather than Portuguese word. Finally, the inscription on Henri Gordes' gravestone states that he was a native of Marseilles.

Another *carte de visite*, this time one representing both the Osaka and Kobe studios, shows the name of "A Gordes" and this suggests that Henri's activities were restricted to the Nagasaki studio and, possibly, the management of the art export business (Figs. 182, 183).

Although almost nothing of their personal lives is yet known, plotting their movements over the years is helped due to their regular appearances in the contemporary directories. Some brief but useful information concerning their dates of death, nationality, and place of burial is also found in L. Earns and B. Burke-Gaffney's *Across the Gulf of Time* (1991).[66] As this book was going to press, the collector and writer Christian Polak, an expert on early French–Japanese relations, passed me a copy of an article by Paule Giron, "Le descendant des marquis de Gordes est Japonais," which appeared in the French magazine *Historia* (1983). The article covers the history of the noble family of Gordes, which can be traced back to the year 1008 to the town of Gordes, France. Although Henri and Auguste are briefly mentioned, there is no reference to photography. Nevertheless, it does throw some additional light on the Gordes brothers and a number of lines of future research suggest themselves.

The *Nagasaki Kiyouyuchi*, a publication which reprinted a number of early primary records from the period and is quoted in Earns and Burke-Gaffney's website, states that Henri, the elder brother, was in Nagasaki by October 1862. Giron's article suggests the brothers left Marseilles, France, for Japan around 1869, but this probably refers to Auguste. In any case, by 1863 Henri is working for Glover and Co., and later at a Chinese warehouse. Around this time he was living at No. 7 Minamiyamate. From April 1867 the firm Henri Gordes & Co. is shown as operating from No. 10 Deshima. He is listed as a merchant and resident of Nagasaki in the 1866 and 1869 editions of the *Chronicle and Directory for China, Japan and the Philippines* (1864–92). We know that Henri returned to Nagasaki on June 2nd, 1870 from a visit to Shanghai, since he appears in the passenger list of the *Oregonian*, a fact that is noted in the *Nagasaki Express* on June 4th. The February 18th, 1871 issue of the *Nagasaki*

Express (p. 230) carried a report about a serious fire on Deshima at Henri Gordes' residence at No. 10 that began at 1 a.m. on the 13th and also destroyed the neighboring property of No. 11. "We regret that Mons. Gordes, who occupied No. 10, has been severely burnt about the body...."

Japanese sources, notably Umemoto and Kobayashi in their 1952 publication, *Nihon Shashin Kai no Bukko Korosha Kenshoruku*, refer to Henri's giving photographic instruction to several Japanese. The authors state that although they do not know when this French photographer came to Japan, he was living in Nagasaki during the early Meiji period. In 1868 he taught photography to Hanabuchi Tamesuke, and then to Wakabayashi Koka and Moriwawa Shinshichi in 1869. It was also in Nagasaki that Tomita Juhan (Shigenori) learned photography from Anryu Gorudo (Henri Gordes) in 1871, and after his training he opened a studio in Shimonoseki in either 1871 or 1874. Earlier, in 1867, Henri visited Kobe and rented property from the Hiramura family. This afforded the opportunity to Hiramura Tokubei to learn photography and he subsequently opened a Kobe studio in 1872.

These references suggest that Henri Gordes was involved in commercial photographic activity by 1867 at the latest and may well have had a studio in operation at that time. However, it is not until 1872 that the *Japan Directory* for that year lists the Gordes brothers and gives their occupation as photographers, based at 20 Mmemotocho (Umemoto-cho), Osaka. But given the small community in Osaka of only around seventy in 1872, it is more likely that Auguste maintained the studio in Osaka and Henri in Nagasaki. The date that the brothers first opened a Nagasaki studio is not known. However, it is almost certain that the Gordes brothers were the first Western studio in Osaka, although for a short while they had competition from a former employee – C. Parant: "We have now two foreign photographic establishments here, which is rather curious, seeing that there is not one in Kobe. Mr. Parant, who was formerly with Messrs. Gordes Brothers, has now started on his own account, and I hear is likely to be a formidable competitor to the older established house. I have seen some photographs which were said to be Mr. Parant's work, and they were to my thinking very well done. A really well executed photograph is as superior to a common one as a first class steel engraving is to a coarse wood-cut" (May 31st, 1871 issue of the *Hiogo News*, carrying a report from its Osaka Correspondent.)

It is not known when Auguste arrived in Japan or opened in Osaka, but it could have been in 1870, and this would tie in with the Giron article. In any case, 1873 still shows the studio operating at Osaka, but Henri is simultaneously listed as a merchant in Nagasaki. The following year a studio is opened in the Native Town area of Kobe, according to the 1874 *China Directory*, and from 1875 the Osaka operation is no longer listed. There is a brief glimpse of Henri when he is listed as a passenger on the *Hiroshima Maru*, arriving at Nagasaki on August 8th, 1876 from Yokohama (*Rising Sun and Nagasaki Express*, August 19th, 1876). In this year Giron states that Auguste wrote to his uncle in France. The extracts which follow have been translated from the original French: "In this country it is easy to succeed and, with a little, you can live like a powerful lord.... I asked my mother for 7 to 8,000 Francs, and with this amount of money, I can live quite happily, work and earn lots of money. Here you can make a fortune and within three or four years, I could come back to France and live quite comfortably...."

The brothers then seem to concentrate on Kobe until around 1877, but it has not been possible to trace their movements for the subsequent three years. This may be explained by Giron, who says that Auguste was in Vladivostok in 1877 where a son, Eugene, was born. It is quite possible that both brothers stayed there for two or three years but it is far from clear whether they were involved in photography or general trading. At around this time, Auguste wrote home about Russia, stating that the country lacked everything and that with a small amount of capital it was possible to increase this by 200 per cent.

Nevertheless, by 1880 the *Japan Directory* picks up the scent again and the brothers have a photo studio based in Nagasaki, where it would operate until at least 1888. From 1880 there is no mention of a Kobe or any other studio. The position is confused slightly by the *Nagasaki Kiyouyuchi* as it lists Henri as a photographer at Umegasaki No. 9, Nagasaki from 1881, with Auguste joining him in the list for 1883.

It is very likely, however, that the following editorial comment, which appeared in the *Rising Sun and Nagasaki Express*, refers to the establishment of the new Gordes Brothers Nagasaki studio. For some reason the tone of the piece is somewhat dismissive, if not hostile: "We notice the new photographic studio, now being erected in the Settlement, is drawing near completion. Much cannot be said in favour of the site or of the outward appearance of the structure, and we doubt if it will exist long in opposition to the well-established and very enterprising native artist, Mr. Uyeno, of Nakasima" (May 24th, 1879, p. 2).

Summarizing, it seems likely that the brothers were in Vladivostok from 1877 until 1879. Upon their return they focused their efforts on Nagasaki, opening a studio there in 1879.

Earlier, whilst in Osaka, Auguste placed two interesting advertisements in the Kobe-based *Hiogo News*. The first was in the issue for July 15th, 1871, just five days after the devastating typhoon which rocked Kobe:

FOR SALE. SPLENDID PHOTOGRAPHIC VIEWS OF THE DISASTERS IN HIOGO, TAKEN BY A. GORDES, PHOTOGRAPHER OF OSAKA. A LARGE PHOTOGRAPH ON BRISTOL CARD-BOARD, 24½IN. BY 14IN.... $3. FOUR PHOTOGRAPHS ON BRISTOL CARD-BOARD, 16IN. BY 12IN., EACH $2. THE WHOLE SERIES FOR $10. E. VINCIENNE. NO. 11, OLD BELLEVUE BUILDINGS HIOGO, JULY 15TH 1871

The second was placed in the October 31st, 1871 issue and offered photographs taken at the Kobe Races held on October 26th to 28th:

FOR SALE, PHOTOGRAPHIC VIEWS OF THE RACE GRAND STAND, TAKEN BY A. GORDES, OF OSAKA. GANDAUBERT & CO. HIOGO. OCT. 31ST 1871

It is not clear exactly when they ended their photographic activities, but Henri died after a short illness on June 18th, 1889 at the age of forty-seven.

DEATH. AT HIS RESIDENCE, NAGASAKI, AT 4 A.M. ON THE 18TH INST., HENRY EUGENE MARIE GORDES, AGED 48 [SIC], OF PARALYSIS. *THE RISING SUN AND NAGASAKI EXPRESS*, JUNE 19TH, 1889.

The *Japan Directory* lists them as merchants for that year, so it is possible that their studio activities finished sometime in 1888. The *Nagasaki Kiyouyuchi Gaikokujin Meibo* shows that in December 1889 Auguste is living at 10 Umegasaki with four children, two girls and two boys. The *Japan Directory* for 1891 records that Auguste is living at the same address and is in business as a baker. The *Nagasaki Kiyouyuchi Gaikokujin Meibo* also shows that in addition to the four children, by 1891 Auguste is living with a foreign dressmaker. Auguste died on November 29th, 1894 at the age of forty-eight. The December 12th, 1894 issue of the *Rising Sun and Nagasaki Express* announced that the Nagasaki merchant Victor Pignatel would act as executor of Auguste's estate and guardian of his infant children.

DEATH OF AN OLD FRENCH RESIDENT. MR. AUGUSTE GORDES, A VERY OLD MEMBER OF THIS COMMUNITY, SUCCUMBED TO THE EFFECTS OF A LONG AND SERIOUS ILLNESS ON THURSDAY NIGHT LAST, AT THE AGE OF FORTY-NINE [*SIC*] YEARS, AND WAS BURIED THE FOLLOWING AFTERNOON IN THE URAKAMI CEMETERY, IN ACCORDANCE WITH THE RITES OF THE CATHOLIC RELIGION, THE FIRST PORTION OF WHICH, AS USUAL, WAS PERFORMED IN THE CATHEDRAL. *THE RISING SUN AND NAGASAKI EXPRESS*, DECEMBER 5, 1894.

The Gordes brothers were commercial photographers in Japan for at least seventeen years, probably for longer. This is a remarkable achievement and clearly makes them the longest running Western studio in nineteenth-century Japan. They appear to be the first Western photographers to have a commercial studio based in Osaka (1871–4), and they were certainly one of the first to operate in Kobe (1874–7). They are also the earliest known Western commercial studio based in Nagasaki. Yet, despite these achievements, they are virtually unknown, with very little photography so far attributed to them. Their contribution to Japanese photo-history may prove to be much more significant than we can yet know.

JOHN REDDIE BLACK AND *THE FAR EAST*

When discussing Japanese photography of the 1870s, it is impossible to overstate, in resource terms, the importance of *The Far East* (1870–8) journal (Figs. 186, 188, 189). Initially published as a fortnightly newspaper, it later changed its frequency to monthly and in content became more like a magazine. Throughout its existence, it carried illustrations of some 750 pasted-in original and vintage photographs of Japan and China, contributed by at least twenty different photographers.

The editor and inspiration behind the publication was John Reddie Black (1826–80).[67] He had been born in Scotland, of English parents, and had studied at Christ's Hospital in London destined for a career in the Royal Navy. Realizing that a career as a naval officer was not to his taste he decided, in 1854, to emigrate with his wife to Australia to start a new life. Black also had a fine singing voice, and when his Australian business interests failed, he embarked on a singing career and toured the Australian colonies, India, and China before arriving in Japan. What Black's intentions were at this stage are not clear, but he said later that when he arrived in Japan he had not intended to stay. It has been suggested that he was returning to England with his wife and son, Henry James, who had been born in Adelaide in 1858.

There has hitherto been no consensus amongst historians as to when Black first arrived in Japan.[68] However, by a careful reading of Black's *Young Japan: Yokohama and Yedo* (1968), the periodical *The Far East*, and the notices given in contemporary newspapers, July 1864 emerges as the probable date. On page 150 of the first volume of *Young Japan*, Black records witnessing a review of British and Japanese troops at Yokohama, an event which took place on October 22nd, 1864. On page 249 he states: "... the settlement with Satsuma brought to a satisfactory climax; when I arrived on a visit, without an idea of becoming a permanent resident." In the July 1876 issue of *The Far East* (pp. 8–12), Black recalls his first visit to Shanghai in June 1864 (more likely to have been May), twelve years earlier, and mentions that he had not previously visited a Chinese city. After leaving Australia with his wife and son, probably in early 1864, Black traveled to India. It is likely that he arranged a series of singing concerts there in order to improve his financial situation. He must have received considerable encouragement because he decided to travel to China, leaving his family to continue on to England.

He arrived in Hong Kong on March 25th, according to the *Overland China Mail* (April 1st, 1864), and the same newspaper was praising Black's singing performance in its April 29th supplement. After a series of concerts which were also highly praised (see the May 13th issue, for example), Black left for Shanghai and arrived on May 13th. Contemporary issues of the *North China Herald* also enthusiastically reviewed his performances and the 18th June issue noted with regret Black's intention to leave on a trip to Hankow. Whether Black did make this trip is unclear, but the Yokohama newspaper, the *Japan Herald*, in its issue of 30th July (supplement, p. 336a), was equally fulsome in its praise for Black's

Below Fig. 186. *The Far East,* May 30th, 1870. Author's Collection. The first page of the first issue of this important periodical.

Left Fig. 187. "Caricature of John Reddie Black." *Japan Punch,* October 1865.

first concert in the port. Several more performances were given, and reviewed, but it was clear that Black's visit to Japan was temporary. He returned to Shanghai in September or October.[69] It is likely, however, that Albert Hansard, resident entrepreneur and the proprietor of the *Japan Herald,* had made Black an offer. On November 8th Black had returned to Yokohama (*Japan Herald,* November 12th) and as soon as the 11th, Hansard had issued a notice in his newspaper that Black was now involved with his auction business.

In 1865 Hansard offered Black a partnership in the *Japan Herald,* the first English-language newspaper in Japan, which Black was happy to accept, and a notice to that effect appeared in the paper on April 29th, 1865 (p. 641). Subsequently, the *Japan Herald* ran into severe financial problems and Black and Hansard were declared bankrupt in 1867. A report of the bankruptcy proceedings was given in the *London and China Telegraph* (November 27th, 1867, p. 611). However, this did not stop Black's nascent publishing career from taking off. That same year he launched the *Japan Gazette,* a daily evening newspaper, which was an immediate success. He subsequently launched *The Far East,* which began life with its first issue on May 30th, 1870. Black, a talented amateur photographer, was no doubt influenced by the short-lived periodical, the *China Magazine,* which was published between 1868 and 1870 in Hong Kong and contained original photographs, many of which were provided by the famous British photographer John Thomson.[70] Black determined that his new publication would also be illustrated in this way.

The idea behind *The Far East* was expressed in the first issue: Black wanted to cultivate "good-will and brotherhood between the outer world and the subjects of the most ancient imperial dynasty in the world." He would therefore write about the history, arts, and manners and customs of the Japanese. His original intention was to include China and other Far Eastern countries. Although, as we shall see, the journal received photographic contributions from various photographers, there has been speculation as to who the "staff" photographer was. From a close reading of all of the volumes of the journal, it is clear that Black himself contributed many of the photographs. However, the identity of the journal's staff photographer is revealed in the December 1st, 1870 issue as the Austrian Michael Moser, who worked with Black until February 1873 (see page 150).

In the May 16th, 1871 issue, Black reflected on the difficulties encountered in putting together the first volume. He complained about the weather conditions affecting the photography, inferior or unobtainable chemicals, and sub-standard paper. These circumstances often made it difficult to meet publication deadlines. On the bright side, Black was expecting imminent delivery of a higher grade of paper; and he said that a number of "excellent views" of Edo, Osaka, and other interesting places had arrived. Moser was also making good progress in putting together a number of "character pictures" which would start appearing in future issues.

Black complained, however, about the unreliability of the native Chinese photographers. In particular, he bemoaned their failure to understand the need for sending more than one negative per picture – essential for a magazine that was printing and mounting literally hundreds of photographs for each issue. He was more forgiving of Western photographers, however: "European artists in China cannot supply us, their time is too valuable." Clearly Black was not prepared to pay the "going rate," and this would no doubt have discouraged the European photographers from contributing. Black announced that he shortly intended to dispatch Moser "on a tour through the open Ports of China, in hopes of securing a large and valuable series of views." Judging by the illustrations in future issues, this journey did not take place.

The above notes explain why the quality of the journal's photographs is so variable. It has also been noticed that some views have variants and this demonstrates that Black was often using more than one negative. Where circumstances

THE FAR EAST;
MONTHLY JOURNAL
OF
CHINA AND JAPAN,
Photographically Illustrated.

THE First Edition of 300 Copies of the July Number (No. 1 of the New Series) being now quite exhausted, a Second Edition is in preparation, and will be ready for delivery about the 26th instant.

The August Number (No. 2 of the New Series) now ready, and contain is an excellent portait of

Sir Thomas E. Wade, K.C.B.,

H. B. M.'s Envoy Extraordinary and Minister Plenipotentiary to China, for which His Excellency sat specially to Mr. Fisler, at the request of the proprietor of the *Far East*.

September Number (No. 3 of the New Series) will contain a portrait of

Li Hung-chang,

for which he sat last year at Tientsin to Mr. Fisler.

Persons wishing to subscribe to the *Far East* will oblige by sending their names to the Office of this Paper, or the undersigned, as early as possible, that it may be known approximately how many copies to print; as the preparation of each subsequent Edition not only adds vastly the trouble, but also to the expense of the production.

Single Numbers cannot be sold.

Subscription:—$4 a Quarter, $7 Six Months, $13 a Year—
Payable in Advance.

J. R. BLACK,
1m.   *Proprietor and Editor.*

---

dictated, he was also not averse to using copy prints or copy negatives.

The issue of October 16th, 1871 gave a complimentary review of the newly opened Stillfried studio, and this was mentioned earlier. However, just a fortnight later, on November 1st, Black launched a scathing criticism of the work of native Japanese photographers: "... only the faintest notions of perspective ... some are clever manipulators ... but hardly one ... has the slightest idea of posing a sitter, or of selecting the best point of view for a landscape ... no thought of the effect of foreground and distance ... none of these men can be called artists ... they are merely mechanics...." Whilst there was no doubt some validity in Black's general observations, he clearly, at this stage, was not familiar with the particular work of artists such as Uchida Kuichi or Ueno Hikoma.

By the May 1st, 1873 issue, Black had recanted: "Those we now give are copies from some very excellent views taken by Mr. Uchida, a Japanese photographer of singular ability, who has a great variety of views of all parts of the country most interesting to foreigners. His studio is to be found at Asakusa, Yedo, and is quite worth a visit." It is worth noting that Uchida does not seem to have released the negatives to Black.

The July 1st, 1873 issue brought the news that Moser had left the journal the previous February, to accept an appointment accompanying the Japanese delegation to the International Vienna Exhibition. This would have been unwelcome news for Black, since he had hired Moser as a teenager and undoubtedly paid him much less than he would have had to pay an experienced professional. Although Moser returned to Japan, he did not rejoin the staff of *The Far East* and instead accepted a post offered by the Japanese government. As confirmation, we can jump to the June 30th, 1875 issue when Black is reflecting on the events of 1873 and states: "Mr. Michael Mozer [*sic*], previously the photographer for this journal, accompanied them as an interpreter, and now continues in the employ of the 'Exhibition Department', as photographer to the government."

However, reverting to the July 1st, 1873 issue, we can see that the journal had by then enjoyed some tangible success. Black stated that he was surprised by how "important" the journal had become to subscribers, many of whom carefully bound the issues and requested back copies; the first volume was completely out of print and "commanding a very considerable premium." He also announced that the publication frequency would in future be monthly. Fortunately, bearing in mind Moser's departure, Black went on to say that he now felt able to pay a proper "honorarium" to those who made photographic contributions. He mentioned, apologetically, that in the past he had only been able to pass on his thanks. He also reported that he now had a large number of ethnic views – sufficient for three years. As will be discussed later, it is likely that these photographs were the work of Suzuki Shinichi I.

The excellent but extremely rare Yushodo seven-volume 1965 reprint of *The Far East* ends with the issue for August 1875. However, after a break of almost a year, the journal continued with what Black called the New Series, commencing in July 1876 and continuing to December 1878 when it abruptly

ceased publication. The first series had been published in Yokohama at the offices of Black's English-language paper, the *Japan Gazette*. When he sold this latter paper in 1874, the printing and publication of *The Far East* switched to the Tokyo offices of his Japanese-language newspaper, *Nisshin Shinjishi*. But by early July he had moved to Shanghai and restarted the journal from the offices of the *Celestial Empire*.

In the introduction to the first volume of the New Series, Black looked back on the first series and the "great inequality in the illustrations." He mentioned that the first series continued until October 1875, and hinted that some issues later than October may have appeared: "... the few numbers that were published, the proprietor takes no count of, and makes no charge for...." Black went on to explain that the first series failed to obtain photos of China and that he could not go himself to get any. The New Series would illustrate as many Chinese as Japanese pictures (in fact, there was to be a majority of Chinese photographs), and Black was hopeful that the New Series would enjoy the largest circulation of any English-language newspaper throughout China, Japan, Hong Kong, etc. The subscriptions, to be paid in advance, were $4 a quarter, $7 half yearly, and $13 yearly.

There has been much speculation about the actual number of subscribers. In the October 16th, 1871 issue, Black mentioned that overseas readership was as much as that in Japan, and in November 1876 he boasted that the circulation had grown fourfold since 1874. An unnamed correspondent in the July 1876 issue predicted that the journal would have a future circulation of many thousands. In the November 1876 issue, we get the first direct clue regarding the actual circulation. Black complains of "the difficulties attending the printing [of] so many hundreds of pictures from each

The " Far East."

IN A FEW DAYS will be published, the JUNE number of this Illustrated Magazine, the last of the second volume; and the final number of the first twelve-month's subscription of the New Series. Although the Proprietor is quite aware of its many short-comings, he can confidently point to the improvement in the present over the former series; and to the later numbers over the earlier ones in this. This improvement shall continue. He is able to acknowledge, with, he believes, justifiable pride, the very great favour with which the *Far East* has that received wherever it has penetrated: and that includes almost all the civilised countries in the world.

His ambition is, however, to do far better than he has hitherto succeeded in accomplishing; and to make his little periodical a real Journal of fine Art, high-class Literature, and reliable Information, connected with the countries of which it professes to treat. What has been done must speak for itself. What he hopes to do, may be gathered from the fact, that not only has he received, and still continues to benefit by, the sympathetic assistance of Mr Saunders and Mr Fisler, the widely-known Photographers of Shanghai, but he has received offers of a large supply of negatives of characteristic pictures from Baron Stillfried in Japan, whose artistic productions admittedly surpass any that have ever been taken of the natives and the scenery of that country, and are justly celebrated over Europe and America.

Further, negatives have been promised by eminent Photographers in other parts; and though they "are lang o' comin," doubtless they will come. And, added to this, a special Chinese artist has been well-equipped and sent out to the north-west provinces, by the proprietor; and his pictures, taken specially for this Journal, are daily expected.

As regards the literary work, hitherto dependence has had to be placed on a few very kind and willing helpers, whose papers have imparted a high tone to the magazine. But now that it is so well known and appreciated throughout these regions, and so favourably received elsewhere, it is but reasonable to expect that the number of contributors able and willing to enrich its pages with valuable information, or to adorn them with well-written essays, tales and translations, will increase.

So much for the contents of the *Far East*.

With regard to its circulation, the proprietor thankfully acknowledges the very liberal support he has received—far exceeding the most sanguine expectations that such an Illustrated Journal, if properly conducted, artistically and literarily, reflects credit on the community from whose midst it emanates. He has previously promised "to make perfection his aim." He is sure that if improvement has marked its course in the past he will be credited with a desire for further improvement in the future; and this he confidently relies on being enabled to attain, by the continued generous support of all residents in the Far-East.

In accordance with the above, the undersigned begs to announce that

The Terms of Subscriptions will in future be:—

Quarterly—Payable in advance—$ 3.50,
Half yearly— do do $ 6.00,
Yearly— do do $ 10.00.

N.B.—Of the past year—i.e. from July 1876 to June 1877, there are very few entire copies left. These will continue at $ 13 until June 15th next; after which, if any sets remain, the price will be $ 15.
Annual Subscribers may have the addresses to their friends abroad, printed, and their papers posted direct, on the day of publication, postage free, on payment of One dollar extra.
Subscribers wishing to discontinue at the close of the present volume, will oblige by sending notice to that effect to the office: where the names of new subscribers will be gladly received.

J.D. CLARK.

Far East Agency,
23, Keangse Road.

---

negative." Stephen White, in his article "The Far East" (1991), estimated the circulation figure as no more than 1500, and probably much smaller. We now know that when Black prepared the first issue of the New Series (July 1876) he anticipated sales of no more than 300. This is made clear by the advertisement which appeared in the September 2nd issue of the *Rising Sun and Nagasaki Express* (Fig. 188) .

By 1876 there were probably between 6,000 and 10,000 foreign resident families living in China and Japan. Judging by the text of the advertisement, the periodical was growing in popularity. It seems reasonable to assume, however, that the maximum number of subscribers between July 1876 and its closure in December 1878 was between 500 and 1000.

By the beginning of the third volume of the New Series in July 1877, Black was undoubtedly confident about the journal's future prospects. The circulation had been steadily increasing and, in a bold attempt to expand his subscription base outside China and Japan, he reduced the price of the journal from $13 to $10 per annum. An advertisement issued with the May 1877 issue outlined Black's hopes for the future (Fig. 189). He mentioned that Baron Stillfried had promised him a large supply of negatives but there is no evidence that these materialized, or that any of Stillfried's photographs had been previously published in the journal.

In the issue for September 1876, Black mentioned the setting up in Shanghai of The Far East Art Agency. This enterprise of Black's was for the sale of photographs "and other works of art." He went on to claim that "in a short time extensive and interesting Portfolios and Albums of Pictures of Interesting Localities and Characters in China and Japan will be on view." Clearly, Black was marketing prints taken from his extensive stock of negatives. This would explain

why occasionally it is possible to come across a group of images which seem to be the work of various photographic artists whose work has previously appeared in *The Far East*. In effect, Black was putting together his own souvenir albums.

There are quite a few references to William Saunders in the New Series, and a number of his photographs taken in China appear. Black thanked him for a number of unsolicited contributions. It does seem that as the popularity of the journal grew, so photographers were more prepared to provide contributions. They no doubt saw benefit in having their names publicized. In the September 1877 issue, Black turned his attention to the photographic work of the Chinese: "After waiting seven months, we have at last received some negatives from the artist we sent up to obtain views of the upper Yangtze; and we must admit that we are disappointed with the number and the nature of the views we have to hand. All we can say is they show us that there is plenty of fine scenery to be taken, fully justifying our expectations, but that Chinese artists have not the slightest idea of selection. This is universally recognised; for it is a rare thing to see any views taken by them; their efforts being confined to the studio."[71]

The focus of the journal for the whole of 1878 was China. After the final issue in December 1878 (no issues later than this have come to light), Black started another newspaper, the *Shanghai Mercury*, on April 17th, 1879. This paper was to last forty years. But by this time Black's health was deteriorating. He went back to Yokohama in the hope of recovery but never returned to China, dying there of apoplexy on June 11th, 1880. As a consequence, he did not quite finish his highly regarded book, *Young Japan*, which chronicled the early years of Japan's modernization. Black left behind a widow and three children.

In assessing *The Far East*, we should not forget that Black never devoted his time exclusively to it and was always involved in other simultaneous publishing ventures. His friend Samuel Cocking described Black in his article "1869–1909: Philosophies of an Early Rover to Japan's Shores" (1909) as "an accomplished amateur photographer like myself brought us much together [sic]. *The Far East* was one of his hobbies and was illustrated by his photographs, now valuable and interesting." In lasting eight years, the journal must be considered a success. It was not the first periodical in the East to use original photographs, but the venture was nevertheless imaginative and ambitious. It has also provided us with a priceless resource for the study of photography in 1870s Japan (not to mention China), documenting as it does the country's dramatic transformation from a feudal to a modern state. Black, as a talented photographer himself, was refreshingly critical of the illustrations which appeared in the journal. His comments are all the more enlightening for that.

Frustratingly, Black does not always identify the author of the photographs. It is true that a number of these will have been his own handiwork, and a careful reading of the text will often enable the photographer of a given image to be identified. For those who wish to study further the wealth of information contained within the journal's text, there are reproduced in *OJP* the main references to Japanese photography which appeared.[72]

Below left Fig. 190. Anonymous, "Portrait of Michael Moser," ca. 1870, large-format hand-colored albumen print. Courtesy of Alfred Moser.

Below right Fig. 191. Michael Moser, "Large Lantern for the Austrian 1873 Exhibition," 1872, large-format albumen print. Author's Collection.

MICHAEL MOSER

The Austrian Michael Moser (1853–1912) came from humble beginnings but left his own distinctive footprint on the history of nineteenth-century Japanese photography (Fig. 190).

He did not turn out to be one of the truly great photographers of his age but his precocious talent, combined with resourcefulness and determination, did enable him to carve out a unique photographic career, which started when he was apprenticed to Wilhelm Burger.

Born on May 3rd, 1853 in the beautiful lake district of Altaussee, the son of a salt mine worker who practiced woodcarving to supplement the family income, Moser came into contact with Wilhelm Burger through fortuitous circumstances. Burger, whose reputation as a photographer was growing, was on a photographic tour of the Altaussee in the early 1860s when he made contact with Moser's father because he needed a wooden frame for his camera. On a subsequent visit to the area, he met Michael and was impressed by the boy's willingness to help. In 1867 he accepted Michael's request to become his photographic apprentice in Vienna.

In 1868 Burger was engaged as the official photographer to the Austria-Hungary trade and diplomatic mission to Siam, China, and Japan. The mission left the port of Trieste on

August 18th, 1868 with the fifteen-year-old Moser on board as photographic assistant. Siam was reached in April 1869, Saigon in May, and Hong Kong and Shanghai in June. The mission arrived in Nagasaki in September and in Yokohama on October 2nd. After a month the mission was ready to leave, although Burger had been asked to stay on awhile to photograph Japanese works of art. For some unknown reason, Moser did not continue as Burger's assistant.[73]

His choice now was to take up the offer of working as a cabin boy on the arduous journey home, or alternatively trying to find employment in Japan. He chose the latter but was reduced to accepting any work in order to survive. Moser graphically described his experiences in the following translation from articles written by him later in life and published in the *Steirischen Alpen Post*, January 1st and 8th, 1888: "I found a job as a serving boy in an inn which belonged to a Russian, who also spoke German. When he was drunk he would shoot at the wall or ceiling with a loaded pistol or rifle, in order to amuse his guests – mainly rough or depraved sailors; or he would find a guest with a similar sense of humour, hold a pistol to his ear and then pull the trigger. Here, for six months, I worked for my board and lodging. I used to stay up until two or three almost every night and work behind the bar. I was woken again before six in the morning to scrub the floor in the bar."

Below Fig. 192. Michael Moser, "Studion Garten in Tana," ca. 1871, cabinet-size albumen print. Author's Collection.

Bottom Fig. 193. Michael Moser, "The Graves of William Adams (Miura Anjin) and His Wife at Henmi, Yokosuka," 1872, large-format albumen print. Author's Collection. Adams (1564–1620) was born in Kent, England, and reached Japan in 1600 when a Dutch ship he was piloting was

wrecked off Kyushu. Surviving attempts by the resident Portuguese Jesuits to have him executed, he found favor with the Shogun, Tokugawa Iyeasu, who gave him money and land. Eventually, Adams lost his yearning to return to his wife and children in England, and died in Japan.

Costumes of Tokio, Japan.

A French visitor to the bar had some camera equipment but did not know how to use it. He and Moser set up a studio together in Yokohama, but almost immediately a typhoon hit the town and destroyed their small enterprise. Moser was desperate and approached John Reddie Black, whom he had known for a while. Black took a fatherly interest in Moser, put him up at his house, and employed him as the staff photographer on his new publishing initiative *The Far East*, probably from the very first issue in May 1870, but certainly no later than November 1870. Moser traveled throughout Japan with two assistants, photographing wherever he went. After a while he had made enough money to have a small wooden house built in Yokohama.

Moser had worked hard at learning Japanese, and he was rewarded by being asked to act as interpreter to the Japanese delegation which was to attend the 1873 International Exhibition in Vienna. Moser seized this opportunity to visit his homeland, from which he had been away for five years. Although busy with the exhibition for some months, he was able to find time to visit his family between June 12th and 16th, 1873 and again from March 27th to 28th, 1874. On the return to Japan, the delegation stopped off in Venice where Moser was given lessons in night-time photography by the well-known photographer Carlo Naya, whose fee for the instruction was paid by the Japanese. On returning to Japan, Moser was employed as a "photographer in Government service" and also seems to have mounted some exhibition of works of art from around the world which he acquired in Vienna. He was also honored by an audience with the Emperor and Empress.

At the beginning of 1876, Moser was again asked to interpret, this time at the Centennial Exhibition in Philadelphia. According to Johann Von Linortner's "Michael Moser: Ein Altausseer als Fotograf in Japan" (1987), because of the excessively hot weather in Philadelphia, Moser was hospitalized from June until September. Still convalescing, he felt too weak to return to Japan and decided instead to visit his family in Austria. He arrived home in Altaussee in February 1877 and never returned to Japan. Moser set up a local studio with his brother Eusebius, and won several national awards for his photography. In 1889 he married a photographer's assistant and they had an only child, Philipp (1890–1978), who became a professor of music. As a reminder of his time in Japan, the backs of Moser's mounted photographs carried a design of a Torii gate and Mount Fuji.

Gert Rosenberg, the Austrian photography expert, described Moser's Japanese village and landscape scenes in his article "Michael Moser: Photographer (1853–1912)" (1985). He characterized them as particularly striking and full of mood, and praised the depth-creating lines in the foreground. He went on to say that Moser's portraits had a documentary style, almost certainly a result of his being influenced by his time with Burger, where the expedition's portraits were primarily of ethnographical interest. Despite Moser's poor education and humble background, Rosenberg felt that Moser was able to use his industry and intelligence to become an extraordinary achiever. There can be no argument with that.

HERMANN ANDERSEN

Hermann Andersen, the German half of the Stillfried and Andersen partnership, first appears on the Yokohama scene in 1874. The *China Directory* for that year lists him as a clerk/book-keeper working for the Belgian merchants Bavier & Co. He may also have had some legal training since he is reported in the *Japan Daily Herald* of November 14th, 1874 as being acting attorney in a case before the German consular court. He acted in a legal capacity in a number of cases over the next ten years, and this work would no doubt have provided a useful supplement to his other earnings.

As we have seen, by 1876 Andersen was in partnership with Stillfried, but prior to this it is not known whether he had had any experience with the camera. Following the acrimonious split in June 1878, Andersen appears to have taken a more active role in photography, whether out of interest or necessity. In a September 1878 court case, described in Gartlan's "Stillfried Chronology" (p. 153), he is introduced as "Mr. Hermann Andersen, photographer," while in *The Voyage of the Vega round Asia and Europe* (1885), an 1879 travel account written by A. E. Nordenskiold, the writer stated: "... a grand dinner was arranged for us by the German Club, the photographer Andersen being chairman." Finally, Gartlan (p. 154) refers to another 1880 court case where Andersen himself stated: "I am a photographer, living at No. 17, Yokohama." At this time Andersen's only serious opposition from foreign studios would have come from Stillfried's brother Franz, and it seems that the two of them competed fiercely (Fig. 196).

In April 1882 Andersen left Japan and was away for a year. On his return in March 1883, he seems to have decided to call it a day. Within a year he is no longer listed as a resident of Japan and almost certainly left the country for good in 1883. Before doing so, it is possible he sold his business to Franz, who subsequently sold everything to Adolfo Farsari in 1885. It is too early to assess whether Andersen's photography had any independent worth since none of his work has yet been attributed. We first need to separate his output from both of the Stillfried brothers. Andersen's work is likely to appear in Stillfried and Andersen albums which can be dated between July 1878 and before the end of 1883.

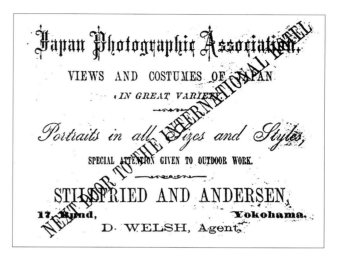

Right Fig. 197. Stillfried and Andersen Studio, "Portrait of Mrs Charlotte Brent," ca. 1881–3, cabinet card lightly hand-colored albumen print, Inscribed on the back: "Charlotte Brent in Patience G&S Yokohama." This must refer to an amateur dramatic performance in Yokohama of the newly written Gilbert & Sullivan opera "Patience," which had opened in London in April 1881. Charlotte Brent was the wife of the prominent British merchant Arthur Brent, who worked at the Yokohama offices of Walsh, Hall & Co. The Brents left Japan some time in 1883 and did not return until 1889. If Andersen was in Yokohama when this picture was taken, it is likely that he would have personally photographed the wife of such a prominent member of the community. In any case, the studio would certainly have been under Andersen's ownership.

BARON FRANZ VON STILLFRIED-RATENICZ

Baron Franz von Stillfried-Ratenicz (1837–1916) was Raimund's older brother and seemed destined to follow his father's military career. In 1861 he had risen to the rank of captain in the Austrian army. At some stage he left the army, and according to Gartlan's "Chronology" (p. 141), in 1875 he lived and worked in Philadelphia as a merchant and married a French woman, Jeanne M. E. Chizelle. His activities between leaving the army and moving to Philadelphia are not well documented. However, some years ago the writer came across an unpublished diary written in 1881 by a Mrs Alice Rea, a tourist traveling in Japan. An entry referring to Franz throws a little light on this period: "We bought some costume photos at Baron Stillfried's – an Austrian who had lost his fortune at Monaco and came here to retrieve it. He has a large staff of artists under him, who colour most beautifully."[74]

He was listed as a resident of Philadelphia in 1877 when his brother, on a trip to America and Europe, met up with him after several years (Gartlan, p. 147). It is likely that the two brothers discussed the possibility of Franz's moving to Japan. Whether at this time they then concocted the plan that was to have such negative consequences for Andersen is not known, but just a couple of weeks after Raimund's return to Yokohama, in June 1878, after an absence of more than a year, the Stillfried and Andersen partnership was dissolved. It is worth recalling here that the terms of the agreement prohibited Raimund from practicing photography in Japan for ten years, and allowed Andersen to continue to trade under the name Stillfried and Andersen. In July 1879 the bitterness between the ex-partners grew when the Imperial German Consular Court upheld Andersen's complaint that Raimund had opened a studio in Tokyo in contravention of the dissolution terms.

Just three months later, on October 25th, 1879, Franz arrived in Yokohama after a three-week voyage in a steamer from San Francisco. On November 17th the local press carried the announcement that Franz was opening his own studio under the name Baron Stillfried! As we saw earlier, this understandably created great friction between the Stillfried brothers and Andersen. It also created confusion amongst the local residents. Franz's early adverts consequently denied any connection with any other studio in Japan.

In the advertisement below, note the reference to prices being 50 percent lower. This is clear evidence that foreign studios were coming under increasing price competition from Japanese studios such as Usui's. An advertisement placed in the June 8th, 1880 issue of the *Japan Daily Herald*, illustrates both the price-discounting policy employed by Franz, and the continuing connection with his brother Raimund (Fig. 199).

Despite the previous acrimony existing between them, it is quite possible that Franz acquired Andersen's business some time in 1883 or 1884. He certainly moved into the premises of his former rival, as a cartoon from the October 1884 issue of Charles Wirgman's *Japan Punch* shows. If he did buy Andersen's business, perhaps by auction, then he very quickly sold it on to Adolfo Farsari in 1885. There is no evidence to date that Franz von Stillfried was anything other than, at best, an amateur photographer when he first arrived in Japan. It makes sense to assume that at some stage he received lessons from his brother before starting the new studio, which was to be in operation for five years. His work is yet to be separated from his brother's, but examples will undoubtedly exist in the albums carrying the name Baron Stillfried. The advertisement below is critical for identifying Franz's work. Although Franz was gifted some of his brother's negatives, many of the images pictured look as though they could well be his own.

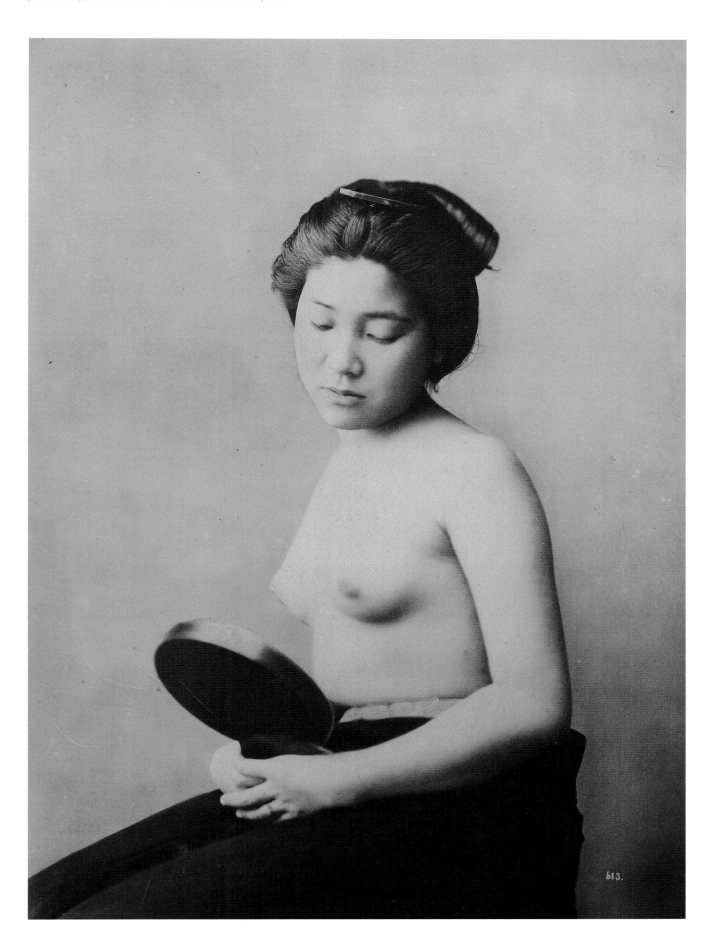

DAVID WELSH

It is very difficult to chronicle the life and movements of the peripatetic David Welsh who worked for at least four different Yokohama studios before eventually setting up his own in 1890. Nothing is known of his personal life, other than that he was British, but the 1864 *Chronicle and Directory* shows him working in Hong Kong as a clerk for the merchants Smith Kennedy & Co. He is probably the D. Welsh noted in the October 5th, 1861 issue of the *North China Herald*, as being expected to depart from Southampton, England, on September 4th, 1861 with Hong Kong as his destination. And, in fact, the *Overland China Mail* (October 15th) does record a D. Welsh arriving at Hong Kong on October 9th. There is then a fleeting reference to a Welsh leaving Shanghai for Hong Kong in 1865 (*North China Herald*, December 9th, 1865). It is likely that Welsh settled in Shanghai for a time because he is mentioned as a member of the visiting Shanghai cricket team when they played Hong Kong in 1866 (*Overland China Mail, Supplement*, p. 3). He probably stayed in China until 1869, when he moved to Japan. The 1870 *Japan Herald Directory* records Welsh as a resident in Yokohama staying at Felix Beato's studio address at No. 17. However, there is no proof to date that he actually worked with Beato. By January 1873 he was certainly a bill collector for the watch-making firm of E. Berger & Co., since Welsh appeared as a witness in a case brought by Berger in the United States Consulate Court, Yokohama (*Japan Weekly Mail*, December 13th, 1873). In 1874 he is listed as a bill collector for the *Japan Gazette* newspaper. He was the unsuccessful plaintiff in the Kanagawa Court on December 28th, 1876, when he alleged that an offer of employment made to him in the middle of December 1875 (this might be a printing error for 1876) by the company Sanriku-Shoko had been unfairly withdrawn. His action for $1020 damages was dismissed on the grounds that the offer had not been formerly put to him. The role would have seen him representing the company in Yokohama, marketing Japanese works of art.

In October 1876 he is employed by Stillfried and Andersen as a bill collector. This ended acrimoniously in an August 1877 court case when he is accused by his employers of not rendering accurate accounts. Welsh seemed to attract controversy since there is a report of yet another court case (Gartlan, "Stillfied Chronology," pp. 155–6) which tells us that Welsh, in 1879, was working as an agent for the Japanese photographer Usui Shusaburo. On December 9th, 1879 Welsh joined Baron Franz Stillfried, but mysteriously left six days later to rejoin his old firm, Stillfried and Andersen, as agent (Gartlan, pp. 148, 158). Whilst with his new employers, Welsh acted as an interpreter and guide to the wealthy Charles J. Lambert who was on a two-year world cruise with his family. Welsh was with the family from December 11th to 21st, 1881. It is possible that this service was part of the studio's marketing activities in the hope that the visitor would feel obliged to purchase photographs: "We were guided by Mr. Welsh, whose services we were lucky in securing during our stay in Yokohama, Yeddo and the neighbourhood; he is a most excellent guide and adviser, having a good knowledge of the Japanese language, and being very active, obliging, and trustworthy" (Lambert, *The Voyage of the "Wanderer"* (1883)).

He now settled for a few years and it seems he became more involved with photography itself; in 1882 he was listed as "assistant" to Andersen. It is likely that he left the business some time in 1883, as the *Japan Directory* for 1884 lists him as working with Usui Shusaburo again, at the Otemachi studio address. This studio, the Yokohama Photographic Co., relocated to No. 16 Bund in 1884, and the *Japan Directory* for 1885 indicates that Welsh was working there as Usui's agent. Whether by accident or design, the premises were positioned next door to the Stillfried and Andersen operation at No. 17. However, both Andersen and Franz Stillfried had left Japan by then and Farsari would acquire the business at the beginning of 1885. The rivalry between the two studios was satirized in the *Japan Punch*[75] (Figs. 203, 204). But any rivalry would be short-lived: a severe fire in February 1886 consumed Farsari's studio at No. 17, destroying all of his stock and negatives. One or two other buildings were similarly damaged, and although there is no record of Usui's studio having suffered, he nevertheless closed down No. 16 and moved back to his old Otemachi address.

This ended Welsh's involvement with Usui. The 1888 *Japan Directory* then advertised what appears to be Welsh's first business enterprise. Trading under the name Fine Art Store at 37 Water Street, D. Welsh & Co. employed a Japanese assistant and marketed Japanese curios and works of art. "Also the largest, finest and cheapest photography can only be had at the above." The boast in the 1889 *Japan Directory* extended to "Many years experience and a thorough knowledge of the business has permitted us to gather together an assortment that is not equaled in this country" (Fig. 202).

From 1890 he was trading as D. Welsh & Co. from No. 37 and living with his wife on the Ishikawa Bluff. The very first indication that Welsh operated his own photo studio is contained in the 1891 *Japan Directory*. This advertises Welsh & Co.'s Studio at No. 39. His curio business was now separated

from the studio and operating at No. 86 as D. Welsh & Co. (trading as the Fine Art Store) and employing two Japanese assistants. According to Gartlan's "Stillfried Chronology" (p. 175), the State Library of Victoria, Australia, has in its collection a photograph of a traveler on a *jinrikisha* with the inscription "Edward D. Brock, Yokohama Japan, 10th April 1890." On the back of the mount is printed "D. Welsh & Co., Photographic Studio, No. 39 Yokohama."

David Welsh and his various businesses are no longer listed after 1892; the addresses referred to above are by then occupied by other firms. However, perhaps by way of a dying echo, the 1893 third Scribner edition of B. H. Chamberlain and W. B. Mason's *A Handbook for Travellers in Japan* mentions that photographs can be bought from Welsh & Co. at No. 86. But this is the New York edition, which contains identical text to the London 1891 third Murray edition; so it seems likely that Welsh finally left Japan in 1891 or 1892. For a short one- or two-year period, Welsh was probably running the only owner-managed foreign studio in Japan. Given his involvement with so many of the studios in Yokohama, his memoirs, were they available, or even any contemporary letters, would make very interesting reading indeed! They would undoubtedly throw much-needed light on the personalities of many of the Yokohama photographers, both Western and Japanese.

Below Fig. 202. David Welsh Advertisement. *Japan Directory*, 1889. Reference to the "largest" photographs suggests that Welsh is selling mammoth-plate, or larger, prints. He is also clearly acting as a dealer in photographs originally produced by other studios. He is also offering a wide range of Japanese works of art and is not solely dependent upon the sale of photographs in which, by this time, there was fierce competition.

Above Fig. 203. "Caricature of David Welsh." *Japan Punch*, October 1884. In this cartoon Charles Wirgman provides evidence that Baron Franz von Stillfried-Ratenicz acquired the Stillfried and Andersen studio and moved into those premises. His tenure there was short-lived, however, since the business was, in turn, acquired by Adolfo Farsari in February 1885.

Above Fig. 204. "Caricature of David Welsh." *Japan Punch*, February 1885. In this cartoon Welsh, who then was working for Usui Shusaburo's studio at No. 16 Bund, is presumably uncomfortable with the new competition next door! Over the years No. 17 had accommodated a number of different studios. Perhaps Welsh is suggesting that there had been too many!

Below Fig. 205. William Willmann, "Japanese Officer," ca. 1873–4, hand-colored albumen-print *carte de visite*. Author's Collection.

Below Fig. 206. William Willmann, "Japanese Woman," ca. 1873–4, hand-colored albumen-print *carte de visite*. Author's Collection.

OTHER WESTERN PHOTOGRAPHERS

William Willmann, an Austrian, first appears on the Yoko-hama scene on September 1st, 1866 when he is admitted as a partner to the general merchants firm Ladage, Oelke & Co. His appointment was announced in the *Daily Japan Herald* on October 2nd, 1866 (p. 1850). Willmann and a colleague left that firm shortly afterwards to form a rival operation, Rothmund, Willmann & Co., on January 1st, 1867, which was advertised the same day in the *Daily Japan Herald* – although a printing error gives the date as 1866. We can see from an advertisement in the 1870 *Japan Herald Directory* that by then Willmann was trading under his own name as a general storekeeper and commission agency business at 61 Main Street, specializing in the importation of wines and liquor.

In the summer of 1871 Willmann joined forces with Stillfried and worked as an assistant in the newly formed Stillfried & Co., which started its life in Willmann's premises at No. 61. In the 1874 *China Directory*, he is still described as an assistant, but sometime around 1873–4 he briefly set up his own studio, W. Willmann's Photographic Establishment, at No. 59 Main Street. This was probably with Stillfried's sup-port, since Stillfried & Co. was also operating from the same address. Willmann stayed until 1875, but then presumably left Japan as his name no longer appears in lists of residents.

Work by this artist is exceptionally rare; the writer has only ever seen a few examples of *cartes de visite* or cabinet photo-graphs with Willmann's studio name on the reverse. It is very likely that he was an amateur enthusiast who tried and failed to succeed as a commercial studio operator.

The American amateur photographer and philanthropist **William H. Metcalf** (1821–92) is known for an excellent series of twenty-six stereos of Japan taken in 1877 during a six-month visit (Fig. 208). These were then published by a friend, the photographer and publisher Henry H. Bennett, and titled "A Summer in Japan." In 1843 Metcalf and another friend, Charles Bradley, moved from New York City to Milwau-kee, Wisconsin, and in 1845 set up Bradley & Metcalf, a shoe manufacturer. According to the *National Cyclopaedia of American Biography*, Metcalf enjoyed great success and was able to spend time traveling and supporting the work of local painters. This enabled him to accompany Henry Bennett on photographic trips. According to Larry L. Hess in "H. H. Bennett of Wisconsin" (1991), Metcalf provided his friend with encouragement and financial support, and in 1875 made available a loan which enabled Bennett to construct a new studio. Bennett built a stereo camera for Metcalf, which the latter used during the trip to Japan. According to a biography written by his daughter Julia Metcalf Cary, *William Henry Metcalf* (1937), during the 1870s Metcalf entertained many

353 Village of Enoshima.

visitors at his large house in Milwaukee. These included Professor Edward Morse of Salem and Oliver Wendell Holmes. In 1870 Metcalf had become "very much interested in photography and was developing the dry-plate process. He took a great many pictures in Texas of the tropical growths, trees, vines and the old missions.... At this time father began contributing articles to the photographic journals in England and in this country, his success in making dry plates having won him a certain recognition." When Morse decided to visit Japan, Metcalf decided on short notice to join him. "So together they made the memorable trip, the most interesting father ever made.... Professor Morse went with a definite object on view, to explore their 'shell heaps' for fossils, et cetera, but father from curiosity alone" (Fig. 207).

A photographer named **A. Schleesselmann** is known to have operated a portrait studio in Yokohama in the late 1870s from No. 61 Main Street. From Gartlan's "Stillfried Chronology" (p. 153) we know he was the defendant in a case heard in 1878 at the German Consular Court. The plaintiff was one Hans Friebe, who had worked as an artist for Schleesselmann from June 25th to July 18th, 1878, hand coloring the photographs, and was claiming unpaid wages. Friebe won the case and was also awarded costs.[76] This appears to be the only record we have of this photographer, who does not appear in any of the usual directories. There is a photograph in Boyd and Izakura's *Portraits in Sepia* (2000) which has the studio name and address on the back of the mount (Figs. 209, 210).

Below Fig. 209. A. Schleesselmann, "Japanese Woman," late 1870s, cabinet-card albumen print. Boyd and Izakura Collection.

Below Fig. 210. Reverse of Fig. 209.

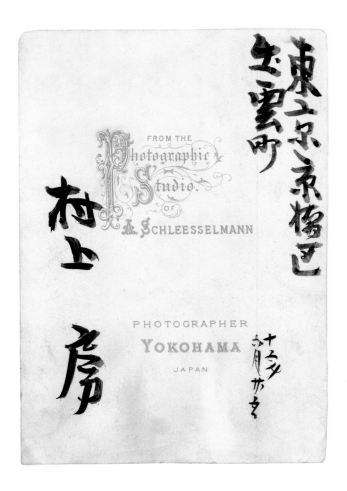

The conclusion is that his studio can only have operated for a few months in 1878. A probable connection lies with a **G. A. Schleesselmann**, a photographer who ran a studio in Singapore from March 1875 to June 1877 (see John Falconer's *A Vision of the Past*, 1987, p. 191). As the Boyd and Izakura photograph has "A. Schleesselmann" on the mount, it is possible that the two were brothers.

Nothing much is known about the Kobe studio **E. Parant & Co.**, which opened for a short time and was advertised in the *Hiogo News* on August 20th, 1870:

Opening of Messrs. E. Parant & Co.'s Photographic Studio, No. 40 Main Street Cartes De Visite Taken At Moderate Prices. Views in Japan. Jewel Boxes, Albums, Pocket Books and Photographic Jewellery. A large assortment of frames of all kinds Sittings from 7 till 10am and from 2 till 5pm

The advertisement was repeated on August 24th, 27th, and 31st. It seems that the photographer was a C. Parant, who shortly after the above advertisement closed the studio and joined forces with Auguste Gordes in nearby Osaka. But by May 1871 he parted company with Gordes and set up a rival studio in the same city, much to the astonishment of the local newspaper, the *Hiogo News* (see page 145). Not surprisingly, with a foreign resident population of approximately only seventy, Osaka proved unable to support such competition and Parant seems to have moved on.

According to Clark Worswick's *Japan Photographs* (1980), a C. Parant worked for Stillfried in 1872–3. In this connection, there is the following listing in the 1870 *Japan Directory*: "E. Parant & Co. (House Decorators), C. Parant & B. Laurent; 166 Yokohama." There is also one reference to a C. Parant arriving in Kobe on April 30th, 1870 from Yokohama. He is reported as a passenger on the *Golden Age* in the May 4th issue of the *Hiogo News*. If nothing else, Parant, who was probably French, may well have been the first foreigner to open a commercial studio in Kobe.

John Douglas was an American who worked for Stillfried and Andersen and subsequently tried to open his own studio. The first we hear of him is when the 1877 *Japan Gazette Hong List and Directory* shows him resident at the Temperance Hall, Yokohama. The directory for 1878 lists him as Hon. Secretary of the Total Abstinence Society of Japan, as well as working for the Japan Photographic Association and Stillfried and Andersen. He obviously survived the partnership dissolution since he continued to work with Andersen until 1883. He set up his own studio towards the end of that year, but a serious fire destroyed it in December (Gartlan, "Stillfried Chronology," p. 170). Perhaps disheartened, Douglas must have left Japan since his name no longer appears in the Japan directories.[77] It has been suggested that Douglas taught photography to Usui Shusaburo from December 1876 to March 1877. This would mean that Douglas was an experienced photographer before arriving in Japan.[78] However, some of the dates associated with Usui leave room for doubt. He also met Francis

Bottom Fig. 211. D. R. Clark, "Temple in Japan," 1874, albumen-print stereoview. Author's Collection. This is No. 52 in the series of "Asiatic and Tropical Views" taken by Clark as chief photographer of the Transit of Venus party on its way to the Russian Station. The view here is presumably taken in Nagasaki and is one of approximately five Japanese scenes.

Below Fig. 212. Reverse of Fig. 211.

Guillemard in 1882 and helped him develop his dry plates taken in Okinawa and Kamchatka (see page 224, Guillemard).

Lieutenant **John Henry Sandwith** (1846–95), an amateur photographer, was a royal marine stationed in Yokohama in the early 1870s. Perhaps because his tour of duty was over, he advertised the sale of his photographic equipment in the local press in January 1875. In 1872 he had published a journal, *A Trip into the Interior of Japan*, covering an 1871 trip to the Hakone Mountains which had contained a few original albumen prints (Gartlan, "Stillfried Chronology," p. 140). Another amateur, **Lieutenant Swinton C. Holland** (1843–1922), was present during British Minister Sir Harry Parkes' visit to the *daimyo* of Wakayama in 1870. The *Hiogo News* issue of December 14th, 1870 reported the event and referred to Holland's photographic work which occurred on November 24th, 1870: "During the morning some very successful groups and views of the grounds were taken by Lieut. Holland." In 1871 Holland traveled to Hokkaido and took photographs of the scenery and indigenous tribes, the Ainu.

Between the years 1869 and 1873 Felix Beato employed a British assistant, **John Goddard** (ca. 1824–1903), who according to his obituary in the *Japan Weekly Chronicle* (July 15th, 1903, p. 65), first arrived in Hong Kong from England in 1842 where he joined the British trading house Jardine Mathesen at the age of eighteen. He was later transferred to Jardine's Yokohama branch in 1868 (the *Japan Times and Overland Mail* on September 5th, 1868 records a J. Goddard arriving from Hong Kong on August 23rd), but subsequently went into business on his own account. It is not clear when he first settled in Yokohama, but sometime in 1869 he accepted an appointment at Beato's studio.

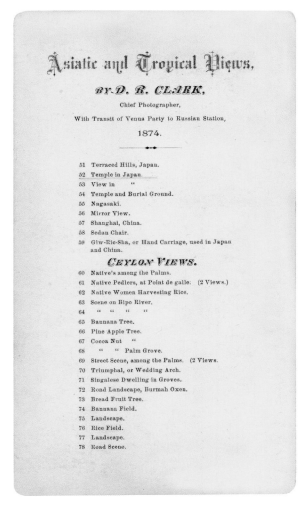

Asiatic and Tropical Views,

BY D. R. CLARK,

Chief Photographer,

With Transit of Venus Party to Russian Station,

1874.

51 Terraced Hills, Japan.
52 Temple in Japan.
53 View in "
54 Temple and Burial Ground.
55 Nagasaki.
56 Mirror View.
57 Shanghai, China.
58 Sedan Chair.
59 Giw-Ric-Sha, or Hand Carriage, used in Japan and China.

CEYLON VIEWS.

60 Native's among the Palms.
61 Native Pedlers, at Point de galle. (2 Views.)
62 Native Women Harvesting Rice.
63 Scene on Bipo River.
64 "   "   "   "
65 Bannana Tree.
66 Pine Apple Tree.
67 Cocoa Nut "
68 "   " Palm Grove.
69 Street Scene, among the Palms. (2 Views.
70 Triumphal, or Wedding Arch.
71 Singalese Dwelling in Groves.
72 Road Landscape, Burmah Oxen.
73 Bread Fruit Tree.
74 Bannana Field.
75 Landscape.
76 Rice Field.
77 Landscape.
78 Road Scene.

PUBLISHED BY D. R. CLARK. INDIANAPOLIS, IND.

NORTH PENNSYLVANIA STREET.

No.

Copyright 1875, by D. R. CLARK.

Below Fig. 213. William Pryor Floyd, "Japanese Woman in Hong Kong," ca. 1870, large-format albumen print. Author's Collection.

Right Fig. 214. William Pryor Floyd, "Japanese Man in Hong Kong," ca. 1870, large-format albumen print. Author's Collection.

In Christine Wallace Laidlaw's *Charles Appleton Longfellow* (1998, p. 42), we find, on September 6th, 1871, that Goddard and his bride Isabel were on the ship *Ariel* heading for Hakodate, which also contained Charles Longfellow, the son of the famous American poet. Longfellow recorded in his journal: "We have the steamer almost to ourselves, for besides our party there is only Mr. Goddard and his wife on a wedding tour having been married yesterday ('while there is life there is hope', he being only 45)."

After leaving Beato in 1873, Goddard is absent from Japan for a couple of years. The *Japan Directory* has him listed as a resident again in 1876, but he does not seem to take employment until 1878 when he is a clerk at the Yokohama United Club until 1882. He then, according to his obituary, went with his wife and family to Australia where he stayed until 1901 or 1902, after which time he returned to Japan and stayed with his son-in-law. His health was deteriorating, and he died at Yokohama General Hospital on July 6th, 1903. He left a widow and three sons and three daughters. According to the listing in Patricia McCabe's *Gaijin Bochi* (1994), he and his wife are buried at the Foreigners' Cemetery in Yokohama. It is hard to say whether Goddard had any photographic experience before joining Beato.

Another Beato assistant was **H. Woollett**, who was employed between 1871 until the sale of the business in 1877, in which year he was the manager. According to the October 29th, 1870 issue of the *Japan Weekly Mail*, H. Wollett [*sic*] arrived in Yokohama from San Francisco on October 26th. Apart from accompanying Beato to Korea as a photographic assistant in 1871, and a mention on an 1873 Yokohama passengers' arrival list (*Japan Weekly Mail*, August 16th, 1873, p. 594), we know almost nothing else about him. The 1874 edition of the *China Directory* mentions Woollett as still being Beato's assistant, but by 1877 he is no longer listed as a resident of Japan. There is one mention of Woollett in the October 17th, 1874 issue of the *Japan Weekly Mail* (p. 830), when he photographed a Yokohama social gathering: "During the afternoon [October 10th] a photograph of the visitors who were present was taken by Mr. Woollet [*sic*], which will doubtless form a pleasant memento of the occasion."

The Australian **Samuel Cocking** was a long-term Yokohama resident, merchant, and amateur photographer. He was also a founding member of the Nihon Shashin Kyokai (Photographic Society of Japan). As a consequence he knew most, if not all, of the local photographers and was particularly friendly with Shimooka Renjo and John Black. Gartlan's "Stillfried Chronology" (p. 146) refers to a long letter written by Cocking on February 27th, 1877, which was published in the *British Journal of Photography* (April 13th, 1877, pp. 173–4). Although not directly referring to Shimooka by name, Cocking remarked that the famous photographer and all of his family were committed Christians. He also referred to his business as a photographic equipment importer, and went on to boast that of the 240 photographers in Tokyo, 180 were his customers – together with many others throughout the country. Cocking, who spent forty years in Japan, was also the first to import the Kodak camera, in 1890–1.

The French engineer **Lieutenant Louis Kreitmann**, in Japan as part of the Second French Military Mission, traveled throughout the country during his stay from October 1875 until May 1878. Kreitmann taught surveying and fortification at the newly established military academy, Rikugun Shikan Gakko, in Ichigaya, Tokyo. He collected many souvenir photographs, but as an enthusiastic amateur photographer he also took many himself. Dated, and with detailed captions, this important archive of some 600 images, which was discovered in France just a few years ago, is now at the Edo-Tokyo Historical Museum.

No research seems to have been done on the American photographer **D. R. Clark**, who arrived in Japan in August 1874 as a senior photographer for the expedition which was recording the transit of Venus in December of that year. Clark was assigned to the Vladivostok station, but found time to produce a series of stereoviews in Japan and in other countries (Figs. 211, 212).

The British photographer **William Pryor Floyd** worked for studios in Shanghai and Hong Kong before opening his own in the British Colony in 1867. He is better known for his Chinese work, and at one stage provided serious competition to the famous John Thomson. He was active until 1874. Whilst operating his Hong Kong studio, he photographed members of the local Japanese community. Judging from his identified Chinese photography, Floyd seems to have been an extremely talented artist, both in portrait and landscape work. There is no evidence that he worked in Japan.

HUNG CHIONG,

MARINE, SHIP, AND PORTRAIT PAINTER, PHOTOGRAPHER,

CHART COPIER,

AND PICTURE FRAME DEALER,

No. 165, HOMURA ROAD, YOKOHAMA, JAPAN.

Very little seems to be known about the Shanghai-based photographer **L. F. Fisler**, who was a major competitor to William Saunders from 1866 until 1885. In an advertisement carried in the October 1877 edition of *The Far East*, Fisler mentioned that he had a " Fine Collection of Negatives of Chinese and Japanese Persons and Places, taken by himself during a lengthened residence in the Far East." None of his Japanese work has so far been identified.

E. Warren Clark was an American missionary and amateur photographer in Japan 1871–5. Clark gave the Emperor and Empress a magic lantern slide show at the palace in 1872.

Although not a Westerner, it is worth mentioning here the Chinese photographer **Cheong Hung**, who ran a studio at No. 165 Yokohama from 1875 to 1885. His advertisements in the directories state that he was an artist, chart copier, portrait painter, and photographer. He left Japan in 1885, and according to Boyd and Izakura, (p. 294) he opened a studio in Hong Kong. His name was variously rendered as Chong and Chiong.

HUNG CHEONG, JAPAN.

ESAKI REIJI

Born into a wealthy farming family in Gifu, central Japan, Esaki Reiji (1845–1910) learned the principles of photography from a local chemist who had spent time in America (Fig. 218). Fascinated by the technology, Esaki determined on a career in photography and moved to the capital in 1870. He initially secured employment through the introduction of a friend, and saved as much money as possible whilst studying photography from a contemporary instruction manual. Using this, together with some cheap equipment he managed to purchase, he was able to produce some poor quality photographs, but otherwise made fast progress. He succeeded in securing a short-term apprenticeship with Shimooka Renjo in Yokohama, following which, in 1871, he opened his first studio in Shiba, Tokyo, on borrowed capital of $180. This enterprise failed, but he managed to secure a bigger loan of $1000 to open a second Tokyo studio in Asakusa. This was much more successful, and within a few years he became one of the best-known photographers in Tokyo and was able to move to a very grand studio in 1889 which cost $18,000.

Esaki is credited with being the first Japanese to commercially employ dry-plate technology.[79] According to an article he wrote in 1896, "Professional Photography in Japan," Esaki claimed that the first gelatin dry plates were imported into Japan in 1879 (March 20th) but that he and the other Japanese photographers initially failed to master the new process. Persevering, he finally managed to understand the necessary procedures and became the first to photograph a moving object; the subject was the funeral procession of Iwakura Tomomi on July 1st, 1883. According to Anne Tucker et al. in *The History of Japanese Photography* (2003), Esaki managed to photograph a column of water caused by the detonation of a mine in the Sumida River on May 19th, 1883 (*Yubin Hochi*, June 6th, 1883). In fact, Esaki may not have been the first Japanese to successfully use the new gelatin dry-plate technology in Japan. The British amateur photographer Francis Guillemard used the technology in Okinawa in June 1882 (see page 224). Furthermore, from July of the same year he traveled throughout Japan with Usui Shusaburo and it is possible that Usui took at least one dry-plate photograph on behalf of Guillemard.

Esaki mentioned in the 1896 article that dry-plate technology produced significant commercial benefits, since parents now found that their children could be photographed without any difficulty because of the shorter exposure times. Within just three years, he produced 3000 negatives of children, and for publicity purposes he produced a famous photographic collage of some 1700 babies (Fig. 221). There are two variants: mainly clothed and unclothed. In his article "Sketches of the Lives of a Few of the Leading Professional Photographers in Japan" (1896), Izawa Shuji, the editor of the contemporary *Shashin Sowa* photographic journal, stated that Esaki was asked by the government in 1884 to photograph the eclipse of the sun but failed because of poor weather conditions. However, later that year he became the first to photograph a lunar eclipse in Japan.

Only a handful of Esaki's photographs have so far been attributed, and no real assessment of his work has therefore taken place. However, he appears to have produced souvenir albums of views and costumes, and it is to be hoped that his work will soon be identified amongst the host of such albums which remain without attribution.

SUZUKI SHINICHI I

There has been considerable confusion about the key biographical facts concerning Suzuki Shinichi I (1835–1919) and Suzuki Shinichi II (1855–1912). This is not surprising given that both photographers adopted these names, leaving their birth names behind. Furthermore, both were apprenticed to Shimooka Renjo at the same time and Suzuki II married Suzuki I's daughter. What follows is an attempt to untangle some of the historical details and to point out some of the areas in which more research is required.

For Suzuki Shinichi I, the writer has relied largely upon information provided in Saito Takio's recent work *Bakumatsu Meiji* (2004). There is also an extant Suzuki family ornamental vase, which has some biographical information printed on it, together with a self-portrait.

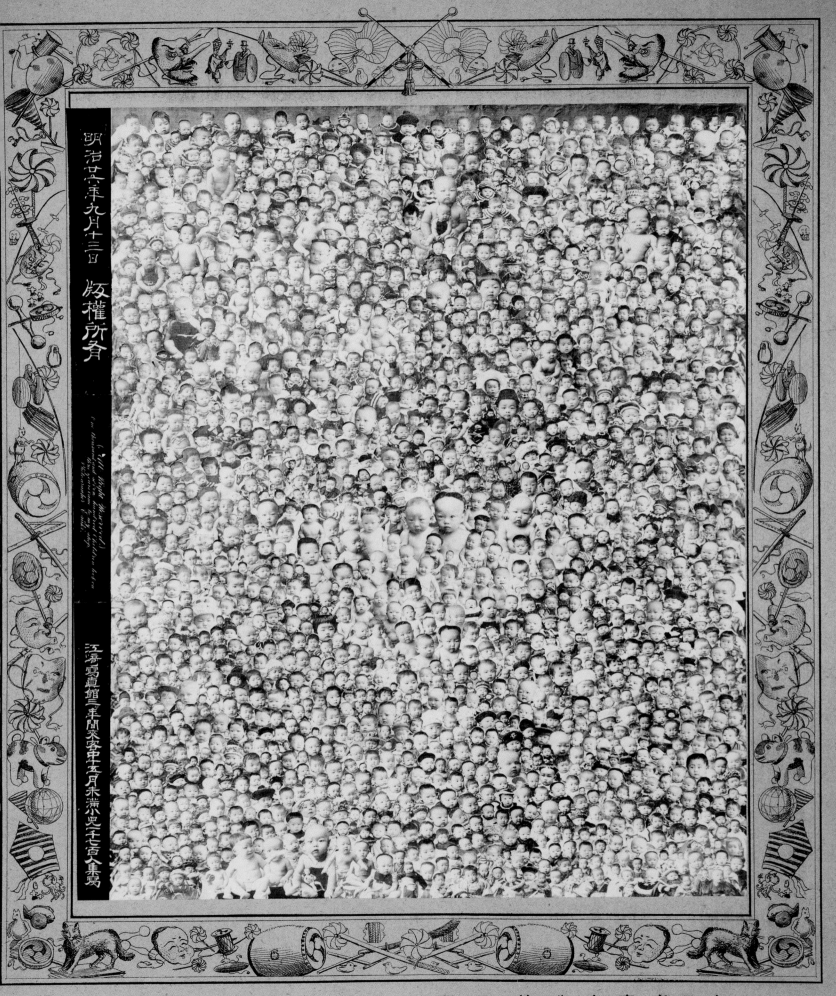

Esaki
ARTISTIC PHOTOGRAPHER,
ASAKUSA-PARK TOKYO, JAPAN.

大日本東京淺草公園
早取寫真師
江崎禮三製

Suzuki was born Takahashi Yujiro in Iwachi, Iwashina village in Kamogun, Izukuni. In 1854 he married the daughter of Suzuki Yoshichi and moved to Shimoda, whilst also assuming the Suzuki name. That year a huge tidal wave hit Shimoda and Suzuki lost everything he owned. Along with many others from the area, he and his wife migrated to Yokohama to start a new life. There is then a dearth of information until 1866 when he becomes apprenticed to fellow Shimodian, Shimooka Renjo, at the age of thirty-one. In October 1873 he left and set up his own studio at No. 112 Benten-dori. That year he also changed his given name to Shinichi and saw his daughter married to Okamoto Keizo, who was apprenticed to Shimooka. Okamoto would later become Suzuki Shinichi II.

Suzuki operated a portrait studio in Yokohama and also sold souvenir albums. He pioneered a technique for printing photographs onto porcelain and found a ready market for these productions amongst foreign residents and visitors.

SUZUKI,
PHOTOGRAPHER.

No. 112, Honcho-Dori, Roku-chome, Yokohama, near Railway Station.

Branch Studio — Kudan-Zaka, Tokio.

COLORED VIEWS OF PLACES OF NOTE IN JAPAN.

ALBUMS FILLED TO ORDER.

Costumes, Groups, Cartes de Visite, Cabinet and Imperiales,

Taken in the Best Style, at the Lowest Prices.

CABINET-SIZE PHOTOGRAPHS
TAKEN ON PORCELAIN,
— AND —

Artistically retouched .... 12 Yen each.

SARGENT, FARSARI & Co., No. 80, MAIN STREET,
Are Agents for the Sale of above Views & Costumes.

Below Fig. 226. Suzuki Studio Advertisement. *Japan Directory*, 1893. This is the first time the name I. S. Suzuki is mentioned and reflects the fact that Suzuki's actual son, Izaburo, has taken over the studio from his father who now retires. Suzuki Shinichi II, meanwhile, continues to manage the branch studio in Tokyo

Bottom Fig. 227. Suzuki Studio Advertisement. *Japan Directory*, 1903. For the last ten years the wording in the advertisements had been practically unaltered. Now, there is the cryptic statement: "Note 'I. S.' Suzuki"! It seems that Izaburo is trying to differentiate himself from another "Suzuki." Meanwhile, the branch studio in Tokyo is no longer listed from this year and Suzuki Shinichi II disappears from the scene. What the relationship had been between Izaburo and his father's adopted son can only be surmised.

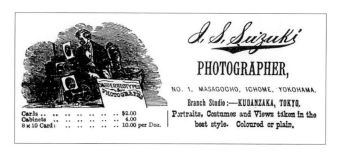

In 1884 he is said to have moved to a Western-style two-story photo studio which he had built in Masagocho, Yokohama. Suzuki retired in 1892 and his son Izaburo became head of the family. Suzuki died in 1919 at the age of eighty-three.

The earliest reference to Suzuki's studio that the writer has been able to trace is in W. E. L. Keeling's *Tourists' Guide to Yokohama* (1880), which gives the address as No. 112 Honcho Dori. Although this would seem to be a direct contradiction of the No. 112 Benten-dori address above, in fact these streets at that time converged near the railway station where the studio was apparently based. Keeling also mentions Suzuki's specialty of printing on porcelain and a branch studio in Kudanzaka, Tokyo. The 1884 *Japan Directory* advertises the new Yokohama studio at Masagocho and the manager as "I. S. Suzuki." Undoubtedly the name refers to Izaburo Suzuki. The Yokohama and Tokyo addresses remain unchanged until 1903, when the Kudanzaka branch no longer appears. The Masagocho studio continues until 1908, after which Suzuki's studio is no longer listed. Throughout this period, Izaburo is shown as the studio head. There is a curious, and temporary, alteration to the regular wording of the studio advertisement in 1903. The additional words "Note 'I. S.' Suzuki!" appear. Perhaps there had been some kind of dispute over the studio name. It is hard to say.

There is an interesting group of photographs which the writer has attributed to Suzuki. This group was christened the *shajo* series by Clark Worswick and many of the images were illustrated in Hugh Cortazzi and Terry Bennett's *Japan: Caught In Time* (1995). The book centered on a collection of Japanese photographs brought back to Russia in the 1870s. Amongst the photographs was a fine series of "ethnic views" arranged on an improvised outdoor photo studio (*shajo*). The scenes were expertly composed to document as authentically as possible the life and customs of rural communities. The series had been known for years but its authorship was a matter of debate amongst photo-historians.

It turned out that Alexander Grigoryev, the Russian botanist who had brought the collection back to Russia, had written on the back of one of the photographs in Russian: "photograph by Luca Sudzuki." In studying these photographs for the abovementioned book, this writer attributed the series to Suzuki Shinichi I based on the following circumstantial evidence. It is known that Shimooka Renjo, Suzuki's teacher, was baptised in 1872, around the time that the *shajo* group was taken. It is possible that Suzuki was also influenced to become a Christian. The Grigoryev collection is held by the Russian Geographical Society in St. Petersburg. The curator, Vitaly Naumkin, has suggested that "Luca" is the Christian name Luke, which Suzuki may have been given. The presence in the photographs of numerous Japanese farm and kitchen utensils, together with the apparently random placement of props, strongly suggest a Japanese photographer. The "native feel" is further enhanced by the presence of the dual English and Japanese numbering which appears on the prints.

It looks very much as though the shrewd editor of *The Far East*, John Black, commissioned this series in the early 1870s, and this would support his claim in the July 1873 edition that "we have already in possession photographs of 'groups of the people' from life, sufficient for our work for the next three years." That issue, and subsequent ones, then proceeded to publish selections from the series. Black was candid enough to say that whereas in the past he had not been able to pay his contributors – literary or photographic – he was now able to financially reward them because of the success of the publication.

There is no doubt that the series, stylistically, bears a distinct semblance to a number of the portrait groups seen in known Shimooka Renjo *cartes de visite*: they have a certain zest which is characteristic of Shimooka's style. Black and Shimooka must have known each other well, if only through their mutual friend and amateur photographer Cocking. Black probably approached Shimooka about the proposed series and asked for his help. Shimooka at that time was not particularly active as a photographer and most likely introduced Black to his talented apprentice Suzuki. The series was published in July 1873, and according to Saito, Suzuki set up his own studio in October. Perhaps he had already left Shimooka. The series would have taken some weeks to complete since the negative numbers indicate more than 250 images. Perhaps the series represents Suzuki's first commercial assignment. In any case, despite Black's newfound confidence in being able to pay for photographic contributions, he would not have been willing (or able) to pay the going commercial rate for this extensive, highly professional, and therefore costly series. He would also have required the negatives themselves in order to produce the hundreds of prints needed for each issue of *The Far East*. Shimooka was perhaps returning a favor and providing Black with the series at a heavily discounted price – or perhaps he just caught Suzuki at the right time. Whilst this series is exceptionally rare, the writer has seen some of the *shajo* images continue to appear in Suzuki albums into the 1880s, but by then the subject matter probably seemed outdated and not reflective of a fast-modernizing country.

Below Fig. 228. Anonymous, "Portrait of Suzuki Shinichi II," ca. 1885, small-format albumen print. Old Japan Picture Library.

Below Fig. 229. Suzuki Studio Cabinet Card, 1884. Boyd and Izakura Collection. Suzuki Shinichi I is on the right, his adopted son Suzuki Shinichi II on the left.

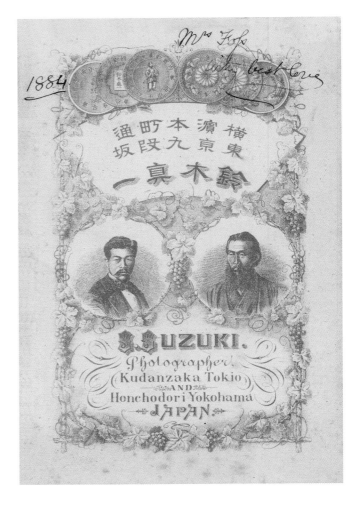

SUZUKI SHINICHI II

When preparing notes on Suzuki for *Early Japanese Images* (1996), and in trying to reconcile the apparent confusing existence of Suzuki I and II, the writer put a lot of store in the accuracy of Izawa's "Sketches of the Lives of a Few of the Leading Professional Photographers in Japan" (pp. 234–5).

In reading this brief but seemingly authoritative commentary on Suzuki's life, it seemed that the reason for the previous confusion over the photographer's identity was simple: there was only one Suzuki! Izawa characterised Suzuki as being "one of the best [photographers] throughout the Japanese Empire." No mention was made of any connection with any other photographer named Suzuki. Izawa seems to have been a reliable commentator, an amateur himself, and editor of a respected photographic journal, *Shashin Sowa*. Suzuki was still living when the article was written, and it is likely that Izawa verified his facts. The two were certainly in communication because Izawa had requested some photographs to accompany the article. It now seems clear to this writer that Izawa was sketching the life of Suzuki Shinichi II (1855–1912). Looking at the article again, and considering the information contained in Saito's *Bakumatsu Meiji*, it does seem that Izawa's contribution could be crucial in clearing up some of the confusion, at least in this writer's mind!

Izawa states that Suzuki, the eldest son of a Mr C. Okamoto, was born in Izu in 1855 (Saito gives 1859, his birthplace as Setagun, Joshu, and his birth name as Okamoto Keizo), and demonstrated an early talent for drawing and painting (Fig. 228). At the age of thirteen or fourteen he made the short journey to Yokohama with the intention of becoming an artist. There he became a student of the well-known English artist Charles Wirgman, who at that time was the correspondent for *The Illustrated London News*. Given Wirgman's friendship with contemporary photographers such as Felix Beato, it is not surprising that Suzuki was exposed to photography at an early stage. Enthralled, he asked Wirgman to explain the rudiments of the art, and following this determined to forsake painting and to embark on a career in this new field.

In 1870 (Saito gives 1867, but Okamoto would have been too young then) he became an apprentice to the famous Shimooka Renjo, and was with him for seven years. In 1876 (Saito gives 1875) he left and opened his first studio in Nagoya, which operated successfully for the next three years. However, not satisfied with the level of his technical knowledge, he decided to study in America becoming, as far as the writer is aware, the first Japanese photographer to study abroad. Leaving the studio in the care of his assistant, he left Japan in 1879 and apprenticed himself to the San Francisco-

based photographer Isaiah West Taber (1830–1912), who at that time was the leading photographer of the West Coast.

Suzuki returned a year later (1881, according to Saito), and had a new studio built in Kudanzaka, Tokyo. This is presumably the "branch" studio referred to in Keeling's 1880 *Tourists' Guide to Yokohama*. Assuming this to be the case, then a clear link is established with his father-in-law, Suzuki Shinichi I. Further evidence is provided by the cabinet card back, illustrated in Fig. 229, which would seem to show both of the Suzukis. Within a very short time the younger Suzuki was winning prizes at Japanese and European exhibitions, and his reputation was growing. In his Tokyo studio he photographed many famous statesmen and dignitaries, including Louis Napoleon and the Hawaiian king in 1881. In 1888 (Saito gives 1889) Izawa claims that Suzuki was honored by receiving a request to photograph the Emperor and Empress. Clearly appreciative of the results, the palace then asked him to photograph the Crown Prince later that year. This was followed in 1890 by a further request to take the Emperor Dowager's portrait.[80]

Around 1890 Suzuki was asked by the government to prepare special presentation albums of views and scenery, which were given to various senior officials in America and Europe by a high-level Japanese delegation sent to study foreign constitutional law. In 1891 the Russian Crown Prince, the future Tsar Nicholas II, visited Japan but had to cut short his trip after being wounded in a failed assassination attempt. At the time, this was a major political embarrassment, and as a further indication of how highly regarded Suzuki had become, the government asked him to prepare a special commemorative album to be presented to the Crown Prince. This album would contain views of all of the hotels on the Tokaido which had been specially prepared to receive him, had his trip gone to schedule.

Izawa's article was written in 1896 when Suzuki was at the height of his fame. According to Saito, Suzuki's success did not last much longer. He apparently lost everything after speculating in the shipping business and died in 1912. It seems that Izaburo, the son of Suzuki Shinichi I, then took control of the Kudanzaka business.

Suzuki was undoubtedly one of the most polished, professional, and famous photographers of the mid-Meiji era, and yet photo-history books today barely give him a mention. Although more research is required before the somewhat complex web of relationships and conflicting dates can be untangled, judging from Izawa's little-known account a reassessment of Suzuki's contribution is overdue. It is perhaps optimistic to expect that in the short term, however, given the existing confusion over the respective identities of Suzuki and his father-in-law.

USUI SHUSABURO

Usui Shusaburo was a fine photographer who operated a successful studio in Yokohama in the 1870s and 1880s aimed specifically at foreign visitors and residents. His aggressive price discounting (see Fig. 231) would have been an assault on the profitability of firms such as Stillfried and Andersen, especially as lower prices did not, in Usui's case, mean lower quality. Quite a few of his souvenir albums containing views and portraits survive. The hand coloring used was often subtle and understated and he was adept at both portrait and landscape work.

However, Usui is another example of an artist about whom very little is known, especially as Japanese sources regarding his life and career are, as in the case of Suzuki, confusing to say the least. It had been thought that Usui opened his first studio in Yokohama in 1878, based on an advertisement placed in that year's *Japan Directory*. However, an advertisement in the January 30th, 1875 issue of the *Japan Weekly Mail*, which was repeated periodically over the next few months, shows that Usui had opened a studio from the beginning of 1875, at the latest. Furthermore, Usui includes in his portfolio a photograph of the opening, in 1872, of Japan's first railway at Yokohama. In fact, according to Saito Takio's *Bakumatsu Meiji* (2004), Usui's studio first opened in 1869.

By 1879 we can see from the *Japan Directory* that Usui is no longer operating as just a portrait studio and has diversified into offering souvenir albums of views and costumes. In addition, he is employing the energetic marketing agent David Welsh, and will become a serious commercial threat to those other Yokohama studios that were also concentrating on the "foreign" market. Gartlan, in his "Stillfried Chronology" (p. 155), cites an interesting court case held on June 28th, 1879, which provides evidence of this growing competition. A resident named John Scott is defending a claim by David Welsh in the sum of 19 yen. Scott, in his defence, states: "When plaintiff presented me his bill in the International Hotel, I told him that I did not owe him 15 yen.... He told me at that time that he would bring me before the Consul, because, when I was bookkeeper at the International Hotel, I had told the guests that his employer, Usui's photographs were not as good as Stillfried and Andersen's. The lawsuit is vexatious."

Welsh's association with Usui was short-lived, because the *Japan Daily Herald* of December 9th, 1879 carried an announcement that Welsh had severed his connection with the studio. Directly, and conveniently beneath this notice, was an advertisement from Baron Franz Stillfried stating that he had that day appointed Welsh as his agent (Gartlan, p. 158).

As an indication of how Usui was beginning to consolidate his reputation, the *Tokio Times* announced on November 1st, 1879 that Ulysses S. Grant (the former US President and war hero) had visited Usui's Tokyo studio: "During General Grant's stay in this capital he sat for his photograph to the well known artist, Mr. Usui, who, having received from the government a copyright for his work, has now on sale cartes de visite of the illustrious visitor" (Gartlan, p. 156). This is the first indication that Usui is also operating in Tokyo.

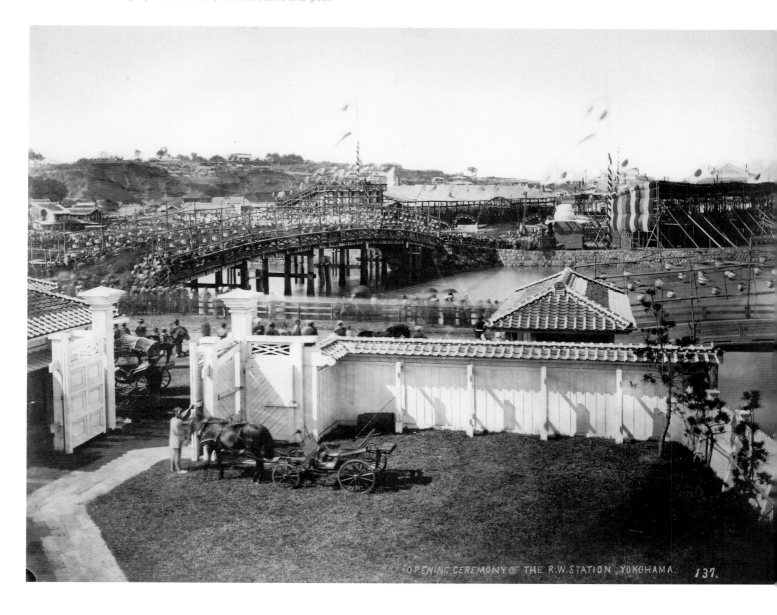

OPENING CEREMONY OF THE R.W. STATION, YOKOHAMA.   *137.*

In July 1882 Usui may have became the first Japanese to successfully take a dry-plate photograph when he and his brother accompanied the British travel writer, naturalist, and amateur photographer Francis Guillemard on two photographic tours of Japan lasting five months in total (see page 226). At this stage, however, there is no proof of Usui's involvement with the process and further research needs to take place.

In 1885 Usui opened up another studio called the Yokohama Photographic Co., with David Welsh once again re-established as his agent. The location at No. 16 Bund was next door to the Stillfried and Andersen studio at No. 17, which had been sold to Adolfo Farsari. Why, exactly, Usui chose to provocatively site his studio in this location is not known. However, any friction was destined to be short-lived as a serious fire in 1886 wiped out Farsari's studio. Farsari would temporarily decamp to No. 61. Usui, "the best and cheapest photographer in Japan," would be back in his Otemachi studio, and Welsh would move to set up his own

fine arts business. Usui continued to advertise until 1889, after which he seems to disappear.

There appears to be no other Western source material on Usui, and when we turn to Japanese sources for details on his life we find them few in number, and contradictory. There is agreement, however, that Usui was born in Shimoda, although the date is unknown, and at some stage he apprenticed to Shimooka Renjo. One photo-historian suggests that Usui was taught by Shimooka during the years 1865–8 when the latter made frequent trips home to Shimoda from his base in Yokohama. Another holds that Shimooka married Usui's sister Mitsume, and took Usui as his apprentice in the early 1860s, with the latter opening his own Yokohama studio between the years 1865 and 1868. A third version suggests that Shimooka did not have time to properly teach Usui in Shimoda, and that Usui therefore moved to Yokohama some time between December 1876 and March 1877, where he studied under the American photographer John Douglas. Shortly after this, he set up his own Yokohama studio.[81]

KEMCHOJI KAMAKURA

Above left Fig. 234. Usui Shusaburo, "Kemchoji Kamakura," ca. 1880, large-format albumen print. Author's Collection.

Left Fig. 235. Usui Shusaburo, "The Entsu Bridge, Kyoto," ca. 1880, large-format hand-colored albumen print. Dr Joseph Dubois Collection. The bridge was built in 1856 to commemorate the 600th anniversary of the death of Shinran, a famous Buddhist philosopher and religious reformer. The pond beautifully reflects the only circle-arch bridge in Japan, and is also known as Megane (spectacles) bridge.

Above Fig. 236. Usui Shusaburo, "Oiran and Attendants," ca. 1880, large-format hand-colored albumen print. Dr Joseph Dubois Collection. An Oiran, a high-class courtesan (prostitute), being carried to her next assignment.

Right Fig. 237. Usui Shusaburo, "Young Man Holding Pipe," large-format hand-colored albumen print, ca. 1880. Dr Joseph Dubois Collection.

It is clear that the above accounts and dates contain contradictions and do not, in some cases, tie in with the known facts outlined earlier. There must be some reason behind the confusion. The answer may lie in the recent discovery by Koyama Noburo that Shusaburo had a brother working in the business. This came out when he was researching Francis Guillemard's journal (page 224), and further study into Usui's life may answer many of the questions which remain. Certainly, Usui Shusaburo was one of Japan's finest photographers and deserves greater recognition.

168.

Left Fig. 238. Usui Shusa-buro, "Geisha and Tea House Girls Relaxing," ca. 1880, large-format hand-colored albumen print. Dr Joseph Dubois Collection.

Above left Fig. 239. Usui Shusaburo, "The Kamibashi Bridge over the River Daiya, Nikko," ca. 1880, large-format albumen print. Author's Collection.

Below left Fig. 240. Usui Shusaburo, "Rural Scene Showing Mount Fuji," ca. 1880, large-format albumen print. Author's Collection.

Below Fig. 241. Usui Shusaburo, "Tattooed Man," ca. 1880, large-format hand-colored albumen print. Dr Joseph Dubois Collection.

NAKAJIMA MATSUCHI

Nakajima Matsuchi (1851–1938) is all but forgotten these days (Fig. 242). However, during the 1880s and 1890s he had a very high reputation, and in 1889 was one of the founding members of the Nihon Shashin Kyokai (Japanese Photographic Society). According to Izawa Shuji in "Sketches of the Lives of a Few of the Leading Professional Photographers in Japan" (1896), he was particularly famous for his lantern slides which were exquisitely hand colored by his wife Sonoko, a very talented artist.

Nakajima, whose given name was Seiichi, was the son of a merchant and born in Shimosa, a coastal village not far from Edo. Like many nineteenth-century Japanese photographers,

he displayed a fondness for painting. A famous artist, Naka-bayashi, visited the village for a few days in 1864 and gave lessons to Nakajima and agreed to take him back with him to Edo as a pupil. Living there with his teacher, he received an education in foreign languages as well as painting.

As a boy, he had been fascinated by a photographic portrait shown to him by a foreigner. Never having forgotten this, he decided at around this time to construct a camera using the lens from a telescope. Lacking any knowledge about chemistry, he acquired a Dutch book which contained the necessary instructions. Presumably, one of the languages he studied was Dutch, because after lengthy experimentation over a period of several years he managed to achieve results, albeit in the form of "fuzzy" images. The onset of the Civil

War in 1868 meant he had to flee back to his native village, but in 1869, at the age of nineteen, he returned to Tokyo but found his teacher had died. Renting a house at Mukojima, opposite Matsuchi Yama, he decided the hill was a good subject for landscape study and every day would point his camera in that direction in attempts to secure good pictures. In view of the time he spent looking at the hill, his neighbors anointed him with the name "Matsuchi." Nakajima decided to adopt this name to be used in all photographic business matters.

At this time there was a large export trade in Japanese paintings, centered in Yokohama. Nakajima spent half his time producing such paintings and the rest in photographic experiments. After inspecting some photographic apparatus in Yokohama, he realized that his results would improve

Below Fig. 245. Ichida Sota, "Street in Kobe Foreign Settlement," early 1870s, albumen-print *carte de visite*. Author's Collection.

Bottom Fig. 246. Ichida Sota, "View of Part of the Foreign Settlement, Kobe," early 1870s, albumen-print *carte de visite*. Author's Collection. One of the distinguishing characteristics of Ichida's work was the occasional appearance of an assistant in the photograph wearing a "happi" coat with the Chinese characters "Ichida Shinko." On the back would sometimes appear a white panel with the word "Photographer" in Roman letters.

were he to invest in a better lens. Not being able to afford to purchase one, he made one himself by visiting a spectacles maker and learning how to grind glass. Although not perfect, it was better than what he had been used to working with and he was able to produce quite good prints.

After overcoming a number of other obstacles, in 1875 he was able to secure some proper apparatus and open a studio in Tokyo. According to Boyd and Izakura's *Portraits in Sepia* (p. 259), Nakajima first took the intermediate step of becoming a student of Yokoyama Matsusaburo. It certainly seems plausible that Nakajima would seek to gain experience in this way. Ever the perfectionist, he would think nothing of asking his customers to return for further sittings even if the customers themselves were otherwise satisfied. In the early years, this amount of dedication helped his reputation to grow and prosper, and he was soon able to build a new studio in Azumabashi-kiwa. In 1894 he moved to sumptuous premises in Gofuku-cho, Nihonbashi.

Nakajima received many honors for his work. At the first and second National Exhibitions in 1877 and 1881, he collected the high class awards on both occasions. The education department also commissioned him to make lantern slides for teaching purposes. He is known to have produced lantern slides, stereographs, *cartes de visite*, and cabinet-size photographs, and it is in these formats that his work has so far been identified. His large-format work may exist in some of the many unidentified souvenir albums waiting to be discovered. It is difficult to assess his work at this stage, although the quality of his lantern slides is exceptionally high (Figs. 243, 244).

ICHIDA SOTA

Ichida Sota (1843–96) was born in present-day Hyogo Prefecture but moved to Kyoto in the early 1860s. After devoting himself to the study of photography, he established a studio there in 1868. Two years later he reasoned that he would be more successful in the newly opened treaty port of Kobe. Accordingly, he transferred his studio there and began to cultivate connections with the foreign community. Ichida seems to have been very successful in doing so, and his work has found its way into many Western collections. He was a regular advertiser in the English-language newspapers and was always looking for opportunities to market his photographs of key events and sporting activities.

An early indication of his ability was given by the editor of the *Hiogo News* in its issue of May 10th, 1871 (p. 146): "Those who wish to possess a memento of the recent Race Meeting, or of the late Athletics Sports, would do well to visit the Photographic studio of Mr. Itchida [*sic*]. It is situated in the Main Street of Kobe, on the right hand, a few doors past the new Government office. Several views were taken of each of the above events, some of which reflect much credit upon the operator."

When the city of Kyoto was opened to foreigners for the duration of its first exhibition (April 17th to July 5th, 1872),

Ichida saw a marketing opportunity and issued the following advertisement in the April 13th issue of the *Hiogo News*, which ran until June 12th:

S. ICHIDA Photographer, of Main Street, Kobe, (formerly of Kioto), Begs to inform his numerous Patrons and intending Visitors to the KIOTO EXHIBITION That he will establish himself at Kioto during the time the Exhibition remains open, and will have on hand a complete assortment of splendid PHOTOGRAPHIC VIEWS of Kioto, Osaka, Hiogo, Kobe, Suma, Akashi, and their neighbourhood, and hopes his well-known style of work will ensure him a visit.

Ichida, now well established, began to extend his business into the import of photographic supplies. In 1877 he exhibited at the first National Industrial Exhibition, along with Ueno Hikoma and Matsuzaki Shinji. In 1882 a local Japanese directory illustrated Ichida's studio at Motomachi 2-chome, and by 1887, when he retired and handed the business over to his adopted son Kojime Hidejiro, the studio was by far the most successful in Kobe and continued well into the 1920s.[82]

Ichida's work is slowly beginning to be identified, and it is becoming clear that his photography was of an exceptionally high standard. Equally adept at portrait and landscape work, it is understandable why he managed to dominate the Kobe region for so many years.

Above Fig. 247. Ichida Sota, "View of Osaka from Yodogawa," early 1870s, large-format albumen print. Tom Burnett Collection.

Right Fig. 248. Ichida Sota, "View of the Kyoto Exhibition at Nishi Honganji," ca. 1871–2, large-format albumen print. Author's Collection. Until 1871 foreigners, other than authorized diplomatic staff, had been prevented from visiting the ancient capital of Kyoto. Access was temporarily given during the Kyoto Exhibition of 1871–2 when Japanese and Chinese antique objects and Japanese "arts and manufactures" were displayed. A number of photographers took advantage of this opportunity to add images of Kyoto to their portfolios, amongst them Felix Beato and Baron Raimund von Stillfried.

YAMAMOTO

Another puzzling studio is that of Yamamoto (his given name is as yet unknown), which appears to have been a prolific producer of souvenir albums in 1870s Yokohama. Most of his work seems to consist of studio shots of exceptionally attractive geisha or *maiko*, or of artisans practicing their trades. Torin Boyd feels that his work is easy to identify from the characteristic studio props. Often a thick, horizontal wooden plank is shown leaning against the baseboard. A variant is a horizontal backdrop board, approximately two feet (60 cm) in height, with a lattice-like design. The plain wooden studio flooring sometimes has stones or pebbles scattered over it. Yamamoto may have died early, or given up photography, because his work subsequently appears amongst the 1880s portfolios of other photographers such as Tamamura Kozaburo and Kusakabe Kimbei. This, in turn, has led to confusion in respect of attributing the work of those two artists.

There is a very important Yamamoto album in the collection of the JCII Camera Museum, Tokyo. It is a small, concertina style souvenir album bound in traditional Japanese cloth. The photographs, approximately 5 x 3 1/2 inches (130 x 90 mm), are hand colored in the usual way. Pasted on the front endpaper is a photographic label, illustrated in Fig. 249, which shows the name and address of Yamamoto's studio. Many of the photographs are contained in other similar albums – all appear to be from the mid- to late 1870s – and exist, previously unidentified, in collections around the world. These can now be attributed to the Yamamoto studio. The studio props are quite distinctive, and a number are illustrated here. Sometimes the Yamamoto name can be seen chalked in Japanese characters on the background wall or screen, or on the clothing of the subjects of a photograph.[83]

Yamamoto also issued larger albums where the photographs were approximately 10 x 8 inches (260 x 210 mm). The JCII album, most unusually, contains the Yamamoto studio name and address. The evidence of the photographs themselves suggests that Yamamoto was an extremely talented operator whose portraits, in particular, are most striking. Unfortunately, we currently know nothing more about this artist.

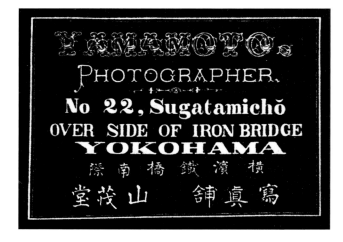

Above left Fig. 251. Yamamoto Studio, "Women Spinning," ca. 1870s, large-format hand-colored albumen print. Dr Joseph Dubois Collection. Notice the characteristic lattice-design studio backdrop.

Below left Fig. 252. Yamamoto Studio, "Cooper," ca. 1870s, large-format hand-colored albumen print. Author's Collection.

Above Fig. 253. Yamamoto Studio, "Woman in Kago," ca. 1870s, large-format hand-colored albumen print. Dr Joseph Dubois Collection.

Right Fig. 254. Yamamoto Studio, "Lady with Attendant," ca. 1870s, large-format hand-colored albumen print. Dr Joseph Dubois Collection.

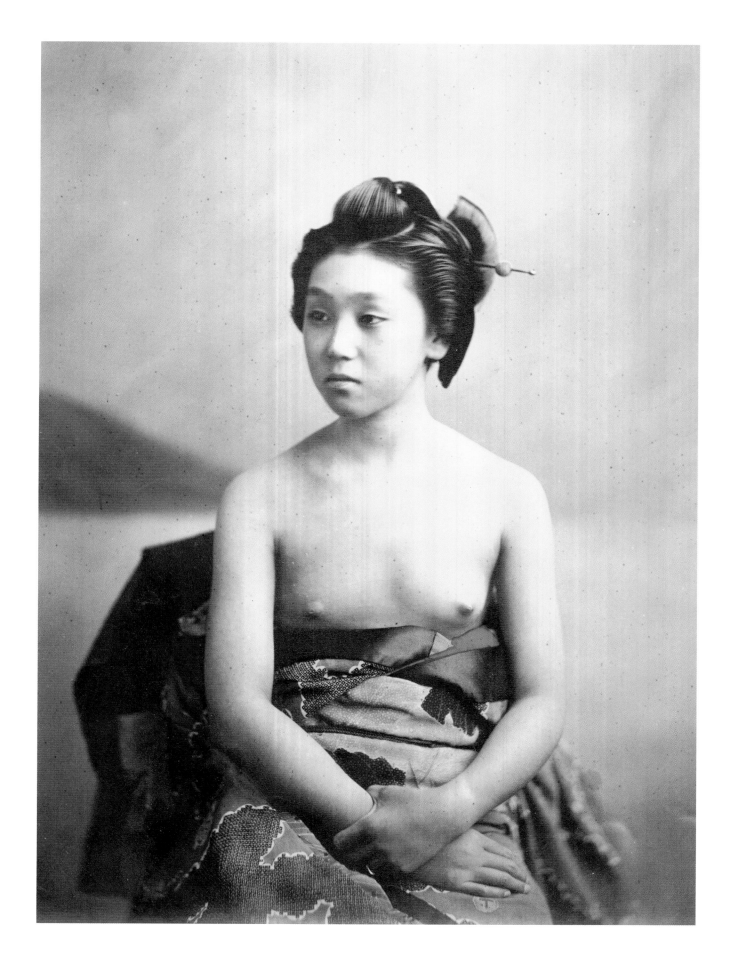

OTHER JAPANESE PHOTOGRAPHERS

Futami Asama (1852–1908) was apprenticed to Kitaniwa Tsukuba (see below) for four years from 1869 (Fig. 257). Thereafter he worked with Stillfried until 1876. He then decided to set up his own studio in Tokyo, and this was opened in 1877. At this time he was commissioned by the government to photograph the peak and crater of Mount Fuji, and the results were exhibited at the National Industrial Exhibition. Futami also received a lot of patronage from the foreign community and advertised extensively in the travel guides and trade directories. Like Nakajima, it is very likely that his work is lying undiscovered amongst the mass of currently unidentified souvenir albums. His name is also rendered as Asakuma (Fig. 258).

Kanamaru Genzo (1832–?) was an early pioneer in Tokyo, where he opened his studio in Asakusa, Umayabashi. He is recorded as taking on Tamamura Kozaburo as an apprentice, but once the latter left in 1874 nothing more is known of the studio. Kanamaru's work can occasionally be found in the smaller-sized accordion-style souvenir albums from the 1870s.

Endo Rikuro operated a studio in Sendai, northeast Japan, from 1878. He assisted Esaki Reiji in 1884 when the latter was trying to photograph the eclipse of the sun.[84] He was well situated to photograph the eruption of nearby Mount Bandai in 1888, and this early example of photo-journalism proved to be a good marketing opportunity for Endo, who successfully sold sets of twenty-eight photographs of the disaster. Three years later, in 1891, he was the official photographer on an expedition to the Kuril Islands, and in 1902 he moved to Taiwan and opened a studio there.

Photographer **Shimizu Tokoku** (1841–1907) is forgotten today. However, during the first decade of the Meiji era, he was considered the equal of Uchida Kuichi and Yokoyama Matsusaburo. The 1875 guidebook *Santo miyage* (Souvenirs of the Three Cities), recommended the Tokyo studios of Shimizu and Yokoyama as being the best. The Parisian journal *Le Moniteur de la Photographie* remarked in its September 15th, 1875 issue that "the Yokohama photographer Shimizu exhibits great skill in portrait work which is the equal of that produced by Europeans."[85] In 1877 the publication *Shashin mitate kurabe* (Graded Evaluation of Tokyo Photographers), mentioned in Tucker et al.'s *History of Japanese Photography* (2003, p. 24), placed Shimazu in the same top rank as Uchida, Yokoyama, and Kitaniwa. This is praise indeed! His studio is listed in E. M. Satow and A. G. S. Hawes' *A Handbook for Travellers in Central and Nothern Japan* (1881). According to Yokohama's *Saishoku Arubamu* (1987), Shimazu studied photography in the late 1850s at the naval college in Nagasaki before opening his first studio on Bashamichi, Yokohama, in 1868. He transferred to Nihonbashi, Tokyo, in 1872 and had branch studios in the city at Gofukucho and Hamacho. In 1881 he received the medal of merit at the second National Industrial Exhibition. Shimizu seems to have concentrated on taking portraits of the rich and famous, and there is no record of his issuing souvenir albums.

Ida Kokichi (1846–1911) was born in Hakodate and apprenticed to Tamoto Kenzo. According to Tucker et al. (p. 344), he assisted Tamoto in photographing Sapporo, Otaru, and other places in Hokkaido in 1871, becoming the first to photograph in that region. He was also the first to photograph in the northernmost Kuril Islands when, in 1878, at his own expense, he accompanied an official settlement office ship traveling there and took a number of ambrotypes. He opened his own studio in Hakodate in 1884. A pioneering photographer in all senses of the word, in 1897 he became the first to open a studio on the remote island of Sakhalin, where he stayed until the start of the Russo-Japanese War in 1904.

The city of Nagoya's best-known early studio was run by **Miyashita Kin**, who studied photography under Yokoyama Matsusaburo in Tokyo. Miyashita's studio operated at various locations in the city and began life some time in the 1870s. Listings in the *Japan Directory* show that the successful studio was still in operation in 1912. Miyashita is best known for photographing the aftermath of the devastating earthquake which struck the prefectures of Gifu and Aichi in 1891 – the worst natural disaster to afflict Japan in the whole of the Meiji era. Four examples of his work were reproduced in the book of the event by J. Milne and W. K. Burton, *The Great Earthquake in Japan 1891* (1892) (Fig. 265).

Left Fig. 257. Anonymous, "Futami Asama," ca. 1890. Old Japan Picture Library.

Below Fig. 258. Futami Asakuma (Asama) Studio Advertisement. *Japan Directory*, 1882. The wording here is the only evidence that has so far come to light that Futami may have been offering souvenir albums of views and costumes.

Left Fig. 259. Kanamaru Genzo, "Japanese Archer," ca. early 1870s, small-format albumen print. Author's Collection.

Above Fig. 260. Kanamaru Genzo, "Relaxation," ca. early 1870s, small-format hand-colored albumen print. Author's Collection. Kanamaru's work appears to have been first identified in *Old Japan Catalogue* 29, issued in February 1999, where six signed images were listed.

Below Fig. 261. Kanamaru Genzo, "Ladies at Their Toilet," ca. early 1870s, small-format hand-colored albumen print. Author's Collection.

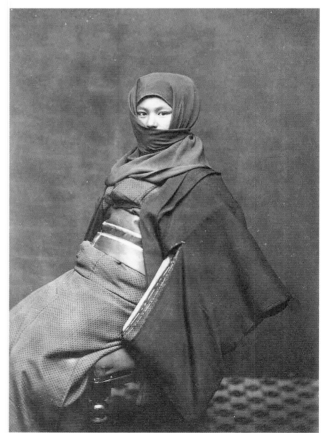

Matsuzaki Shinji was an interesting photographer whose activities span the 1860s to 1880s. Very little is known about his life, but in the 1860s we know he operated a studio in Nakahashi Izumi-cho, Tokyo. In May 1874 he traveled with the military expedition to Taiwan as an official photographer. His photographic colleague **Kumagai Shin** was fatally wounded there by a stray bullet. The photographs taken at the time have unfortunately not come to light despite a notice of their sale the following year: "The photographer, Matsuzaki Shinji, who went to Formosa with the Japanese Expedition, has commenced the sale of the views, costumes, and portraits taken during his stay there" (*Japan Gazette Mail Summary*, February 25th, 1875, p. 38). In *The Far East* issue for March 1875, there is a curious portrait entitled "The Formosan Captive Girl." Frustratingly, there is no more detailed explanation, nor mention of the photographer. It may well have been Matsuzaki.

In 1875 the Japanese government felt the need to reassert its claim over the Ogasawara Islands, and in October Matsuzaki accompanied Meiji government officials as official photographer. A number of these images have survived and illustrate how photography was able to be used to help the government in its political aims of establishing Japan's territorial limits. In 1877 Matsuzaki won an honorable mention at the first National Industrial Exhibition in Tokyo. He also produced photographs of the exhibits and exhibition grounds in Ueno Park, and advertised their sale in the *Japan Daily Herald* on March 7th, 1878, from his Tokyo studio at 5, Umezono-cho, Yushima. In April 1880 he and others, including Esaki Reiji, established the short-lived photography magazine *Shashin zasshi*. In 1886 Matsuzaki published the first Japanese manual on studio portrait photography, *Shashin Hitsuyo Shakyaku no Kokoroe*. We hear nothing about him after this date.

Takebayashi Seiichi (1842–1908) was born in Hirosaki, Aomori Prefecture. He apparently opened a studio in Hakodate in 1871, which almost immediately was destroyed by fire. The following year he acted as Stillfried's assistant for some fifty days when the Austrian was commissioned by the Hokkaido Settlement Office to photograph the area. When this work was finished, Takebayashi purchased some of the surplus photographic equipment and continued to photograph in Hokkaido, including portraits of the Ainu. He opened a studio in Sapporo in 1876, but shifted the main focus of his activities to Tokyo where he set up his main studio in Kojimachi in November 1884 (Tucker et al., p. 363).

Kitaniwa Tsukuba (1842–87) was, as we have seen above, considered to be in the first rank of Tokyo photographers in 1877. Again, however, his career to date does not seem to have received much attention. He was born Ii Konosuke, the son of an oil wholesaler in Edo, but changed his name when aged around thirty. His training was exceptional since he was apprenticed to Yokoyama Matsusaburo in 1868, and then served at various times with Ukai Gyokusen and Shimooka Renjo. He opened his first studio in 1871 at the Asakusa flower gardens, Tokyo, and a second in the same city shortly afterwards. At around this time, he received lessons from Stillfried in fixing and lighting techniques and thereby

further improved his knowledge. In 1874 he established *Datsuei yawa* (Tales of Photography), which is believed to be the first photographic magazine. His business prospered, and in 1875, following the early death of Uchida Kuichi, he somehow acquired a major portion of the estate, including the late photographer's main residence. From there he operated a studio which he named Kyu Uchida-sha (former Uchida studio). The following year he began to sell medical photographs and he also opened a photographic school. He seems to have suspended all photographic activities in 1885.

High on the list of tourist venues were the Hakone lakes and mountains and, of course, Mount Fuji. A very popular hotel in the vicinity then, and now, was the Fujiya Hotel, which opened in Miyanoshita in 1878. The owner persuaded the Yokohama-based photographer **Shima Shukichi** (1850–1917) to open a studio within a short walk of the hotel (Fig. 266). It is still in operation and being run by Shima's descendants. In his article "A Traveler's Paradise" (2004), the collector and researcher F. A. Sharf wrote that Shima offered the usual studio portrait facilities and the standard souvenir albums of views and costumes. The studio majored in photographs of the surrounding Hakone district, but was not averse to buying in views of other parts of Japan from other studios. As a result, it is very difficult to attribute Shima's work.

1880s
Western Studios
Give Way

By the year 1884 both Felix Beato and Raimund von Stillfried had left Japan, never to return. Their departure is symbolic and indicative of the declining fortunes of Western photo studios in Japan. Always a precarious business at the best of times, only the exceptional quality of their work had enabled them to survive, although this did not prevent others from trying to emulate their success. However, with the exception of Farsari in Yokohama and the Gordes brothers in far-off Nagasaki, no Western studio generated enough business to prevent displacement by the increasing number of Japanese studios opening in the treaty ports. Many of these new studios were run by Japanese who were comfortable dealing with foreigners, having been apprenticed themselves to Western photographers, or even having traveled abroad. Moreover, the studios of operators such as Usui, Esaki, Kusakabe, Tamamura, Ogawa, and others were by now well versed in the latest photographic techniques and able to produce quality photographs at a much lower price than their Western counterparts.

Hermann Andersen would run out of steam after trading off the Stillfried and Andersen name for a few years, and Franz von Stillfried would also fail to match the success of his more talented brother. In an inauspicious start to his photographic career in Japan, he felt obliged to join in the price discounting war started by the Japanese. This was not a good sign, and was a clear indication that the commercial environment for Western photo-studios in Japan was becoming intolerable. Farsari, showing infinitely more imagination and business acumen than he would later claim, refused to compete on price and, instead, offered a quality product that was expertly marketed. He survived the decade and may even have continued successfully into the next had he not returned to Italy in 1890. But it is more likely that he left at the peak of his success; disappointment and frustration may well have awaited him had he stayed on. In Nagasaki, Henri and Auguste Gordes, Japan's only other significant Western studio, would fail to make it into the 1890s.

Apart from the steady transfer of technical know-how from West to East, the other major development which made it so much easier for the Japanese to compete was the introduction into Japan of the new and practical gelatin dry-plate photographic process. This technology had proved itself to be far more reliable than the earlier, experimental collodion dry plates. Now less equipment had to be carried, and fewer chemicals purchased. Farsari was an early beneficiary and was able to tell his sister that photography was just a "mechanical process." In 1882 Francis Guillemard would be the first to use these dry plates in Japan, followed closely by Hugues Krafft and Esaki Reiji. By the end of the 1880s Japanese photography had developed into an industry that was rapidly maturing, self-sufficient, and increasingly self-confident. After 1890 there were no significant Western-run studios in Japan.

TAMAMURA KOZABURO

Few photographers were as successful as Tamamura Kozaburo (1856–19?) in marketing their work to foreign residents and visitors (Fig. 268). In 1909 the editors of the business publication *Yokohama Seiko Meiyokan* wrote that Tamamura and Company was the largest tax-paying photographic business in Japan. The year before, on March 11th, 1908, the company had advertised a 50 percent discount in the local newspaper *Yokohama Boeki Shimpo* to celebrate the twenty-fifth anniversary of its Yokohama studio. The same newspaper carried an article stating that Tamamura was the best photographer in Japan. Was this appellation justified, and what were the reasons behind Tamamura's success?

Tamamura was born in Edo in 1856. He was the eldest child born into a family of hereditary retainers to the Hoshinno of Rinnoji, a branch of the imperial family whose head had served as chief priest of the main temple in Nikko since 1654. His early life is not well documented, but it is known that in 1867 he took an apprenticeship with the photographer Kanamaru Genzo, based in Edo's Asakusa district.

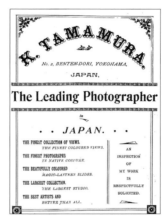

Unfortunately, even less is known about Kanamaru, whose studio seemed to disappear at the same time that Tamamura's seven-year apprenticeship ended in 1874. It was then that Tamamura opened his first studio in the Okuyama area of Asakusa – a simple outdoor *shajo*.

As can be deduced from the 1908 advertisement mentioned above, Tamamura opened his Yokohama studio in 1883. The first mention of this studio appeared in the 1883 *Japan Directory* (Fig. 269). The address, No. 2 Benten-dori, would be the center of his operations for the next thirty years until a move to 1498 Nakamura, Bluff, in 1913. A major branch was opened in Kobe in 1899 at No. 193 Motomachi, and later Kobe addresses were at No. 16 Sannomiya and No. 42 Nishi-machi. The manager at the No. 16 address from 1903 was one Takagi Teijiro who is shown, by the 1904 *Japan Directory*, as the proprietor and continuing to trade under the Tamamura name (until 1914 by which time it has been phased out) but only acting as an agent for Tamamura's work. Tamamura's son Kihei (?–1951) took over the family business in 1916 and the studio is listed, apparently for the last time, in the 1925 *Japan Directory*. The business may not have recovered from the disaster of 1923 when a devastating earthquake of that year destroyed many businesses in Yokohama and Tokyo.

Tamamura's business strategy was clear from his first Yokohama studio advertisement issued in 1883: his main line would be to sell souvenir albums of views and costumes to foreigners. And in this he was remarkably consistent. It

quickly became a winning formula, and there seemed no need to change it. He commissioned album covers which were lacquer covered and decorated with painted Japanese landscape scenes containing typical motifs such as Mount Fuji, *jinrikishas*, and geisha. Many designs were expensively overlaid with cloisonné, pieces of ivory, gold leaf, and mother-of-pearl. The more elaborate the design, the higher the cost.

Tamamura also made great play in his advertisements of offering photographs that had been produced using the best chemicals so that the customer would be purchasing images that "would not early deteriorate." His photographs were almost always colored, and he emphasized the great care in doing so. An advertisement in the 1891 *Japan Directory* summarized matters in this way: "The largest and the best stock of the finest views of celebrated places in Japan.... My colouring has been pronounced by competent judges to be unsurpassed by any in this country, although my charges are much lower than those made by other photographers. Attention is also called to the fact that as I use only the best chemicals

9 TORII AT NIKKO.

my photographs are durable and do not fade." The late nineteenth century was a time when photographers need not be overly constrained by any false sense of modesty, let alone by any dubious advertising statements. But to be fair to Tamamura and, for that matter, to his two great rivals of the time, Farsari and Kusakabe, the photographs in many of the albums produced by his studio have lasted remarkably well, exhibiting fresh, bright coloring. Moreover, his studio would not have been able sustain its customer base for thirty years without a great deal of attention being given to the quality of the finished product.

Among the lucrative commissions received from private organizations, his Tokyo studio was asked, in 1882, to produce a series of "tea industry" photographs for a Japanese tea company, which were to be used to promote the company's product overseas. As these proved successful, according to Ogawa Dosokai's *Sogyo Kinen Sanju Nenshi* (1913), the studio was asked to produce similar material for other industries.

Silk must have been one of these, since Tamamura in his 1883 advertisement offered sets of tea and silk industry photographs for sale. Another supposedly unique set of pictures was some photographs "of the interior of the Nikko temples [which] can only be purchased at our store." These were advertised in the 1893 edition of Tomita Gentaro's *Stranger's Handbook of the Japanese Language* (1893).

Other commissions around this time came from the universities of Cambridge and Chicago who sent in large orders for glass slides. After moving to Yokohama, Tamamura's business continued to grow and he occasionally traveled abroad on photo assignments and also won prizes at domestic and international exhibitions. By 1896 *The Practical Photographer* was able to assert: "Mr. Tamamura is one of the most popular, perhaps the most popular of the professional photographers in Yokohama...."[86] It was at this time also that Tamamura received what must have been one of the most profitable commissions ever received by a photographer from a publisher.

The *Mainichi Shimbun* of July 19th, 1896 reported that Tamamura had just exported 40,000 photographs of various sizes to the Boston publishing house J. B. Millet. These were required for insertion in the work *Japan: Described and Illustrated by the Japanese* by Captain Francis Brinkley. But this was only the first instalment of what turned out to be an enormous order for more than one million(!) hand-colored albumen photographs. Tamamura used over 350 assistants over several months to help with the printing and coloring. The book was issued in at least sixteen different editions over the next few years (see Tucker et al., p. 28), with the Edition de Luxe alone requiring just under 200,000 photographs.[87] Other less expensive editions, such as the Orient Edition, only required approximately 7000 photographs, but arriving at a figure of one million photographs is not as difficult as it might appear. Although no doubt a highly lucrative exercise for Tamamura, it is likely that he cut corners as far as the production was concerned. Because so many of these books were produced, it is not difficult to come across copies today. Invariably, the illustrations are pale, either as a result of poor coloring, printing, or both. It also looks extremely likely that extensive use of copy photographs was made. It is easy to criticize from this time and distance, however, and there may well have been no other way to satisfy the requirements of the publishers. Nevertheless, it would be interesting to consult the Millet archives to see whether any specific directions given at the time still exist.[88]

Tamamura is mentioned in the diaries of Richard Gordon Smith, the globetrotter and amateur photographer who spent some years in Japan. Smith was not satisfied with the studio's hand coloring of photographs he himself had taken in Burma. In a diary entry for March 15th, 1900, reproduced in Victoria

Manthorpe's *The Japan Diaries of Richard Gordon Smith* (1986, p. 48), he states: "Went to Tamamura this morning for my coloured photos of Burma. They were badly done. The moment a Japanese leaves his own country he can neither paint nor think...." A few weeks later, in Kobe, he complained that his photographs had been spoiled whilst being developed at the Tamamura studio there: "Developed photographs with Tamamura; the ass let in too much light and spoiled most of them. I would have given a good deal for the privilege of knocking him down, but here in Japan this means from between three and six months' imprisonment, without the option of a fine" (May 1st, 1900). However, the final photographic reference we come across in his diaries indicates that he had perhaps developed a more friendly relationship with Tamamura: "Mrs. Tamamura came to tea in the afternoon."[89] Reproductions of Tamamura's photographs can be found in, amongst other publications, the September 1896 issue of *The Practical Photographer* and in E. Burton Holmes' *Burton Holmes Travelogues* (1910).

Tamamura's photographic enterprise was a huge commercial success and he can only have achieved this by delivering on the promises made in his advertisements. The mainstay of the business was always the sale of souvenir albums to foreigners, but he always insured that these were of high quality and offered at competitive prices. There is no doubting the artistic excellence of his work, but if there is a criticism it would be that the selection of views in the albums is not anywhere near as varied as one might think, given his assertion in the 1893 *Japan Directory* advertisement to having in excess of 1200 landscape views from which to choose. Tamamura, in the final analysis, was not only a shrewd and successful business man, but also a fine photographer.

KUSAKABE KIMBEI

Kusakabe Kimbei (1841–1932) remains one of the most underrated Japanese photographers of the nineteenth century (Fig. 276). Because of his concentration on producing souvenir albums containing hand-colored views and costumes for foreigners, he is better known today in the West than he is in Japan (Figs. 277, 278). For today's collectors of early photograph albums, pride of place will always be given to Felix Beato and Raimund von Stillfried for their respective output in the 1860s and 1870s. However, from the 1880s onwards, no studio comes close to matching Kusakabe's for the consistent quality and variety of its output.

Kusakabe was fortunate in having worked for both Beato and Stillfried, although when he did so and for how long is not quite clear. He certainly had time, however, to master the intricacies and technical demands of wet-plate photography. He would also have understood how, stylistically, the two men differed in their approach and yet still produced work of the highest order. Given this experience, it is interesting to see how Kusakabe's own style evolved.

Left Fig. 277. Kusakabe Kimbei Souvenir Album with Lacquer, Ivory and Shibiyama Design, ca. 1880s. Author's Collection.

Below Fig. 278. Kusakabe Kimbei Souvenir Album, ca. 1880s. Author's Collection.

K. KIMBEI,

No. 3, Benten-Dori, Yokohama.

PHOTOGRAPHIC

Views of Japan and Costumes of the Japanese
Neatly and Cheaply Executed.

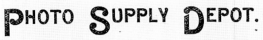

PHOTO SUPPLY DEPOT.

Wholesalers and Retailers of Eastman's Kodaks, Films, Dry plates, etc.

The largest and cheapest photographic suppliers in town.

Developing, Printing, and Colouring for Amateurs.

ALSO

DEALER IN

Japanese Coloured Photographs and Coloured Magic Lantern Slides.

K. KIMBEI. Telephone No. 161.

Main Store :—No. 7, Honcho, Yokohama.
Branch Store :—No. 22, Ginza Sanchome, Tokyo.

Photographer AND PAINTER. **K. KIMBEI.** No. 7, HONCHO-DORI, (Next door to the Town Hall), YOKOHAMA.

FINEST AND BEST PHOTOGRAPHS.

A choice of 2,000 Views and Costumes, 8 inches by 10 inches ∴ ∴ $2.00 per dozen.
Coloured Photographs 17 inches by 22 inches ∴ ∴ ∴ $2.00 each.
Beautifully Coloured Magic Lantern Slides. ∴ ∴ ∴ $6.00 per dozen.

Coloured views of places of note in Japan, Costumes, Groups, &c. Portraits taken in the best style in Card, Cabinet and Imperial size, &c. Albums filled to order, and made up with Choice Pictures, Richly Lacquered and Tastefully Painted in gold, &c., and strongly bound. Also reproduction and outdoor work accurately executed at the lowest possibl prices.

PHOTOTYPE MACHINES WILL ARRIVE EARLY IN JANUARY, 1892.

Below left and right Fig. 283. Kusakabe Kimbei Studio Price List, ca. 1893. Fred Sharf Collection. Although this price list (which forms part of the Kusakabe catalogue of photographs) is not dated, from the listed price of the mammoth plates, which increased in 1894 from $2 to $2.30, we can infer a date of ca. 1893. It is interesting to see the relative

expense of lantern slides, and that Kusakabe produced "giant" prints of 32 x 24 inches (81 x 61 cm)! The writer is not aware of any of these prints having survived.

PHOTOGRAPHIC PRICE LIST.

PRICE LIST OF PORTRAITS.

Sizes.	First order 1 dozen.	First order ½ dozen.	First order 3 Copies.	2nd order each.	Colored Extra each.
Carte de Visite.	$ 2.50	$ 1.80		cts. .15	cts. .15
Cabinet	„ 4.00	„ 3.00		„ .25	„ .20
Boudoir	„ 6.50	„ 4.50		„ .40	„ .35
10 × 8	„ 9.00	„ 6.50		„ .50	„ .50
12 × 10	„ 10.00	„ 7.00		„ .60	„ .60
16 × 11			$ 12.00	„ 1.00	„ 2.00
22 × 17			„ 25.00	„ 3.00	„ 3.00

In case only one or two copies are required charge will be the same as for ½ dozen (exception of 11 × 16 & 17 × 22 inches.)

PHOTOGRAPHS OF 2000 CHOICE VIEWS AND COSTUMES OF JAPAN AND ALSO BEAUTI-FULLY COLORED PHOTOGRHPHIC SILK FANS.

10 × 8 Colored Photographs ...... Each	$ .20
„ Uncolored „ ...... „	$ .15
„ Colored „ ...... Per Dozen	$ 2.00
„ Uncolored „ ...... „ „	$ 1.50
13¾ × 10¾ inches Lacq'd Cover Album with 50 photos	$15.00
„ „ „ „ „ „ 100 „	$25.00
15½ × 12½ „ „ „ „ 50 „	$40.00
„ „ „ „ „ „ 100 „	$31.00
22 × 17 Colored Photographs ...... Each	$ 2.00
„ „ „ ...... Per Dozen	$22.00
„ Uncolored „ ...... „ „	$ 1.20
„ „ „ ...... „ „	$13.00
Beautifully Colored Magic Lantern Slides Per Dozen	$ 6.00
Uncolored „ „ „ „ „	$ 3.00
32 × 24 Composite Photographs ...... Each	$ 3.00
Beautifully Colored Silk Fans ...... „	$ .50
„ „ „ „ ...... Per Dozen	$ 5.00

Tourists favouring us with a visit will receive every attention and courtesy,

Yours faithfully,

K. KIMBEI,
PHOTOGRAPHIC STUDIO,
7, Honcho, Yokohama.
(NEXT TO TOWN HALL.)

Kusakabe's landscapes are particularly fine and his series on the beautiful Nakasendo scenery demonstrates his skill in this area (Fig. 291). In his portrait work he appears to have focused on Stillfried's fondness for extracting the sitter's personality. Intuitively, he seems to take this one step further. No doubt benefiting from being Japanese himself, his best portraits seem to convey a heightened and deeper sense of connectivity between us and the subject – sometimes with a jarring psychological intensity. However, a word of warning. In his early career, Kusakabe was not averse to acquiring the negatives of other photographers and reproducing prints from them as part of his portfolio. That is why his albums often contain the work of artists such as Uchida, Beato, Stillfried, and Yamamoto.

Not that much is known about Kusakabe's life. He was born into a family of textile merchants in Kofu, Yamanashi Prefecture, and his family name was Matsuya. He left home at eighteen to become an artist in Yokohama, and some time in the 1860s he joined Felix Beato, initially to assist in the hand coloring of photographs, but than as a fully fledged assistant. At the end of 1867 he accompanied Beato on a photographic trip to Shanghai, according to Kusakabe's 103-year-old granddaughter, Uchida Tama, in a 1992 interview she gave to Matsumoto Itsuya, who then wrote about it in his book *Bakumatsu Hyoryu* (1993).[90] Later, in the 1870s, he joined Stillfried but it is not known how long he stayed. There is a reference in the January 16th, 1872 issue of *The Far East*, which refers to an artist of high quality silk paintings, going by the name 'Kimbey': "... the patent pre-Raphaelism of the artist can be shown ... the artist, Mr. Kimbey, has other pictures of a kindred character for disposal: and those who would like to possess good specimens of Japanese Art, should become possessors of them." Kusakabe always used "Kimbei" as his studio name. When doing so, he undoubtedly had it in

mind that his foreign clientele would find the name easier to pronounce and remember. This reference suggests that Kusakabe left Beato and attempted to run his own art studio before joining Stillfried.

What we know for sure is that Kusakabe had opened his own Yokohama photographic studio or shop by 1880 at No. 3, Benten-dori, because his advertisement appears in W. E. L. Keeling's *Tourists' Guide to Yokohama* for that year (Fig. 279). The advertisement offers views and costumes of Japan, but it is not clear whether a portrait studio is in operation. An advertisement in the 1883 *Japan Directory*, by which time the business is located at No. 36, still avoids the term "photographer" or "photographic studio" and, significantly, Kusakabe describes himself as a dealer in photographic views. Experience shows that Kusakabe's early albums do indeed include prints from other photographers' negatives – or copies of the prints themselves. He would have known very well that foreign customers would often request albums of views from all parts of the country, and satisfying their demand in this way would give him time to extend his own portfolio outside the confines of Yokohama and district.

According to Saito's *Bakumatsu Meiji* (2004), Kusakabe was baptized a Christian in 1885 at the Yokohama Kaigan Church. That same year the *Japan Directory* shows that he expanded his business to occupy Nos. 27 and 36 Benten-dori. By 1887 the advertisements show that he operated as a photographer from 36 and as a dealer from 27. We can surmise that albums put together at the 27 address would most likely contain work from other studios. Interestingly, the 1887 advertisement also mentions the availability of "Screens, Kakemono painted on Silk from Photographs &c &c." which can be purchased at No. 4, Benten-dori. This could well be a continuation of his art business advertised in the 1872 issue of *The Far East* mentioned above. In 1889 (or possibly early 1890), the

Above Fig. 284. Kusakabe Kimbei, "Yokohama Foreign Settlement," ca. 1880s, three-plate large-format albumen print. Author's Collection.

Below Fig. 285. Kusakabe Kimbei, "512. Main Street Yokohama," ca. 1880, large-format hand-colored albumen print. Author's Collection. This atmospheric print of early Yokohama can be dated to the years 1880–1. This is because two shop signs can be seen in the picture: "G Blass Pioneer Store" and "Kiln(er & Handel)." These businesses were at 70 and 72 Main Street respectively only during this period. The scene represents, therefore, one of Kusakabe's first views of Yokohama.

Below Fig. 286. Kusakabe Kimbei, "109. Samurais [*sic*] in Armour," ca. 1880, large-format hand-colored albumen print. Author's Collection.

110. BASKET SELLER.

Above left Fig. 287. Kusakabe Kimbei, "110. Basket Seller," ca. 1880, large-format hand-colored albumen print. Author's Collection. Note the trademark Kusakabe studio handles to the far right of the back screen.

Below left Fig. 288. Kusakabe Kimbei, "530. Creek, Yokohama," ca. 1880, large-format hand-colored albumen print. Author's Collection. The shop sign just left of center reads "Pianos & Organs, J. G. Doering."

Below and right Figs. 289, 290. Kusakabe Kimbei, "218. Figures," ca. 1880s, large-format hand-colored albumen print. National Gallery of Victoria, Melbourne. This photograph, with its cryptic title from the Kusakabe catalogue, is most curious. It appears to be an example of the genre known as "Shinrei Shashin" or ghost photograph. Here we appear to have two Kabuki actors with one holding a cabinet card. It is likely to be the portrait of a dead lady, who unbeknown to the actors is standing behind them. The Kimbei studio name can just be made out on the back of the card.

studio made its final move and consolidated its main business at the prestigious address of No. 7, Honcho-dori (Main Street), which was next door to the Town Hall.[91]

The following year we see Kusakabe describing himself as a photographer and painter. In 1892 the studio advertises a selection of some 2000 views and costumes, and in 1893 offers hand-colored mammoth-plate photographs measuring 17 x 20 inches (43 x 56 cm). That same year the *Japan Directory* mentions K. Kimbei as being the manager of the Yokohama-based Akitsu Co. Fine Art Depot. This seems to have been a very short-term appointment, however. By 1897 Kusakabe has embraced printing and collotyping, and in 1901 we have the first mention of the sale of hand-colored, photographically illustrated silk fans – a specialty of Kusakabe's. It should be noted, however, that this technique was first announced by Kajima Seibei at a meeting of the Photographic Society of Japan on September 27th, 1889, as reported in the *Japan Weekly Mail* of October 12th. In the 1901 edition of the *Japan Directory*, Kusakabe was able to state that his studio was the largest in Japan. And by 1907 the business styled itself as a Photo Supply Depot where film, cameras, and general photographic supplies were offered wholesale and retail (Fig. 280). Photographs were mentioned, but seemed to be taking a lower profile.

Kusakabe's son was not interested in taking over his father's business, and Ogawa Sashichi, Kusakabe's son-in-law, would have been the natural successor. However, Ogawa died in 1909 and Kusakabe retired five years later, in 1914, and spent his later years painting. By 1930 Kusakabe's health was worsening and he went to live with his granddaughter, Uchida Tama, in Ashiya City, near Kobe, where he died in 1932. Tama herself, who was Ogawa's daughter, died in Ashiya City in 1995 at the age of 106. She had survived the 1923 earthquake and would also experience the Hanshin earthquake in her final year.

OGAWA KAZUMASA

Ogawa Kazumasa (1860–1929) was, in so many ways, a pivotal figure in the history of Japanese photography (Fig. 292). A consummate professional, and arguably the most complete Japanese photographer of the Meiji era, he succeeded in acquiring cutting-edge Western technology and using it to build one of the most successful photographic businesses in Japan. Always innovative, he developed techniques which insured his collotype work was the equal of anything to be found in the West, and he was instrumental in introducing Japanese art to a mass international audience. Equally comfortable with portrait and landscape work, he was undoubtedly a match for any of his contemporaries. Significantly, his three main rivals for the foreign market, Kusakabe, Tamamura, and Farsari, all found themselves co-operating and contributing to his photographic publications. By example alone, Ogawa dispelled any lingering feelings of inferiority held by Japanese studios towards their Western counterparts.

We are fortunate in that Ogawa's life and career are well chronicled in an exceedingly rare 1913 publication (discovered some years ago by Boyd and Izakura), edited by Ogawa Dosokai and called *Sogyo Kinen Sanju Nenshi*, which celebrated the Tokyo studio's thirty years of existence.

Ogawa's father was a samurai and retainer of the Matsudaira clan in present-day Saitama Prefecture. Born in 1860, Ogawa said he could just remember the civil war of 1868–9 which brought an end to the 250-year rule of the Tokugawa shogunate. In an interview with his friend and amateur photographer William Burton, who summarized the conversation in his article "A Japanese Photographer" (1890, pp. 181–5), Ogawa recalled being on the battlefield with his father and sister and suffering a minor injury to his foot from a stray bullet. He also remembered his sister carrying a *naginata*, a spear used by women when learning to fence.

In 1873 he was sent to school to learn architecture at the Arima Gakko in Tokyo. It was there that he also developed an interest in learning English. By the age of fifteen he had also become interested in photography, having come across some photographic illustrations in a school book. From that moment on, he was obsessed with learning how to produce such pictures. He acquired an English book on photography, but his limited knowledge of the language meant he made little progress. An acquired second-hand camera enabled him to undertake some rudimentary experiments with the aid of a lens from an old opera glass, but no real progress was made until he apprenticed to a local photographer, Yoshiwara Hideo, with whom he stayed for around six months and acquired some knowledge of the wet-plate process.

Having managed to save some money, Ogawa acquired the necessary equipment to enable him to open his first portrait studio in Tomioka, Gumma Prefecture, in 1877. The studio was reasonably successful, and after two years he was able to buy a better camera. However, he felt that in order to make real progress he would have to deepen his technical knowledge. Believing that his photographic education could only come from foreign sources, he used his savings to

Below Fig. 292. Anonymous, "Portrait of Ogawa Kazumasa," ca. 1910. Old Japan Picture Library.

Below Fig. 293. Ogawa Kazumasa Studio Advertisement. Chamberlain and Mason, *A Handbook for Travellers in Japan*, 5th edn, 1899.

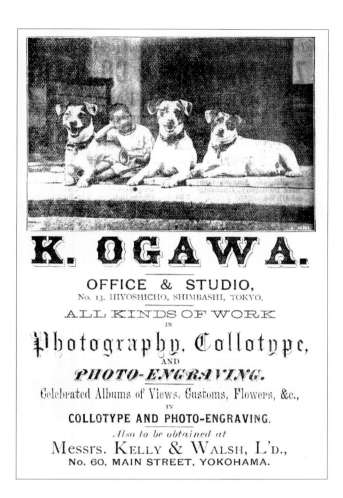

move to Tokyo and enrolled in an English school run by the American missionary James Ballagh, where he studied for the next twelve months. Still frustrated at the end of that time, Ogawa, like Suzuki Shinichi II before him, made the decision to go to America to learn the advanced photographic techniques at first hand.

Having virtually no money, this was easier said than done. But with the help of some friends he managed to get hired as a sailor on board the American frigate *Swatara*, which sailed on July 26th, 1882. Ogawa was very grateful for the kindness he received from the ship's officers, particularly Captain Cooper and the Lieutenants Tyler and Spicer. Burton, however, was not surprised and put this down to Ogawa himself, "whose nature is such that it inclines all men to him."[92] He remained in service for six months, but was then discharged and landed at Washington. According to Ogawa, the ship's officers went out of their way to introduce him to those who could teach him what he wanted to learn.

For the next fifteen months or so, Ogawa systematically studied photographic and printing technologies. In Boston he was the taught the finer points of portraiture, carbon printing, and plate making, and it was in that city that he was also introduced to the intricacies of the collotype. Moving on to Philadelphia, he studied dry-plate photography before leaving America and arriving back in Japan in January 1884. Burton wrote another article about his friend, "Japanese

Photographers, No. 1–K. Ogawa" (1894). In this article (pp. 146–8), Burton explained that before leaving America Ogawa was introduced to Viscount Okabe Nagamoto, who was a man of some means. Okabe was also a photography enthusiast who would later become vice-president of the Photographic Society of Japan. It was he who, in 1885, would provide the capital for Ogawa to open a large studio in Tokyo, the Gyokujun-kan. From this point on, Ogawa's career gives the impression of being one of uninterrupted success.

Almost immediately, he was appointed as photography instructor to the Army General Staff Office. In 1886, according to Burton, he was appointed a committee member for the National Exhibition in Ueno. In 1887 (and again in 1898) Ogawa was commissioned to accompany an American scientific team led by D. P. Todd, which was monitoring the Japanese solar eclipse at Shirakawa. In the preface to her 1898 book *Corona and Coronet*, Mabel Loomis Todd acknowledges Ogawa's photographic support "and to Professor Burton and Mr. Ogawa warm thanks are due for fine views of the Ainu and Northern Yezo." Later in the book she says: "The photographer, Mr. Ogawa (also our photographer during the former Japan eclipse at Shirakawa in 1887), was to follow within a few days, and the interpreter detailed by Government would join the Expedition at Sapporo." For the rest of the decade, Ogawa received several Japanese government commissions, each of which boosted his growing reputation.

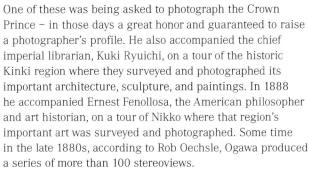

One of these was being asked to photograph the Crown Prince – in those days a great honor and guaranteed to raise a photographer's profile. He also accompanied the chief imperial librarian, Kuki Ryuichi, on a tour of the historic Kinki region where they surveyed and photographed its important architecture, sculpture, and paintings. In 1888 he accompanied Ernest Fenollosa, the American philosopher and art historian, on a tour of Nikko where that region's important art was surveyed and photographed. Some time in the late 1880s, according to Rob Oechsle, Ogawa produced a series of more than 100 stereoviews.

The year 1889 was a particularly busy one. In February he launched the magazine *Shashin Shimpo* (Photographic News) and became its editor. This was actually a relaunch as he had helped to found it in 1882 only for it to be suspended when he left for America. He continued to edit it until 1894, but then had to give it up due to other business pressures.

In May 1889 he was a founder-member of the Photographic Society of Japan. In a meeting of the society held on December 12th, 1889, and reported on the 21st in the *Japan Weekly Mail*, Ogawa amazed members by exhibiting a giant camera: "Mr. K. Ogawa exhibited the colossal camera with which he had made photographs direct measuring 38 by 30 inches for the forthcoming exhibition, and an enormous tripod intended to be used with it in photographing interiors. The top of the tripod reached the roof of the hall. A monster printing frame for making the pictures on paper measuring 4ft. 6in. by 3ft. 6in. was also shown."

Above left Fig. 294. Ogawa Kazumasa, "Yuri (Lilies)," ca. 1890s, large-format hand-colored collotype print. Old Japan Picture Library.

Above right Fig. 295. Ogawa Kazumasa, "Kiku (Chrysanthemum)," ca. 1890s, large-format hand-colored collotype print. Old Japan Picture Library.

Right Fig. 296. Ogawa Kazumasa, "158. Maid of Honour," ca. 1890s, large-format hand-colored albumen print. Author's Collection. Ancient court costume.

The same year he realized a long-held ambition and launched a photo-engraving company specializing in collotype printing, Ogawa Shashin Seihanjo. He first demonstrated his collotype process at the September 27th, 1889 meeting of the Photographic Society of Japan and this was reported in the October 12th issue of the *Japan Weekly Mail*. It was also the year that he launched *Kokka*, an art magazine, which initially used collotype illustrations and is still published today.

It is the 1890s, however, when we find Ogawa at the peak of his fame. The decade started with a first prize at the Third National Industrial Exposition in Ueno Park.[93] In July 1891, in commemoration of the recently opened Ryounkaku in Asakusa, Ogawa exhibited 100 photographic portraits of geisha from the major pleasure quarters of Tokyo, including Shimbashi and Yoshiwara.[94] Visitors were invited to vote for their particular favorite, with prizes being awarded to the five most popular girls (Fig. 297). In October 1891 Ogawa, along with his friends John Milne (the seismologist) and William Burton, photographed the devastating earthquake in the Gifu region of central Japan and published a book of the event in the following year (Fig. 300). In 1893, on his second trip to

158 MAID OF HONOUR.

Left Fig. 297. Ogawa Kazumasa, "Portrait of a Geisha," 1891, large-format hand-colored albumen print. Author's Collection. A contestant from Japan's first beauty contest held in 1891 at the Ryounkaku (twelve-story tower), Tokyo. Ogawa was commissioned to photograph all 100 of the geisha, who came from the major pleasure quarters of Shimbashi and Yoshiwara.

Right Fig. 298. Ogawa Kazumasa, "Ancient Warrior," ca. 1890s, large-format hand-colored collotype print. Old Japan Picture Library.

Below Fig. 299. Ogawa Kazumasa, "Old Couple," ca. 1890s, large-format hand-colored albumen print. Old Japan Picture Library.

the United States, he attended and exhibited his work in the Chicago World Exposition.

During the early 1890s, as we have seen, the influential Burton had been writing eulogistic articles about his friend in the foreign photographic periodicals. Ogawa's international reputation, as a result, was growing. In 1895 he became the first Japanese to be elected as a fellow of Britain's prestigious Royal Photographic Society. In 1899 the Nippon Bukkyo Shimbi (Japanese Art Society) started publishing the *Selected Relics of Japanese Art*, edited by Tajima Shi'ichi, a comprehensive art survey published in twenty volumes. The work, which would not be completed until 1908, contained Ogawa's photographs and was printed by his firm. Perhaps Ogawa's only reversal at this time was the destruction of his printing factory by fire in 1896, as mentioned in the September edition of *The Practical Photographer* (p. 243).

In 1900 Ogawa photographed the aftermath of the Boxer Rebellion. Whilst in Beijing, he also participated in a survey of the city's cultural properties and later published *Shinkoku Pekin kojo shashincho* (Photographs of a Palace Building). Further national recognition arrived in 1910 when he became the first photographer to be elected to the Imperial Art Committee. In 1912 he helped set up a photography department at the Tokyo School of Fine Arts, and in the same year photographed the funeral of Emperor Meiji. Together with Maruki Riyo, he photographed the Emperor Taisho in 1915. Ogawa was active for a few more years, but died in 1929.

According to Boyd and Izakura in *Sepia Portraits* (2000, p. 263), Ogawa published more than 300 collotype and photoengraved books using various state-of-the-art printing processes, and it is for these productions that he is so well known in the West. Many of these were exquisitely hand colored and provided real competition to the popular but more expensive souvenir albums. Ogawa also produced some of his own souvenir albums – colored and uncolored – but the main thrust of his marketing efforts was directed towards the production and sale of his collotype books, a process in which he excelled. The writer's two favorites are *Some Japanese Flowers* and *Types of Celebrated Geysha of Tokyo*.[95]

Ogawa produced very little albumen-print photography after opening his highly successful collotype printing business in 1889. The collotype publications he produced show substantial contributions from Kusakabe, Tamamura, Farsari, Kajima and Enami – probably because Ogawa was not competing with them in the area of studio souvenir albums.

Of all the photographers of the Meiji era, Ogawa was the best exponent of photography as an art form. In writing about his friend in 1894, Burton considered him to be the leading professional photographer in Japan. He rated his studio portrait work very highly but felt that Suzuki (Shinichi II), Esaki, and Maruki could compete in that area. Where he excelled, according to Burton, was in landscape and genre subjects. He also pointed out that Ogawa had taken the highest honors at nearly every exhibition in which his work was shown.[96]

Left Fig. 300. Attributed to Ogawa Kazumasa, "1891 Gifu Earthquake," 1891, large-format albumen print. Author's Collection. This earthquake was the worst natural disaster to afflict Japan in the whole of the Meiji era (1868–1912). Although the event occurred in central Japan, many buildings in Tokyo and Yokohama were shaken and badly damaged. At the center of the disaster, 10,000 people were killed and another 20,000 injured. More than 128,000 homes were destroyed.

Below Fig. 301. Maruki Riyo Studio Advertisement. *Japan Directory*, 1910.

OTHER JAPANESE PHOTOGRAPHERS

Very little is known about **Maruki Riyo** (1850–1923), other than that he was one of Japan's finest portrait photographers whose studio was sought out by Japanese and foreigners alike. The astute commentator William Burton, in his June 1894 article, "Japanese Photographers," considered Maruki's portrait work to be exceptional, with only Esaki and Suzuki (Shinichi II) mentioned as worthy competitors in this field. Maruki opened his first studio in the Uchisaiwaicho district of Tokyo in 1880, and his business continued up until the early 1920s. In 1888 he was asked to help in producing a new official photograph of the Emperor, as the one then in use was ten years old. But rather than a "live sitting," the Italian Edoardo Chiossone, who was employed by the Ministry of Finance printing bureau, was asked to make a drawing which Maruki then photographed. According to Tucker et al.'s *The History of Japanese Photography* (2003, p. 28), the result was then distributed throughout the empire.

An interesting advertisement appeared in the 1889 *Japan Directory*. In perhaps his first attempt to cultivate foreign custom, Maruki announced that his brother "who has for so many years thoroughly studied photography under one of the most distinguished artists in Europe, has recently returned from a tour in America and will skilfully execute all orders.... Photographs entrusted to his care for painting will be carefully finished." This does, of course, raise tricky questions about attribution as far as Maruki's work is concerned. In a later 1903 *Japan Directory* advertisement, Maruki emphasized his skill with flashlight photography. He also stressed his pedigree as a portrait taker: "We have long been favoured with the patronage of Imperial Household Department, the Imperial Princes and their Families, and the high class people. We cordially invite you to visit our Studio." In 1914 Maruki was appointed chairman of the Nihon Shashinshi Rengo Kumiai (Allied Union of Japanese Photographers), which was the first national organization of photographers. The following year he received his greatest honor when he and Ogawa were chosen to photograph the Emperor Taisho.

There is still much to learn about **Azukizawa Ryoichi** who was taught art and photography by Yokoyama Matsusaburo in the 1870s. He operated a studio in the 1880s at No. 9, Sanjuken-bori, Nichome, Kyobashi-ku, Tokyo (Fig. 302). He described himself as a "Patent Oil-Painter on Photograph and Lithograph, and Common Oil-Painter and Photographer."[97] It is this special photographic oil-painting process which is Azukizawa's main claim to fame (Fig. 303). In 1885 he was granted a fifteen-year patent and he applied this strange technique to the standard photographs of views and costumes usually found in souvenir albums. Although this novel art form did not seem to win many admirers, a number of Meiji-era photographers seem to have experimented with similar methods and with mixed results. The writer has seen a number of examples, and it is difficult to tell whether the pictures are photographs or paintings. This whole genre, starting with the early hand coloring of photographs in the 1860s, would be an interesting field of research for art historians.[98]

When Usui Shusaburo moved his studio from Otemachi to No. 16 Bund, a Japanese photographer named **C. Sugawara** set up a portrait studio in the vacated premises. Keen to target foreigners, he placed an advertisement in the 1885 *Japan Directory*. It is doubtful he enjoyed much success, and Usui took back the studio the following year. Sugawara reappeared as a photographer for Farsari & Co. in the 1909 *Japan Directory*. In 1880 Keeling's *Tourists' Guide* advertised **Sudzuki Toocoku**'s Yokohama-based portrait studio at No. 12, Otamachi, Ichome. According to Boyd and Izakura's *Portraits in Sepia* (p. 274), his studio was in operation until 1906.

Mizuno Hanbei is famous for having invented gold- and silver-lacquered photographs. He initially operated a studio in the 1880s in Shizuoka, and then moved to Yokohama in around 1890. According to Saito's *Bakumatsu Meiji*, Mizuno was friendly with Kusakabe and had joined Farsari & Co. for two years in 1885. The 1892 *Japan Directory* gives his studio name as Fukusuisha, at 28 Sakaicho, Ichome, Yokohama. Chamberlain and Mason's *Handbook for Travellers* for 1891 shows the address as 23, as does the 1893 edition which also includes an advertisement for lacquer photographs: "Lacquer Photographs, Invented by Mr. H. Mizuno, and best kinds of Scenery and Costumes coloured, At Reasonable Prices. Photographs Taken at Low Prices" (Fig. 304). The lacquer process was exhibited for the first time in 1890 and reported by Burton in his article "Japanese Photographs in Gold": "I have reserved for the last notice of what is an exhibit perhaps the most interesting of any, because it is quite new. The exhibitor is A. H. Mizuno, of Yokohama, and what is shown is a series of photographs in gold on dark coloured lacquer. The intention is to produce, photographically, the equivalent of hand-done pictorial work in gold in lacquer – one of the fine arts in which Japan far excels any other country in the world. The effect, considered decoratively, is very pleasing. The process has, as yet, been kept secret." Boyd and Izakura give a brief description of the process in *Portraits in Sepia* (p. 255).

Narui Raisuke (1858–1902) was one of Kyoto's most successful photographers in the 1880s and 1890s. Known for his skill in portraiture, his studio became fashionable with many of the city's top geisha, kabuki actors, and socialites. Today, Narui is no longer remembered, but his work seems to have been of exceptional quality.

AZUKISAWA RYOICHI.

Patent Oil Painting on Photographs.

By this process the color never changes, and lasts as long as ordinary Oil Paintings. Photographs of all sizes Painted at the shortest notice.

Patent granted on the 7th day of the 10th month of the 18th year of Meiji (1885) for 15 years.

COLOURED MONOGRAMS PUT ON HANDKERCHIEFS, ETC.

☞ The Colour Warranted not to Fade, however much washed. ☜

TANAKA KOTARO, SOLE AGENT,

NO. 53, BENTENDORI, SANCHOME, YOKOHAMA.

HEAD OFFICE: NO. 9, SANJUKEN-BORI, NICHOME, TOKIO.

Yokohama, January, 1887.

Lacquer Photographs,

INVENTED BY MR. H. MIZUNO,

AND BEST KINDS OF

SCENERY
AND
COSTUMES
COLOURED,
At Reasonable Prices.

PHOTOGRAPHS
Taken at Low Prices.

DAGUERREOTYPES & PHOTOGRAPHS

FUKUSUISHA, No. 23, Sakaicho, Ichome, Yokohama.

ADOLFO FARSARI

"If you cannot understand why my works are more valuable than other photographers', this is no place for you. Go and shop somewhere else."

The Italian Adolfo Farsari (1841–98) was one of the most colorful and remarkable photographers of nineteenth-century Japan (Fig. 305). It has been possible to piece together the details of his adventurous life due to the discovery, in 1988, of a collection of letters written to his family, mainly from the US and Japan.[99] By the time that Farsari turned his attention to photography in 1885, the commercial environment in Japan was fiercely competitive. One by one the Western studios, no longer able to compete on price, had been driven out of Japan. The technical complexities of wet-plate photography had given way to the much more easily managed dry-plate process, and this development had encouraged the growth of local studios. Photography was now easier and cheaper and souvenir photographs were trading as commodities, rather than precious works of art. This commercially hostile environment would have deterred many a seasoned professional, let alone a newcomer to the field. The business strategy that Farsari employed to succeed is very interesting – as was his life.

Farsari was born into a comfortable middle-class home in Vicenza, Italy, on February 11th, 1841. His mother Ortensia was a Frenchwoman from Marseilles and his father Luigi an accountant and court-appointed receiver. The couple had a daughter, Emma, who was born in 1848. She would marry Guido Garbinati, a notary, in 1866 who died in 1875. After that Emma returned to the family home for good. The Farsaris also owned a country house in Arcugnano, in the hills overlooking Verona, and it is from this villa that most of the family papers were recovered.

After studying with a tutor, Farsari went to the Cordellina School in Vicenza before leaving home in 1859 to enrol in the Modena Military Academy. This was the time of the Risorgimento and the Wars of Independence, which ultimately led to the unification of Italy. Farsari showed promise and became an officer in the 5th Grenadier Regiment of Naples. He campaigned in Pisa, Orticoli, and Florence where his father at one time received an urgent call to visit his son. Rushing to his wounded son's bedside, he found there was also the need to satisfy a number of creditors. After "a number of events, the consequences of an adventurous nature," as his father later wrote, Farsari resigned his commission without consulting his family. Possibly to escape a growing number of creditors, Farsari traveled to his mother's home city of Marseilles, and in June 1863 embarked on the Austrian ship *Aquila* for *New York*, with little money and some letters of introduction which he would never use.

Just a few months after arriving, and without informing his family, he married an American widow of independent means, Mary Patchen. Ever restless, and anxious to resume his military career, on December 9th, 1863 Farsari enlisted in the Federal Army to fight in the Civil War and became a member of the 12th New York Cavalry Regiment. In September 1864 he was again wounded by exploding shrapnel, but

wrote to his father about enjoying "the precariousness of military life." In March the following year, during a brawl, he received a sword cut to the head and spent time in the military hospital in New York. The war ended in April 1865, and on July 19th he was discharged.[100] His wife gave birth to his first son, Edward, in August.

By August 1866 he was living in Brooklyn and in business with two Italian partners in placing ships' cargo. By November he must have felt reasonably settled because he became an American citizen. In August 1867 his second child, Henry, was born, and by now his family knew about his wife. In December of that year he wrote a confused and hesitant letter to his parents, cryptically referring to a New York trade crisis and his own illness. After that, as far as his family was concerned, he disappeared without trace. They would not hear from him for twenty-one years.

Farsari is never clear about his activities during the next few years. In August 1865 his wife's stepson from her first marriage was drowned, and in June 1868 his newly born son died of pneumonia. He claimed that this was the start of all his troubles and that his wife had become a "chronic drunk" and their relationship had deteriorated. He left home and spent the next five years traveling with the US Army. He apparently went to South America, West Africa, and Asia and it is very likely that he visited Japan, because following his return to America and his discharge his intention was to join the Japanese army. In what capacity is not clear, but upon traveling to Yokohama he decided to make his home there. However, the final move did not apparently take place until 1874, although his name does not appear in the *Japan Directory* until 1878, when he is named as a manager of the Yokohama Cigar Company.

The directory for 1879 shows that Farsari has taken an American partner and the firm, Sargent, Farsari & Co., is in business selling imported books, magazines, maps, and other luxury goods. Based at No. 60 Main Street, a serious fire in July 1879 destroyed their premises. But the 1880 directory shows that they moved to No. 80 and continued to operate there until late 1883, or early 1884 when the partnership was dissolved and Farsari moved on to other things.

Before continuing to follow Farsari's business activities, it is worth quoting from a letter Farsari sent from Yokohama to his sister Emma in Italy and dated April 12th, 1888 (all letters translated from the original Italian): "Please, do not remind me of my past. I suffered a lot and my past still haunts me. My wife came twice to Japan to make it up with me, but I sent her back to New York where she is living now and I

hope she will never come back. Our older son died about ten years ago of typhoid fever – he was a good, handsome boy, according to his guardians; I think I had not seen him for about five years."

Gartlan, in his "Stillfried Chronology" (p. 155), quotes the *Japan Gazette Mail Summary* of May 15th, 1879 as including in the list of passengers from San Francisco, arriving on the previous 10th, "Mrs. Farsari and son." The 1880 *Japan Directory* has Mrs Farsari living with her husband at his Yokohama residence. We also know that "Mrs. Farsari and infant" departed Yokohama on August 26th, 1880.[101]

Upon locating Mrs Farsari's gravesite in New York, it was possible to understand much more of the Farsari family history. Mary G. Burke (ca. 1847–1900) left Ireland with her family and emigrated to America in around 1860 and settled in New York. By her sixteenth birthday, at the latest, she was married to a Mr Patchen who had a son from a previous marriage, Henry, who was born in July 1857. By the time that she married Farsari in late 1863, Mary was a widow of independent means. Evidence of this is provided in October 1866 when Mary paid $300 for a large burial plot in the exclusive New York cemetery of Green-Wood in Brooklyn. Henry Patchen had died on July 10th, 1866 and his death certificate gave the cause of death as drowning. Farsari's first son, Edward, was born on August 6th, 1865, and died of typhoid aged twelve on September 30th, 1877. Henry, the second son, was born

on August 30th, 1867. According to his death certificate, he died of pneumonia aged nine months on June 19th, 1868. Farsari had a third son, William H. (1868–1924), and it was he who accompanied his mother on the trip to Yokohama in 1879–80. Mary, now impoverished, died of pneumonia in Brooklyn, New York, in 1900. She is buried at Green-Wood with her three sons and Henry Patchen.

Returning to 1884, Sargent, Farsari & Co. is still listed in the *Japan Directory* for that year. The next year's directory, however, shows E. A. Sargent as working for the American Trading Co., and Farsari remaining at No. 80, trading as A. Farsari & Co., and still selling "books, maps and photographs." Despite the usual timing delays between placing advertisements and having them printed in annual directories, we can safely assume that the partnership finished some time between late 1883 and early 1884. The second edition of Keeling's *Tourists' Guide to Japan* was published by A. Farsari & Co. on May 1st, 1884, so that is the very latest date for the old partnership to be running. The mention of "photographs" should not be taken to imply that Farsari was already operating a studio, as these photographs would have been supplied by other studios on an agency basis. An 1880 advertisement in Keeling's guidebook, placed by the Suzuki Shinichi studio, clearly states that Sargent, Farsari & Co. were agents. It is not hard to see why Farsari would become tempted to set up his own studio. After all, his firm had been selling maps and guides as well as photographs for a number of years and he would have had close and regular contact with many tourists and been able to determine their buying habits and preferences, not to mention the fact that he had shared the same address with the Baron Franz Stillfried studio since 1879, albeit in separate units of the same building.

Some time in 1885 Farsari did set up his own studio (Fig. 306). He acquired the stock, negatives, and goodwill of the Japan Photographic Association (Stillfried and Andersen was the trading name for this company).[102] Some scholars have suggested an earlier date, but future studio advertisements clearly show the year of commencement as 1885.[103] Farsari duly moved into No. 17 Bund and enjoyed immediate commercial success. In Farsari's first letter to his parents in twenty-one years, he wrote, on January 17th, 1888: "I am now an artist, photographer, painter etc., and at present I am doing very well in business. If a fire in February 1886 had not caused me a $6,000 loss and had not obliged me to start again at the bottom, I am sure that within a year from now I could have wound up my business and retired. It took me about one year of travelling around Japan and straightening up things before I could start my business again. It is now about twelve months since I re-opened my studio, and business is already very satisfactory."

The fire of 1886 destroyed all of Farsari's negatives, including, tragically, those from Beato and Stillfried, since theirs had been amongst the acquired stock. The consequence of this was that he then spent five months on a photographic tour in order to replenish his stock. This, of course, was a test of his photographic ability, and we will turn to an assessment of this shortly. The fire was localized and Nos. 17–20 were

destroyed or damaged. A full report of the conflagration was given in the February 13th, 1886 issue of the *Japan Weekly Mail* (p. 146). There appeared to be no damage to No. 16, where Usui's Yokohama Photographic Company was based but, nevertheless, Usui moved back to his previous premises at Otemachi and so the short-lived rivalry was at an end. Ironically, Farsari would move into these vacated premises at No. 16 the following year, and this would be the studio's base for the next decade. By the end of 1890 Farsari's studio employed thirty-two staff and was enjoying great success.[104] Now increasingly homesick, Farsari made a sudden decision to visit his family in Italy. The *Japan Weekly Mail* for April 12th, 1890 shows that he left on the steamer *Congo* on April 6th.

Farsari had one more surprise for his family. He returned with his daughter Kiku, born in 1885 of a liaison with a Japanese woman, Nagashima Hona. Farsari intended to return to Japan to resume his business but he never did and died a few days before his fifty-seventh birthday on February 7th, 1898. His sister Emma wrote to his old partner, E. A. Sargent, and asked him to wind up her brother's affairs. Sargent was to report that there was little money to remit back to Italy. The studio was then taken over by the Japanese manager, Tonokura Tsunetaro, who was still listed in the 1900 *Japan Directory* as proprietor. By 1913 the owner is a Mr I. Fukagawa, with a C. Sugawara as chief of operations. There appears to be little change in the management until the 1923 earthquake which destroyed much of Yokohama. From 1926 the studio is listed in the *Japan Directory* as being based in Kobe, and it continued there until at least 1929 under the ownership of a Mr S. Fukagawa.

In his letters home, Farsari maintained that he was not a good businessman. From what he has told us of his early life and the letters of admonishment from his father, he certainly seemed to acquire the habit of getting into debt. However, the partnership with Sargent seemed to be reasonably successful and he did run, single-handedly, one of the most successful photo studios in Japan. Entering an industry when price cutting had become endemic, he adopted the classic business strategy of offering a higher priced, higher quality product – and energetically marketing it as such. Being able to trade off the residual goodwill inherent in the Stillfried and Andersen name was not unhelpful. Indeed, as late as 1887 he styled himself as A. Farsari & Co., Late Stillfried and Andersen (Fig. 308). In his advertisements he had no compunction about illustrating the photographic gold medal which the previous firm had been awarded at the Calcutta International Exhibition in 1884. But that would not be enough: Farsari would need something different in order to compete with the growing number of Japanese studios.

Fortuitously, for one with no previous photographic experience, he discovered a unique and superior form of photograph painting where the colors themselves apparently did not fade. He also trained his colorists to use colors that accurately reflected the actual colors in Japanese costumes, scenery, and architecture, and he said this training lasted from two to four months, during which he would not pay them. A "qualified" painter, however, would then be paid twice as

much as he could earn at other studios. He would also work a six-day week from eight to five and would get extra pay for working Sundays.[105] It seems likely that Farsari himself must have had some degree of artistic talent.

Farsari's marketing approach was direct and systematic. He did not hesitate in his advertising to imply that his competitors used unnatural colors which would, in any case, quickly fade. Even in a time when there was a fairly liberal approach to claims and statements made in advertisements, this was a strong challenge. Were Farsari's claims true?

Rudyard Kipling, in 1889, is unequivocal about the coloring, as the extract from the H. Cortazzi and G. Webb's *Kipling's Japan* (1988) shows: "... in Japan ... you must buy photographs, and the best are to be found at the house of Farsari & Co.... A coloured photograph ought to be an abomination. It generally is, but Farsari knows how to colour accurately and according to the scale of lights in this fantastic country. On the deck of the steamer I laughed at his red and blue hill-sides. In the hills I saw he has painted true." In Burton's article "Photography in Japan" (1887), we hear that the author had visited and talked to Farsari in 1887: "Farsari's artists were very slow and careful in their work. He informed me that he was satisfied if each coloured two or three prints in a day. This allows time enough for each print to be really well coloured, and indeed I have seen no better work in the way of coloured photographs anywhere than some of Farsari's productions."

More than a century later, with the benefit of hindsight and the relatively high number of surviving Farsari albums, we can weigh the evidence for ourselves. The photographs in albums produced by the Farsari studio certainly do seem to have retained remarkably vivid coloring and are very pleasing on the eye. As a general rule of thumb, other studios' coloring is not so good. However, it is not difficult to come across albums by Beato, Raimund von Stillfried, Kusakabe, or Tamamura where the coloring is just as good as Farsari's best work and has not noticeably deteriorated. In fact, albums produced by his studio after Farsari went home in 1890 are much more variable in their quality. As to whether the colors used by Farsari were any more "natural" than those of his rivals, this seems to be a potential field of study for Japanese art experts. Where Farsari undoubtedly scores is in the consistent quality of his pre-1891 coloring.

From his letters we learn that Farsari did not consider himself a great photographer, rather he was able to take good pictures because "taking pictures is just a mechanical thing." Despite the advent of the immeasurably easier dry-plate processing, this is excessive modesty. Farsari was more than just a competent photographer, with an artist's "eye" for the right scene or portrait. Whilst his work might look a little "mechanical" at times, and is certainly not in the same class as a Beato, Uchida, or Stillfried, there is no doubting he was a clever and skillful photographer.

Other points of interest emerge from his letters which were, incidentally, written in Italian. He says he benefits from the fact that 50 percent of tourists are amateur photographers, and he offers them a darkroom for their free use. His studio

is next door to the popular Grand Hotel. His portfolio consists of around 1000 photographs, which is interestingly only half the number that Kusakabe was boasting. Farsari employs his own craftsman for making the lacquer albums, and he imports his printing paper from England. He claims, incorrectly, that he is the only European photographer in Japan but adds that there are so many Japanese photographers that you cannot throw a stone without hitting one. Because his studio was hit more than once by fire, he had duplicates of all his negatives stored in a place far from his studio. All of his photographs have the Farsari name printed at the bottom. However, if the photograph is to be placed in a "better-class" album, this signature is trimmed off. He points out that his album prints are smaller than other studios. This ties in with the writer's own experience: Farsari's print sizes approximate to 9 1/2 x 7 1/2 inches (245 x 195 mm) whereas other studios are usually at least 10 x 8 inches (260 x 205 mm). Farsari explained to his sister that there was no secret about his painting technique: water was applied to the photograph with a brush, and when the paper was damp "rubber colours" were applied. The result was not varnished, he stressed, and the shining effect was produced by the paper, which he imported.

Farsari appears to have been on good terms with the local community and outwardly sociable. However, he seems more comfortable in his own company and his employees describe him as "the serious one." He is also a little eccentric. He tells his sister that he is invariably ill in the winter and only feels better when lying down. Consequently, he would frequently receive customers and visitors to his office lying down and wearing a dressing gown. He is constantly shouting and beating his employees, who seem otherwise incapable of maintaining high work standards, and is proud of the sign above the door which encourages customers to go away if they cannot appreciate his photographs. Proud of being Italian, he succeeded in regaining his Italian citizenship by presenting the Italian king with a special album of photographs. He was also awarded the title of Cavaliere. In a letter to his sister in 1889, Farsari explained proudly that he had taught himself photography from books, without the help of anyone else.

Adolfo Farsari's life was certainly eventful, and led him down a number of unexpected paths. Ending up running a photo studio in 1880s Yokohama is presumably an outcome that he would not have predicted for himself. The surviving letters to his family back in Italy give us glimpses of his personality – although they also seem to hide more than they reveal. It is still not clear why he fled Italy, why he avoided contact with his parents for over twenty years, or why he treated his wife so callously. Perhaps he had good reasons, perhaps not. He was a talented, but not great photographer. What he achieved commercially, however, was quite remarkable. He single-handedly, for several years, delayed the total Japanization of the photo studio industry in Japan. In addition, because of the innovative coloring techniques employed, he has left us a truly enduring testimony to his commercial and artistic endeavors. Many of his photographs are reproduced in the book by Del Mar, *Around the World through Japan* (1903).

Below Fig. 310. Francis Guillemard, "Leaving Naha for Shuri," June 29th, 1882, large-format albumen dry-plate print. Syndicate of Cambridge University Library (MSS Add. 7957). This view, taken on Okinawa, is now considered to be Japan's earliest recorded gelatin dry-plate photograph. It shows Guillemard's traveling companions and a crowd of interested Okinawan onlookers. Crowd scenes had previously been very hard to capture clearly using wet plates.

Opposite Fig. 311. Anonymous, "Francis Guillemard and Party at Kamakura," July 1882, cabinet-size albumen print. Syndicate of Cambridge University Library (MSS Add. 7957). Guillemard is shown standing on the left. This photograph may well have been taken by Usui Shusaburo (see page 174). It is not yet clear whether the photograph was taken using a gelatin dry plate. If so, it would be the earliest recorded use of the process on mainland Japan.

FRANCIS GUILLEMARD

It had been thought, for many years, that the Frenchman Hugues Krafft was the first to use dry plates in Japan. The writer and historian Koyama Noboru has now convincingly shown that the English travel writer and naturalist Francis Henry Hill Guillemard (1852–1933) was taking dry-plate photographs in Japan's southern prefecture of Okinawa some two months earlier.[106]

Guillemard graduated from Cambridge University with a medical degree in 1881 but never practiced medicine. He became a lecturer in geography at the university in 1888,

but left a year later and worked for many years as an editor for Cambridge University Press. Between graduation and starting his working career, he embarked on a two-year world cruise on the schooner yacht *Marchesa*, which was owned by his friend and traveling companion, Charles Kettle.

The yacht left England in April 1882 and stopped off in Ceylon before reaching Singapore in June. The next stop was Formosa (Taiwan), and the party arrived in Ryukyu (Okinawa), Japan on June 28th, 1882. After just a few days, they moved on to Yokohama where they spent around a month visiting the local sites. They left for Kamchatka on July 29th and returned to Yokohama on October 6th. The touring party then traveled around Japan for the next four months, finally leaving Nagasaki on January 31st, 1883 for the voyage home.

Guillemard, an amateur photographer, took what must now be considered the earliest extant dry-plate photograph in Japan on the very first day of his arrival on Okinawa. He wrote in his journal for June 29th, 1882: "Landed at 8am and went straight to Governor's house…. Then they told us the chairs were ready. We went out into a sort of front courtyard & found them – curious looking vehicles, something like a Japanese Kago but made of basket work of very pretty pattern. Outside, thousands were gathered to see us, so I took the opportunity of photographing them and our cavalcade at the same time. At last we got off, & words fail to describe the excitement we caused. We were told that 20 years ago they had seen a European woman for the first and only time, which may account for the persistent way in which they glued their eyes on Mrs. K." The party, including Mrs Kettle, had been advised to land at Unten Harbor before going to the governor's house, and the photograph shows them about to leave Naha for a visit to Shuri (Fig. 310).

The same day at Shuri Castle: "I then took a photograph, and he [Japanese guide] ascended still further to above the magazine which commanded splendid views all round." The party then paid a short visit to Tokiwa and then left to return to Naha. "En route we stopped to take a photo of the curious tombs of the Liukiuans." These three photographs, which are present in the collection, were not the only ones taken. However, in a letter he wrote to his uncle dated October 29th, 1882, he explained what had happened to the rest: "I am sorry that most of the photographs I took turned out failures owing to my plates having become mildewed."

The party arrived in Yokohama on July 4th, and the key diary entry reads: "Photographic agent came off & settled to get dry plates developed. Went ashore with Ross & K., but came off after finding photo shop shut. Much cholera about." July 5th, 1882: "In afternoon I went off to the photographer Stillfried & Andersen & developed some dry plates." Ross was one of the traveling party and "K" was Charles Kettle.

These last two diary entries raise interesting points. The photographic agent was probably David Welsh, whilst John Douglas (both of them were working for Stillfried and Andersen at the time) was probably the person who developed the plates. Hermann Andersen was out of the country then, and Raimund von Stillfried had left Japan two years earlier. An undated page of notes in Guillemard's hand is loosely

inserted in one of the journals. This *aide memoiré* includes the following list beneath the name "Douglas": "get photo things; print 10 copies each decent photo; make dark boxes & return negatives in them; negative of self in Kamsch. dress." This last reference means that the note must have been written in October 1882, before the party left Yokohama for the last time. Although dry-plate technology was new to Japan, we can assume that Stillfried and Andersen, or rather John Douglas, had been recommended to Guillemard as having the necessary technical expertise to satisfy his requirements. This raises the possibility that others in Japan had already taken successful dry-plate photographs. For example, had the photographer John Douglas done so?

Except for Okinawa, Guillemard does not seem to have used dry-plate photography in Japan for either the July 1882 or the October 1882 to January 1883 tours. Instead, he commissioned the professional photographer Usui Shusaburo and his brother to travel throughout Japan with the party to take photos. This is confirmed in a letter dated December 12th, 1882, written in Kobe by Guillemard to his brother Arthur: "As in our last trip too, a professional Jap. Photographer accompanies us everywhere – a great thing, as it saves me a lot of work." There are more than 200 photographs of Japan in the collection concerned with these tours of Japan. All of them measure 8 x 10 inches (210 x 250 mm) and have been taken by Usui using wet plates. Some of them are clearly from Usui's studio stock, and were no doubt supplied to Guillemard's order to supplement those taken on the tours. It is possible that Usui did not attempt any dry-plate photography, and perhaps Guillemard's equipment was left in Yokohama.

However, there is one photograph that requires further research. Smaller than the others, it shows Guillemard and party by the Daibutsu at Kamakura on July 25th, 1882 (Fig. 311). This could well be from a dry plate. Did Usui take this photograph and thereby become the first Japanese to use the process successfully – beating Esaki Reiji by one year?

The phrase "Usui Brothers" is mentioned in Guillemard's typed, unpublished autobiography, "The Ears That the Locust Had Eaten," held at the Cambridge University Library. There are also several, albeit short, references to photography scattered throughout the journals and letters. For example, a journal entry for July 15th, 1882, when the party was passing through Tokoni: "Lovely morn. Usui took photo of valley." On returning to Yokohama from Kamchatka, where Guillemard had used his dry plates, a journal entry for October 9th, 1882 reads: "In afternoon took off Kamchatka photographs to Stillfried & Andersens but found him unable to do them until tomorrow." October 18th, 1882: "Went to photographers etc. & settled up as best could about various things." On October 30th, 1882, there is a cryptic journal entry: "Usui is delighted at the [illegible] conceit of photographing a peculiarly obtrusive Japanese stench." And on November 3rd, 1882, near Miogi-San: "Usui returned with some photos; none particularly good." On November 7th, 1882: "Usui had been sent back to photograph the Suwa Lake." On November 10th, 1882, Guillemard made a journal entry which tells us the size of the party: "We are 28 coolies, 16 boatmen, 2 Usuis, ourselves,

Below Fig. 312. Hugues Krafft, "Bonze du Monastere Bouddhique de Sabutsudo, à Nikko," ca. 1883, large-format phototype. Krafft, *Souvenirs de notre tour du monde*, 1885.

Below Fig. 313 Hugues Krafft, "Le Village de Hatta, sur Le Tokaido," ca. 1883, large-format phototype. Krafft, *Souvenirs de notre tour du monde*, 1885.

Louis & Hakodadi – 51 in all!" In Nagoya on December 5th, 1882, the journal reads: "Usui photographed it & two other scenes & we then thought seriously of lunch." Finally, an entry for January 3rd, 1883 off Shikoku suggests that Usui's work is under Guillemard's direction: "I cruised off in search of photos for Usui to take, and got one or two pretty ones."

Apart from Okinawa, Guillemard did not enjoy his visits to Japan. He complained constantly in his letters home and to his journal. For example, in commenting on Japanese *bonsai*: "Nothing, for instance, can be more unpleasing than the custom of cutting and dwarfing their trees and shrubs, and producing thereby little stunted vegetable miseries which no one can pretend to admire." He did not like the food or the scenery, and to his mother wrote: "On the whole I shall be infinitely glad to get out of Japan. It is the dirtiest, smelliest country I ever saw … it always rains, and the mists are as bad as I have known them in any country. Everything testifies to the dampness of the country." Guillemard did, however, concede that the Japanese people were "kind, civil, and industrious," but it is not surprising that in his book *The Cruise of the Marchesa* (1886), the only part of Japan he wrote about was Okinawa. In the preface to the book, he explained this omission: "To such countries as Ceylon and Japan, and others which lie in the beaten path of the tourist round the world, I have not thought to allude." He never returned to Japan.

OTHER WESTERN PHOTOGRAPHERS

The wealthy French tourist and amateur photographer **Hugues Krafft** (1853–1935) was thought until recently to have been the first in Japan to use the new dry-plate process, in August 1882, a year before Esaki Reiji. Krafft spent five months in Japan during an 1881–3 world tour and he brought back over 250 negatives[107] (Figs. 312–314). However, a recent discovery has shown that the British travel writer and naturalist Francis Guillemard used dry-plate photography on Okinawa at least one month before Krafft (see page 226). See also Annette Beaulieu's *Hugues Krafft (1853–1935)* (2005).

The English writer and explorer **Isabella Bird** (1831–1904) visited Japan four times between 1878 and 1896. A keen amateur photographer, she took numerous photographs during her excursions to the Far East, which included trips to Malaya, China, and Korea. When she took photographs in Japan is not clear, but she did commission a private collotype book in the late 1890s.[108] Her photographs were deposited with the Royal Geographical Society in London.

Emma Lasenby Liberty (1846–1920) was another female amateur who spent four months in 1889 traveling in Japan with her husband Arthur, the founder of Liberty's of London. She took over 1000 photographs, of which fifty were selected for her book *Japan: A Pictorial Record* (1891).

Below Fig. 315. Georges Bigot, "Military Post at Fusan Korea," ca. 1894–5, cabinet-size albumen print. Old Japan Picture Library. A scene from the 1894–5 Sino-Japanese War.

Bottom Fig. 316. "Portrait of Georges Bigot." *The Graphic*, October 27th, 1894. An engraving of a photograph taken by the Tokyo photographer Yamamoto Sanshichiro.

The French artist and cartoonist **Georges Bigot** (1860–1927) was in Japan from 1883 until 1899 (Fig. 316). Like many artists, he liked to record a favored scene with his camera in order to draw or paint it at a later date. An accomplished photographer, a number of his photographs have survived, particularly those of the 1894–5 Sino-Japanese War, a number of which are illustrated in the writer's book, *Korea: Caught in Time* (1997) (Fig. 315).

E. H. M. Kuhardt was a storekeeper in Kobe who also acted as an agent for Stillfried and Andersen from 1881. The *Japan Directory* lists him as being based at 31 Settlement, Kobe, from 1876 to 1882, after which he is no longer listed. It is worth noting that the two editions of E. M. Satow and A. G. S. Hawes' *A Handbook for Travellers in Central and Northern Japan* (1881 and 1884), both state that photographs can be bought from Kuhhardt [*sic*] & Co., 31 Settlement, Kobe. It looks as though the 1884 edition is in error.

Finally, it is worth mentioning here the little-known Yokohama-based Chinese photographer **Cheong Tong**. His studio operated for just one year, judging by the single entry in the 1884 *Japan Directory*. There, his operation is described as Book and General Job Printer and Photographer. In the same directory, an advertisement was placed offering the usual souvenir albums of views and costumes. The address

given is No. 55 Main Street. Revealingly, the directory for 1885 describes the operation as General Printers and Bookbinders, with the reference to photography having been dropped. The business name is now Tong Cheong Brothers and a total of twenty employees are involved. The diversion into photography was not a success. Whether Cheong was related to the only other Yokohama Chinese photographer, Cheong Hung, mentioned on page 164, is not clear.

[CHAPTER 5]

1890s Japanese Studios Dominate

ENAMI TAMOTSU
KAJIMA SEIBEI
OGAWA SASHICHI
OTHER JAPANESE PHOTOGRAPHERS
HENRY STROHMEYER
WALTER CLUTTERBUCK
WILLIAM BURTON
OTHER WESTERN PHOTOGRAPHERS

By the end of the 1880s Japanese photographers must have known that the technology gap between West and East was closing. Dry-plate photography was now a routine matter, and a general all-round improvement in quality was remarked upon by Professor William Burton in an article, "Photography in Japan," published in *The Photographic News* on March 27th, 1891. He also said, however, that the variety in printing methods still lagged behind the West; there was little employment of platinotypes or carbon processes, and bromide paper was used only for the occasional enlargement. Nevertheless, Ogawa Kazumasa was producing collotypes that were equal to anything in the West, and within a few short years Japan would be successfully experimenting with photographic printing on silk, crepe paper, and other materials. In 1890 Japan's first unique photographic invention would be patented when Mizuno Hanbei introduced gold and silver lacquer photographs.

William Burton, who had set up the Japan Photographic Society in 1889, had written books on photography and was respected throughout the photographic world. Because of his presence in Japan and personal friendships with a number of the photographers there, he must have been a tremendous source of encouragement and stimulation. It was just as well that it was he who organized, in 1893, Japan's first foreign photographic exhibition. Many photographers who visited the exhibition, which was dominated by the works of the pictorialists, were shocked. The art photography on show made them feel that although *technically* they might have caught up, they were still far behind the West in *artistic* endeavor.[109] But Burton must have realized that contained in this apparent threat were the seeds of opportunity: Japan's own artistic heritage would surely enable the same fusion between art and photography to take place. It was just another challenge. Burton's early death in 1899 was a great loss to Japanese photography, but by then the student no longer needed the master – the lessons had all been learned. Moreover, this progress was being echoed in political affairs, where the hated extraterritoriality would be swept away in 1899.[110] In military capability, too, Japan was making rapid strides; she would summarily defeat China in the 1894–5 War and, shockingly, Russia in 1904–5.

ENAMI TAMOTSU

Enami Tamotsu was one of the most artistic and broad-ranging commercial photographers of the late Meiji era (Fig. 318). Surprisingly, almost nothing is known of his life and there has been great confusion concerning his relationship with a certain Enami Nobukuni, about whom we also know very little. An article by Ono and Wright entitled "Tourist Photographs of the 1930s: The work of 'T. Enami'" (1997) discussed Enami's work and the uncertainty surrounding his identity. For a number of years it has been the contention of the collector and Enami expert Rob Oechsle that N. Enami and T. Enami are one and the same person. What follows is an outline of the available data in order that the reader can reach his or her own conclusions.

Almost nothing has been published on Enami to date. According to Boyd and Izakura in *Portraits in Sepia* (2000), Enami Nobukuni trained under Ogawa Kazumasa before setting up his Yokohama studio at No. 9, Benten-dori in 1892. The authors go on to say that research has so far failed to establish a family relationship between Nobukuni and Tamotsu, or whether they were the same person. The book *Saishoku Arubamu* (1990), edited by the staff of the Yokohama Kaiko Shiryokan, states that Nobukuni's studio operated from 1892 to 1926, after which it passed to Tamotsu who ran it from around 1929 to 1938. That is just about all there is on this studio. What other information can we go on?

The earliest reference the writer has found to the name "T. Enami" is in the 1902 *Japan Directory* when the studio took a half-page advertisement and promoted a comprehensive range of goods and services from its address at No. 9,

Left Fig. 318. Anonymous, "Portrait of Enami Nobukuni (Tamotsu)," Ogawa Dosokai (ed.), *Sogyo Kinen Sanju Nenshi*, 1913.

Above Fig. 319. Enami Tamotsu Studio Advertisement. *Japan Directory*, 1902. This is the earliest known Enami advertisement. From the wording, however, it would appear that the studio had been established for some time. Note the mention of a branch studio in the Philippines and the wide range of goods and services on offer.

Below Fig. 320. "T. Enami Photographic Studio," ca. 1910, hand-colored postcard. Old Japan Picture Library.

Bentendoori at Yokohama　　横濱辨天通リ

Benten-dori (Fig. 319). Apart from offering the standard portrait studio facilities and help to amateurs, Enami was also offering souvenir albums, lantern slides, and stereoviews of Japan, Manila, Singapore, Hong Kong, and Shanghai. A year later, Pekin and Tientsin would be added. A branch office in the Philippine Islands is also mentioned. Umemoto's *Nihon Shashi* (1852) also refers to a Hong Kong branch. Despite the studio's sudden appearance in these advertisements and listings of 1902, this is undoubtedly a substantial, mature operation. For the first time in the *Japan Directory*, the name N. Enami also appears: an entry is shown under the list of Japanese firms operating from Benten-dori. It reads: "9, Itchome. N. Enami. Photographer. Telephone No. 961." There is no mention of T. Enami, but the address and telephone number are the same. The name N. Enami, with a similarly worded entry, continues to appear intermittently in the *Japan Directory* until 1912 – but never as an advertisement.

This seems most strange; it begs the question: who is the photographer at No. 9? On the face of it, this information would imply brothers working together, or a father and son relationship. If so, why not make this clear in either the advertisement or the listing? No attempt is made over the next ten years to clarify the position. If they were two people operating from the same address, then why not style themselves as Enami & Co. or Enami Brothers?

In fact, the N. Enami name only appears in the *Japan Directory* as described, and never anywhere else. As far as the writer knows, no photograph has yet been found with an N. Enami studio imprint. T. Enami, however, appears in several advertisements and in some years replaces N. Enami in the list of Japanese firms. In all cases, the No. 9 address is shown. There exists a late Meiji photographic postcard which depicts T. Enami's studio in Benten-dori (Fig. 320). As we saw in his 1902 advertisement, T. Enami makes reference to a branch office in the Philippine Islands. Rob Oechsle has an undated cabinet-format photograph with a T. Enami Manila studio imprint. The photograph depicts American soldiers from the 1898 Spanish-American War. There have also been several early twentieth-century books illustrated with photographs by "T. Enami."[111]

Top left Fig. 321. Enami Tamotsu, "Japanese Junks," ca. 1890s, albumen-print half-stereo. Rob Oechsle Collection. A full half-negative crop of this beautiful image adorned the front cover of Jane Livingston's *Odyssey: The Art of Photography at National Geographic* (1988). The book celebrated 100 years of the *National Geographic* and reproduced 299 of the best art photographs selected from the thousands of images in the journal's archives. The cover image is a posthumous recognition of Enami's talents.

Top right Fig. 322. Enami Tamotsu, "Mount Fuji above the Clouds," ca. 1900, hand-colored glass lantern slide. Rob Oechsle Collection.

Above Fig. 323. Enami Tamotsu, "Woodland Scene," ca. 1900, hand-colored glass lantern slide. Rob Oechsle Collection.

Below Fig. 324. Enami Tamotsu, "Sannenzaka Steps at Kioto," ca. 1895, hand-colored gelatin silver-print stereoview. Rob Oechsle Collection.

Bottom Fig. 325. Enami Tamotsu, "Fox Temple Gate at Inari, Kioto," ca. 1895, hand-colored gelatin silver-print stereoview. Rob Oechsle Collection.

Below Fig. 326. Enami Tamotsu, "Mount Fuji through the Trees," ca. 1895, hand-colored gelatin silver-print stereoview. Rob Oechsle Collection. Note that the publisher's caption on the mount is wrong. The exact location is unknown.

Bottom Fig. 327. Enami Tamotsu, "Wrestlers in Uniforms," ca. 1895, hand-colored gelatin silver-print stereoview. Rob Oechsle Collection.

Rob Oechsle has collected and researched Enami's photographs for almost thirty years. He believes that under Japanese regulations the government would have required registration using the studio owner's real name, in this case Nobukuni Enami. The trading name used in all advertisements, letter headings, studio imprints, and published photographs was always "T. Enami" and Oechsle does not think that this would have been prohibited; in fact, it is common practice today in Japan's photographic, art, and entertainment industries. It certainly seems possible that any questionnaire sent by the *Japan Directory* to existing or potential advertisers would ask for both names: the business owner's legal name as well as the business (trading) name.

It is sometimes suggested that Nobukuni was the father of Tamotsu. However, Oechsle points out that a portrait of Nobukuni in the Ogawa Kazumasa studio memorial book *Sogyo Kinen Sanju Nenshi*, written and compiled by the Ogawa Dosokai (Ogawa Alumni Association) and published in 1913, shows a man aged about forty. Tamotsu, were he to be the son, would have been too young in 1892, or even 1902, to be running a studio. He further suggests that there are a number of reasons why Enami might have used the initial "T." It was

not uncommon, for example, to take the first name of a former teacher. Alternatively, Nobukuni might have had a son named Tamotsu whom he hoped would inherit the studio in later years – or Tamotsu may simply have been Enami's childhood pet name. As the many examples in this book show, it was not unusual for Japanese to change their names and the practice is still prevalent today. In any case, in 1926 the studio's proprietor is listed as Tamotsu, and the name Nobukuni has disappeared.

Oechsle's arguments seem compelling. If there is one area of doubt, it might center on the question of who might have been running the branch offices in the Philippines and Hong Kong? They could, of course, have been locally hired managers, but it is equally likely they were family members. If so, this might raise questions again about the true identities of "N" and "T." Nevertheless, the one-person theory seems to be the front runner at this point in time. If Oechsle is right, and he probably is, he will have solved one of the most vexing mysteries of Japanese photo-history.

Regardless of the mystery surrounding his name, an often overlooked aspect of Enami's studio was its tremendously wide variety of activities and the broad range of photographic formats produced. Other contemporary and well-known studios, such as Farsari's and Tamamura's, were focused on souvenir album and portrait production. Many others operated as just portrait studios catering exclusively to the Japanese, whilst still others specialized in the stereoview or glass lantern slide market. Amongst all of them, both famous and forgotten, Enami stands alone as the only photographer who consistently produced *all* formats in *all* sizes for *all* customers, from complete albums to single views and portraits, as well as stereoviews and glass lantern slides. He also acted as a photo-finisher for amateurs in these varied formats as well as operating overseas branches in key Asian cities.

Global popularity of the stereoview peaked between the years 1900 and 1910, and Enami had aligned his business strategy with this increased demand and became Japan's foremost producer of Japanese stereoview scenes. The sheer quality of his work is attested to by the many international stereoview publishers, such as Ingersoll, Sears, and Griffith & Griffith, that sold Enami's work under their own labels. Travel was a privilege afforded to relatively small numbers of Westerners, and for those less fortunate the stereoview was the chief photographic medium through which many millions of others could vicariously "travel" to foreign countries. Given Enami's dominance in this field, as far as Japanese images were concerned, his role in shaping Westerners' perceptions of Japan should not be underrated and may well repay further study. When Enami also dominated the production of Japanese glass lantern slides between the years 1890 and 1930, it should be remembered that he often produced these using half-negatives from his stereoviews.

Enami's business operated from 1892 until at least 1938, outlasting almost all other major Japanese studios. His success should be attributed to the quality, consistency, and variety of his production. Although his larger-format photography and lantern slides are highly regarded, it is as Japan's most productive and greatest Japanese stereo photographer that he is likely to be remembered.[112] But that recognition depends upon stereoviews themselves receiving great attention. Although a number of Enami's stereoviews are illustrated on these pages, it is not really possible to appreciate the sheer artistry of their composition without looking at the originals through a dedicated viewer. Otherwise it is the same as looking at a photograph of a piece of sculpture – interesting, but inanimate. If, as seems possible, 3D is the future of the visual media, then perhaps more people will become interested in its past – and in Enami.

Below Fig. 329. "Portrait of Kajima Seibei," ca. 1890. Old Japan Picture Library.

Right Fig. 330. Kajima Seibei, "112. Winter Evening," ca. 1890s, large-format hand-colored albumen print. Author's Collection.

KAJIMA SEIBEI

The Kajima family's extreme wealth had arisen due to their ownership of the Kajimaya wholesale saké distribution operation. Born in Osaka, Kajima Seibei (1866–1924) was the second son of the Osaka branch of the family (Fig. 329). In 1885 he married Nobu, the eldest daughter of the Tokyo-based Kajima family and was adopted by them and took the name Seibei. He moved to Tokyo and became the heir-apparent to the business. From an early age he seems to have suffered from indifferent health, and this led him to pursue less strenuous interests such as lacquering, rifle shooting, and music. His father had dabbled a little in photography but with no real success, but Kajima's interest in the subject was nevertheless kindled at that time. After taking control of the business, he looked out the old quarter-plate camera and started experiments.

Needing to improve his knowledge, he sought instruction from the Asakusa, Tokyo-based photographer Imatsu Seijiro. In addition, he befriended the British expert William Burton, and consulted him on a number of technical issues. Displaying great natural talent, he was very soon spending virtually all of his time behind the camera. Despite the recent introduction of dry-plate processes, photography was still a demanding and expensive pursuit, particularly as Kajima was not satisfied with anything but the best and latest chemicals and equipment. Drawing on the considerable resources of the Kajimaya, he financed a number of his friends' photo projects as well as his own photographic tours around Japan.

In 1889 Kajima financed the Ogawa Shashin Seihanjo – Ogawa's venture into photo-engraving and collotype printing.

The same year he gave, as a founder-member, support and encouragement to the Photographic Society of Japan. The Society organized a Foreign Photography Exhibition in May 1893 in Tokyo, where around 300 pictorialist art photographs were exhibited. These created a sensation at the time and inspired Kajima to help set up the Dai Nihon Shashin Himpyokai (Greater Japan Photography Critique Society) just one month later.

One of Kajima's special interests was in working with cameras that enabled him to produce giant-sized prints. In the late 1880s–early 1890s, enlargement techniques were not highly developed and so huge cameras were necessary, with all the associated expense and inconvenience of transportation. As Kajima was one of the richest men in the country, he was not to be deterred.[113] In 1894 he embarked on a photographic tour of Nikko and the Koshu district with a camera capable of producing *zenshi*-size prints – 18 x 22 inches (457 x 560 mm). Kajima required the assistance of more than twenty coolies to transport the equipment around. He used the camera to take pictures of Mount Fuji the same year and had one print enlarged to 8.8 x 5 feet (2.7 x 1.5 meters). This was presented to the Emperor in celebration of his twenty-fifth wedding anniversary. The following year he commissioned the construction of a special camera that would accommodate a dry plate to enable him to successfully produce a life-size photograph of the Kabuki actor Ichikawa Danjuro IX. The related order to the British company Marion for the dry plate itself, was at first met with incredulity.

In the early 1890s Kajima was producing a great number of hand-tinted Japanese photographs of views and costumes. By 1894 at the latest his sole agent for their sale was Okamoto Rokuhei, whose studio was at Kyobashi-ku, Tokyo. In an advertisement for that year in B. H. Chamberlain and W. B. Mason's *Handbook for Travellers in Japan*, Okamoto made what appears to be an extravagant claim: "Japan, the garden of the world, has been reproduced in the unrivalled photographs of the celebrated Amateur, Mr. Kajima Seibei, in such a manner as to make his work the wonder and admiration of every visitor to our studio. Millions of examples of Japanese Scenery and Costumes from the negatives kindly lent by him were submitted to the *Photographic Society of Japan* ... and the selection made from them has earned for Mr. Kajima the title of 'King of Amateur Photographers'." Even assuming "millions of examples" was an exaggeration, there is no doubt that Kajima's output at this time was prolific.

Kajima had also become the proprietor of the photo magazine *Shashin Sowa*. His obsession with his various photographic activities meant that he was devoting less time to the saké business. This created tension within the Kajima family. In February 1895 he went too far. Whether or not it was with the intention of converting his photographic status from amateur to professional, he fulfilled a long-held dream by opening his own studio in Tokyo. Kajima had previously insisted that his younger brother Seizaburo should go to England to study photography and now, on his return, he was reluctantly persuaded to manage the studio. In fact, it was too grand to be called a studio; it was a major photographic

112. WINTER EVENING

Below Fig. 331. H. E. Bottlewalla, "Kajima Seibei's Kyoto Studio," ca. 1897–1900, large-format hand-colored albumen print. Tom Burnett Collection. The signboard next to the studio (bottom center) reads "Photographic Studio The Genrokukwan Kioto Branch."

Bottom Fig. 332. Genroku-Kwan Studio Advertisement. *Japan Directory*, 1902. There is still much to learn about this studio and its changing relationships with Kajima Seibei and others. Nothing appears to be known about Koda & Co., the firm mentioned in the advertisement.

GENROKU·KWAN,

KODA & Co.

Photographic Studio,

No. 1, BENTENDORI ICHOME, Side Street, Yokohama.

DEALERS IN

The Best Coloured Photographs

OF

Scenery, Costumes, Flowers, etc.

Collotypes and Bromide Photographs.

Screens, Kakemonos, Silk Pictures & General Curios.

ARTISTIC ALBUMS

OF EVERY DESCRIPTION.

PRICES VERY MODERATE.

enterprise which was billed as being "The Most Complete Photographic Establishment in the Orient."

The Genrokukan (also Genro-kwan) – for so it was called – was an imposing two-story Western-style building with a frontage of 59 feet (18 meters), a revolving stage lit by the latest lighting technology, and an elevator connecting the first and second floors. Western and Japanese costumes were provided for customers whilst having their photographs taken, and all forms of commercial and amateur photography were catered for. An extensive range of "photographic works of art" was available for sale, and this eclectic mix included such items as lampshades, handkerchiefs, and ceramics – all decorated with printed photographs. A photo-mechanical department catered for collotype printing, copper-engraving, and photo-lithography, whilst a "photo-scientific" department was devoted to the production of micro- and tele-photographs. Not content with this, an art gallery was added just a few months later.

This hugely ambitious, ostentatious, and loss-making enterprise was the catalyst which saw a complete breakdown in his relations with the Kajima family. In March 1896, in a series of ruthless actions, Kajima was stripped of his control of the family business, forced to leave his wife, and disinherited. It is very likely that he ceased his involvement with the Genrokukan at the same time. By way of consolation, he was given the sum of 250,000 yen and a monthly allowance. Kajima used some of the money to redeem a well-known Shimbashi geisha known as Ponta (Tanida Etsu), and moved with her to Kyoto where he operated a photo studio known as the Tokyo Genrokukan (Fig. 331). The studio was not a success, and neither was his attempt to set up a printing company in Osaka. He then turned his attention to opening a studio in Hongo Harukicho, Tokyo, but this also failed. Although he famously photographed the 1897 funeral of the Empress Dowager at night, using magnesium flash, his photographic career was in decline. Indeed, magnesium was to finally bring it to a halt when, shortly afterwards, an explosion whilst working with the substance was to take away the thumb from his left hand.

Kajima's money and luck were running out. There were apparently problems with the monthly allowance, and in order to make a living Kajima turned to performing as a musician in the Umewaka School of *no* drama. Although in this new field he achieved some modest success, the *shashin daijin*, or "millionaire photographer" as he had been known, would spend the rest of his life in obscurity and poverty. The geisha Ponta was Kajima's companion until his death in 1924, and she herself died eight months later.

Identification of Kajima's work has, paradoxically, been hindered by the enormous number of prints he produced. He distributed his photographs not only through his own studios, but also through those of other photographers who would sometimes mix his work with their own when compiling souvenir albums of views and costumes. Kajima also co-operated with Ogawa Kazumasa in producing a number of collotype albums where the work of both artists, and sometimes other contributors, is not clearly identified. A further complication is that when his Genrokukan studio failed, he may have lost the rights to his negatives since the studio name, rather than Kajima's, seems to be credited in some publications which used his work. An example of this would be J. Stafford Ransome's *Japan in Transition* (1899). Japanese photo-history books have only formally identified a small number of Kajima's works. Perhaps, as a result, his reputation has not risen above that of a reasonably talented amateur. However, there are a number of publications which do contain photographs clearly credited to Kajima, and enough of these exist to enable a more measured assessment of his work to be carried out. From what the writer has seen, Kajima seems to have been seriously underestimated.[114]

Kajima Seibei's enthusiasm and financial support were key ingredients in promoting and furthering the cause of Japanese photography in the 1890s. For a few brief years, he was the driving force behind a number of initiatives, publications, events, and exhibitions. He was also most influential in helping to establish photographic societies in a number of Japanese cities. A keen experimenter, he was always at the forefront of the latest advances in photographic technology. Burton described Kajima in his August 1894 article as "not only the most enthusiastic amateur photographer of Japan, but also the most enthusiastic amateur that it has been my privilege to meet anywhere."[115]

OGAWA SASHICHI

Ogawa Sashichi was a Yokohama-based photographer who was married to Kusakabe Kimbei's daughter Matsu, and was expected to succeed Kusakabe whose own son had shown no interest in his father's business. A few details about Ogawa's life are given by Saito Takio in *Bakumatsu Meiji* (2004), but there is not much to go on. It is possible to add some pieces of the jigsaw by consulting the studio listings and advertisements in the contemporary directories and guidebooks.

Saito says that Ogawa was initially trained by Kusakabe before setting up his own studio around 1896. In fact, Ogawa did have a studio in existence by 1895 since it is mentioned as one of the agencies for Kajima's Genrokukan studio. His address then was 13, Otemachi, I-chome, Yokohama. Saito tells us that Kusakabe and Kajima were close friends, so it does seem likely that between them they provided Ogawa with a sufficient stock of photographs to start his operation in 1895. Further confirmation of this is provided by Saito, who also mentions the existence of an Ogawa album with this studio address, containing predominantly images from Kusakabe's portfolio. In 1896 a move was made to No. 24, Sakaicho, I-chome, and the studio's first advertisement, placed in the *Japan Directory* for that year, shows a full offering of souvenir albums and lantern slides depicting views and costumes of Japan (Fig. 333). Ogawa was clearly competing

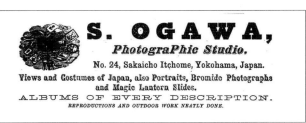

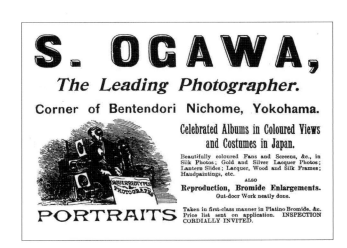

Benten dori at Yokohama.

リ通天辨濱横

Benten-dori, Yokohama.

リ通天辨濱横

Above Fig. 335. "Y. Watanabe Studio," ca. 1910, hand-colored postcard. Rob Oechsle Collection. Watanabe took over Ogawa's studio when the latter died in 1909.

Left Fig. 336. "Ogawa Sashichi Studio," 1908, hand-colored postcard. Rob Oechsle Collection. In this image Benten-dori is decorated with flags and lanterns as a welcome to the American Great White Fleet, which visited Yokohama in 1908. The street number "44" can be seen painted on the "S. Ogawa. Photographer" sign.

Left Fig. 337. Ogawa Sashichi, "1570. Samurai Dressed Long Trowser [*sic*]," ca. 1900, large-format hand-colored albumen print. Author's Collection.

Below Fig. 338. Ogawa Sashichi, "Geisha Making Music," 1908, large-format gold-lacquered photograph laid on wooden board. Author's Collection. The address on the back of the board is 25 Benten-dori. Although this process was invented and patented by Mizuno Hanbei in 1890, it is possible the patent protection had lapsed by the time Ogawa first advertised the sale of such photographs in 1908.

Below Fig. 339. Y. Watanabe Studio Advertisement. *Japan Directory*, 1911.

Below Fig. 340. Yamabe Studio Advertisement. Chamberlain and Mason, *A Handbook for Travellers in Japan*, 6th edn, 1901.

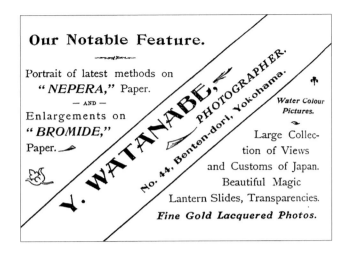

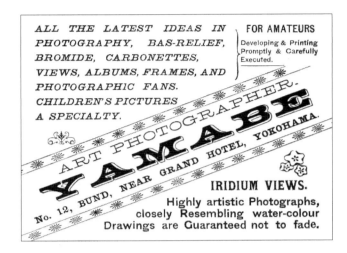

in the space occupied by studios such as Farsari & Co., Tama-mura, Enami, Kusakabe, and Genrokukan.

The studio continued at No. 24 for the next four years, but then moved to No. 25 Benten-dori in 1900, and then to No. 44 Benten-dori in 1908. There is a Yokohama street-view photograph in the November 21st, 1908 issue of *The Illustrated London News* commemorating the welcome given to the American Great White Fleet, in which it is possible to make out the studio sign "S. Ogawa Photographer." Oechsle has a postcard of the event, which also shows the studio with a confirmed address of No. 44 Benten-dori.

Further strong evidence of a link with Kusakabe is indicated by the very similar wording given in their respective advertisements (Fig. 334). Both were keen to emphasize, for example, the availability of platinotypes, colored photographic silk fans, lantern slides, and price lists. In 1908 the studio name changed from S. Ogawa Photographer to Ogawa & Co. Photographic Studio.[116] Ogawa never did take over from his father-in-law and mentor because, according to Saito, he died in July 1909. From 1910 until at least 1920, a certain Y. Watanabe was advertised as the successor and owner of the studio, which continued to operate from No. 44 (Fig. 339).

Identifying Ogawa's work has proved difficult. On three occasions the writer has come across albums where the front endpapers contained small, blue, oval-shaped studio name wet stamps. The numbers and captions shown on the photographs, however, did not demonstrate any great consistency, and the suspicion is that many of the prints originated from the Kusakabe and Kajima studios. During the fifteen or so years that Ogawa's studio was in operation, numerous albums of photographs would have been issued, and it should eventually be possible to isolate and identify his portfolio. Until then, an assessment of his work will have to be postponed. One final point of interest is that in 1908 and 1909 his studio advertised the sale of gold- and silver-lacquered photographs. This was a process invented by Mizuno Hanbei in 1890 (see page 217), and it may well be that the patent had run out by the time that Ogawa started to market the novelty. Alternatively, Ogawa may have benefited from his father-in-law's friendship with Mizuno (Fig. 338).

OTHER JAPANESE PHOTOGRAPHERS

A number of Japanese photographers covered the 1894–5 Sino-Japanese War, but the best known is **Count Kamei Koreaki** (1861–96). According to Tucker et al.'s *The History of Japanese Photography* (2003, p. 346), Kamei was born in Kyoto, the third son of a court noble. He went to England in 1877 to study at the University of London, and during his three-year stay there he also enrolled at an art college. Following his return to Japan, he joined the Imperial Household Ministry in 1883, but left in 1886 to study art and aesthetics in Berlin. Whilst in Germany he became interested in writing and also studied photography. When Kamei did return again to Japan, in 1891, he studied lithography and other printing techniques. As soon as the war with China began, he organized – at his own expense – a private photographic unit to cover the conflict. Between October 1894 and May 1895, during severe winter conditions in China, he took more than 300 photographs. On his return he presented the Imperial Household with an album of his work entitled "Meiji 27-8 nen sen'eki shashincho" (Photograph Album of the 1894/5 Campaign). Never having enjoyed robust health, he had been badly affected by the harsh conditions at the front and he died just a few months later. His photographs and archive are kept at the Kamei Onkokan in the town of Tsuwano, Shimane Prefecture.

The Yokohama studio of **Yamabe Zenjiro** was very well located at No. 12 Bund and seems to have been successful in operating not only as a portrait studio but also in the supply of frames, photographic fans, and the traditional souvenir albums (Fig. 340). One particular speciality was the production of "photographic paintings" – "Highly artistic Photographs, closely Resembling water-colour Drawings." This particular art form, which was a hybrid between oil- or watercolor-painted portraits and photography, is a genre that does not seem to have been adequately researched. The studio had a long run of success from 1898 until 1913, the last two years of which were at No. 3. It is not known whether Yamabe created his own portfolio of commercial views or whether he acted more as a dealer and distributor for others.

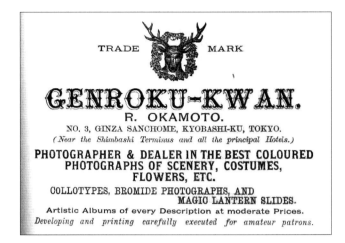

The Akitsu Co. traded as the Fine Art Depot and Manufacturing Association from No. 14 Bund, Yokohama, between 1892 and 1896. It placed several advertisements in the *Japan Directory* and offered a range of art objects, including bronzes, ivory, and wood-carvings, Satsuma porcelain, and photographs. There must have been a connection with Kusakabe Kimbei since a K. Kimbei is mentioned as the manager in 1893. In addition, the company boasted of a portfolio of more than 2000 photographs of views and costumes of Japan from which to choose, and this matches the number that Kusakabe himself was advertising at this time.

Tamemasa Torazo (1871–?) operated one of the most successful photographic dealer businesses in late Meiji Japan. A fair number of his souvenir albums have survived but the photographs are likely to have all been produced by other photographers. He also advertised a general fancy goods business and maintained a portrait studio. His main business was based at Nagasaki, and opened in the early 1890s (Fig. 341). His studio was advertised in the 1893 edition of Chamberlain and Mason's *Handbook for Travellers in Japan* and was still listed in 1913. The 1899 *Handbook* also listed a branch in Kobe.

Like Tamemasa, the dealer and photographer **Okamoto Rokuhei** played an important role in distributing souvenir albums to Western audiences in the late Meiji era. Unfortunately, very little information is available on him or his studio, and the first mention the writer has been able to trace is an advertisement placed in the 1894 Chamberlain and Mason *Handbook*. In that publication, the Tokyo-based Okamoto promoted himself as a "Photographer and Dealer in the Best Coloured Photographs of the Scenery And Costumes Of Japan." In additon, he offered collotypes, bromide photographs, and glass lantern slides, all "at moderate prices." Significantly, however, the advertisement proclaims him as "SOLE AGENT for the Magnificent Art Photographs of Mr. Kajima Seibei." As we know, Kajima was a prolific producer of commercial views, and it is likely that Okamoto did not need to supply his own. Kajima, at this time, was at the height of his fame. It is likely that Okamoto would have focused on exploiting his monopoly over distribution.

Okamoto's exclusive arrangement did not last very long. When Kajima opened his Genrokukan studio in February 1895, agencies were given to an additional six studios. As we saw, however, Genrokukan got into financial difficulties and Kajima's involvement with the enterprise probably ended by 1896 at the latest. What had been happening to Okamoto in the meantime is not clear, but by 1901 he appears to be in control of the similarly named Genroku-kwan.[117] Although the address is not the same (although it was still based in Ginza), some connection with Kajima's old establishment is likely. It is possible, though, that Okamoto acquired no more than Kajima's negatives – or most of them. There is strong circumstantial evidence for this as a number of Kajima's photographs were reproduced in Stafford Ransome's 1899 book, *Japan in Transition*, credited to Genroku-kwan.[118] In addition, *The Illustrated London News* of October 24th, 1903 (pp. 618–19) carried a double-page montage of thirteen of what all appear to be examples of Kajima's work under the caption "Photographs R. Okamoto."

Okamoto's 1901 advertisement is styled "Genroku-kwan R. Okamoto Photographer & Dealer … in scenery, costumes, flowers, etc. … and Artistic Albums of every Description" (Fig. 342). In 1903 this has changed to "R. Okamoto (Genroku-kwan) Photographer" and the advertisement also promoted the sale of silk pictures on *kakemono*. Four years later, in 1907, the studio has become "Okamoto & Co. Genro-kukwan Artistic Photographs, Silk Pictures (Kakemono)." The address of No. 3 Ginza remained constant from 1899, at the latest, until at least 1913.

If Okamoto's studio had been short-lived, it would have been possible to dismiss him as a peripheral player, at best dealing in the work of other photographers. However, his studio's very longevity raises questions. He certainly issued composite souvenir albums which included the work of Kajima Seibei – and perhaps others. He described himself as a dealer and photographer, and this may have meant more than just operating a portrait studio. We may also never know whether he controlled all or just some of Kajima's negatives. Further research into Kajima's Genrokukan brand may yield some answers.

HENRY STROHMEYER

Henry Strohmeyer was a fine American photographer and stereoview publisher who visited Japan in the spring of 1896 and probably took around 200–300 negatives (Fig. 343). Later that year a selection of seventy-two was made and published by Strohmeyer & Wyman as a boxed set but distributed by Underwood & Underwood. Strohmeyer had a close working relationship with the Underwoods, and in 1901 sold out to them and became a director and vice-president on their board.

According to Oechsle, no significant research has been carried out on this photographer and almost nothing is known about his life. We do know, however, that he was a partner in his own firm, Strohmeyer & Wyman, and in 1896 seems to have entered into a major contract with Underwood & Underwood to bring back images from Japan, China, India, the Middle East, and Europe. An insight into Strohmeyer's status with Underwood & Underwood, and into that firm's marketing strategy, is contained in a surviving letter from the photographer sent from Kyoto on April 16th, 1896, addressed to Underwood & Underwood's salesmen back home in America.[119] In this letter, which would be received by the legions of young college men who would soon be on their summer break canvassing homes throughout America and selling countless numbers of Underwood & Underwood stereoviews of home and abroad, Strohmeyer writes from the ancient capital that he "takes pleasure in sending you this note from the city in the land of the Rising Sun that for 1200 years was the capital of the Mikado."

By this time Strohmeyer had already visited Yokohama, Tokyo, Nagoya, Kobe, Osaka, and Nara. He would have been seeking out images that not only captured the essence of Japan but would also play well as three-dimensional photographs when placed in a viewer and shown in the homes of prospective buyers. Strohmeyer mentioned that he found himself "searching diligently for characteristic views of the country such as street scenes, temples, and the beautiful gardens for which the Japanese are so famous."

The 1896 set is highly appreciated by collectors of Japanese stereoviews, and the artistic compositions compare favorably with Herbert Ponting's best work. The experienced Strohmeyer must have known that he was accumulating a store of fine images likely to be well received by his sponsors. Aware of this, and wanting to motivate the firm's salesmen, as well as helping them obtain some leverage with potential customers, he wrote of the forthcoming exotic views that would make their work "easier this year, and not only easier, but pleasanter as well, for surely with such a subject to talk up you should have no difficulty in winning the attention of your people."

Strohmeyer delivered on his words, and gave Underwood & Underwood the world's first stereoview *Tour of Japan*. A review of the original set of seventy-two views shows a balanced mix of people, places, and objects, all artistically rendered and revealing of a positive and happy experience whilst traveling throughout the country. The many additional negatives brought back allowed the Underwoods to offer nonstandard extra views, including custom-made sets of a hundred or more. It would be another four years before any other stereoview publisher offered anything significant on Japan, and between the years 1896 and 1900, if you wanted to tour Japan three-dimensionally, Strohmeyer's views were the only ones available for that purpose.

In 1901, when Strohmeyer formally joined the Underwoods, no less than five other major stereoview publishers brought their own sets and series of Japan views before the public. Although this broke the Underwoods' monopoly on Japan, such was the quality of the original Strohmeyer set that it remained on the market for eight years before the Underwoods felt moved to update the content and feel.

In 1903 Herbert Ponting, who had already finished his stereo work in Japan for C. H. Graves and the Universal Photo Art Company, was commissioned for the job. The resulting 100 view famous set, published in 1904, still retained six of Strohmeyer's original images as well as a few new ones by T. Enami. In the few short pleasant months that Strohmeyer spent in Japan, he had been able to capture many unique views that eluded the redoubtable Ponting – in spite of the latter's stay of several years. Henry Strohmeyer would no doubt have been delighted at this silent tribute to the enduring quality of his work.[120]

Strohmeyer's sought-after 1896 stereoview set of Japan is now extremely rare – more so in its original custom-made box. It is as popular with collectors today as it was when first produced. When Strohmeyer arrived in Japan he was a seasoned, professional stereo-photographer. The set is delightful.

Below Fig. 344. Henry Strohmeyer, "A Washerwoman of Yokohama, Japan," 1896, albumen-print stereoview. Rob Oechsle Collection.

Bottom Fig. 345. Henry Strohmeyer, "Dotombori or Theatre Street, Osaka, Japan," 1896, albumen-print stereoview. Rob Oechsle Collection.

A Washerwoman of Yokohama, Japan.
Copyright 1896 by Strohmeyer & Wyman.

Dotombori or Theatre Street, Osaka, Japan.
Copyright 1896, by Strohmeyer & Wyman.

WALTER CLUTTERBUCK

Walter John Clutterbuck (1853–1937) was a wealthy English-man born in Chippenham, Wiltshire, who spent much of his time traveling the world and indulging in his favorite pas-times of plant collecting and photography (Fig. 346). He also authored, or co-authored, four travel books on Norway, British Columbia, Ceylon and Borneo, and the Arctic.[121] Clutterbuck was an early pictorialist in style, having been inspired by the work of Robert Demachy. Not currently placed in the first rank of art-photographers, a recent discovery of some thirty-two albums of his photographs, held by the Norfolk and Norwich Millennium Library, England, may well change that since he seems to have been a very fine photographer indeed.

During his travels he often used a stereoscopic camera, which was disguised to look like large field glasses or binocu-lars (Fig. 347). The camera lenses were built into one side, and he was thereby able to appear to be gazing at right angles to his subjects who would not suspect they were being pho-tographed, and in this way he was able to obtain some very relaxed and natural poses. Having obtained his glass-plate stereo negatives, he would cut them in half and then set about obtaining prints from them of the required dimensions.[122]

Photographs of nineteenth-century Okinawa are very rare, but the writer recently came across an album of seventy photographs taken by Clutterbuck in Okinawa during a brief visit to the islands from December 1898 to January 1899. The gelatin silver photographs are all approximately 3 1/2 x 2 1/2 inches (83 x 65 mm). At the beginning of the album are a further nine photographs of Nagasaki and south Kyushu. From other photographs in the collection, it is clear that Clutterbuck was in Tokyo during May 1898 and the Hakone area in September and October. Presumably, he began his Japan trip in the east and slowly made his way towards Kyushu from where he journeyed to Okinawa in December.

The Okinawan photographs are roughly evenly split between Naha and Shuri. All of the images are interesting and representative of life on the island and include images of people, street and village scenes, ships and boats, houses, potteries, paper makers, market stalls, tombs and cemeteries, Shuri Castle walls, temple grounds, a pigsty, and a group of Luchuan musical instruments (Fig. 350). There are also views of Mrs Clutterbuck in a rickshaw, her female "model" (Mrs Violet Clutterbuck was a talented amateur painter who had studied in Italy and married Walter in 1892), and an interpreter named Masuda. Very little information on Clutter-buck's life and career has yet emerged and it is not known, for example, whether he visited Japan more than once. He remains one of only a handful of photographers to have worked in Okinawa during the Bakumatsu and Meiji eras (Figs. 348, 349, 352, 353).[123]

The photographer and writer Arthur Hacker owns an album of Clutterbuck's photographs of Hong Kong taken during a visit in 1901. He wrote about this album, and Clut-terbuck's style, in the *Hong Kong Tatler* of June 1999 in an article entitled "Eastern Exposure." Hacker, a Hong Kong

resident, has been able to determine that Clutterbuck left England on November 2nd, 1901 aboard the *Malacca*. En route he took pictures in Malta, Port Said, and Singapore, and arrived in Hong Kong on December 2nd, 1901. In Hong Kong he visited Kowloon, Stonecutters Island, Taipo, and Lantau Island where he took pictures of the Tung Chung Fort and Tai O. He went to the Happy Valley Race Track and also pho-tographed Hong Kong yacht races. After that he went to Macau for a few days, but his subsequent movements are not clear.

In the catacombs of the British Library, buried in the pages of an obscure short-lived travel journal, *Travel and Exploration* (1910), lies an article that Clutterbuck penned about his visit to Okinawa, albeit some ten years after it had taken place, entitled "The Lu-Chu Islands." In this delightful eight-page article, which the writer found by chance whilst searching for other material, Clutterbuck records his first impressions on arriving at Naha: "We crept up to the shores of Okinawa in a Japanese steamer, just when the day was breaking.... By the time the anchor-chains rattled at the moorings, the faint yellow gleam in the sky had changed to a flood of dazzling light, though the outlines of the land were softened by morning mist. It was a beautiful morning, so warm, so sunlit, almost like a dream."

During his six weeks' stay, the temperature averaged a pleasant fifty-five degrees, despite it being the coldest time of the year. However, he felt that the absence of a hotel was a disincentive for travelers from China or Japan who would otherwise find the islands a delightful spot to winter in. Clutterbuck stayed with his wife in a Japanese inn, the Ikebata tea house, before renting a house in the capital Shuri, three miles inland. The locals were fascinated by the sight of a woman in Western dress.

Clutterbuck is very complimentary about the Luchuans whom he described as very friendly and "a much finer race than their conquerors [the Japanese], taller, broader and apparently more healthy in physique; the women, too, seem much bigger and stronger, and many of the young girls were very pretty, with their big, soft, brown eyes."

He also found the scenery charming, consisting so much of light and color, which must have been conducive to securing good photographs. Most regrettably, Clutterbuck does not discuss photography in the article, which is nevertheless illustrated with photographs from the album mentioned above. It was most unusual for a Westerner to travel to Okinawa at this time, and photographs of the islands are exceptionally rare. It is fortunate that Clutterbuck's images survive since they, together with the written account he has left us, give a rare insight into life in this remote but beautiful corner of Japan.

In conducting research into Clutterbuck, the writer was reminded of the difficulties faced by the early photographers in China and Japan. One problem was in trying to photograph people's everyday activities without their getting excited and not remaining still. Paul Champion and Henry Woods both comment on this in Appendix 2. What would they have given, one wonders, for Clutterbuck's Physiographe Stereo Camera?

Above Fig. 347. Clutterbuck's Physiographe Stereo Camera. Courtesy of John Benjafield. This is the 1898 model which was made by Edmond & Leon Bloch, Paris, and also sold in England as "Watson's Stereo Binocular." See page 248 for a description of its properties and how it enabled Clutterbuck to catch his subjects unawares.

Below Fig. 348. Walter Clutterbuck, "Boats at Naha Harbour, Okinawa," December 1898/January 1899, small-format gelatin silver print. Okinawa Prefectural Museum.

Left Fig. 349. Walter Clutterbuck, "A Deserted Street in Naha," December 1898/January 1899, small-format gelatin silver print. Okinawa Prefectural Museum.

Above Fig. 350. Walter Clutterbuck, "Luchuan (Okinawan) Guitar," December 1898/January 1899, small-format gelatin silver print. Okinawa Prefectural Museum.

Below Fig. 351. Walter Clutterbuck, "Instantaneous in Tokeo [*sic*]," May 1898, large-format gelatin silver print. Norfolk and Norwich Millennium Library and by permission of Norfolk County Council Library and Information Service.

Above Fig. 352. Walter Clutterbuck, "Natives (Naha)," December 1898/ January 1899, small-format gelatin silver print. Okinawa Prefectural Museum.

Right Fig. 353. Walter Clutterbuck, "Market Women, Naha," December 1898/January 1899, small-format gelatin silver print. Okinawa Prefectural Museum.

Below Fig. 354. Anonymous, "Portrait of William Burton," ca. 1890s. Old Japan Picture Library.

Right Fig. 355. William Burton, "Ainu," ca. 1890s, large-format albumen print. Courtesy of Ken and Jenny Jacobson.

WILLIAM BURTON

Despite being of amateur status, Professor William Kinnin-mond Burton (1856–99) was one of the most technically competent photographers to have visited Japan, and was instrumental in the introduction of many new photography techniques (Fig. 354). Prior to arriving in 1887, his book *Burton's Modern Photography* (1885) had just gone through its seventh edition. A few years later, in 1892, another of his books, *Practical Guide to Photography,* would be published and remain in print for many years. In 1889 he founded the Photographic Society of Japan (Nihon Shashin Kyokai), and an announcement of its inaugural meeting on May 10th, 1889, was given in the form of a letter from Burton to the editor of the *Japan Mail,* which was published in the weekly edition on May 11th. Burton also formed mutually beneficial relationships with key Japanese photographers such as Ogawa Kazumasa and Kajima Seibei, and in 1893 organized the first international photographic exhibition to be held in Japan. This was a hugely influential event, which introduced art photography to the country. An engineer by training, Burton

designed the water supply systems for most of Japan and Taiwan's major cities, and also drew up the plans for the twelve-story Ryounkaku which, on its opening to the public in 1890, would become Japan's first skyscraper (see Fig. 400).

Thanks to Olive Checkland's research, summarized in her article "W. K. Burton, 1856–99: 'Engineer Extraordinaire'" (2002), we are able to understand something of his early life before he came to settle in Japan. Burton was born in Edinburgh in 1856 and his father was a lawyer and writer. His mother's father was a respected figure in Edinburgh's legal and cultural circles. After his education at the Edinburgh Collegiate School, Burton wanted to pursue a career in engineering, and in the absence at that time of any formal university courses for engineering undergraduates he became, in 1873, apprenticed for five years to a local firm of engineers. Burton progressed to becoming resident engineer of the London Sanitary Protection Association, and on the strength of successful engineering projects in both Edinburgh and London, was offered the post of Professor of Sanitary Engineering at the Tokyo Imperial University and took up his position on May 5th, 1887.

Burton immersed himself enthusiastically in Japanese society. He learnt the language, and was one of the first Westerners to marry a Japanese. A daughter was born in 1892. He traveled extensively throughout the country and photographed the aftermath of the 1891 Gifu earthquake (Fig. 356). When his term at the university expired in 1896, Burton accepted a role in overseeing the development of Taiwan's water supply system. It was there, in Japan's new colony, that Burton's health broke down due to overwork. He returned to convalesce in Japan but died there of a fever in 1899 at the age of forty-three. He did, however, manage one last photographic and scientific assignment when he, perhaps unwisely in view of his health, accompanied the Todd Expedition to Hokkaido to observe the Japanese eclipse. There, according to Mabel Loomis Todd's article "In Aino-Land" in *The Century* (1898), he photographed the Ainu, and a number of these photographs were illustrated in the article and her book *Corona and Coronet* (1898) (Fig. 355).

The many contributions that Burton made to Japanese photography would take too long to enumerate, but mention should be made of his relationships with Japanese photographers. A lasting friendship was formed with Ogawa Kazumasa, for example, and in the preface to his 1892 *Practical Guide to Photography* Burton was anxious to express his appreciation for the time the two had spent in carrying out various photographic experiments.[124] Burton gave technical assistance to Kajima Seibei from time to time, who in turn assisted financially in setting up the Photographic Society of Japan. Burton brought both photographers to the attention of the international photographic community when he wrote about their careers in the early 1890s.[125]

During his time in Japan, Burton was a prolific writer and produced numerous articles and publications.[126] His importance to the development of Japanese photography was recognized by the Japanese themselves, and a tribute was published in the *Shashin Sowa* where the writer stated: "As it is we do not hesitate to say that Japan owes much to Professor W. K. Burton in photographic matters, and that the present popularity of photography in Japan is greatly due to Professor W. K. Burton."[127] Although unequalled in his understanding of photographic technology, Burton is unlikely ever to be recognized as one of the greatest photographers to work in the country. There is no doubt, however, that had Burton not gone to Japan, the development of photography in that country would have been that much slower.

Forgotten today in the West, Burton is nevertheless remembered in Japan – but not so much for his contribution to photography, although that is valued. He is revered as an engineer who introduced fresh water and sewage systems throughout Japan, that at a stroke all but eliminated cholera which, together with other epidemics, was killing as many as 100,000 people a year. He built a sand-filtering system in Shimonoseki which enables the city today to manufacture and sell pure bottled water, and Burton's picture is on the label. As this book was going to press, a monument to commemorate the 150th anniversary of Burton's death was being erected in Edinburgh.

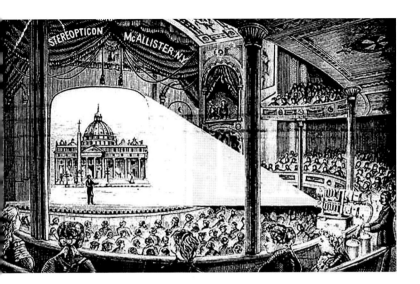

OTHER WESTERN PHOTOGRAPHERS

The English Anglican missionary and Alpinist **Walter Weston** (1861–1940), known as the "Father of Japanese Mountaineering," spent three periods of residency in Japan totaling fourteen years. According to A. H. Ion's "Mountain High and Valley Low" (1991), Weston first arrived in Japan in 1888 and was initially posted to Kumamoto, but was quickly transferred to Kobe where he took charge of St. Andrew's Church. On his second posting to Japan in 1902, Weston looked after St. Andrew's in Yokohama. Being a keen mountaineer, he spent his summer holidays during 1891 and 1894 climbing Mount Fuji and various peaks in the Chubu mountain region. Some, like Mount Hotakadake, were scaled for the first time.

A keen amateur photographer, Weston took some of the finest photographs of alpine Japan, and a selection of his work appeared in his famous 1896 mountaineering book, *Mountaineering and Exploration in the Japanese Alps* (1896). A later book, *The Playground of the Far East* (1918), also contains photographs by his friend Otis Poole, whom we will consider in the next chapter. Of particular interest are Weston's photographs of the tough bear hunters, many of whom had never before been captured on camera. Weston had a great affinity with the local communities, and regarded the mountain areas as *Kunshi no Koku* (the country of gentlemen). Finally, mention should be made of some of his climbing companions who were also amateur photographers: **H. W. Belcher** (1891), **H. J. Hamilton** (1894), and **Otis Manchester Poole** (1905). Some of the photographs they took are included in Weston's books.

Another amateur photographer was the seismologist **John Milne** (1850–1913), who was appointed to the post of Professor of Geology and Mining at the Imperial College of Engineering in Tokyo. Prone to severe bouts of seasickness, Milne traveled overland from England, and arrived in Japan in 1876 after an epic eleven months' trek. He would spend the next nineteen years of his life attached to the college, which became part of Tokyo University in 1886. Over the years Milne made his reputation as the foremost world expert on the study of earthquakes. He continued teaching in Japan until 1895 when he went home to England and lived on the Isle of Wight with his Japanese wife Tone, whom he had married in 1881. He died in 1913 and was affectionately known as the "Father of Seismology."

Milne took many photographs in Japan, a number of which were converted into hand-colored lantern slides. Some of these are illustrated in the biography by Herbert-Gustar and Nott, *John Milne: Father of Modern Seismology* (1980). He is known to have done some early documentary work amongst the Ainu in northern Japan, and he made the first of several trips to the region in 1877. There are some Ainu photographs included in those he presented to the Royal Geographical Society in 1892, but it is difficult to date them.

Milne, along with his friend and colleague William Burton, and also Ogawa Kazumasa, rushed to the scene of the 1891 earthquake, which centered on the prefectures of Gifu and Aichi. They arrived just two days later and witnessed and photographed the aftermath of what had been, up until that time, the most devastating earthquake recorded by seismology. A collaborative effort, it is not possible to separate Milne's photographs from Burton's in the jointly authored book of the event, which was published the following year as *The Great Earthquake in Japan*. However, the preface to the book states: "The greater number of the photographs that are reproduced in this book were made by one of the Authors, for the Imperial University of Japan." The strong suspicion is that Burton was the photographer, leaving the seismologist Milne to concentrate on the aftermath of the earthquake. Certainly, Burton had the greater reputation as a photographer, and a natural division of labor suggests itself.

Below Fig. 359. Elias Burton Homes, "Mount Fuji," ca. 1890s, hand-colored glass lantern slide. The Burton Homes Collection.

Wilson Le Couteur (1853–1925) was an Australian amateur photographer and writer who spent two months in Japan during 1899. A number of his photographs were reproduced in the account of his tour, *To Nippon: The Land of the Rising Sun* (1899), which was published by the Japanese shipping line Nippon Yusen Kaisha in the form of a guidebook.

The American traveler, public lecturer, and author **John Lawson Stoddard** (1850–1931) made his living by trekking

around the globe and writing about and lecturing on his experiences (Fig. 358). Born in Brookline, Massachusetts, he attended public school in Boston and then entered Williams College from where he graduated in 1871. He then spent two years at the Yale Divinity School, but abandoned the ministry to take up a teaching post in the classics at the Boston Latin School. It was at around this time that he started to visit other countries for pleasure and found that he could entertain his

Taylor says that Stoddard obtained many of his images from an agent in Paris. According to the photo-journalist Richard Barry in his book *Port Arthur: A Monster Heroism* (1905, p. 110), it was James Ricalton who provided most of Stoddard's photographs, though probably not the ones of Japan. According to Herbert Croly in his biography of Willard Straight (1925), Ricalton worked for T. H. McAllister, the New York firm of lantern slide manufacturers and distributors. It is likely, therefore, that this firm had a formal or informal connection with the Paris agent.

During his first Japan trip, Stoddard bought photos from a number of different studios judging by several of the illustrations in his *Lectures*. For the rest, it seems that one of his traveling companions operated a camera; certainly many of the illustrations were not of the usual commercial studio type. In *Lectures*, Stoddard describes his arrival in Japan and the custom house baggage inspection at Yokohama: "A slight examination of our trunks was made by officers polite enough to beg our pardon for the trifling delay. There is a duty in Japan on photographic cameras. One of our party was, therefore, called upon to pay the stipulated sum."

Stoddard's young protégé, **Elias Burton Holmes** (1870–1958), was a remarkable man (Fig. 360). Taking over from his mentor and inspiration John Stoddard, Holmes developed a new genre known as "travelogues," which consisted of educational and entertaining lectures based on his travels to all corners of the globe. Unlike Stoddard, Holmes was a fine photographer, and during his career he gave more than 8000 lectures illustrated with his photographs, which were converted in Japan to hand-colored lantern slides. He also used photographs from artists such as James Ricalton, Otis Poole, Tamamura Kozaburo, Kusakabe Kimbei, Enami Tamotsu, and Ogawa Kazumasa. A collection of Holmes' original slides, numbering some 18,000, is held today by the University of California, Los Angeles. It is said that Holmes visited almost every country on earth and went six times around the world.

He thought of himself more as a performer than a lecturer, giving talks to packed audiences in venues all over America, including Carnegie Hall, New York, and the Symphony Hall, Boston. An immensely popular ten-volume series based on his lectures was published in 1901 as *Burton Holmes Travelogues*.

Born in Chicago, the son of a wealthy banker, Holmes discovered an early passion for photography, buying his first camera at the age of thirteen. His other passion was travel and he had an insatiable curiosity for people and places. His formal education became a casualty and he dropped out of school at sixteen and went on a European tour with his mother and grandmother. According to Genoa Caldwell's book, *The Man Who Photographed the World* (1977), Holmes first traveled to Japan in 1892 at the age of twenty-two, coincidentally meeting John Stoddard on the outward voyage, also on his first visit. He fell in love with the "Old Japan," which in later life he described as "inconceivably picturesque, strangely and curiously beautiful. There were no ugly areas, no unfinished raw edges anywhere visible. All things Japanese

audiences by lecturing to them about his travels. He gave up teaching and embarked on a career as a public lecturer in 1879 (Fig. 357). After a highly successful career, and almost eighteen years of non-stop travel visiting "nearly every part of the habitable globe," he retired in 1897.

There is little detail about his travel schedules other than that contained in his biography written by D. Crane Taylor, *John L. Stoddard: Traveller, Lecturer, Litterateur* (1935), but it is clear that he made the first of several visits to Japan in 1892 because he writes about it in Volume 3 of his well-known ten-volume publication *John L. Stoddard's Lectures* (1897). Stoddard did take some of the photographs used in his lectures, particularly in the later years of his career, but in Taylor's biography it is clear that Stoddard was content to secure views from local photographers or from other sources, thereby giving him more time to study and research the places he visited.

were bound together into a satisfying mellow unity." Of all the cities in the world he visited, it seems that Kyoto was a particular favorite, and it was in that city, in 1899, that Holmes used movie film for the first time in Japan's history. When he returned to America in 1893, he mailed out 2000 invitations on Japanese poem cards inviting people to illustrated lectures entitled "Japan: The Country and the Cities." The performances were oversubscribed and Holmes' professional travelogue career was launched. He was able to convey his enthusiasm for the country using lantern slides which he had had hand colored in Yokohama, and his contribution to increasing the numbers of American tourists to late Meiji Japan should not be underestimated.

Mention should be made of **John Alfred Vaughan**, an engineer on HMS *Undaunted*, who took pictures of the landing of the Japanese army at Chemulpo (present-day Inch'on), Korea, during the 1894–5 Sino-Japanese War. His photographs appeared in *The Illustrated London News* on November 10th and 17th, 1894, and were also illustrated in the writer's *Korea: Caught in Time* (1997) (Fig. 361).

A number of photo studios in the 1890s would make a brief appearance, only to disappear without trace once the competitive pressures from the growing number of Japanese studios had asserted themselves. One example is that of the unknown **L. Brouwer**, who first appeared on the Japan scene in 1891 when the *Japan Directory* listed him as a resident.

By 1893 he is shown as the manager of the Yokohama Invest-ment Co. and living with his wife on the Bluff. The 1894 directory has the same entry but additionally mentions him as an agent for the horticultural firm Messrs. L. Boehmer & Co. In the appendix to the same directory, however, Brouwer advertises the sale of "my large and fine collection of views of Japan, China, Corea and Java, coloured and uncoloured … also stereoscopic views and magic lantern slides." The ad-dress given is 52 Main Street, Yokohama, which is the same address as the Yokohama Investment Co. There is no indica-tion that a studio is operating at this address, or that Brouwer is a photographer. It is even possible that he was a collector simply seeking to offload his collection, and the advertise-ment is the last we hear of him. There is an interesting link with Alfred Unger (see endnote 123), which raises the possi-bility that Brouwer took photographs in Okinawa (Fig. 363).

The 1895 *Japan Directory* listed a **J. Himen**, who is shown as managing the Japan Photographic Co. (not to be confused with Stillfried's Japan Photographic Association nor Usui's Yokohama Photographic Co.) at No. 77 Yokohama and living there with his wife. Whether this was a studio or photo-graphic supplies outlet is not clear. A second and final listing appears in the *Japan Directory* for 1896 after which the busi-ness and J. Himen are no longer mentioned.

William Henry Jackson (1843–1942) is famous for his landscape photographs of the American West. In the years 1894–6 he was commissioned by *Harper's Weekly* to undertake a world tour, which was organized by the World's Transportation Commission in order to gather information about foreign transportation systems. He arrived in Japan in 1895, and the photographs he took there are retained by the Library of Congress, Washington.

The French missionary **Michel M. Ribaud** was an amateur photographer whose photographs of the Ainu and Hokkaido are illustrated in his book *Japonais et Ainos Dans Le Yeso* (Kokkaido), published in 1897, which refers to an earlier 1892 journey.

For a period of some thirty years, **Baron Adolf de Meyer** (1868–1949) was a famous pictorialist photographer, said to be the founder of fashion photography. For some inexplicable reason, his work today is largely forgotten despite there being holdings of his photography in museums all around the world. Due to his impressionistic style, Cecil Beaton referred to him as "the Debussy of Photography."

In 1899 de Meyer married into nobility. Olga Caracciolo, his bride, was commonly held to be the illegitimate daughter of King Edward VII. She lost no time in introducing de Meyer to her high society friends, and many of them sat for their portraits. This gave real momentum to de Meyer's career, which was also helped in 1901, when he was given the title of Baron. His career as a fashion photographer was very suc-cessful but, unaccountably, he died in poverty and obscurity in California. It seems there is much more to learn about his life. Of particular interest here is that he and his new bride visited Japan in 1899 as part of a honeymoon trip around the world (Fig. 364). The platinum print photographs that he took in Japan are represented in the Worswick Collection, Tokyo, and in the Metropolitan Museum of Art, New York.

Opposite Fig. 362. Japanese Military Photographic Unit, "Japanese Army in China during the Sino-Japanese War 1894–5," large-format albumen print. Author's Collection.

Left Fig. 363. L. Brouwer Advertisement for Sale of Photographs. *Japan Directory*, 1894. It is not clear from the wording whether Brouwer is selling photographs taken by himself or by others.

Below Fig. 364. Baron Adolf de Meyer, "Portrait of Baroness Meyer in Japan," 1899, large-format platinum print. Worswick Collection. The former Olga Caracciolo on honeymoon in Japan.

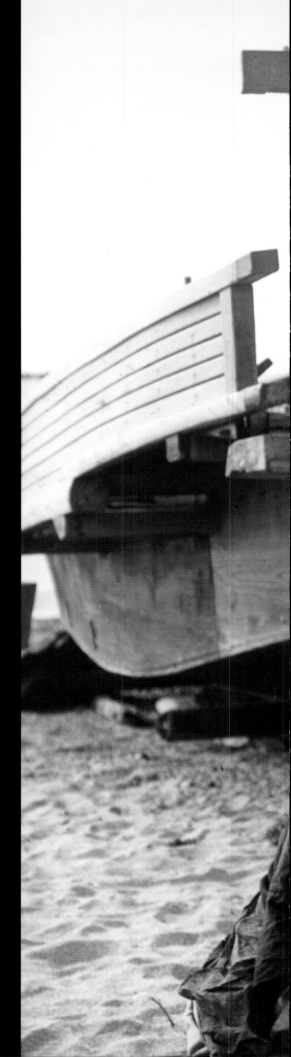

1900s
In Full Control

At the beginning of the twentieth century, the West had very little left to teach Japan about photography – apart, that is, from art photography and the manufacture of cameras and equipment. There had been no serious Western photo studios in Japan for ten years, and supplies of chemicals and equipment were readily available. Full sovereignty had been re-established in 1899 with the removal of extraterritoriality, and Japan – and the Japanese – were becoming more self-assured and confident about their place in the world.

It is instructive to recall the departure of the Western studios, and to understand the commercial imperatives which brought about their demise. Adolfo Farsari had built his business around the demand from foreign tourists for attractive souvenir albums of hand-colored views and costumes. When he started, in 1885, there was already intense and growing competition from Japanese studios. Farsari was the exception that proved the rule, and we saw earlier how he managed to buck the trend and operate a successful and remunerative business, albeit for just a few short years.

Above Fig. 366. "Tokura Photo Studio," ca. 1910, hand-colored postcard. Rob Oechsle Collection. A typical photographer's studio in late Meiji Japan. Nothing is known, incidentally, about T. Tokura.

Previous page Fig. 365. Takagi Teijiro, "Fisherman's Family," ca. 1910, hand-colored glass lantern slide. Rob Oechsle Collection.

Below Fig. 367. Herbert Ponting, "Peering into the Awful Crater of Aso San, a Volcano in Southern Japan," 1906, gelatin silver-print stereoview, published by H. C. White Co. Rob Oechsle Collection. Here we see Ponting himself, at 5,216 feet (1590 meters), leaning into Mount Aso's crater, which has seen more explosive eruptions than any other volcano in the world. Seemingly innocuous as a two-dimensional print, the sense of danger is considerably heightened when viewed stereoscopically.

But the commercial storm clouds were gathering. If Farsari's studio had opened in the year 1900, things would have been quite different. The first problem would have been finding artists to color his photographs to the standard for which he had become famous. Growing economic prosperity and alternative employment options would have meant that either the quality of his product would have suffered, or he would have had to pay rates that would, as a consequence, make his albums prohibitively expensive. In addition, foreign travelers increasingly brought their own portable Kodak cameras along and had less need, therefore, for "ready-made" souvenirs. They enjoyed taking their own photographs, and following the lifting of travel restrictions were able to move inland and obtain views which were previously only available in typical souvenir albums.

Photo-mechanical processes such as collotype printing were turning out their own form of color souvenir albums – but at a much lower price. These commercial pressures were bad enough, but the introduction of the picture postcard in October 1900 was decisive. Here was a way in which tourists could obtain hand-colored souvenirs of all parts of the country for a fraction of the cost paid for the larger albumen print photographs. Most commercial studios supplying tourist photographs therefore had no choice but to offer postcards as well. Stereoviews and hand-colored glass lantern slides were also extremely popular, and the cheaper bromide print photographs were also becoming more widely available.

We can see how the successful Japanese studios adapted to these market forces by looking at Kusakabe Kimbei's early studio advertisements. Initially, he was content to focus on the promotion of his albums of views and customs, together with the usual studio portrait facilities. It was not until 1892 that he felt compelled to offer colored lantern slides, and by 1897 we can see that he had broadened his offering to include colored collotype photographs and silk and paper hand screens

decorated with colored photographic prints. By 1901 he was offering lacquered wooden photographic frames, colored photographs printed on silk fans, and platinotypes and carbon photographs. In 1904 he was supplying Eastman Kodaks and other cameras and supplies, as well as offering full developing, printing, and coloring services to amateurs.

What we did see, however, was a parade of very fine Western photographers passing through Japan towards the end of the Meiji era. Some, like Herbert Ponting, were on commercial missions whilst others, such as Arnold Genthe and Adam Vroman, were on vacation. The Russo-Japanese War also brought expert photo-journalists such as James Ricalton and James Hare. We can now consider the contribution that these photographers made to the history of late Meiji photography.

HERBERT PONTING

At the beginning of the twentieth century, the *Japan Times* reviewed the work of an English photographer who had taken pictures of Mount Fuji: "It would scarcely be an exaggeration to say that Mr. Ponting has discovered a new mountain; for no one has ever seen the great quiescent volcano depicted from so many points before, except, indeed, from the pencil of Hokusai. But then, this great painter gave representations that were half true, half fanciful, whereas the pictures before us are pure and unadulterated truth"[128] (Figs. 368, 372).

Herbert George Ponting (1870–1935) was a perfectionist, determined to obtain the best results wherever in the world he was working. That he was not easily satisfied can be seen from the description given in his book *In Lotus Land Japan* (1910), of how he tried to capture a particular view of Fuji. Particularly struck by the beauty of a winter's view of the mountain near Lake Motosu, he wanted to illustrate a cloudless Fuji through shoots of Kaia grass in the foreground. It was a prerequisite that the grass be completely still in order to avoid the inevitable blurred image. In achieving the perfect combination of a cloudless and windless moment, he had to tramp back and forth to the nearby village of Nakano-kura-toge, a distance of some 14 miles (22.5 km). It required more than a dozen journeys before the now world-famous photograph of "Fuji and the Kaia grass" could be taken.

Ponting worked tirelessly to illustrate a mountain for which he had genuine and deep affection. He photographed it in all seasons, and from all positions, circling the base on a number of occasions in order to obtain the desired views, and taking views from the summit, which he reached twice. In *Lotus Land* he declared: "Every hour of every clear day the mountain was a different picture. There was Morning Fuji, shaking off mists of night; the Midday Fuji, with a belt of cumulus cloud floating across its waist; the Sundown Fuji, a symphony of pink and violet; and a hundred other phases, for the mountain is never twice alike."

In experiencing sunset from the summit he wrote: "When the sun sank to the level of the surging vapours, flooding their waves and hollows with ever-changing contrasts of light and shade, the scene was of indescribable beauty. Never in any part of the world have I seen such a spectacle so replete with awesome majesty as the sunset I witnessed that evening from the topmost cubic foot of Fuji."

In stark contrast, Ponting gave a graphic account of how potentially dangerous a place Fuji could be. He described his first journey to the summit accompanied by a Japanese friend and four mountain guides. Between them they had the dubious privilege of carrying Ponting's 80 lbs (36 kgs) worth of

photographic equipment, including a darktent, a supply of glass plates, and enough food and clothing to facilitate a stay for up to a week on the summit, if that was how long it needed in order to capture the best views. On arrival at the summit, the party was caught in a severe storm and involuntarily marooned for several days. During a brief lull, Ponting ventured alone to the highest point of Fuji, Ken-ga-mine, to witness the sunset. Just as he was about to negotiate the half-mile return journey to the rest hut, he was suddenly enveloped in swirling mists, darkness, and a howling icy wind which "moaned and whistled amongst the crags which loomed like ominous moving phantoms in the turbulent vapours and dying light." He was completely disoriented and groped his way along a perilous path, almost falling over a precipice. After shouting for some time, he was eventually rescued by one of the guides.

An energetic, restless, and ultimately tragic figure, Ponting had great technical competence in photography, combined with an artist's intuitive understanding of composition. Famous for his stunning, large-format pictures of Scott's 1910 Antarctic Expedition, it is not so well known that he was also one of the world's finest stereo-photographers and produced many exceptional images in this medium. In addition, he published a number of books and articles on Japan, a country he loved above all others.

Ponting was born in Salisbury, England, on March 21st, 1870. One of eight children, he appears to have had a reasonably happy childhood. Certainly it was comfortable, since the family lived in large houses in London, Watford, Ilkley, and Southport and employed several maids and servants. Ponting

(14)-3853-Snow-capped Fuji, the superb, (12,365 ft.) mirrored in Lake Shoji—looking S. E.—Japan. Copyright 1904 by Underwood & Underwood.

(100) Coaling the Pacific Mail S.S. "Siberia" at the fortified naval station of Nagasaki, Japan. Copyright 1904 by Underwood & Underwood

Above Fig. 369. Herbert Ponting, "Coaling the Pacific Mail 'S.S. Siberia' at the Fortified Naval Station of Nagasaki, Japan," 1904, albumen-print stereoview, published by Underwood & Underwood. Rob Oechsle Collection.

Below Fig. 370. Herbert Ponting, "Ponting Photographing the Crater of the Volcano, Aso-san," 1904, albumen-print stereoview, published by Underwood & Underwood. Rob Oechsle Collection.

An Underwood stereoscopic photographer at the crater of the largest active volcano in the world, Aso-san, Japan. Copyright 1904 by Underwood & Underwood.

had an adequate, if not exceptional education, initially at Carlisle and Preston grammar schools, and then at Wellington House College, Leyland. Leaving at eighteen, he attempted to follow in the footsteps of his father's successful banking career. But after four years he had had enough and set out for California with the advantage of generous financial support from his father. Ponting had great affection for his parents, and wrote and visited them whenever he could. He stayed close to them until his mother's death in 1919 and his father's fatal illness in 1923.

His father's financial support was sufficient for Ponting to purchase a fruit farm in Auburn, California, as well as to speculate with others in local gold-mining enterprises. In June 1895 he married Mary Elliott, a local girl who came from a successful and prominent family, who bore him two children. The fruit farm was soon in financial difficulties and the gold mining ultimately proved unsuccessful. According to H. J. P Arnold's *Herbert Ponting: Another World* (1975), it seems that Ponting had little talent for business, and indeed achieved no lasting commercial success throughout his life.

Below Fig. 373. Herbert Ponting, "Charming Youth and Hoary Age – A Fair Devotee Counting the Stone Lanterns, Kasuga, Nara, Japan," 1904, albumen-print stereoview, published by Underwood & Underwood. Rob Oechsle Collection.

Bottom Fig. 374. Herbert Ponting, "Group of Ainu, Hokkaido," ca. 1904, gelatin silver-print stereoview, published by Keystone View Company. Rob Oechsle Collection.

(77) Charming youth and hoary age—a fair devotee counting the stone lanterns, Kasuga, Nara, Japan. Copyright 1904 by Underwood & Underwood.

W33912 A Group of Pure-blooded Japanese Aborigines—Ainus on the Island of Hokkaido.

Below Fig. 375. Herbert Ponting, "Charming Geisha Girls of Japan, in a Lovely Garden at Hiroshima," 1906, hand-colored gelatin silver-print stereoview, published by H. C. White Co. Rob Oechsle Collection.

Bottom Fig. 376. Herbert Ponting, "Ito Hirobumi and Family at Their Tokyo Home," ca. 1904, small-format gelatin silver print. Author's Collection.

3865 Charming Geisha Girls of Japan, in a lovely Garden at Hiroshima. Copyright 1905 by H. C. White Co.

Ponting took up photography seriously in 1900, although it is not clear what induced him to do so. He immediately became obsessed with stereo-photography and won a number of competition prizes. He enjoyed great good fortune in having one photograph, entitled "Mules at a Californian Round-Up," displayed as a centerpiece at the 1900 Worlds Fair in St. Louis. It is an understatement to say his rise to fame was meteoric, because within a year he was regularly selling his work to publishing companies. In 1901 he was asked by the American journal *Leslie's Weekly* and the stereo-view publishing company Universal Photo Art Co. of Philadelphia to go on a Far Eastern stereo-photo assignment. After completing this photographic tour of Japan, China, and Korea in the spring of 1902, he received similar commissions, and so began a decade of frenetic globetrotting, at the end of which he would be one of the best-known and most famous photographers in the world.

Unfortunately, not enough is known about his movements during this time and it is difficult to determine the precise chronology of his subsequent assignments in Europe and North America.[129] Ponting does not seem to have kept a diary, and other sources are sparse, although further information might well be found in the archives of the magazines and stereoview publishers which sponsored his photographic assignments.[130] Ponting traveled extensively in Japan, photographing everywhere he went, and made five visits between the years 1901 and 1906. He emerges as an intelligent and sympathetic observer of Japanese life and customs, and seems to have acquired a basic level of conversational Japanese, a more than passing interest in the country's history, and a deep appreciation of Japanese arts and handicraft.

Ponting liked Japan and the Japanese and was quite intoxicated by the fairer sex, affording them a whole chapter in *Lotus Land* (Fig. 375). Ainu women, however, did not seem to get quite the same Ponting seal of approval: "The lot of the Ainu woman is not a happy one ... dirty, slovenly, barefoot ... disfigured by tattoo-marks ... a wretched drudge, to whom life holds out none of the pleasures and diversions known to women of other parts of Japan. But in common with her sex the world over, she loves jewellery ... she loves to adorn her scanty attractions with rings, sometimes on her fingers, sometimes in her ears." Nevertheless, Ponting is seldom uncharitable, and finished: "And yet she has charms – that I had almost overlooked: she is gentle and submissive as a child, and her voice is low and musical" (Fig. 374).

Ponting was now in great demand and constantly traveling. His long absences from his wife and young children, however, must have put a great strain on his marriage. In either 1905 or 1906 he returned home to Berkeley, and according to Arnold's biography of Ponting, *Photographer of the World*, apparently informed Mary that the responsibilities of marriage were holding back his artistic career. This seemingly cold, indifferent approach to his family does appear to belie his friendly, affable personality. The facts, however, are that he never saw his wife again, refused her subsequent request for a divorce (possibly because he feared the financial consequences), and specifically excluded her from his Will, which was made on February 5th, 1935, just two days before he died: "I declare that in no circumstances is my wife, whom I have not seen for upwards of thirty years, to receive any benefit from my estate." Ponting's father did not approve of his son's actions, and supported Mary both morally and financially up until his death.

Ponting, an excellent conversationalist, had many friends and acquaintances, but he seemed incapable of forming long and deep relationships and rarely took anyone into his confidence. He was a loner. In 1910, just before going to the South Pole, he sent a message to his children who were in Europe at the time, to meet him in London because he wanted to say goodbye. They came, as arranged, only to find their father absent and a note saying that he had decided not to meet them because he feared he would be weakened in his resolve to go with the expedition.

The photographs taken of the Antarctic by Ponting are considered to be unsurpassed by any photographer of any expedition, before or since. They certainly represent the crowning achievement of Ponting's life, and sealed his reputation for all time as one of the world's great photographers. Ironically, however, his obsession with insuring their wider distribution and recognition was to cost him his health and financial security.

Ponting was unable, to any great extent, to commercially exploit his Antarctic photography. There were many reasons for this, amongst them being a lack of clarity in the agreement between Ponting and Scott regarding the use of the photographic prints. The arrival of World War I was also a distraction. Ponting seems to have wasted a lot of money and energy in trying to raise the stature of the expedition in the eyes of the British public, and always felt aggrieved that his photographic monument was not more appreciated. Other disappointments followed in the lack of success derived from a series of photographic inventions. By 1935 his financial position and health were deteriorating fast. He suffered a coronary thrombosis and died.

Ponting's later life had been full of frustration and disappointment. On his death, his net estate was minimal. Certain debts emerged and his photographs and equipment were sold to meet them. He considered himself to be a "camera artist" rather than a "photographer." Although he appears to have had no formal art education, his intuitive understanding of composition and lighting helped him to produce pictures that have placed him in the photographers' Hall of Fame. More than most photographers, Ponting tried to capture the "mood" and "feel" of a scene. It is too simplistic to describe, as others have done, some of his Japanese garden scenes and portraits of women as being contrived and unimaginative. Most of these photographs were taken with the stereoscope in mind: an apparently flat and uninteresting image is often transformed into a stunning three-dimensional scene when viewed as intended. The illustrations in *Lotus Land*, for example, were originally intended as stereoviews. This is also true of his later work, *Japanese Studies* (1906). There is no disagreement, however, regarding the timeless quality of his Mount Fuji and Antarctic work. These are the real monuments to the life and memory of the camera artist Herbert George Ponting.[131]

OTIS POOLE

The American amateur photographer Otis Manchester Poole (1880–1978) certainly led a full and eventful life (Fig. 377). Born in Chicago, the youngest of three children, the family moved to Yokohama in 1888. His father, whose business was in trading China and Japan teas, had decided that a permanent move to Japan would be a good business decision, as well as providing the family with an agreeable lifestyle. A house was taken at No. 89 Bluff, which was to remain the family home for the next thirty years. In his unpublished memoirs, written in 1962, he reflected fondly on his early recollections of Yokohama:[132] "I still recall with nostalgia the booming temple bells at night, the wailing call of the ama-san (blind masseurs) and soba vendors, the wooden clack of the night watch-man. I picture the rikisha stands at every twist of the winding Bluff road their idle pullers crouched in a fragile lean-to over a charcoal fire or playing 'Go' (chess) awaiting the next call 'Hai! Kuruma!' I see again the oblong-sailed fishing sampans gliding down the bay in the pearly morning light and hear their conches blowing as they returned at dusk.... All that has 'gone with the wind' now, but not from memory."

Poole enrolled with his brother at the newly established Victoria Public School, where amongst the sixty other English and American boys he made lifelong friendships. One of these friends, Halstead Lindsley, nearly ended Poole's life: "I shall never forget one morning in our workshop as I sat cleaning my rifle, and Halstead picked up my revolver, its six chambers loaded alternately with bullets and dust-shot, clicked it several times with his thumb on the hammer, held it to my head and fired. By the Grace of God it was a dust-shot that fired and a thick double seam of my tweed cap stopped the fine pellets so that I was only pricked. But Halstead went white as a sheet and vowed he would never touch a firearm again. Ten Summers later he was a Deputy Sheriff in Telluride, Colorado, with two colts in his belt."

Left Fig. 377. Anonymous, "Portrait of Otis Manchester Poole in the Japanese Alps," 1917, small-format gelatin silver print. Courtesy of Jillian and Richard A. Poole.

Below Fig. 378. Otis Manchester Poole, "Kashiba," 1917, small-format gelatin silver print. Courtesy of Jillian and Richard A. Poole.

Poole left school at the age of fourteen and was given private tuition in French, Japanese, shorthand, and typing. In 1895 he joined the Yokohama office of Dodwell, Carlill & Co., a British merchant house engaged in trade and shipping and headquartered in London. He would spend fifty-three years with the firm, and when he left Japan for good in 1925, the last twenty would be as a main board director based at the company's New York office. For a few months in 1899 he was posted to the Hong Kong office, and from there made a short excursion to Macau with some friends. He recalled seeing there, for the first time, his future wife, "a fair little 3 year old in a red dressing gown, summering there with her mother from Hongkong."

Poole described his life in Yokohama at the time as "singularly pleasant" with every type of sport readily accessible. He shared his brother's enthusiasm for swimming, rowing, sailing, bird shooting, and bicycle riding, but not his interest in music. Instead, Poole developed a lifelong passion for sketching and painting. He was also fascinated by mountaineering. It was in connection with his love of climbing – he had climbed Fuji with his father and brother in 1892 – that we find his first reference to photography: "[Mountain climbing] became my keenest interest and so many were the trips I organised in my twenties that I came to be regarded by fellow-enthusiasts as something of an institution. An aptitude for photography inherited from father [Otis Augustus Poole]

added interest to these explorations, of which accounts often appeared in the local papers. Walter Weston, the Alpinist, in his book *The Playground of the Far East,* [which] contained several of my photographs of the Japanese Alps, refers to me as 'my friend Chester Poole, the European doyen of artistic landscape photography of the Kamikochi region.' I was elected a Fellow of the Royal Geographical Society and enlargements of some of my photographs of the Japanese Alps taken during the scaling of Yarigatake in 1905 hung on the walls of its headquarters in London for many years."

Poole goes on to describe the numerous trips he took to America, Europe, and Asia, many for business purposes. He recalled one assignment at the close of the 1904–5 Russo-Japanese War, when a shipload of "hulking" Russian prisoners was repatriated to Odessa: "They were always hungry and would eagerly pluck a round loaf from a barrel, break it open, insert a handful of salt and eat it like a hamburger."

In 1916 Poole was promoted to manage the Yokohama office, and in the same year he married Dorothy Campbell, the three-year-old he had seen playing on the beach at Macau some fourteen years earlier. They moved into No. 68 Bluff, and a year later the first of three sons was born. Poole was in charge of Dodwell's entire Japanese operation and enjoying a settled family life when the worst earthquake in recorded Japanese history struck on September 1st, 1923. Almost the whole of Yokohama was destroyed, and much of Tokyo. The Poole family were fortunate not to be amongst the 150,000 killed. He described, in harrowing and graphic terms, how he made three terrifying trips up the cliff face to bring his children down from the burning homes on the Bluff: "... people risked their lives in a hazardous scramble down to a not quite perpendicular cliff face, transferring half way down to a slide where the cliff had avalanched.... Time had run out and as the fire struck the Naval grounds, people panicked and overwhelmed the rope, which broke before our eyes. Sheets of fire appeared above the brim like a Niagara and as it licked those who had feared to go over the cliff, many threw themselves over in flaming pinwheels, thudding in piles on the beach below. A sickening sight."[133]

For the next two years, the Poole family lived at the company's house in Kobe. In 1925 Kobe suffered a severe earthquake: "Kobe forgot its historic immunity from earthquakes and suffered one so violent that at its height I thought we were in for another Yokohama disaster." Poole's wife Dorothy, caught downtown, had run back up the hill terrified for the safety of her children. After finding them safe, she collapsed from exhaustion and was hospitalized. Dodwell's granted the family a three-month rest in Victoria, British Columbia. Whilst there news came that the company's New York manager's health had broken down and Poole was asked to take over. The family moved to America and Poole never returned to Japan.

Poole took many photographs of Japan. Weston was complimentary about those which appeared in his aforementioned book, and Burton Holmes used approximately seven for the 1910 edition of his *Travelogues.* Given that both Weston and Holmes were expert photographers themselves, it is a tribute to Poole's ability that they should have wanted to include his

work in their publications. Indeed, his photography shows remarkable versatility: the books mentioned above include his photographs of mountain scenery, seascapes, cloud formations, and children. It is a little surprising, therefore, that Poole said very little in his memoirs about his photographic activities, and it may be that any passion for the subject died with his prints and negatives when the earthquake struck in 1923. He described on p. 85 of his book *The Death of Old Yokohama* (1968) the scene of desolation at his former home: "We poked around among the ruins, unearthing blobs of melted silver and glass, all that was left of our lovely wedding presents. And in one spot, where a Korean chest had stood in our drawing-room, filled with twenty-two albums of photographs illustrating thirty years of life in old Japan, just a neat pile of perfectly foliated ashes. For safety's sake, I had kept my negatives out in the stables, but they too had been burnt beyond redemption, as were all my records of countless trips and explorations up country in the mountains of Central Japan and among the disappearing Ainu of Yezo, the Northern Island."

At the age of eighty-two, looking back on his life and sitting in his retirement home in Virginia, he wrote: "And so it has come about, after all of our wanderings, that 1962 finds Dorothy and me living by ourselves in happy retirement.... Sometimes, looking back upon our changeful lives, we wonder by what kind fate our paths were shaped to lead us eventually to this lovely corner of Virginia."

A final point worth noting is that Poole's father, Otis Augustus (1840–1904), not only taught photography to his son but was very talented in his own right. Evidence for this comes from the inclusion of no less than thirty-seven of his photographs in Burton Holmes' 1910 *Travelogues* (Fig. 379). Although not mentioned by Poole the younger in his reminiscences, father and son were clearly very successful in having their photography published – perhaps as a serious commercial pursuit on their part, or simply an interesting diversion.

ARNOLD GENTHE

The photographer Arnold Genthe (1869–1942) was born in Germany into a comfortable middle-class family of academics who had produced a long line of able scholars, architects, and teachers. Genthe wanted to become a painter, but a family member persuaded him to follow the family tradition and a safer career in academia. He graduated in philology and was literate in Latin, Greek, Hebrew, French, and English. In 1895 Genthe accepted a position as tutor to the son of a wealthy German aristocrat who owned land in San Luis Obispo county, just outside San Francisco. Initially, he stayed in San Francisco itself, and wandering the streets as a tourist became fascinated with the sights and sounds of the Chinatown district. In letters home to his family, he was disappointed not to be able to enclose pictures of the area to complement his descriptions. He had tried sketching but found the inhabitants would take flight on seeing his sketchbook. It was then that he decided to try photography.

Never having used a camera before, he bought some books and made a study of the subject. Knowing that the Chinese were superstitious about having their pictures taken, he bought a small, unobtrusive camera which he could conceal in his pocket. When not teaching, he would stroll around Chinatown taking pictures and developing them himself in a small darkroom which had been fixed up by a previous occupant of the house in which he was staying. His early results were disappointing: his inexperience, combined with the slow camera speeds at that time, meant that many of his shots were out of focus or underexposed. But after a while his technique improved and the local camera club included some of his enlarged pictures in their annual exhibition. The favorable comments received encouraged him to continue his experiments.

It had occurred to him that conventional portrait taking did not capture the sitter's natural "radiance and spirit," particularly in the case of women. He wondered whether the artificial stiffness of pose could be eliminated by employing the same techniques he had, of necessity, used when photographing the Chinese – capturing them unawares. He began experimenting with friends, using the camera club's portrait studio, and the results were surprisingly good. So much so that when he was faced in 1897 with the prospect of returning to Germany following the completion of his teaching assignment, he decided instead to stay in San Francisco and open a studio. The successful portrait technique he employed there was described in his autobiography, *As I Remember* (1936): "I was determined to show people a new kind of photography: there would be no stilted poses; as a matter of fact, no poses at all. I would try to take my sitters unawares, at a moment when they would not realize that the camera was ready. I would show them prints in which a uniform sharpness would be avoided and emphasis laid on portraying a person's character instead of making a commonplace record of clothes and a photographic mask."

It soon became the fashion for the city's wealthy socialites to have their pictures taken at his studio. However, his

A. Genthe.

studio and work – apart from the Chinatown images that had been stored in a bank vault – were totally destroyed in the 1906 earthquake and fire. Genthe recovered, nevertheless, to become one of the leading commercial photographers in America, with studios in San Francisco and New York. Interested in oriental art from an early age, a chance meeting with the Japanese art scholar Ernest Fenellosa awakened an interest in *ukiyo-e* prints. Genthe was already a serious collector of prints and other Japanese artifacts when he traveled to Japan in 1908, where he spent six months touring the country and taking photographs.

The methodical Genthe had prepared well for his trip. Being a natural linguist, he had mastered a reasonable amount of colloquial Japanese. He had studied, and learnt, 300 kanji, but in a testament to the difficulty of learning written Japanese Genthe found that after putting them aside for one week he had forgotten them. A chance meeting with a Japanese family at Shuzenji, on the Izu Peninsula, considerably eased his travel difficulties. Finding an elderly gentleman on vacation with his son and daughter-in-law, he convinced the man, who came from an old samurai family, that the three of them should accompany Genthe on his travels through central Japan as his guide and companions. In return, Genthe would meet all expenses. This proved to be a good arrangement, and Genthe later recounted in his autobiography that their presence meant that he "saw and learned a great deal about the real Japan that without my new friends would have remained unknown to me."

Although Genthe does not detail his exact itinerary, he mentions visiting Kyoto, Shikoku, and Hokkaido. He climbed Mount Fuji in August, but was trapped at the summit for two days and nights due to a snowstorm. He had obtained an official permit to use his camera from the Japanese Minister of War, but noted that this came with a long list of restrictions. Amongst these were a prohibition on photography within a 30-mile (48-km) radius of any fortifications and a ban on photographing any place visited by the Emperor. Furthermore, no photographs could be taken without first notifying the local chief of police who would then detail an officer to accompany him. Genthe found that these officers, whilst always courteous, would never permit the slightest deviation from the official rules.

In Hokkaido, Genthe spent an enjoyable four weeks with the Ainu in their main village of Piratori. He got on well with the inhabitants and spoke fondly of them in his autobiography. He was introduced to the Ainu chief Penri II, and seems to have been well accepted into the community. He managed to take a number of photographs, including one of Ainu women performing the erotic crane dance. Penri II's wife asked to be photographed with Genthe. He therefore arranged the camera and tripod and got the Ainu chief himself to click the shutter. He recounts one amusing episode aboard a canoe in which he was seated taking photographs. The Ainu oarsman had apparently been intoxicated with too much saké and the boat overturned, with Genthe having great difficulty in getting himself and his camera to shore safely. Fortunately, the camera was in a waterproof case.

The famous photographer Alfred Stieglitz was an admirer of Genthe's Japan work, and a number of examples form part of the Stieglitz Collection in the Metropolitan Museum of New York. Asian photographic expert Clark Worswick believes that Genthe's contribution to and influence on Japanese art photography of the 1920s and 1930s have not been fully understood or appreciated. Worswick points out in his article "Notes on Japanese Collections of Photographs" (1988) that Genthe was himself influenced by Japanese art and also by the photographic pictorialists of the 1890s. By the early part of the twentieth century, he had become part of Stieglitz's circle in the new photography of the Photo Secession. He goes on to say that Genthe's Japan work, exemplified by "out of focus" trees and artistic cloud formations, undoubtedly influenced Stieglitz himself, and certainly the later generation of Japanese photographers in the 1910–30 art photography or salon period.

KARL LEWIS

The last Western commercial studio of the Meiji era was operated by the American Karl Lewis (1865–1942), who opened for business in Yokohama in 1902 (Fig. 381). At that time, picture postcards had just arrived on the scene, and Lewis dealt in these as much as he did in photographs (Fig. 384). His published postcards at around this time carried the statement "The only Western Photographer in Japan." Apart from operating a portrait studio, Lewis also acted as a commercial agent

for a British photographic supplies firm, and in 1910 he started stocking Eastman cameras and supplies. It appears he did not make enough from his studio work, since at around this time he also worked for two years as manager of the United States Navy Coal Depot followed, in 1913, by a position as general manager of an American roller-skating rink.

His photographic activities continued until 1917, but he then closed his studio and joined the automobile import division of the merchant firm Sale & Frazar, where he became sales manager, staying until at least 1922. At some stage, and certainly by the early 1930s, he set up a postage stamp dealership selling Japanese and Asian stamps and hand-colored "covers" to collectors around the world. This business continued until 1939 when, at the age of seventy-four, Lewis suffered a stroke. He died in Yokohama in 1942 and is buried next to his wife in the grounds of the Shinkoji Temple at Kamioka, Yokohama.[134]

Lewis was born in Bell County, Kentucky, and seems to have been an only child. Nothing is really known about his

parents, but shortly after his birth he and his father migrated west to Kansas, and then after a while continued to San Francisco. It is unlikely that he received a formal education, and judging from letters he sent in later years to his customers, he embarked on a career at sea whilst still a teenager. He traveled around the world for the next twenty years, and between ships found time to acquire a number of self-taught skills, including writing and photography.

It was not the first time he had visited Japan, but when he arrived at Yokohama in July 1901, he decided to stay. And stay he did, for there is no record of his leaving the country until his death some forty years later. He opened a photo studio some time in 1902, and the 1903 *Japan Directory* lists him as a photographer operating from 136-D Honmura Road, which is now part of the Chinatown district. In August 1903 he took a common-law wife named Sasako Sadako, who at just seventeen was twenty years younger than Lewis.

The novelty of being the only Western studio in Japan was no doubt helpful in bringing custom his way, and a number

Below Fig. 384. Karl Lewis, "Benten-Dori, Yokohama," ca. 1910, hand-colored postcard. Author's Collection.

of his Japanese photographs were published. Some appear in D. C. Angus's *Japan The Eastern Wonderland* (1904) and others were included in *The Illustrated London News*.[135] In the 1906 *Japan Directory* he advertised himself as a "photographer and postcard manufacturer," and by 1912 was also selling "Hotel labels of all cities in the Far East." It is thanks to his stamp-dealing activities from the early 1930s that the little information we have on his life has emerged. Lewis seemed to enjoy writing lengthy letters to a number of his customers, and some of these have survived. Although largely concerned with matters philatelic, some of the content would touch on his private life.

In the compulsory biennial re-registration with the American consulate in Yokohama, Lewis, in 1934, stated that he was supporting himself and his wife by stamp dealing and the sale of silk goods and dolls by mail order. In December 1939 he suffered a paralytic stroke which severely limited his movements. In March 1940 Lewis filed the necessary papers with the consulate confirming his allegiance to the United States; in his previous submission he stated that the reason he had not been back to America since 1901 was "lack of funds." The records indicate he had no friends or relations resident in America.

On March 16th, 1940 Lewis's wife of thirty-seven years died. Lewis, now aged seventy-four, was in poor health and heartbroken. In a poignant letter the following month to a long-standing customer he wrote: "Sada died like a little child going to sleep, not even a murmur.... We had no children; I am all alone; and could not realize before, my loneliness and sorrow.... Sada was nearly twenty years younger than I, and I never thought she would die before me, would that I had."[136]

In 1941, following Pearl Harbor and the outbreak of war between Japan and the United States, Lewis was arrested as a suspected spy. The police could not understand why he was mailing letters to the US containing no correspondence. Of course, Lewis was supplying his customers with stamped envelopes franked by the Japanese post office, but what made matters worse were the apparent codes he was using. It had been Lewis's practice to mark the outside of the letters with "O," which meant the letter was to be opened; the letter "N" meant that it should not be as the envelope was empty. Other "unusual" markings were evident. In order to satisfy demand, he had a network of contacts mailing similar letters from various Pacific islands, and this also baffled the authorities. He was locked in a police cell for several days, but representations from his brother-in-law proved successful in convincing the police that Lewis was no threat to anyone. He was released to the Sasako family, but was nevertheless placed under house arrest until his death, on May 19th, 1942, six months after Pearl Harbor.

Karl Lewis was one of the pioneers of stamp collecting in Japan and was the first there to offer first-day covers. His was the last Western commercial photo studio to operate in Meiji Japan, and as far as the writer knows, the first and last Western photo studio to operate there throughout the whole of the twentieth century.

No. 1834. Japan. "Benten-Dori" (Curio Street) Yokohama.
Published by Karl Lewis, Photographer, No. 136-D, Honmura Road, Yokohama.

JAMES RICALTON

At the beginning of the twentieth century, James Ricalton (1844–1929) enjoyed a deserved reputation as one of the finest war correspondents and photo-journalists (Fig. 385).

He was also a popular travel writer, naturalist, and schoolteacher. In addition, as well as being one of the pioneer motion picture cameramen, he also assisted the famous inventor Thomas Edison in sourcing materials for his incandescent lamp. Between 1879 and 1914, when travel was rough and photographic equipment heavy, Ricalton traveled over 500,000 miles (805,000 km). He visited almost every country in the world at least once, and returned with 100,000 photographs and 30 miles (48 km) of motion picture film. Alice Bennett, a contemporary newspaper columnist for the *Watertown Daily Times*, was moved to write in her article "Has Weapons, Trophies and Pictures of Far Off Lands": "This is the man who has spent 20 years or more of his life exploring the far ends of the earth. This is the man who is known as the greatest traveller the world has ever known, living or dead, and the most daring photographer."

Nevertheless, James Ricalton was forgotten, and today his name is known only to a handful of photo-historians and stereoview collectors. Why is this? Posterity seems so capricious when it comes to deciding whether or not to remember those who led extraordinary lives. Perhaps it was because Ricalton was a quiet man, unassuming and modest. Perhaps it was because only a small proportion of his published photographs carried his name.

According to Susan Kempler's "America 'Discovers' the World" (1991), Ricalton was born into a farming family in upstate New York, and his Scottish immigrant parents insured that he and his nine other brothers and sisters were brought up believing in the Calvinist principles of piety, restraint, and thrift.[137] These, together with the overriding Protestant work ethic, influenced and shaped his attitude to life and provided a set of core values which he would unfailingly follow.

Approaching the end of his common school education, Ricalton wanted to extend his studies by entering the local prepatory academy. Perhaps reluctant to incur the expense, Ricalton's father refused. Showing a determination and obduracy that would become noticeable traits to his character, Ricalton went anyway. Having saved enough from the money he earned working for other farmers to defray the expenses of tuition fees and rent, he was able to enrol in around 1859. However, with very little money left over for food, he practically starved himself during the first term.

During his time at the academy, Ricalton developed a yearning for travel, and without informing anyone other than his roommate he set off to see Niagara Falls with just $10 in his pocket. Later that year, having taken a job during the summer vacation in his uncle's axe handle factory, he had saved enough to finance another trip to Niagara and surrounding areas. He slept rough, and encountered interesting travel companions wherever he went, and these experiences increased his determination to see more of the world.

Left Fig. 385. Anonymous, "Portrait of James Ricalton in Rhodesia, Africa," ca. 1910, detail from a gelatin silver-print stereoview, published by Keystone View Company. Rob Oechsle Collection.

On finishing studies at the academy, he enrolled at St. Lawrence University, Canton. Although the surviving records are not complete, he was certainly there in 1865 and is listed as one of eleven non-graduates in 1871. This implies that his time there was not continuous and that breaks may have occurred through financial necessity. He taught for a year in 1866–7 at the common school he had attended, and in 1866 or 1867 he married Christine Rutherford (1854–78). A son, Robert, was born in 1868 but unfortunately lived for just a short time. In 1870 a daughter, Elizabeth, was born followed three years later by twin boys, Charles and Thomas. After a couple of short-term local teaching posts in November 1871, he was taken on to teach at the village school in Maplewood, New Jersey. In those days, teaching appointments were usually short-term and precarious and his initial contract was for one twelve-week term. Nevertheless, he stayed at the school for twenty years, and according to Kempler became the principal in 1878 before finally resigning in 1891.

Ricalton loved teaching and built a good rapport with his pupils. Many years later, former students recalled with affection "a strict but kindly schoolmaster" who always seemed interested in their welfare. According to Lucas in *James Ricalton's Photographs of China*, Ricalton was a keen naturalist who imbued lessons with a greater interest by bringing back flora from the surrounding countryside. But, despite his full-time teaching career, he did not, as we shall see, cut back on his traveling.

Ricalton's wife Christine died in 1878 leaving him to take care of their eight-year-old daughter Elizabeth and her two young brothers. Nevertheless, in 1879 he arranged for his children to be looked after whilst he took his first trip abroad – a 500-mile (800-km) walking tour of the British Isles. In his parents' native Scotland, he met a young Barbara Campbell whom he was later to marry. Throughout the next ten years, during the summer vacations, Ricalton went on six further overseas trips.

In 1885, at the age of forty-one, Ricalton returned to Scotland and married the twenty-five-year-old Barbara Campbell. Over the next seventeen years they had five children together, and along with his other three children settled down into family life at Maplewood. His second marriage and the additions to the family, however, did not mean that Ricalton would change his travel habits. On the contrary, just one year after their marriage, he made an epic 800-mile (1280-km) trek across Russia, starting at Archangel on the

White Sea coast and finishing at St. Petersburg. He wrote about his adventures in one his many travel articles, entitled "My Travels on Next to Nothing" (1887).

Thomas Edison, one of the world's greatest inventive geniuses, had read Ricalton's travel accounts and had been impressed. In 1888, despite having invented the electric light, he had yet to develop a filament with sufficient heat-resistant properties capable of transforming his invention from a brilliant idea into a viable commercial proposition. After extensive trials, he had decided that bamboo was the best substance. There were, though, over 1000 different varieties of the wood, mainly to be found in the Far East. He financed various expeditions which brought back numerous different types, but none provided the complete answer. Edison knew that Ricalton was an experienced traveler and an amateur botanist, and asked him if he would like to help. Ricalton, flattered, obtained leave of absence from the school and sailed from New York on February 22nd, 1888.

The 43-year-old had agreed to an open-ended trip that Edison said would take anything from five months to five years. His first stop, via England and the Suez Canal, was Ceylon. He spent three and a half months covering the whole island and almost 100 different species were tested. He moved on to India, where he toured extensively, and then to Burma. In Singapore and the Malay Peninsula, he stopped to take stock: his tests had indicated that one particular fiber which grew in both Ceylon and the Malay Peninsula was already a 100–200 percent improvement on anything Edison had previously worked with. Although he had planned to go to Java and Borneo, his exciting discovery meant he could now go home, searching China and Japan on the way. Ricalton's first visit to Japan, therefore, was either late 1888 or early 1889.

Ricalton arrived home on February 22nd, 1889, exactly a year after leaving Maplewood. The whole town came out to welcome him. Edison, however, had lost interest in bamboo and had discovered that a form of cellulose filament was more successful. His financial backers had expended $100,000 on the "bamboo quest" which, ultimately, came to nothing, and Ricalton never did learn whether Edison had been able to make use of his bamboo. After being reinstated at Maplewood school, Ricalton became restless and determined on a new career. He resigned in 1891 and spent the next twenty years as a traveling professional photographer working for Underwood & Underwood and others. During this time, he circled the globe at least six times, and visited almost every country. Reminiscing in later life, he only regretted never having been to Greenland, Antarctica, Tibet, some of the South Pacific islands, and just a few other places.

Exactly when Ricalton took up photography is not known, but he did take pictures during his 1882 trip to Iceland, which were converted to glass slides and sold. One glass slide still exists from his 1884 trip to the Amazon. In a 1921 article, "Strange Sleeping Places in 500,000 Miles of Travel," which looked back on his 1888 trip for Edison, Ricalton confirmed that he was encouraged to take up photography more seriously when the photographs he took whilst away were noticed and praised on his return.

According to Lucas, Ricalton was taken on as one of the staff photographers for the New York-based stereoview publishers Underwood & Underwood in 1891. It is certainly true that a number of boxed sets featuring the work of Ricalton were issued by the firm, and we know from Ricalton's published comments and writings that these sets included the Spanish-American War (Philippines) 1898, China 1900, India 1902, and the Russo-Japanese War 1904–5. However, whether he actually worked for Underwood & Underwood between the years 1891 and 1898 is not so clear.

Kempler states that Ricalton photographed in Europe and the Middle East in 1891–2, France and Switzerland in 1894, and the Middle East again in 1896. We know that he was also providing photographs for John Lawson Stoddard, the travel writer and lecturer. In his 1905 book *Port Arthur: A Monster Heroism*, Richard Barry states that "[Ricalton] took most of the photographs for John H. [sic] Stoddard's lectures."[138] As we have seen, Stoddard traveled all over the world and retired in 1897. It is therefore possible that Ricalton did not join Underwood & Underwood until 1898, when he accepted the assignment to the Philippines.

When we take into account further research from Kempler, we see that Dr Albert S. Bickmore of the American Museum of Natural History also illustrated his lectures with glass slides from Ricalton's portfolio. In addition, the New York State Department of Visual Instruction distributed Ricalton's slides of Hawaii, Ceylon, India, Palestine, and Africa to schools throughout the United States. Finally, Kempler says that Burton Holmes used Ricalton's photographs in his lectures to supplement his own photographic efforts. This is corroborated by E. W. Earle in his article "The Orient Viewed" (1984), wherein he states "Many of his [Ricalton's] photographs were used to illustrate text books or for lantern slides; they were employed by such celebrated travel lecturers as John L. Stoddard and Burton Holmes. He was one of the few photographers to work for a stereo-publishing company [Underwood & Underwood] who received credit as both photographer and author." All of this means that Underwood & Underwood were doing either exceptionally well by selling on their employee's work to these organizations and individuals, or that Ricalton, in 1891, had embarked on a career as a freelance photographer.

On the face of it, Ricalton had many masters. But he was no businessman and was excessively cautious when it came to considerations of career and money. Despite his world-wide reputation as a photographer, he never earned more than $2400 a year in his twenty-five year career, according to Kempler. This was only twice as much as his previous salary at the school in Maplewood. So who was paying Ricalton? Perhaps the mystery is solved by referring to Herbert Croly's little-known biography of Willard Straight (1925, p. 153), the American businessman, war correspondent, and Far East diplomat. Here, Croly cites Straight's diary entry for April 22nd, 1905: "Back from Mukden and the front. At Liaoyang I met the redoubtable Ricalton. For twenty years he told me he had been principal of a school near Orange and then had suddenly started taking pictures for a Macallister [sic]

Below Fig. 386. James Ricalton, "American Giving Water to Japanese after the Battle of Tientsin, China," 1900, albumen-print stereoview, published by Underwood & Underwood. Rob Oechsle Collection. In China to secure a portfolio of views for his employer, Ricalton found himself the only photo-journalist at the Battle of Tientsin during the Boxer Rebellion. As a result, he was able to secure important photographs of the conflict, thereby providing a fortuitous publishing coup for Underwood & Underwood.

Bottom Fig. 387. James Ricalton, "Ministers of Foreign Powers during Negotiations with China Leaving the Spanish Legation – Peking," 1900, albumen-print stereoview, published by Underwood & Underwood. Rob Oechsle Collection. Amongst the ministers we can see Baron Nissi of Japan, and behind him, framed by the doorway, is the British diplomat Sir Ernest Satow who was appointed as Minister to China in 1900.

(57)-4166-Columbia's noble soldier boys—American giving water to Japanese after battle of Tientsin, China. Copyright 1901 by Underwood & Underwood.

(100) Ministers of Foreign Powers during negotiations with China—leaving Spanish Legation—Peking. Copyright 1901 by Underwood & Underwood.

stereopticon view company. He went all over the world for them. There was scarcely a country on the map that he had not done three times at least. Everywhere and anywhere, this old man had gone. Dried and wizened, unclean almost, he had at the age of fifty started out to gratify his appetite for travel and to take pictures. India and the tiger hunts, Ceylon and the elephant drives, the Boxer campaign, the Philippines, wherever there were pictures there was Ricalton. He had stood the Port Arthur show better than any of the rest, up and down the hills like a chamois, wherever his old legs would carry him and the Japanese would let him go, Mr. Ricalton had gone. Nerve, he had of iron. He didn't know what fear was. What he wanted was pictures."

Ricalton was not particularly interested in money, but he was interested in travel. It is possible he came to some kind of semi-exclusive arrangement with the major New York lantern slide manufacturers and distributors T. H. McAllister. Although only speculation at this stage, it is possible that Ricalton was paid a retainer and expenses in return for allowing McAllister to wholesale his photographs to customers such as Stoddard and Holmes. Ricalton may have had an option to accept specific assignments from other sponsors. This might include, for example, coverage of the Spanish-American War of 1898 and China and the Boxer Rebellion of 1900 for Underwood & Underwood and the later assignments for Thomas Edison. It seems unlikely that the self-reliant loner Ricalton would want to accompany Stoddard or Burton Holmes on their own travels around the globe. Their predilection for first-class travel would no doubt have proved anathema to the old veteran. Nevertheless, given the pressure

on these two famous travel lecturers to entertain their public with an extensive range of illustrated presentations, the temptation to supplement their own work with Ricalton's photographs, purchased through McAllister, must have been irresistible. This kind of arrangement would have suited everybody. Another equally plausible theory is that Ricalton worked with McAllister until 1898, but then switched to Underwood & Underwood.

Richard Barry spent time with Ricalton during the 1904–5 Russo-Japanese War and was very impressed. In his aforementioned book, Barry provides us with some interesting insights into Ricalton's character and personality: "The public knows almost nothing of Ricalton, one of its obscure great men ... he has gone through a long life heedless of fame and money. He is original, alone, and has done things no other man has done.... In the Philippines he was the only one to get troops actually firing on the foe. At the battle of Caloocan a soldier near him was winged; Ricalton picked up the useless rifle, grabbed the cartridge belt and went up with the skirmishers."

After the Philippines, Ricalton's next stereo-photographic assignment for Underwood & Underwood was China, where he spent a whole year putting together a comprehensive photographic picture of the land and people. As the 1900 Boxer Rebellion broke out whilst he was there, he was also able to secure some of the most compelling images of the conflict. During the battle of Tientsin, Ricalton believed he was the only photographer in the city. In the accompanying text to the set of stereos entitled *China through the Stereoscope* (1901), Ricalton records (p. 209): Tientsin ... July 13, 1900....

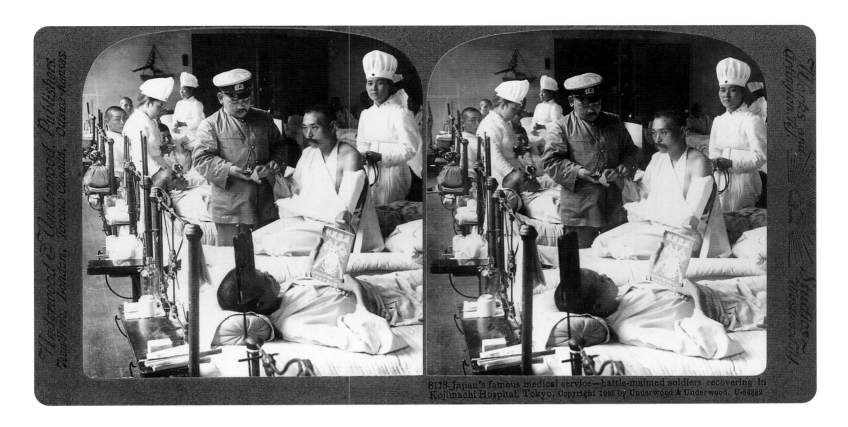

8118-Japan's famous medical service—battle-maimed soldiers recovering in Kojimachi Hospital, Tokyo. Copyright 1905 by Underwood & Underwood. U-64382

"I was, so far as I can learn, the only photographer on the ground to do work of this kind. Correspondents from all over the world tried to secure these views and offered to pay me any sum I would mention for them; but, of course, they were not mine to sell – they were the property of the publishers by whom I was employed."

The set of 100 China views which Underwood & Underwood subsequently published was an immediate success, but most people are unaware that Ricalton was the photographer since his name is not shown on the stereoview mounts. Ricalton's accompanying 358-page text was not an integral part of the set and needed to be purchased separately.

Ricalton covered the Russo-Japanese War for the Underwoods, in particular the siege of Port Arthur. Barry, who was also there, was again impressed: "He is sixty years old, yet he tramps ten and twenty miles a day with a thirty-pound camera under his arm, for he sneers at the snap shot and will carry a tripod ... he goes everywhere ... into captured forts while the corpses are still about, through the most dangerous artillery positions ... into the actual fighting if they would let him."

Barry and Ricalton secured a journalistic scoop together when they were permitted to interview General Baron Nogi, who was then directing the attack on Port Arthur. During the interview, which took place on September 12th, 1904, Nogi discovered that he was three years younger than Ricalton: "The command of the army, then, belongs to me. I'm your senior," said the photographer. The General smiled, and replied: "Ah, but then I should have to do your work and I fear I could not do it as well as you do." That night, Ricalton

received a special hamper of fruit with a card which read: "The General sends his compliments to his senior in command." On reading the card, Ricalton responded: "He is a great man who can so notice, in the midst of colossal labors, a passing old photographer." Ricalton was later decorated by the Japanese imperial government for his bravery on the battlefield. Nogi and his wife, incidentally, would later commit suicide on the death of the Meiji Emperor in 1912 (Fig. 388).

Amongst Ricalton's war portfolio was one photograph that Underwood & Underwood were able to sell newspaper rights for the fabulous sum, in those days, of $5000. It is arguably the most famous picture of the war. For some time Ricalton had been obsessed with trying to obtain a photograph of the firing of a Japanese siege gun at close range, and to simultaneously capture the actual flight of the 11-inch (28-cm) mortar fired. The difficulties in securing such a photograph were enormous, and no photographer had succeeded in doing so. In the first place, there are few more dangerous battlefield positions than being in the close proximity of such gun platforms, as they are a prime target for enemy fire. During one photographic attempt, Ricalton was to witness the decapitation of a Japanese gunner at the point of firing. Several other soldiers were hit by shrapnel and carried off to the field hospital, although Ricalton himself was unscathed. Positioning himself directly behind the gun, and with the camera tilted at the correct anticipatory angle in order to capture the shell in flight, was also not without risk. He needed to be close enough to fill the camera frame with the gun itself, but far enough back to avoid the recoil shock once the gun had been fired. There was also the small matter of avoiding a blurred

Below Fig. 390. Anonymous, "Professor Ricalton with Japanese Officers of the 11th Division, at the Foot of Takushan, Port Arthur," 1904, albumen-print stereoview, published by Underwood & Underwood. Rob Oechsle Collection.

7593-Professor Ricalton, with Japanese officers of 11th Division, at foot of Takushan, Port Arthur   Copyright 1905 by Underwood & Underwood.

image, since each time the gun was fired the ground shook. Ricalton attempted this picture many times before obtaining the desired image, together with considerable recognition and respect from his fellow professionals (Fig. 392).

After the war Ricalton returned to Maplewood and did very little traveling for the next few years. But in 1909, at the age of sixty-four, he decided to go back to Africa for a hunting and photographic expedition of his own. He had decided to travel from Cape Town to Cairo on foot, and he took just a few native porters with him for the 1,500-mile (2400-km) journey. The intrepid Ricalton shot a variety of wild game, bringing back home four lion skins and a buffalo hide. Typically, the cost of the whole trip was very low – just over $200. Nobody knew how to economize like Ricalton.

In 1911 Edison asked Ricalton to embark on a world tour taking with him the recently invented kinetograph in order to bring back movie film of far-off people and places. The Edison studio management personnel made meticulous preparations. Ricalton was instructed in the finer points of moving picture photography, and he experimented by taking film of New York City and Boston. Satisfied with the results, the studio equipped him with two cameras, a portable developing apparatus, and a strong box for returning developed negatives. He was also given 10,000 feet (3048 meters) of film (which approximated to just less than three hours' running time), and letters of credit for $3000.

The studio had acceded to Ricalton's request to take along as an assistant his 22-year-old son Lomond. At the age of sixty-seven, Ricalton set off on his most ambitious expedition to date, one that would take more than three years to complete, and end tragically. The journey took in Mexico, Newfoundland,

Below Fig. 391. James Ricalton, "Admiral Togo, Japan's Naval Hero, at Hongwanji Temple, Tokyo," ca. 1905, albumen-print stereoview, published by Underwood & Underwood. Rob Oechsle Collection.

Canada, India, the Middle East, Africa, Australia, New Zealand, the Far East, and Hawaii. By May 1914, with the expedition almost complete, Ricalton and his son took some time off for hunting in present-day Kenya. Unfortunately, Lomond contracted typhoid fever and died in a Nairobi hospital. Ricalton returned home distraught and depressed.

Despite this, Ricalton continued working for Edison. He photographed the upstate New York area for the state exhibit in the forthcoming Panama-Pacific International Exposition. Whilst in the middle of this assignment, he received a request from Underwood & Underwood to go to Europe and cover the Great War. But due to his commitments to Edison, he had to regretfully decline. In 1915 Ricalton carried out one more assignment for Edison in South America. This proved to be his last overseas tour, and on returning home he retired.

The next ten years were spent quietly at Maplewood. He delighted in showing visitors his little museum attached to the house, which contained numerous trophies, souvenirs, and photographs which he had collected during his life of travel. Active until the end, he was often seen taking long country walks in his early eighties. He died at the age of eighty-five. His daughter, Kathryn Ricalton Murphy, writing in "The Life of James Ricalton" (1948), remembered her father as someone who had "travelled six times around the world, had photographed four wars, added much knowledge to the craft of picture taking, and played an important part in the development of science and exploration. He ... lived the full life, wherein most of his dreams came true."

Just how many times Ricalton visited Japan is not clear. *John L. Stoddard's Lectures* (1897) contain numerous photographs of that country gathered from more than one trip. It is quite possible that these photographs were all, or mostly, taken by Ricalton. We also know that he went to Japan for Edison on at least two occasions. From the 1880s to the late 1930s, Ricalton's photographs, usually unaccredited, were mass-produced as stereoviews, magic lantern slides, and book illustrations and seen by many millions of people. Perhaps we will never be able to positively identify more than a small fraction of his work.

Ricalton's personality was complex. He hated parting with money and would never spend it on what he considered to be extravagances. His list of prohibited items would include tobacco, alcohol, magazines, hotels, restaurants, and theaters. In an obscure publication cited by Kempler, Richard Barry recalled in an article entitled "An Old Fashioned Traveler" (1928) how, during the Russo-Japanese War, Ricalton would keep his expense account noting down every half cent. Kempler refers to Ricalton's preference for "roughing it" as bordering on self-flagellation and as a way of demonstrating his own physical superiority. Given his short and wiry frame, it is possible he might have felt the need to prove himself to others. Certainly, he possessed more energy and reserves of stamina than many of the younger war correspondents he encountered during his travels.

Kempler also believes that Ricalton's self-imposed traveling deprivations may have been an attempt to expiate the guilt he felt in constantly traveling and being away from home and family. In his travel accounts, Ricalton would gleefully write about how little money he had spent on his travels. In 1888 Edison was minded to tell Ricalton: "Never mind the expense. Travel first class and don't want for anything." Ricalton duly ignored this advice and was incapable of spending his employer's money on anything other than the barest necessities. Writing in *India through the Stereoscope* (1907), he considered self-sacrifice to be "the brightest gem in the Christian character."

Ricalton was known to be quiet, modest, and unassuming. These are not the obvious character traits of big-game hunters. In the Philippines, in 1898, Ricalton was not averse to putting down his camera and picking up the rifle of a wounded soldier and continuing to fire at the enemy. In fact, Ricalton's repressed aggression was never far from the surface. An example of this manifested itself in 1885 when he was at home with his family. His 12-year-old son Charles was bitten by a neighbor's dog. Without a moment's thought, Ricalton picked up his gun, sought out the animal, and shot it dead.

Ricalton had discovered early on that using a camera meant he could be paid to indulge in his main passion – travel. He always considered his photography to be less important than traveling itself – and his writing. Ricalton's apparent lack of interest in seeing his published photographs correctly attributed has ultimately prevented his receiving the recognition he deserves. He may not have cared, but posterity should. James Ricalton was a remarkable man and a remarkable photographer.

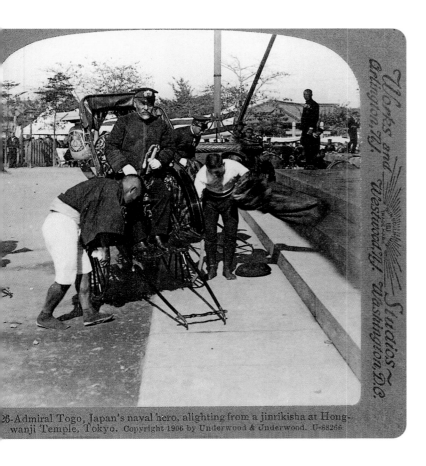

26-Admiral Togo, Japan's naval hero, alighting from a jinrikisha at Hongwanji Temple, Tokyo. Copyright 1906 by Underwood & Underwood. U-88266

JAMES HARE

James Henry Hare (1856–1946) was a celebrated British photo-journalist who first made his name in America by photographing the 1898 Spanish-American War for *Collier's Weekly* (Fig. 393). Well known for his coverage of conflicts, he also photographed shipwrecks, earthquakes, political rallies, and the Wright brothers' early test flights. In 1904 he made his first and only trip to Japan as a correspondent to cover the 1904–5 Russo-Japanese War in Korea and Manchuria.

Hare was born in London on October 3rd, 1856. His father was a well-known camera maker whose Patent Camera, introduced in 1882, was warmly acknowledged in the *British Journal of Photography* in an article entitled "International Inventions Exhibition." The article, contained in the issue for 28th August, 1885 (p. 545), described the camera as "the model upon which nearly all others in the market are based." Not particularly academic, Hare left school in 1871, and was apprenticed to his father until 1879. Following a disagreement over future camera design, Hare joined a competitor and there met his wife-to-be whom he married in August the same year.

By the early 1880s Hare was becoming less interested in making cameras, and more in taking photographs. He successfully sold some of his photographs of public and sporting events to London illustrated journals, and in 1889 was offered the position of technical adviser to the famous New York firm of E. & H. T. Anthony & Co. Hare moved with his family (which by then included two sons and three daughters) to Brooklyn, and America would be his home for the rest of his life. But the company he joined was going through difficult times, and the factory where Hare worked was sold. The new owners could not meet Hare's salary expectations, so he resigned and worked alone on camera manufacturing and freelance photography. He made just enough money to keep going.

Hare had become friendly with Joseph Byron, a noted photographer, who worked for the *Illustrated American*. In 1895, when Byron stopped working for that journal, Hare, who had learned much about news photography from his friend, was appointed as the publication's full-time news photographer. There he captured on camera a variety of sporting events, which he later claimed taught him a sense

of timing. After three years he felt in need of a change, and in 1898 applied to *Collier's Weekly*, where he was taken on to photograph the Spanish-American War. The pictures he sent back sealed his reputation. An American soldier encountering Hare and his camera in the thick of the action, told the photographer that he was a fool. Hare replied: "... you can't get real pictures unless you take some risk!" Nevertheless, the strain of Hare's first combat assignment adversely affected his health and he was unable to work again for several months. After returning to work, he spent the next five years photographing yacht launchings, political rallies, and Latin American affairs. In 1901 he famously covered President McKinley's presidential tour and took his photograph minutes before his assassination – probably the last taken of McKinley alive. In January 1904 he joined other *Collier's* reporters in San Francisco, en route for Tokyo, ready to cover the expected war between Russia and Japan.

Upon arrival, they waited impatiently for permission to leave for the front. However, the Japanese authorities were initially very nervous about military security, and raised many obstacles. One photographer (Jack London) was arrested for

Left Fig. 393. Anonymous, "Portrait of James Hare," 1904. Hare, *A Photographic Record of the Russo-Japanese War*, 1905.

Left Fig. 392. James Ricalton, "Eleven Inch Shell on Its Way to Port Arthur," 1904, albumen-print stereoview, published by Underwood & Underwood. Rob Oechsle Collection. Ricalton finally achieved his ambition of capturing on camera a shell being fired from a siege-gun, something that no photographer had previously been able to accomplish. The difficulties in obtaining this picture, which secured Underwood & Underwood newspaper rights for $5,000 ($102,000 in today's money), are explained on page 283.

Below Fig. 394. James Hare, "Japanese Gunners about to Open Fire during Action at Liaoyang," 1904, gelatin silver-print stereoview, published by H. C. White Co. Old Japan Picture Library.

taking unauthorized photographs. Hare managed to get some clandestine pictures of the Japanese army in training under cover of visiting a Japanese colonel whom he had met in Cuba, and was fortunate to escape with a reprimand. After more than a month of delay, the Japanese, realizing they needed favorable publicity in the US and Great Britain, agreed to a select group of journalists being allowed to go to the fighting in Korea and Manchuria – but only under strictly controlled conditions. Hare was one of those selected. One of the less fortunate journalists, Richard Harding Davis, approached Hare with a financial offer to take his place. Hare declined, using his trademark Cockney accent: "A photographer 'as to be on the spot. A newspyperman can use 'is h'imagination.'"

In April 1904 the select group of journalists joined General Kuroki's First Army, close to the Korea/Manchuria border, and met up with the foreign military observers who were already there. They would have plenty of time to get to know each other since, when the army was camped, the movement of all non-combatants was restricted to within a 2-mile (3.2-km) circle of the base. Hare, at forty-seven, was the oldest of the group, and according to L. L. Gould and R. Greffe's biography, *Photojournalist: The Career of Jimmy Hare* (1977), his cheerful disposition, Cockney accent, and diminutive frame (he was no more than 5 feet 4 inches (1.65 meters) tall) all combined in endearing him to the other correspondents and observers. Hare became friendly with Sir Ian Hamilton, for example, despite the wide gulf in social background. Frederick Palmer, a correspondent, wrote later in "About 'Jimmy' Hare" (1905) that he was the "*enfant terrible* of the camp" and that at Pyongyang in Korea he "ate an whole bottle of olives without getting indigestion." According to C. Carnes in another Hare biography, *Jimmy Hare News Photographer* (1940), when one member of the group was extolling the virtues of treacle, Hare retorted, "Caesar

conquered the world on treacle. I know all about it now. He slid down the Alps on it, and chucked it all over the Gauls and gummed 'em up so they couldn't fight."

General Kuroki, in charge of 42,500 men, marched north to cross the Yalu River and threaten the Russian positions at Liaoyang. Hare and his colleagues followed, and were just in time to witness the two-day battle of the Yalu, which commenced on April 30th. Once again, under strict supervision and censorship, Hare took what pictures he could. Palmer, for one, was very impressed. Hare was "the first of the correspondents' corps" to cross the Yalu and "was up the next morning at daybreak, ill and pale, developing the first photographs of the army at the front to be published." Hare was unimpressed with the amateur camera work of other correspondents who only took photographs to complement their reports: "You can't compete with me.... You button pushers couldn't make a real photograph, anyway."

Kuroki's army pushed on towards Liaoyang, and in August a huge battle between 158,000 Russians and 125,000 Japanese took place. Hare, on horseback, crossed the Tang River with the army and photographed the main body of troops making their way across. He was the first correspondent to enter Liaoyang with the victorious Japanese troops, and *Collier's Weekly* were delighted with this scoop, together with Hare's other work which they lost no time in promoting as "probably the most complete pictorial record of recent events in the Far East." After capturing on camera the last decisive battle at Sha-ho, which lasted from October 5th to 17th, Hare decided that hostilities were unlikely to resume for some time and went home to the US to recuperate. In 1905 *Collier's* published a comprehensive book of the war, *A Photographic Record of the Russo-Japanese War*, edited and arranged by Hare, with some 545 of his and other correspondents' photographs.[139]

DOUBLEDAY PAGE & CO., NEW YORK.
General Agents for America.

THE ALADDIN STEREOGRAPH (Pat. Apr. 14, '03.)
H. C. White Co., Publishers, N. Bennington, Vt.

(18) 8394 Japanese Gunners about to open fire during action at Liao Yang.   Copyright 1905 by James H. Hare.

The Japanese military worked hard to prevent correspondents from mixing with the troops in the trenches. Watching battles from prescribed hillsides was permitted, as was photographing on the ground, but only before and after any fighting. Hare, nevertheless, would always look for opportunities to circumvent these rules and did succeed in getting some close-ups of actual life in the trenches, as did Barry and Ricalton. His bravery (or recklessness) on one occasion was rewarded when he managed to slip his escort and rush directly into the field of fire. The camouflaged Japanese troops furiously waved him away, worried that Hare's camera would draw attention to their position. He retired, but not before getting the desired pictures.

Hare commanded great respect from his journalistic contemporaries. In his article "Photography as a Profession" (1904), Richard Harding Davis stated that Hare had "made the Russo-Japanese War famous." In 1907 Emperor Meiji awarded Hare a medal for his services as a correspondent. After the war Hare settled back down to a series of domestic assignments and photographed the aftermath of the 1906 San Francisco earthquake. That same year he photographed New York from a hot air balloon, and almost drowned when the craft lost control and fell towards the sea. In 1908 he took the first photograph of an airplane in the air when he photographed one of the Wright brothers' training flights. Hare was not finished as a war photographer, and covered the 1911 Mexican Revolution, the 1912 Balkans conflict, and the 1914–18 World War. He finally retreated from active photography in 1922 and spent the next ten years on the lecture circuit before formerly retiring in 1931. He died in 1946, just three months before his ninetieth birthday.

Jimmy Hare had inherited his father's flair for camera design and optical and mechanical innovation. He carried this with him into the field, and captured many images with contraptions of his own making. He had witnessed first hand the transition from wet- to dry-plate photography, and had seen the emergence of the hand-held camera. He was a true photographer in all respects, admired and respected wherever he went, and unquestionably one of the greatest photo-journalists of the twentieth century.

JACK LONDON

It is not widely known that the celebrated American author Jack London (1876–1916) was a war correspondent for a short period of his life, and that one of the conflicts he covered was the Russo-Japanese War (Fig. 395). Commissioned by the Hearst newspapers syndicate, he arrived in Japan in January 1904, already famous due to the publication the year before of his novel *The Call of the Wild*.

As R. O'Conner makes clear in *Jack London: A Biography* (1965), London had a life-long phobia concerning Asia and feared future territorial expansion by the Chinese and Japanese. In a 1910 article, "The Unparalleled Invasion," London first coined the expression "The Yellow Peril." He had traveled to Japan earlier in his life, but during his second visit in

1904 he developed a lasting antipathy towards the Japanese, brought about largely by what he considered to be high-handed and arrogant behavior towards him and the other foreign correspondents. Due to London's restless and impatient temperament, he soon clashed with the understandably terse Japanese military that were at war with an enemy that almost everyone outside Japan thought would defeat them. One of their major concerns was the accidental or intentional leaking of military secrets to the Russians. Had it not been for London's burgeoning fame as a writer, it is very likely that his conduct in Japan would have landed him in far more trouble than was actually the case.

The foreign journalists who gathered in Tokyo were impatient to receive permission from the Japanese authorities to travel to the front in Korea. Tired of waiting, and true to character, the adventurous London, who had arrived in Tokyo on January 24th, set out on his own by *jinrikisha* and train. On the 27th he took a train to Kobe, where he was told that no non-military ship would be leaving until February 3rd. At Nagasaki he received a similar response, and therefore continued on to Moji. There he was able to obtain passage on a steamer bound for Chemulpo (present-day Inchon), due to leave on February 1st. With time to kill, he wandered around Moji taking photographs of the people and buildings, but Moji at this time was a fortified town and he was arrested by the police on suspicion of being a Russian spy (Fig. 396). After eight hours of questioning, he was moved to Kokura,

where he was subjected to further investigation. The respected correspondent Richard Harding Davis and the American ambassador intervened on London's behalf, and the Japanese released him and his camera. However, London was formerly charged and required to pay a fine. This incident was covered in the San Francisco *Examiner* on February 3rd, 1904 under the headline "How Jack London got in and out of jail in Japan." The incident is also covered in Gould and Greffe's *Photojournalist: The Career of Jimmy Hare* (p. 34).

Free again, on February 8th London bought passage on a steamer to Pusan. However, just before departure the ship was requisitioned by the military. Undeterred, London caught a launch to a small steamer whose only accommodation was on the open decks. As a result, he had to endure a rough winter's night crossing. At Pusan he took a coastal steamer to Chemulpo, but this was also requisitioned by the military at Mokpo. Fast running out of options, London, who had navigational experience, chartered a fishing junk, hired three local Koreans as crew, and set off across the Yellow Sea to Chemulpo in sub-zero weather and gales. During a tempestuous crossing, he lost his mast to the winds and his rudder to rough seas. They managed to find safe harbor at Kunsan, and the next day resumed their journey, reaching Chemulpo after six days and nights of battling against the elements.

London was one of the first correspondents to reach Chemulpo, and hearing that the first conflict was likely to take place in Pyongyang, he purchased a horse and hired a Korean servant and a Japanese interpreter named Yamada. His determination was rewarded by being the first correspondent to reach Pyongyang, and he was able to send back a detailed report of the first battle between Japanese and Russian forces – a real scoop for his sponsors, and one that earned the respect of the other correspondents.

His luck ran out, however, when he decided to move north on the Peking road with the advancing columns of the Japanese First Army. His relations with the military were frosty, and when the authorities in Tokyo heard about his unauthorized movements, the security police were instructed to arrest him. He was escorted back to Pyongyang, and then to Seoul, where he was again imprisoned and questioned. Released, he was ordered to remain with the other correspondents who were just arriving. Meanwhile, the Japanese military, following international pressure, had finally agreed to allow the correspondents to get closer to the action. The correspondents therefore went up to the Yalu, and London sent back reports of the Japanese army's heroic crossing of the river. He sent many photographs back to America and his were the first to be published.

Towards the end of May, London was becoming increasingly frustrated by the military's continued restrictions on correspondents' access to the war front, and he had sent in a request to Hearst to be allowed to switch coverage to the Russian side. Whilst waiting for a reply, he got into a fight with a Japanese groom whom he accused of stealing some horse's fodder. For the third time in four months he was arrested, and with the patience of the military exhausted he was in genuine danger of being court-martialed. Davis again intervened, and sensing the seriousness of London's position sought help from the US President, Roosevelt, a personal friend. The Japanese agreed to release him on condition that he immediately left Korea.

Davis caught up with him in Tokyo, just prior to London's leaving for home. Davis's letters from Japan are held by the University of Virginia Library and in one from Tokyo, dated June 13th, 1904, addressed to his mother, he records his impressions of the famous writer: "Jack London turned up to-day on his way home. I liked him very much. He is very simple and modest and gave you a tremendous impression of vitality and power. He is very bitter against the wonderful little people and says he carries away with him only a feeling of irritation. But I told him that probably would soon wear off and he would remember only the pleasant things. I did envy him so, going home after having seen a fight and I not yet started."

London died at age forty of kidney disease at the height of his fame. His life was every bit as adventurous as the lives of the fictional characters about whom he wrote in his books and short stories. An obituary in the *San Francisco Bulletin* on December 2nd, 1916, stated: "No writer, unless it were Mark Twain, ever had a more romantic life than Jack London. The untimely death of this most popular of American Fictionists has profoundly shocked a world that expected him to live and work for many years longer."

OTHER WESTERN PHOTOGRAPHERS

Frank Lloyd Wright (1867–1959), the famous American architect who designed Tokyo's Imperial Hotel, was a proficient photographer who used the medium as a design aid to his architectural work. He first visited Japan as a tourist in 1905 with the aim of adding to his collection of Japanese woodblock prints. He was enchanted by Japan and called it "The most romantic, artistic country on earth." However, he did not return until 1913 following a commission to design the Imperial, but then returned regularly until the project was over in 1922. During his first 1905 trip, which took place between February and April, Wright photographed a number of scenes around the Kyoto and Kobe areas. His personal album of some fifty of these images has survived and was presented by his son to the Frank Lloyd Wright Home and Studio Foundation, Chicago. The album of photographs is illustrated in Melanie Birk's *Frank Lloyd Wright's Fifty Views of Japan* (1996). Despite first taking an interest in photography in 1890, apart from one or two family portraits almost no other work by Wright appears to have survived.

William Herman Rau (1855–1920) was a well-known Philadelphia photographer whose stereographs, lantern slides, and larger-format photographs are in many collections and archives, including the Library of Congress, the Smithsonian's National Museum of American Art, and the Museum of Modern Art in New York. In the 1904 book by Angus, *Japan The Eastern Wonderland*, there are several photographs of Japan credited to Rau and dated 1893. However, it is clear that some – probably all – of these photographs are by other photographers. The writer has not been able to find any evidence that Rau visited Japan and it is more likely that he purchased the negatives and then marketed them under his own name – a commercial practice for which he was known.

133. Richard Barry and Frederick Villiers.
Copyrighted, 1905, by T. W. Ingersoll.

14887—Looking for Something. Japan.

Richard Barry was an American photo-journalist who covered the 1904–5 Russo-Japanese War. His photographs were reproduced as stereoviews by the publishing firm T. W. Ingersoll and his book on the conflict, *Port Arthur: A Monster Heroism*, is also illustrated with his work (Fig. 397). Another American photo-journalist, **Julian Cochrane**, was in Japan just prior to the outbreak of the war with Russia and took photographs on behalf of the stereoview publishers Keystone Company (Figs. 398, 399).

Nothing is known about the Kobe-based amateur photographer **H. E. Bottlewalla** who, according to the *Japan Direc- tory* entries, operated in Kobe as a "Bill and Bullion Broker" from 1899 until 1901, and then as a "Merchant and Commission Agent" until 1905. After this date Bottlewalla disappears from the scene and is no longer listed as a resident of Japan. There would probably have been no trace of his photographic activities were it not for the fact that he produced a fine lacquer-covered album of approximately fifty hand-colored photographs entitled "Scenic Japan, An Album of Photographs of the Chief Places of Interest, prepared by H. E. Bottlewalla Amateur Photographer." Over the years the writer has seen two examples of this album, and it is very likely that Bottlewalla prepared them as gifts to his friends and clients. His Kobe business must have been successful enough to allow him the time to travel around Japan putting together his portfolio. The work is of a very high standard (Fig. 400).[140]

According to the Harold Williams' Archives, held at the National Library of Australia, Canberra, the photographer of the American Southwest frontier, **Adam Clark Vroman** (1856–1916), toured Japan in 1903 and 1909, photographing and collecting Japanese art. His collection of Netsuke carvings was subsequently acquired by the Metropolitan Museum of Fine Art, New York. As far as the writer is aware, Vroman's Japanese photographs have not been published and his glass negatives are stored at the Los Angeles County Museum. According to Vroman's biography, *Photographer of the Southwest* (1961) written by R. Mahood, his Japanese work was done with a small camera and the "negatives have no longer the quality which distinguishes the earlier work."

Born in La Salle, Illinois, Vroman, whose parents were of Dutch ancestry, initially took a job with the railroad in 1874. He married Esther Griest in 1892, and in the same year moved to Pasadena, California, in the hope that the climate there would improve his wife's health. Esther, who suffered from tuberculosis, unfortunately failed to recover and died just two years later.

Following his wife's death, Vroman entered into partnership with J. S. Glassock and opened an art book and photography supply store, which is still in operation in Pasadena to this day. As an enthusiastic amateur photographer, Vroman made several expeditions to the Southwest in order to photograph the Indians in Arizona and New Mexico. He also photographed Pasadena, Yosemite, the California Missions, Illinois, Pennsylvania, and the Library of Congress. But as Webb and Weinstein's *Dwellers at the Source* (1992) makes clear, it is undoubtedly his Southwestern Indian photographs, taken between 1895 and 1904, for which he is famous. He died at the age of sixty from pernicious anemia at a friend's home in Altadena, California. At his request, Adam Vroman's ashes were scattered over his wife's grave in Flora Dale, Pennsylvania.

Richard Gordon Smith (1858–1918) was an Englishman of independent means whose income from family investments was sufficient to enable him to travel around the world indulging in big-game hunting, fishing, and photography. He was so taken with Japan when he reached it in 1898, that he decided to make it his home and settled in Kobe. He kept journals whose pages were adorned with attractive hand-painted illustrations and pasted-in photographs. The illustrations were from commissioned Japanese artists, whilst the photographs were mostly his own. According to Victoria Manthorpe in her book *The Japan Diaries of Richard Gordon Smith* (1986), his own photographs were printed and colored at Tamamura Kozaburo's establishment.

The year before leaving England, Gordon Smith's eighteen-year marriage had collapsed. As divorce in Victorian England was not considered respectable, he did what many estranged spouses did in those days – he traveled. Leaving his wife and three daughters behind, he set off at the age of forty and reached Japan at the end of 1898. He spent most of the rest of his life exploring the country, and supplemented his income by collecting fauna for natural history museums in England, Germany, and Japan. He developed an interest in Japanese folk tales and wrote a book, *Ancient Tales and Folklore of Japan* (1908), which was unfortunately not a commercial success. In 1907, however, the Japanese government had rewarded his services to Japanese museums by presenting him with the Order of the Rising Sun, Fourth Class.

Nothing is known of **Miss C. Burnside-Johnson**, who took photographs of the Ainu in Hokkaido in around 1904. Three of her Ainu photographs appear in *The Illustrated London News*, December 24th, 1904 (p. 962). The same jour-

nal carried a photograph of "Mount Asama" by the **Reverend G. C. Niven**, the British missionary based in Gifu, and which appeared in the issue for November 30th, 1907 (p. 795). A photographer only identified by his family name **Bolak**, took pictures of the Ainu and the Japanese silkworm industry around 1910. These also appeared in separate issues of *The Illustrated London News*: "Ainus," April 23rd, 1910 (p. 601) and "Silkworm Industry," June 11th, 1910 (pp. 916–17). Two other unknown photographers had their work illustrated in *The Graphic*. The first was an **R. J. H. Mittmer**, whose photograph was captioned "Women Labourers in Tokio – Making the Elevated Railway" and which appeared on October 1st, 1904 (p. 433). The other photographer was **J. W. McLellen** and his work "A Japanese Boy Having His Lies [*sic*] Washed Away at a Shrine," appeared in the May 28th, 1904 supplement.

George Rose (1861–1942) was a commercial photographer who specialized in producing stereoviews (Fig. 402). He was born in Clunes, Australia, and after leaving school took a job in his father's shoe shop. According to the collector Ron Blum, who has been researching Rose's life for many years, a talent for photography led to a change of career and he quickly began to specialize in stereo-photography. A prodigious traveler, he photographed the Far East, the Middle East, Europe, North America, his native Australia, and New Zealand. He built a portfolio of more than 9000 views and marketed them through the Rose Stereograph Company, which is still operating. His photographic tour of Japan in 1903 or 1904 secured around 200 views. Of these, according to Rob Oechsle, approximately twenty percent were from Enami Tamotsu's negatives, with whom Rose must have come to some commercial arrangement. Rose's own photographs, combined with some of Enami's finest, together make up one of the best published sets of late Meiji stereoviews (Fig. 401). Unfortunately, the set is extremely rare. Other information on Rose can be found in the book by R. Hall which illustrates Rose's work in Korea: *1904 Korea through Australian Eyes* (2004).

Benjamin West Kilburn (1827–1909) and his brother Edward (1830–84) founded the Kilburn Brothers Stereoscopic Co. in the mid-1860s in Littleton, New Hampshire, USA. After Edward retired from the firm in 1877, it changed its name to B. W. Kilburn. The door-to-door sales distribution method was pioneered by Kilburn, who is also credited with introducing the curved stereoview mount. Whilst this method enhanced the illusion of depth, it also served the more functional purpose of optically matching the view to the curved field of focus. (This same concept can be seen today in the

better cinemas, where the screen is curved in a like manner.) Kilburn traveled extensively, building his portfolio, and by the early 1900s his firm was one of the world's largest producers and distributors of stereoviews. An excellent copyright 1901 series on Japan was produced, and a later series on the Russo-Japanese War illustrated the conflict from the Russian side. The imprint on both sets states "Photographed and Published by B. W. Kilburn." However, Kilburn did not travel to Asia, as Linda McShane makes clear in her book *When I Wanted the Sun to Shine* (1993), and the actual photographer of these views remains a mystery. When Kilburn died in 1909, the negatives were acquired by his distribution partner James M. Davis, who subsequently sold them to the Keystone View Company. These negatives are now held by the California Museum of Photography.

Below Fig. 401. George Rose, "Nagoya Castle," ca. 1903, gelatin silver-print stereoview, published by George Rose. Rob Oechsle Collection.

Bottom Fig. 402. Anonymous, "Portrait of George Rose," ca. 1900. Courtesy of Ron Blum.

6198 Nagoya Castle, Japan. Most Japanese castles are of the same type, five or six storeys high, and surrounded by high stone walls and a deep moat

6198 Nagoya Castle, Japan. Most Japanese castles are of the same type, five or six storeys high, and surrounded by high stone walls and a deep moat

TAKAGI TEIJIRO

More research is required into the life of Takagi Teijiro, a prolific producer of hand-colored lantern slides and collotype albums in the late Meiji era and beyond. As we have seen, he is mentioned in 1903 as the manager of Tamamura Koza-buro's branch store at No. 16 Sannomiya, Kobe, and a year later is shown as the proprietor. He operated as Tamamura's agent for some years, and appeared happy to trade off the celebrated photographer's name until 1914, after which the Tamamura name is no longer used. Evidence of this transi-tion is shown by some surviving collotype publications and lantern slides, which credit the work to "T. Takagi" – even though it is clear that a number of original Tamamura nega-tives have been used.

Takagi's studio continued until at least 1929. In the writer's possession is an undated catalogue of some 455 lantern slides with the T. Takagi Photographic Studio & Art Gallery imprint, and this gives the main studio address as No. 42 Nishimachi, Kobe, and a branch store at No. 1, Sanjo Furukawacho, Kioto. On the back cover is the inscription "The Firm's Name 'The Tamamura' Has Been Changed to 'T.Takagi.' The Work is Carried On Under Exactly The Same Management." The writer's collection also includes a 1917 published collotype book entitled *The Fujiyama*, with the studio address still showing as No. 42 Nishimachi, and a custom-made studio photograph envelope with the No. 16

Sannomiya address but with a printed caption on the reverse. The caption reads "Tamamura Photographic Studio and Gallery of Art. The address after June 1909: No. 42, Nishi-machi, Kobe, Japan, T. Takagi, Proprietor."

According to Boyd and Izakura in *Portraits in Sepia* (2000), Takagi's father was Takagi Kichibei, who operated a studio in Kyoto from 1868 until his death in 1882. The studio was then taken over by Kichibei's brother Kotani Sojiro (1859–1904). Kotani's studio, which became one of Japan's top producers of ambrotypes, was also based in Kyoto and known by the name "Takagi-ho."

It is possible that Takagi Teijiro was destined to take over the family business at around the time of Kotani's death. Perhaps Tamamura, anxious to retain the services of his talented Kobe manager, was also prepared to cede ownership of the Kobe business to Takagi. If this speculation is correct, then it would have been sensible for Takagi to continue acting as an agent for Tamamura's photographs, whilst steadily building up his own portfolio. Takagi's "post-Tamamura" work is of exceptional quality. He produced over twenty-five different titles of hand-colored collotype photo books of Japanese life and customs. These tasteful publications proved to be very popular, and attract avid collectors to this day. Takagi was also a major rival of Enami's in the manufacture of hand-colored lantern slides. Again, the quality of work is outstanding (Figs. 365, 403). Takagi's talents, however, do not seem to have been fully recognized. This is almost certainly because it is difficult to disentangle his work from Tamamura's. However, enough of Takagi's work exists in published form and a comparison with Tamamura's should make attribution easier.

OTHER JAPANESE PHOTOGRAPHERS

Ryoun-do was a Kobe-based photographic studio which was positioned close to the famous Nunobiki waterfall. We only know this from a photograph of the studio taken in the vicinity around 1900 and illustrated in Ozawa Takesi's *Shashin de Miru Bakumatsu Meiji* (1990, p. 100). Painted on the outside wall is "RYO-UN-DO. Photographic Studio. NB Kobe's lovely Nunobiki Taki after that comes rest in the RYO.UN.DO'S rustic rooms and gardens for the cup of tea that cheers and not inebriates...." On the opposite side of the road, a sign on a building reads "Ryoundo's (Fine) Art Depot." It is not clear whether the studio produced its own commercial souvenir albums or, more likely, operated instead as a dealer. The only advertisements the writer has traced appear in the *Japan Directory* for the years 1906–8 when the business promoted itself as a dealer in lacquer wares and was based elsewhere in Motomachi, Kobe. Although the last two years mentioned C. Miyake as the proprietor, nothing more is known about this short-lived studio (Fig. 404).

There were at least two other active Japanese photo-dealers operating in Kobe at this time, although very little is known about their activities. **T. Musumi** was based at Motomachi and advertised himself in the *Japan Directory* as a dealer in photographs between the years 1906 and 1908. The other was **Fukasawa Tadashi**, who was also based in Motomachi and advertised his "Photo Store" in the *Japan Directory* from 1901 until 1904. For the next four years, the business is depicted as a "Dealer in General Curios." After 1908 nothing further is heard. Fukasawa seems to have been quite active for a while, and his souvenir albums of views and costumes turn up from time to time. Whether he also operated a portrait studio is not clear, but it is more likely that he simply concentrated on distributing the souvenir albums of other studios. Fukasawa may well have had some connection with Okamoto Rokuhei and his Genroku-kwan studio since he used the same stag's head trademark logo on the printed labels sometimes appearing on the inside front cover of his albums. An article on Fukasawa's albums appeared a few years ago, and the accompanying illustrations of photographs included at least one Kajima Seibei print. This provides another link to Okamoto, who seems to have acquired a number of Kajima's negatives some time in the mid-1890s.[141]

Another Kobe studio in operation at the beginning of the 1900s was **Shin-E-Do**. The firm described itself as "Photographers" in Chamberlain and Mason's *Handbook for Travellers in Japan* from 1894 to 1901. However, they may have been a portrait studio rather than a manufacturer of their own studio souvenir albums. The firm acted as dealers in composite albums, and often impressed their studio wet stamp on the backs of the photographs handled. Shin-E-Do may have been the main or exclusive Kobe agent for Enami Tamotsu since many of his photographs appear in their albums. It would be interesting to discover the name of the proprietor since there is some suggestion that the composite albums issued by the firm contained some of their own work. The writer has seen one Shin-E-Do album, for example, where a print illustrating the Kobe studio was included.

Above Fig. 404. Ryoun-Do Studio, "693. Panorama of Ryoundo's Store, Kobe," large-format hand-colored albumen print. Worswick Collection.

Epilogue

This book is larger and took longer to write than originally intended. I had not fully appreciated how much information had become available over the past ten years or so. Numerous books and articles on the subject have appeared, especially in Japan. That added to the research load.

In trying to track the movements of the photographers mentioned in these pages, I found myself going down some very time-consuming paths. The English-language newspapers published in nineteenth-century China and Japan, for example, often include lists of ships' passengers – inward- and outward bound. Photographers' inclusion in one or more lists can be a very effective way of piecing together their travel itineraries. But that knowledge comes with a price: most of these old newspapers are on microfilm, and constant use of this retro-technology is very laborious and definitely conducive to promoting eyesight and/or back strain! Yet results can often be achieved and pictures emerge. In the end, the exercise can be addictive. Old newspapers are a wonderful resource, but in the absence of digitization and reliable word-searching facilities, one needs to be very patient – and have an even more patient publisher.

More often than expected, I was able to take advantage of the incredible and growing amounts of genealogical information available on the Internet and elsewhere. This was particularly helpful in tracking down life-event details for some American and British photographers – much less so, however, for other European and Japanese photographers. An increasing number of old periodicals and newspapers are also becoming available and searchable on the Web – a very exciting development. And the nineteenth century is still within touching distance. I was able, for example, to interview or correspond with grandchildren (and even one son) of several of the photographers discussed in these pages.

Museums and libraries across the world hold artifacts and archives of letters, diaries, ships journals, and photographs which, for various reasons, usually financial, have been inadequately catalogued, and therefore unresearched. These potentially vital resources will perhaps, over time, become accessible; but in the meantime it is frustrating to think that the pace of their introduction is generally linked

to circumstances outside the control of the serious researcher. Yet, just knowing the information is out there, somewhere, is in itself a motivation. Missionary archives are steadily becoming more available. These promise much: in researching this book I was surprised to find that so many missionaries had used cameras – and often to good effect.

Many of the photographers in this book, of course, whether Western or Japanese, have been forgotten. Some of them deserve to be remembered, a few revered. Each one of them has left footprints behind although some tracks, over the passing years, have unfortunately faded. Retracing them was often difficult, sometimes frustrating, and occasionally impossible. But more often than anticipated, the efforts proved to be satisfying and rewarding. Future researchers will no doubt retrace some of these steps, and follow new ones, making fresh discoveries along the way. As they do so, the history of Japanese photography will continue to be written – and rewritten.

We reflect sometimes on the daunting number of unanswered questions which remain – and on the legions of missing photographs. And we still know too little about many of the key photographers, particularly of the 1850s and 1860s. It is quite possible that the supposed lost daguerreotypes of Eliphalet Brown, Edward Kern, and Edward Edgerton are, as these words are being written, lying uncatalogued and forgotten in the basements of national and local archives across the world – stored in trunks or boxes waiting to be discovered. And there are old suitcases up in some attics belonging to descendants of photographers, who were once, a long time ago, active with their cameras in Japan. These cases contain letters and photographs. Every twenty years or so the cases are opened; the "dry" letters and "dull" photographs are briefly scanned and replaced. The lids close again. A decision about what to do with them is put off – for another occasion. And those decisions, and those occasions will have a direct bearing on when, and how much we can expand our knowledge of this fascinating subject.

Terry Bennett
London, September 2006

ENDNOTES

Chapter 1

1 The writer is grateful to American researcher Eric Politzer for providing this reference.

2 The writer is grateful to Steven Joseph for the reference to *Craig's Daguerreian Registry* in which details of Marks' career are given.

3 For further information on the life of Sentaro, see Calvin F. Parker, *The Japanese Sam Patch* (2001).

4 The writer is grateful to the American collector Rob Oechsle for pointing out this reference and its significance. Note that Okinawa at that time was known as "Loo-Choo," "Luchu," or "Great Lu-chu." For a work covering historical exposure times for daguerreotype photography, see S. D. Humphrey, *American Hand Book of the Daguerreotype* (1858).

5 It should not be forgotten that apart from Brown's work, the next oldest surviving photograph of Japan is a daguerreotype taken at Shimoda in April 1854 by the Russian Lieutenant Aleksandr Fiodorovich Mozhaiskii (1825–90), who was a member of the rival Russian expedition that arrived in Japan in August 1853, only a month after Perry. See *Old Japanese Photographs* (2006 – hereafter *OJP*) for a full listing of known Japanese daguerreotypes.

6 These are discussed in P. E. Palmquist and T. R. Kailbourn, *Pioneer Photographers of the Far West* (2000). Other sources on Kern quoted in this book are William J. Heffernan, *Edward M. Kern* (1953) and Robert V. Hine, *Edward Kern and American Expansion* (1962).

7 For the background to this photograph and the group of American pioneers who resided in Shimoda from March 15th to June 5th, 1855, see pages 30–1 above.

8 The actual permitted area was defined in October 1857 when additional articles were attached to the January 1856 Dutch Treaty. The full wording is given in J. H. Gubbins, *The Progress of Japan* (1911).

9 It is worth noting a letter written by Elgin from Tien-tsin, China, on July 6th, 1858, to the opticians and camera manufacturers Murray and Heath. The firm published an extract of this letter, by way of advertisement, in *The Art Journal Advertiser*, January 1859. "After referring to a series of negative plates which Mr. Bruce, the bearer of the new treaty, is to bring to England, the letter continues: 'I have not before had the opportunity of telling you how excellent in every respect I have found your apparatus to be. The camera has been subject to violent alterations of temperature and to long exposure in the blazing sun (the thermometer is at this moment 96 degrees in a shaded room), and a few days ago everything was not only damp, but wet, and yet all is in most perfect condition.'"

10 See H. A. James, *The Price Guide to Photographic Cards* (1982, p. 94) and William C. Darrah, *The World of Stereographs* (1977, p. 121).

11 Freiburg State Archives, AEF. census, No. 8, 1845, reg. VI, p. 427. Pierre Rossier's occupation is shown as "regent."

12 Freiburg State Archives, AEF, DPC II, 13,335.

13 I am grateful to the Swiss collector Gerard Bourgarel who drew my attention to a photographic portrait of a young girl taken by Rossier in his home town of Freiburg. The girl died in 1862, the same year the photograph was taken.

14 Freiburg State Archives, AEF, RP582, p. 60.

15 The writer is extremely grateful to Benoit de Diesbach Belleroche and Gerard Bourgarel who drew his attention to this publication.

16 This additional information was discovered by Benoit de Diesbach Belleroche on further research into the Freiburg State Archives.

17 Entered in the Stationers' Hall Copyright Register as *Stereoscopic Views in China Nos. 1–50, published by Henry Negretti & Joseph Warren Zambra, No. 1 Hatton Garden, copyright – the same, date of publication 19th November 1859*. The National Archives hold this under reference COPY 3/10 (see p. 126).

18 See the following photographic periodicals: *The Photographic News*, November 4th, 1859, pp. 99–100; November 11th, pp. 110–12; November 18th, pp. 124–6; the *Photographic Journal*, December 1st, 1859, p. 298; *La Lumiere*, March 17th and 24th, 1860.

19 A ship's journal written by one of the officers of HMS *Sampson*, Henry Purcell Ward, between January 1st, 1858 and October 31st, 1860. The ship was part of the British China squadron and was kept occupied by the disturbances in China during that period. The ship was also instructed to take Rutherford Alcock (first British Minister to Japan) and the other consuls to Japan in June 1859.

20 The writer would like to thank Eric Politzer for this reference.

21 National Archives, F.O. 46.8 contains the correspondence referred to and also Rossier's three-plate and eight-plate panoramas of Nagasaki.

22 See the Negretti and Zambra Appendix 1 (page 305) for more details.

23 The writer is grateful to both Claude Estebe and Gerard Levy for pointing out that Rossier made photographs in Siam for Firmin Bocourt, a French zoologist, who carried out a scientific expedition in Siam in 1861–2. This was reported in a lecture given by Milnes Edwards at the French Académie des sciences, who stated "M. Bocourt utilisa aussi son talent de dessinateur au service de la collection anthropologique du Muséum, et il profita aussi de la présence à Bangkok d'un artiste habile (M. Rossier) pour obtenir une série nombreuse de photographies représentant les monuments et les sites les plus remarquables de cette partie du royaume de Siam." Académie des sciences, Seance du 10 août 1863, cote Y 324, p. 312. [Mr. Bocourt also used his drawing skills for the anthropologic collection of the Museum, and he took advantage of the fact that a good artist, M. Rossier, was staying in Bangkok and was therefore able to get numerous photographs of the most interesting monuments and landscapes of this part of the kingdom of Siam.] Claude Estebe also provided the following background to the mission: "In 1861 the kings of Siam made a promise to M. de Montigny, French Consul-General in China, to give numerous live animals to the French Museum d'histoire Naturelle. A mission, under the supervision of Firmin Bocourt, a zoologist and draughtsman of the museum, was sent to Siam to receive the animals. The mission left Paris on the 5th of September, 1861 with the Siamese Embassy which was returning home. They reached Bangkok on the 10th December. They were greeted by the two kings of Siam and their ministers and were helped by M. d'Istria, the French temporary Consul in Bangkok and the abbot, M. Larnaudie. They left on the 30th of July 1862 with all the animals presented by the kings and they reached Paris on the 15th November."

24 Rossier's China and Japan work was published by Negretti and Zambra at various times between 1859 and 1863. A set of fifty Chinese views appeared first, followed by some twenty-five Japanese views and a further thirty-odd Chinese views at the end of 1861. By 1863 a second series of forty Japanese views had appeared. See the Negretti and Zambra Appendix 1 (page 305) for more details.

Chapter 2

25 *Satow Papers*, National Archives, 30/33/15/1, October 1st, 1862. For an excellent account of early treaty port life in Japan, see James Hoare, *Japan's Treaty Ports and Foreign Settlements* (1994).

26 At the time of going to press, the writer has established a little more information on Duane B. Simmons (ca. 1832–89). Prior to his first visit to Japan, he applied at New York City for a passport on March 29th, 1859 (National Archives, Washington, M-1372, Passport Applications 1795-1905s, Roll #77, ref#12438.) He is shown as aged 27 and 5 feet 6¼ inches in height. A further application dated September 20th, 1865 (M-1372 Pass Apps, Roll#134, ref# 22326), also from New York City to Japan, gives his age as 33, forehead: full; eyes: gray; nose: ordinary; mouth: rather large; chin: oval; hair: dark; complexion: fair; face: full oval; height: same as above. The passport also included his wife and child. This means that the age at death given in the *Japan Weekly Mail* obituary must be wrong. He was buried at the Aoyama Cemetery, Tokyo. It is not known whether Simmons was a skilled photographer, or how much time he spent in the studio. If he successfully took any photographs, they do not seem to have survived.

27 See *OJP*, which contains a summary of the photographic references in his diary.

28 The existence of these letters, of which there are in excess of a hundred, was pointed out to the writer by Eric Politzer. The letters are kept at the G. W. Blunt White Library, Seaport Museum, Mystic, Connecticut (ref. C.118).

29 Unfortunately, there are no earlier letters in the collection which would give a clear picture of exactly when Orrin went to Japan, and why.

30 The writer recently visited the cemetery, and the inscription for the date of birth is indeed September 9th, 1830.

31 The other references cited by these two authors are Nishina Matasuke, "Shashin-jutsu no kaiso wa betsu ni ita: Edo de saisho ni shashin-kan o hiraita, Ukai Gyokusen" (1969); Nishina Matasuke, "Ukai Gyokusen and Utagawa Kuniyoshi" (1969); and "74 nen-mae noshitsuban: Ukai-o no shashin-zuka kara no hakkutsu" (1956).

32 This is often cited by Japanese sources without giving publication details. It seems to have been some kind of pamphlet.

33 With thanks to Sebastian Dobson for pointing out this reference

34 "Fine Art Gossip," *The Athenaeum*, No. 1805, May 31st, 1862, p. 729. This article also suggests that Wilson was able to move around the closed city of Edo because he was attached in some capacity or other to the British Embassy there. In fact, Wilson's relative freedom of movement in Edo was almost certainly due to his being temporarily appointed as photographer to the Prussian Embassy. The reference to the British Embassy could be a mistake. "Wilson's Grand Panorama," as it was called, was advertised in *The Times*, May 20th, 1862, p. 1, through until June 23rd. It also received a mention in *The Illustrated London News*, May 24th, 1862, p. 524. It is worth recording that whilst the British accounts of the exhibition talk of the scroll taking up some 2700 meters (8858 feet) of canvas, Japanese sources, quoted in Saito's *Bakumatsu Meiji* (2004, p. 118), state that the canvas was only around 270 meters (885 feet) long. Perhaps the British accounts were referring to square meters. The report also refers to the photographer as "Captain" John Wilson. This could be a mistake, or might prove useful in tracking down additional data on Wilson. It could also possibly explain why there was some argument over his *bone fide* residential status given that he may have been a naval officer.

35 See Thomas C. Pitkin, manuscript papers, folder 2, fragment 14. Gartlan in his "Stillfried Chronology" (2001, p. 185) estimated the dates of Pitkin's stay in Japan as being between November 1861 and February 1862. This was surmised from the transcript of a lecture delivered in the US (Pitkin, folder 5) in which Pitkin mentions that he visited Japan "during the years 1861 and 1862" and that his stay was "of nearly four months."

36 In a letter written to the *British Journal of Photography*, February 27th, 1877, Cocking writes: "Many a time have I met the old veteran – the father of photography in Japan – going to church, leading his little daughter by the hand...." Cited in Gartlan, "Stillfried Chronology" (2001, p. 146).

37 For a detailed account of the invention and introduction of this vehicle, the best source is Calvin F. Parker, *Jonathan Goble* (1990).

38 This reference was mentioned by Gartlan in his "Stillfried Chronology," p. 172.

39 Although Tucker et al., in *The History of Japanese Photography* (2003) maintains this was Morita Raizo.

40 Mentioned in Gartlan's "Stillfried Chronology." Putting Uchida's prices into perspective, it is interesting to note that Gartlan mentions elsewhere in his chronology that Japanese workers employed by Stillfried earned between $3 and $12 per month depending on the skills required (p. 150). On p. 153 Gartlan cites a court case where Stillfried, in giving evidence, states that he paid his Japanese painter $20 per month and his European photographer $100 per month plus 10 percent per sale.

41 Gartlan also mentions that Griffis' manuscript diary contains references to his visiting Uchida's Tokyo studio on several occasions. Margaret Clark Griffis, Griffis' sister, also mentions Uchida in her unpublished diaries. These documents are kept at the William Elliot Griffis Collection at Rutgers University Libraries.

42 See Appendix 3 (page 306) for a description of Woods' technique and the difficulties he encountered photographing in Japan.

43 Beato had requested permission to travel through Benares, Cawnpore, Lucknow, Agra, and Delhi for a period of eight months with two Maltese servants. The license was issued on March 18th, 1858 by the foreign department at Fort William, Calcutta. See Record Book, "India. Political Consultations, 19 March–9 April 1858," P-202-49, No. 244, India Office Archives, the British Library, London.

44 The company, F. Beato Ltd., was established in London in 1898 and dissolved in 1913. See "Companies Dissolved Before 1930 Volume: D-I" (a typed list compiled and held by Guildhall Library, London Ref: ST 1656). The F. Beato Ltd reference is 58446. Furthermore, in Joint Stock Returns 5A 1897–1898 held by Guildhall Library London, the following information was given concerning the registration of the company: F. Beato Limited, Merchants & Manufacturers of Carvings, 53 Chancery Lane, London W.C. Date of Registration: 3 August 1898, Nominal Capital: £10,000, No. of shares into which divided: 2,000. (Whether this implies that Beato may have been alive as late as 1913 is just speculation at this stage.)

45 Saint Mary Magdalene Church, Woolwich, London, Parish Records, London Metropolitan Archives ref: Microfilm X097/294.

46 The hand coloring of photographs was not new and had certainly been practiced in Europe from the 1850s at the latest. *The Photographic News* carried an article entitled "Lessons on Colouring Photographs: Colouring in Oil." This lengthy article ran to several consecutive weekly issues from March 11th, 1859 to April 8th, 1859. A follow-up article, "Lessons on Colouring Photographs: Albumenised Paper," ran from April 15th to June 10th, 1859. This article advocated using watercolors on albumen prints. In addition, Saito Takio in *Bakumatsu Meiji* draws attention to the review of Saunders' portfolio of Japanese photographs given in the *Japan Herald*, October 25th, 1862. The description of a temple in Kamakura perhaps suggests that Saunders was coloring landscape photographs as early as 1862: "No. 41. A cluster of Temples at Kamakura, the principle [sic] of which shows the double roof – the rafters, &c., are painted red, and show out with great grandeur against the fine grove of surrounding trees" (see *OJP* for the full review). In May 1860 *The Times* carried an advertisement from Negretti and Zambra who had just published one of Pierre Rossier's hand-colored stereoviews of Japan.

47 She died at the family house, 14 Manor Road (now Manor Avenue), Brockley, Kent. The house still stands but is now derelict, having been abandoned some years ago. The properties in this quiet road are "protected" and are all

similar substantial town houses. It is strange that No. 14 is the only one to be empty.

48 Colonel Du Pin was one of the French photographers during the China campaign, attached to the French Topographical Service. A group of his views of Pekin were presented to Sir James Hope Grant, the commander-in-chief of the British forces in China. Grant forwarded these to the Duke of Cambridge with a letter dated January 21st, 1861. According to David Harris' *Of Battle and Beauty* (1999), the letter is held by the Manuscripts Department at the British Library but the photographs have not been located. The letter states: "I have the honour also to forward some Photographic views of Pekin from Colonel Du Pin of the French Topographical Service which he has requested me to present to her Majesty & which I shall feel obliged to your doing if you consider them worthy of her acceptance." In Du Pin's book, he describes Fauchery as a correspondent of Moniteur Universel who was temporarily assigned to assist Du Pin with his photographic work. He said that Fauchery had fulfilled a long-felt wish to visit Japan. He was "steady, reliable and possessed of a talent that had matured during an adventurous life but one tinged with constant misfortune."

49 Father Mounicou's diary was reproduced in the *Bulletin De La Societe Des Missions Etrangeres De Paris*, Hong Kong, 1927. The Harold S. Williams' archives include a transcript for the dates 1859-64 but do not give a place of publication. However, the relevant entry concerning Fauchery's death is as follows: "27 Avril, 1861. Un Francais, Nomme Antoine Faucherie, Recemment Attache a la Legation de France, est mort a l'hopital, en refusant les secours de la religion."

50 Much of the information on Fauchery was drawn from the late Harold Williams' archives held at the National Library of Australia. Williams spent many years piecing together the elusive details of Fauchery's life and summarized his findings in a lecture given to the Asiatic Society of Japan on January 17th, 1972, entitled "The Mysteries of Antoine Fauchery." Although this was unpublished, a transcript forms part of the archives. Another useful source is the entry for Fauchery given in the *Australian Dictionary of Biography, Vol. 4, 1851–1890*, Melbourne University Press, 1972.

51 For more detailed information on Sutton's career, the reader can consult Ishiguro Keisho, *Bakumatsu Shashinshi Satton woo u* (1996); Sebastian Dobson and Terry Bennett, "British Photographers in Japan, 1858–1898" (1998); and Sebastian Dobson, "Frederick William Sutton, 1832–83" (2002).

52 One definite sighting of Miller around this time is contained in the *North China Herald*, June 22nd, 1861, which records "M. M. Miller" departing Shanghai for Hong Kong on June 19th, 1861, on board the *Cadiz*. He may also be the "Miller" recorded in the same paper in the June 8th, 1861 issue leaving Shanghai for Hong Kong on board the *Pekin* on June 4th, 1861.

53 A Mr. Wheel [sic] and a Mr. Howard left San Francisco on November 21st, 1859 on the ship *Black Warrior*. They arrived in Hong Kong on January 19th, 1860 (*Overland China Mail*, January 30th, 1860).

54 The United States 1870 Census, taken on August 2nd, shows Weed as an invalid living in San Luis Obispo, California, and having been born in New York. The 1880 Census describes his occupation as a photo-engraver and shows him living with his sister-in-law in Oakland, California.

55 References to Gower's work appears in Vol. 2 of Sir Rutherford Alcock's *The Capital of the Tycoon* (1863, pp. 74, 110, 132, and 149). Gower's photograph of a temple in Osaka is engraved on p. 280.

56 The fire consumed the whole of the British and Russian consulates and the home of Goshkevich, including all of his personal property. Dr Zalesky's home was also destroyed, although he seems to have been able to save

the bulk of his personal property. The *Japan Herald* also recorded that Zalesky arrived at Yokohama on March 19th from Hakodate on the ship *Bongatyr*.

57 For a full and detailed explanation of early Dutch photography in Japan, the reader is recommended to consult Herman J. Moeshart, *Arts En Koopman in Japan 1859–1874* (2001).

58 Crane's obituaries appeared in the *Japan Weekly Mail*, October 24th, 1903, and the *Japan Weekly Chronicle*, October 28th, 1903.

59 The Worswick and Dubois collections. I am grateful to Dr Dubois for the information concerning Le Bas's naval career.

60 *The Photographic Collector*, Vol. 5, No. 3, 1986, p. 289. According to the collector and researcher Christian Polak, Le Bas was the son of the well-known architect Hippolyte Le Bas (1782–1867), who designed the prison of La Roquette, the church Notre-Dame-de-Lorette, and the obelisque at the place de la Concorde, Paris. See also Clark Worswick, *Japan Photographs* (1980), which carries illustrations of Le Bas's Japanese work. There are also two illustrations contained in M. F. Braive, *The Photograph: A Social History* (1966).

61 See also the *Japan Times*, December 25th, 1978, and a letter to the editor from Robert G. Flersham of Fukui (found in the Harold Williams' archives), headed "Photography in Japan," who argued that Ono Benkichi's pioneering work had been overlooked.

Chapter 3

62 The story first broke in the *Japan Weekly Mail*, January 13th, 1872. See also the January 20th issue; the *Japan Herald Mail Summary*, January 23rd; the *Hiogo News*, January 27th, and Gartlan's "Stillfried Chronology," for a summary.

63 In this respect, see Henry Rosin, "Etudes sur les debuts de la photographie japonaise au 19e siecle" (1987).

64 The Japan Photographic Association would most likely have been the main trading company, whereas the partnership of Stillfried and Andersen would have been a separate entity. Stillfried had a number of business enterprises, and there may well have been tax, legal, or operational reasons to justify the separate firms. For example, Stillfried may have retained a different percentage of shareholding to Andersen in certain companies. Or perhaps Stillfried and Andersen was the photo studio, and the JPA the repository for all other businesses.

65 For future Farsari studio addresses, see page 219.

66 The same authors maintain an informative website on the Nagasaki Foreign Settlement at http://www.nfs.nias.ac.jp/

67 Although all Japanese and Western sources give Black's birth date in Scotland as January 8th, 1827, this is probably wrong. The International Genealogical Index shows a John Reddie Black being born on January 8th, 1826 in Dysart, Fife, Scotland. His parents are shown as John Reddie Black and Sophia K. J. Hurdies (b. 1784 in Seaford, Sussex). This seems to tie in with a UK 1851 Census listing which shows an unmarried John Reddie Black (aged 25) living in Greenwich with his widowed father John Reddie Black (aged 63), both of whom are stated to have been born in Dysart, Scotland. Black's occupation is shown as a merchant and general agent, whereas his father is shown as a lieutenant of the Royal Navy, then on half pay.

68 The Harold Williams' archives give the following alternatives: 1862, according to M. Paske-Smith, *Western Barbarians in Japan and Formosa* (1968, p. 355); 1863, according to the *Japan Chronicle*, October 22nd, which carried an obituary of Black's wife; 1864, according to the *Shanghai Mercury* in its obituary on Black (no date is given, but Black died on June 11th, 1880 and so the paper was almost certainly issued some time in June); 1864, according to the obituary given in the *Japan Daily Herald*, June 11th, 1880. Other very useful sources on Black's life are Neil Pedlar, *The Imported Pioneers* (1993, pp. 135–8) and James Hoare, "British Journalists in Meiji Japan" (1994, pp. 20–32).

69 It should be noted here that Black unaccountably styled himself in his concert advertisements as "John Roderick Black." At first sight this gives the appearance of there being two "J. R." Blacks in the Far East at the same time. However, all of the other facts point, overwhelmingly, to there being just one individual. See the confusing use of the name Roderick in *Japan Herald* concert advertisements for August 27th, 1864; September 3rd, 1864; September 10th, 1864.

70 A critical review of the first issue was given in the *Japan Times Overland Mail*, May 2nd, 1868, pp. 118–20.

71 Probably because most Chinese photographers had previously been portrait painters. In China and Japan, Westerners were able to obtain inexpensive and excellent portraits of themselves or family painted from photographs.

72 Mention should also be made of the excellent reproduction made of the First Series, called *The Far East, May 1870–August 1875* (1965). Note that the actual First Series continued until October 1875, and possibly beyond. This reproduction set is now very hard to find.

73 If there was some disagreement between the two, it was probably not serious. Moser's two brothers would later work in Burger's Vienna studio in 1873. It is also possible that Burger gifted Moser a number of negatives taken during the former's time in Japan. We suspect this because prints from them appear in *The Far East* and similar, variant views appear in the collection which was taken back to Austria by Burger. We should not discount the possibility, however, that Black acquired the negatives from Burger directly. According to a note to the author in April 2005 from Professor Alfred Moser, the photographer's grandson, Michael Moser was reluctant to go home because he felt he had no prospects there. In addition, he dreaded the sea journey and was always ill when traveling by ship.

74 The Mary Alice Rea 1881 private journal is held by the Yokohama Archives of History Museum. Until Gartlan's "Stillfried Chronology," which pointed out the existence in Japan of a second Stillfried brother, it was thought that the references in the journal referred to Raimund.

75 The *Japan Punch*, February 1885, carried a cartoon which is not easy to interpret. David Welsh is shown either complaining about the new competition next door (Farsari's studio) or suggesting that the constant ownership changes in that studio were farcical. There was an earlier *Punch* cartoon of Welsh in the October 1884 issue.

76 The case apparently concerned two colored photographs. Raimund Stillfried was called as an expert witness, appointed by the court, and pronounced that the coloring of the two photographs in question would take a skilled workman twenty days. He said that he paid his own Japanese painter $20 per month, but he would pay a European painter the same salary as he paid his European photographer – $100 per month and 10 percent on the sale. The speed with which the photographs are apparently painted does not tie in with the information that Adolfo Farsari gave to his sister – as we shall see shortly. He claimed (admittedly ten years later) that Japanese studios used artists who painted around sixty images a day! Rudyard Kipling (quoted later in the section on Farsari, page 219) was informed by Farsari that his artists would paint only two or three per day. Stillfried would presumably consider even this to be too fast. Clearly more research is needed in this area.

77 It is worth noting that an R. Douglas, who may well have been John Douglas's brother, is listed in the 1882 *Japan Directory* as working at the Japan Photographic Association. He did not stay long, and in the 1885 *Chronicle and Directory for China* an R. Douglas is listed as

working with the renowned Chinese photographer A. Fong at his studio in Hong Kong.

78 Boyd and Izakura in *Portraits in Sepia* (2000, p. 284) quote two Japanese sources to substantiate this claim: Yokohama Kaiko Shiryokan (ed.), *Bakumatsu Nihon no Fukei to Hitobi* (1987) and *Saishoku Arubamu* (1990).

79 See "The Japanese Dry Plate Factory" in *The Photographic Dealer* (1910).

80 Japanese sources are far from clear about when and how many photographs were taken of the Emperor Meiji. Some hold to the view that the last official sittings were in 1872 and 1873. See Donald Keene, "Portraits of the Emperor Meiji," in *Impressions* (1999).

81 For the differing reports on Usui's early life, the reader can consult the two publications by Yokohama Kaiko Shiryokan (ed.): *Bakumatsu Nihon no Fukei to Hitobi* (1987) and *Saishoku Arubamu* (1990).

82 According to a note in the Harold Williams' archives, the *Go-Sho, Shin-Kyo, Minato-No-Sakigake* (1882) – an illustrated directory of Japanese shops etc. in Kobe – carried this reference and illustrated the studio on page 14.

83 Although Yamamoto's work seems to stop by the early 1880s, and is then reproduced by other studios from that time, there is one puzzling feature about his studio. In *Saishoku arubamu – Meiji no Nihon* (1990), edited by Saito Takio, there is a passing reference (p. 241) to a studio owned by a Yamamoto Ei being in operation in 1898 at 21 Sugatamicho, rather than 22. But the impression given is that the studio was only in operation for that year. Yamamoto is a common Japanese name, but this is a curious coincidence.

84 Anne Wilkes Tucker et al., *The History of Japanese Photography* (2003, p. 315) gives the date as 1883.

85 Gartlan in his "Stillfried Chronology" (p. 141), gives the full text in the original French.

Chapter 4

86 *The Practical Photographer*, September 1896, Vol. 7, No. 81, p. 243. The full reference is interesting: "Mr. K. Tamamura, of Yokohama, has sent a number of examples of his work "outside the studio." [A number were reproduced in this issue.] Mr. Tamamura is one of the most popular, perhaps the most popular of the professional photographers in Yokohama, the principal 'Open Port' in Japan, and had promised us an article on his studio experiences. Readers will be sorry to hear that, at the last moment, he sent word that on account of the sudden death of his wife he was unable to keep his promise. The subject of his communication was to have been 'The Foreign (European and American) Sitter from the Japanese point of view,' and would probably have been very interesting."

87 See Anne Wilkes Tucker et al., *The History of Japanese Photography* (2003, p. 28).

88 Further background to this whole assignment is given in Denise Bethel's article "The J. B. Millet Company's Japan" (1991), and in Elmer Funkhouser's "Japan: Described and Illustrated by the Japanese" (1999).

89 The diary entry is for October 13th, 1900 and clearly Tamamura has remarried. As the diary entry was made in Kobe, it seems that Tamamura and his wife were familiar with the area and perhaps had property there. The Kobe studio would have opened recently. The book also contains (p. 96) a 1901 New Year's Day card from the Tamamura studios in Yokohama and Kobe which shows a portrait of Tamamura, plus one of his sons (or possibly Mr Takagi).

90 See also Matsunobu Yasuke and Yokohama Kaiko Shiryo-kan, *Meiji no Nihon* (1990).

91 The American collector and researcher Fred Sharf has done some interesting, unpublished work on the numbering system employed by Kusakabe. The first point he makes is that following the move to Honcho-dori in 1890, the catalogue of more than 2000 numbers and titles which was issued represents a complete reordering of numbers that existed when the studio operated from Benten-dori.

Photographs sold from the former address generally had handwritten numbers in the negatives, with printed title-captions pasted onto the album page below each image. Following the move, both numbers and titles were printed in the negatives. Although Kusakabe seems to have escaped the ravages of the February 1886 Yokohama fire, Sharf speculates that the move of the studio, together with the reordering of the number sequence, were both motivated by the studio's falling victim to one of the other numerous conflagrations in the town. He makes another interesting observation: Kusakabe's later numbers sequentially follow the recommended tourist routes outlined in the contemporary guidebook, the third Murray edition of B. H. Chamberlain and W. B. Mason's *A Handbook for Travellers in Japan* (1893).

92 Burton, who first met Ogawa in the autumn of 1887, was even more complimentary about his friend in his 1890 article "A Japanese Photographer:" "[He] … is a man of remarkably intelligent and prepossessing appearance. His manner and conversation are as charming as his looks; he is a delightful companion, and a kindly, generous, upright and honorable man in all respects."

93 At the exhibition he showed photographs measuring 38 x 30 inches (965 x 762 mm), which had been produced with the help of a giant camera. See the British periodical *Photography*, February 27th, 1890, p. 134.

94 The twelve-story tower Ryounkaku was designed by Burton as a venue for popular amusement and opened to the public in Asakusa, Tokyo, in 1891. At 220 feet (67 meters) it was the tallest building in Tokyo. Made of red brick, it contained Japan's first elevator. It had to be demolished after the 1923 earthquake.

95 An important and extensive explanation of how these works were produced is given in Burton's "Photo-mechanical Work in Japan," (1891, pp. 117–19). See also the antiquarian print and book dealer George Baxley's website, which contains extensive information on Ogawa and his publications: www.baxleystamps.com/litho/ogawa.shtml

96 In the past there has been some disagreement over Ogawa's actual name. Although there is no dispute about Ogawa's family name, the kanji for his given name can be read as Isshin, Kazuma, or Kazumasa. T. Boyd and N. Izakura in *Portraits in Sepia* (2000, p. 263), settle the matter by pointing out that in the official Ogawa studio's commemorative book, *Ogawa Dosokai, Sogyo Kinen Sanju Nenshi* (A Thirty-year History of the Firm), published in 1913, the studio gives the correct spelling (in English) as Ogawa Kazumasa.

97 The writer, some years ago, saw one of Azukisawa's "photographic oil-paintings" with the following printed caption on the back in English and Japanese: "AZUKISAWA'S PATENT OIL-PAINTING ON PHOTOGRAPH. This is a Patent Permanent Process neither changing nor producing spots on the surface. Enlargement can be made up to the life size by the special order. PATENT OIL-PAINTER AND PHOTOGRAPHER, NO. 9, NICHOME, SAN-JUKKENBORI, KIO-BASHIKU, TOKIO."

98 Fred Sharf has an album of twenty-four oil-painted photographs of Nikko scenery produced by the Azukisawa studio. Each measures 4 x 5 inches (100 x 135 mm). At the back of the album is a printed colophon which reads: "System of Oil-Photography by Azukizawa. Patent for 15 years on the 7th October, 1885. The absence of any colour in ordinary photographs, the insufficiency of correct form in ordinary oil paintings, and the constant change and fading in colour in painted photographs, have long been a cause of disappointment. After long researches, and many failures, I have at length, after some years of labour, discovered a system which I call oil-photography … and which is neither photography alone, nor oil-painting alone, but comprises the advantages of photography as regards form, and of the other as regards colour. The colouring is not only lasting in itself, but is even uninjured by the application of a wet cloth. Several Europeans have complimented me upon the elegance and delicate appearance of this process, and I now confide it to the enjoyment of the public. Ryoichi Azukizawa, No. 9 Ni-chome, Tsukenobori, Kiobashi-ku, Tokio." Sharf describes the process as producing especially vivid colors of black, gold, and red. He judges the coloring of the pictures of waterfalls as "terrible." In the few examples that the writer has seen, it cannot be said that the coloring is aesthetically pleasing. Azukizawa's studio was advertised in the 1887 *Japan Directory*. Perhaps Farsari's claim that the coloring on his own photographs did not fade undermined one of the key attractions of Azukizawa's invention.

99 The letters were discovered by an Italian university student, Elena Dal Pra, who published "A. Farsari: un avventuriero fotografo" in an Italian magazine, *Domina*, in 1991. The article was drawn upon when discussing Farsari in the author's *Early Japanese Images*. The letters themselves formed the basis of a detailed article by Beretta Lia, "Adolfo Farsari: An Italian Photographer in Meiji Japan" (1996, pp. 33–48). The section here is drawn from all three sources and the writer's own research.

100 Roster For Letter F of 12th NY Cavalry is a website dedicated to this regiment, produced by Kenneth Wooster: www.web.cortland.edu/woosterk/12cav.

101 *Japan Daily Herald*, August 26th, 1880, p. 2; *Japan Gazette: A Fortnightly Summary of Intelligence from Japan*, September 2nd, 1880, p. 114; both references are quoted in Luke Gartlan, "A Chronology of Baron Raimund von Stillfried-Ratenicz" (2001, p. 162).

102 It is unclear who Farsari purchased the business from. It is possible that it was still owned by Hermann Andersen. However, he had left Japan in 1883 and may have passed it on to his arch-rival Baron Franz von Stillfried. Given their past enmity, this seems surprising. However, Franz Stillfried is shown in the 1884 edition of the *Japan Directory* as being back at No. 17 and connected in some way with the Japan Photographic Association, with Andersen noted as absent. It looks, on the face of it, that Andersen sold the business to Franz Stillfried and then left Japan in 1883. (Or perhaps the business was auctioned?) Stillfried, in turn, then sold it to Farsari at the end of 1884 and then left Japan himself. A very confusing picture! With regard to the financing of the purchase, it has been suggested that Tamamura Kozaburo was financially involved and helped Farsari acquire the Japan Photographic Association in February 1885. See "Gaijin haiso," *Jiji Shimbun*, September 6th, 1886, cited in Saito Takio (ed.), *Saishoku arubamu* (1990, p. 230). This was slightly expanded on in Saito's later *Bakumatsu Meiji* (2004), which states that Tamamura was Farsari's partner in the enterprise. In 1886 Farsari apparently sued his partner for the alleged theft of $300 worth of silver nitrate. Tamamura, found to be innocent, countersued Farsari that year for slander.

103 See, for example, the studio advertisement in the 1913 ninth edition of Chamberlain and Mason, *A Handbook for Travellers in Japan*. See also the *Japan Punch*, February 1885, which includes a cartoon suggestive of Farsari's having only just taken over the studio at No. 17. The October 1884 edition carried a related cartoon which, like the other, pictures David Welsh as the central character. This latter cartoon implies that No. 17 was still occupied by, or connected with Baron Franz von Stillfried.

104 The *Japan Directory* 1891 listing has "A manager, clerk, operator, four assistants, a printer plus two assistant printers, compositor, bookbinder, painter plus sixteen painter assistants, two younger assistants and a carpenter."

105 As an example of his attention to detail, his albums sometimes included tissue guards with the following printed inscription: "HOW

TO HANG, OR LOOK, AT A PICTURE. In looking at a picture, or hanging it, place it with the light coming from the same place, as the light in the picture is supposed to come from. This rule should be observed with all kind of pictures, oil, or water colors, photographs etc.; especially when they have a glazed surface. – If the portrait you hold in your hands looks towards your right shoulder, and the light on the same, when it was taken, came from the left, look at it having the window at your left (there being no other light to interfere). Always place the picture at any rate in such a way that the inequalities of the surface of the paper or canvass may not be seen. No water color painting, or photograph, ought to receive direct or too strong reflected light, and should be kept in a dry place and in an album, or under glass, as dampness and dust will spoil any picture. The worst possible position, that can be selected for hanging a picture, is over a chimney piece, or any portion of the wall over a fire place. A. FARSARI & Co., Photographers, Painters, and Surveyors, No. 16 Bund, Yokohama, Japan."

106 Koyama Noburo, "The Guillemard Collection (Early Photographs of Japan)," Cambridge University Library. This paper, as yet unpublished, was read at the 14th Annual Conference of the European Association of Japanese Resource Specialists (EAJRS), Valenciennes (France), in September 2003. The photographs and journals from Guillemard's world cruise are in the manuscripts section of Cambridge University Library under shelf marks MSS Add.7957 and 7783 respectively. Accompanying letters are held in the archives of the university's Gonville and Caius College, shelf mark PPC/GU1/04/01. The Japanese portion of the cruise is covered in Koyama's book, *Kenburijji Daigaku hizo Meiji koshashin: Makezago no Nihonryoko* (2005). The writer is grateful to Mr Koyama for the opportunity of looking through the Guillemard collection of photographs and papers and for providing his research notes from which the following account here has been largely drawn.

107 A small proportion of these were included in Krafft's book *Souvenirs de notre tour du monde* (1885). See also Goto Kazuo, *Hugues Krafft* (1998). The original photographs are at the Musée Le Vergeur, Rheims, and include two interesting group portraits which feature Felix Beato.

108 Bird's Japanese book, *Unbeaten Tracks in Japan* (1880), contains engravings from photographs, but the preface implies the photographs are not hers. The private collotype book, *Views in the Far East* (ca. 1896), was published after she had married Dr John Bishop in 1881.

Chapter 5
109 The exhibition also included the work of several Japanese photographers such as Ogawa Kazumasa, Kajima Seibei, Mizuno Hanbei, and others. A good critique of the Western and Japanese works on show was provided in a contemporary issue of the *Japan Mail* and reprinted as "Japanese and Foreign Photographs" in *The Photographic News*, August 4th, 1893, pp. 493–4.

110 Extraterritoriality was, very broadly speaking, the principle whereby foreigners living in certain treaty ports such as Yokohama, Nagasaki, and Kobe were not under the jurisdiction of the Japanese and were accountable for their actions only to their own foreign consuls. This principle had been established in 1859 when treaties between Japan and various foreign powers were signed. By agreement, extraterritoriality ended in 1899.

111 See D. C. Angus, *Japan: The Eastern Wonderland* (1904), A. Lloyd, *Every Day Japan* (1909), and Burton E. Holmes, *Burton Holmes Travelogues* (1910). Others are listed in *OJP*.

112 See *OJP* for an in-depth discussion of Enami's contribution to the world of stereoviews.

113 According to William Burton, Kajima was the highest tax payer in his district and was thus automatically entitled to a seat in the Upper

House of Parliament. See his article "Japanese Photographers. No. 2–Kajima Seibei" (1894, pp. 204–8).

114 A study of the many collotype productions from the Ogawa Kazumasa studio will produce a number of credited examples of Kajima's work. See also Angus, *Japan The Eastern Wonderland* (1904), in which a number appear. Four examples of Mount Fuji appear in *The Practical Photographer*, September 1896, Vol. 7, No. 81. Kajima's portrait and "giant camera," together with two other river and seascapes, appear in Burton, "Japanese Photographers. No. 2–Kajima Seibei" (1894).

115 For more on Kajima, see Anne Wilkes Tucker et al., *History of Japanese Photography* (2003); Nigano Shigeichi, Iizawa Kotaro, and Kinoshita Naoyuki (eds.), *Nihon no shashinka* 2 (1999), and Yokota Yoichi (ed.), *Meiji no Yokohama/Tokyo* (1989).

116 There is no evidence that Ogawa was related to, or connected with the more famous Tokyo-based photographer Ogawa Kazumasa.

117 Chamberlain and Mason, *A Handbook for Travellers in Japan*, 6th edn, 1901. The address shown is No. 3, Ginza Sanchome, Kyobashi-ku, Tokyo, which is the address listed for Okamoto in the 1899 5th edition. Note also the variant spelling in 1901 of Genroku-kwan. Perhaps this was a deliberate change of name, which may have been for legal reasons. The *Japan Directory* of 1902 also advertised a branch of Genroku-kwan, run by "Koda & Co." at No. 1 Benten-dori, ichome, Yokohama. However, nothing is known about Koda & Co., which failed to appear in future listings.

118 Note, however, that at least one caption in the book is incorrect: "A geisha, at home" should be credited to Ogawa Kazumasa rather than Genroku-kwan.

119 This letter was originally discovered by the collectors Kevin and Vicky Hines and now forms part of the Rob Oechsle collection.

120 With thanks to Rob Oechsle for notes supplied on the relationship between Strohmeyer and the Underwoods.

121 J. A. Lees and W. J. Clutterbuck, *B.C. 1887: A Ramble in British Columbia* (1892) and *Three in Norway* (1882); W. J. Clutterbuck, *About Ceylon and Borneo* (1891) and *The Skipper in Arctic Seas* (1890).

122 A description of Clutterbuck's photographic technique was given in his own words in a recently discovered copy letter to an unnamed correspondent. Although undated, his reference to Robert Demachy's work suggests it was written in the 1920s. The writer is very grateful to the English photo-dealer and Clutterbuck researcher John Benjafield for bringing the following letter to his attention. "It has been my happy lot in life to wander about the world with a Camera, hoping to bring away with me memories of beauty & light, of form & even of colour, of types of men & women, of groups grave & gay, of gloomy streets & sun-bathed spaces. Once at home again, these hasty impressions must be searchingly criticised & selected for enlarging. Then again strict selection must set aside many, only reserving a few with possibilities of interest, lighting & composition, which will repay further work. The camera that has helped me beyond words in obtaining natural groups & figure subjects is a French Stereoscopic Camera sold by W Neafson & Sons of High Holborn. [This is almost certainly the "Le Physiographe" made by Leon Bloch.] In appearance it is a large field-glass & in using it the Camera-man escapes suspicion of his wicked intentions, by gazing innocently through it at right angles to his subject the lenses being on the side. Thus the old man goes on chuckling & smoking, the women gossip, the children play, the marketer bargains, all unaware of the fact that you are carrying away those natural records with you. With this excellent camera, given a good light (which is essential) negatives capable of enlargement from 2 1/4 x 2 1/4 (inches) to 15 x 12 (inches) are obtainable. I must add that I do not use this camera stereoscopically, but cut the double glass plates (i.e. 4$_{1/2}$ x 2$_{1/4}$) in half after development. The thinnest possible plates are necessary, only made by Lumière of Lyons. I owe so much to this make of Camera that I must mention it as a most important help to my work. I discovered by degrees that the gum-bichromate process would give me the largest amount of freedom to develop my 'sketches' into Exhibition pictures. It was the beautiful work of M. Robert Demachy about 20–25 years ago that won my admiration for the gum-bichromate process. The painter-like quality of his prints was a revelation at that time. The process necessitates a very small outlay in materials, but a good deal of time & trouble. To begin with an enlarged negative must be made of the same size as the print, passing through the stage of a half-plate *positive*. Unfortunately gum-bichromate pigmented paper is not manufactured in England & the most reliable source is now from Mssrs. Höchheimer of Feldkirchen, Nr. Munich. It should be used within a year of manufacture & must be kept in a dry place. Those who have the time can pigment their own paper, directories for which are easily found, no doubt a wider range of colours could be used. With the pigmented paper from Germany are full directions printed in English, which should be carefully followed. The most difficult part of the process is perhaps the printing, but it is treated exactly like P.O.P paper, & with the help of a Sensometer, the time should be accurately gauged. I have found that good paper is slightly less sensitive than P.O.P. & that the blue & green shades require rather less time than the brown & red tints. These latter require very ample exposure. The process gives one great liberty in development to augment or decrease contrasts, to 'lose' undesirable objects & while the paper is still wet after development a delicate brush can be used now & then with care. Specially prepared sawdust is obtainable with the paper & must be used in development, but lasts a very long time." Wingfield Park, Ambergate.

123 The writer only knows of photographs being taken on Okinawa by Eliphalet Brown (1854), Frederick Sutton (1866), Francis Guillemard (1882), and Walter Clutterbuck (1898–9). None of Brown or Sutton's Okinawan photos has so far emerged. Mention should also be made of some Okinawan photographs taken, presumably in 1879, by an unnamed photographer who was part of the official Japanese delegation which went to the islands at that time. These photographs are illustrated in Ishiguro Keisho's book, *Dai-Nippon zenkoku meisho ichiran* (2001). It is also likely that Edward Kern used his camera on the islands in the 1850s. Finally, mention should be made of an Alfred Unger who may have taken photographs in Okinawa during the 1890s. In B. H. Chamberlain, "The Luchu Islands and Their Inhabitants" (1895), there is the reference: "... and the only other occasional visitor (also to Oshima) was Mr. Alfred Unger, of the firm of Boehmer & Co., florists, of Yokohama." And later, in the same article: "My special thanks are due to ... Mr. Alfred Unger, who has favoured me with several photographs." However, see the earlier reference to L. Brouwer, who may himself have been the photographer.

124 "I must on the whole, declare my indebtedness to Mr. K. Ogawa of this city than to anyone else. It has been my pleasure, and has certainly been to my profit, to be associated with him in much experimental work in connection with various photographic processes, mechanical amongst others. Mr. Ogawa has put in operation the greater number of the photo-mechanical processes described at the end of this book on more than an experimental scale, and he has made me free to publish all results whether of our joint work or of his own".

125 See W. K. Burton, "A Japanese Photographer" (1890), "Japanese Photographers, No. 1–K. Ogawa" (1894), and "Japanese Photographers, No. 2–Kajima Seibei" (1894).

126 Given Burton's importance to early Japanese photography, his various articles in the Bibliography should also be consulted. Other publications of photographic interest include W. K. Burton, "On the Application of Photography to Seismology and Volcanic Phenomena," in J. Milne (ed.), *Seismological Journal of Japan*, Vol. 1, 1893, pp. 21–30; W. K. Burton, *Panorama of Matsushima*, Yokohama, 1894 (this photograph, which the writer has never seen, was 9 x 58 inches (23 x 147 cm) and folded in book form). It is mentioned in Wenckstern, *Bibliography of the Japanese Empire*, Vol. 1, Leiden: E. J. Brill, 1895; W. K. Burton, *Scenes from Open Air Life in Japan*, Yokohama, 1893 (fourteen phototypes of Burton's work, executed and published by Ogawa, text by J. Murdoch; W. K. Burton, *Wrestlers and Wrestling in Japan* (1895) (no place of publication or publisher are given but this was an Ogawa imprint which included Burton's photographs); W. K. Burton and T. Tanaka, *Dai Nihon Tokyo Zen Shigai Shashi* (A Complete Photograph of the City and Streets of Tokyo in Greater Japan), Tokyo, 1890 (a fourteen-plate albumen print panorama of Tokyo measuring in total 14$_{3/4}$ x 190 inches (37.5 x 482 cm) mounted on a paper scroll with a silk border. A copy is held in the Northern Studies Collection, Hokkaido University Library, Sapporo); J. Milne and W. K. Burton, *The Great Earthquake in Japan 1891* (1892) and *The Volcanoes of Japan* (1892); and J. Murdoch, *Ayame-san: A Japanese Romance*, Yokohama: Kelly & Walsh Ltd, 1892 (this book is profusely illustrated with Burton's photographs and was the first publication to have been illustrated with true half-tone photo-mechanical reproductions printed with the letterpress).

127 This article was reproduced in *Photography*, October 17th, 1895 (pp. 665–6) as "Professor W. K. Burton in Japan."

Chapter 6

128 See the foreword in H. G. Ponting, *In Lotus-Land Japan* (1910). The *Japan Times* article by Professor Basil Hall Chamberlain was published some time in 1905, shortly after the publication of Ponting's book *Fuji San*.

129 The writer is grateful to Rob Oechsle for providing the following chronological notes on Ponting's time in Japan: "In his book *In Lotus-Land Japan*, Ponting states that he spent a total of three years in the country. This period seems to cover five visits between the years 1901–6. From other comments made in the book, and from scattered articles, it is possible to draw up a tentative chronology. His first Japan visit appears to have been in the summer or fall of 1901 when he carried out a photo-assignment for C. H. Graves of the Universal Photo Art Company. He then spent some part of 1902 for the same publisher in Korea and China. His second visit to Japan was on behalf of Underwood and Underwood and this was mid-spring to November 1903. At the end of that year he returned to California. The third visit was for H. C. White & Co., and this was during summer of 1904 until spring of 1905. For the same publisher, he accompanied General Kuroki of the First Japanese Army to Manchuria and Mukden where he photographed the Russo-Japanese War. This assignment finished in the summer of 1905 and, still working for H. C. White, he made his fourth trip to Japan where he stayed until November 1905. He then toured India and Burma until May 1906, again on instructions from H. C. White. His fifth and final visit to Japan was in May 1906 when he stayed several months."

130 The stereoview publishers were Universal Photo Art Co., Underwood & Underwood, and H. C. White. In addition, he wrote numerous articles for an impressive list of magazines, including *Century, Cosmopolitan, Country Life, The Graphic, Harper's Weekly, The Illustrated London News, L'Illustration, Leslie's Weekly, Metropolitan, Pearson's, Sphere, Strand, Sunset, Wide World*, and *The World's Work*.

131 For those with an interest in Ponting's Japan-

related articles and published photographs, the following represents a list of those the writer has been able to locate: ARTICLES: "The Adornment of the Sword," *Country Life*, Pt 1, November 14th, 1908, pp. 659–60, and Pt 2, December 12th, 1908, pp. 846–8; "From Japan to Korea," *Harper's Weekly*, Vol. 48, April 16th, 1904, pp. 589–91; "Japan's Highest Volcano," *Century Magazine*, Vol. 46, September 29th, 1904, pp. 697–700; "The Work of a Japanese Craftsman," *The World's Work*, English edn, Vol. 3, 1903, pp. 179–82. PHOTOGRAPHS PUBLISHED IN *THE GRAPHIC*: "Love-Letter," August 29th, 1908; "Sweet Blossoms," October 10th, 1908; "Fair Lilies," February 6th, 1909; "By the Gods," February 13th, 1909; "Geisha," February 27th, 1909; "Fortune-Teller," April 3rd, 1909; "Springtime," April 10th, 1909; "A Buddhist," September 18th, 1909; "Fuji-yama," October 23rd, 1909; "Embroiderers at Work," February 26th, 1910. PHOTOGRAPHS PUBLISHED IN *THE ILLUSTRATED LONDON NEWS*: "Lotus-Land," June 1st, 1907; "Sunrise," June 8th, 1907; "Yamanaka," September 14th, 1907; "Craftsmen," April 25th, 1908; "Japanese Tortoises," August 8th, 1908; "Tea," August 22nd, 1908; "Wisteria," May 22nd, 1909; "Ainu," April 23rd, 1910; "Lotus Land," June 25th, 1910.

132 Now held by a descendant, Antony Maitland, an enthusiastic family historian who maintains a website on http://www.antonymaitland.com/ompoole1.htm

133 Poole wrote the definitive account of the earthquake in his book *The Death of Old Yokohama* (1968).

134 The writer is extremely grateful to the philatelists Charles Swenson, William Collyer, and Bill Burgess for granting access to some photographs and research notes on Lewis. Bill Burgess, in particular, has been researching Lewis's life both in America and Japan for a number of years and has uncovered material of much interest. Swenson's article "Karl Lewis Was Early Cover Dealer in Japan" contains a good overview of Lewis' career. Although undated, the article can be found on the Japanese philately website http:/www.japan-Japan.com/lewispage3.htm.

135 See, for example, "Port Arthur, St. Petersburg," May 14th, 1904 (there is no evidence that Lewis traveled to Russia during the war despite these photographs carrying his credit); "Soldiers at Yokohama," August 27th, 1904; "Model of War," January 21st, 1905; "Yokohama," February 18th, 1905.

136 For the full transcript of this heart-rending letter, see *OJP*.

137 Kempler's excellent work is recommended to anyone who wishes to know more about the life of James Ricalton.

138 The name should read John L(awson) Stoddard, whose career is described elsewhere in this book. The confusion over the name is further compounded by C. J. Lucas's mixing J. L. Stoddard with the writer Charles Warren Stoddard (1843–1909) in his book *James Ricalton's Photographs of China during the Boxer Rebellion* (1990).

139 Numerous photographers, mainly Western, covered the 1904–5 War. During the war period, *The Illustrated London News* and *The Graphic* published photographs from many of those in the following list which, though likely to be incomplete, may prove useful for any future research in this area. Note that those in capital letters are covered elsewhere in this book: Lorenzo d'Adda; James F. J Archibald; E. Ashmead-Bartlett; Grantham G. Bain; RICHARD BARRY; W. H. Briel; Victor K. Bulla C. O.; Ingram Collingwood; W. Dinwiddie; Revd G. Douglas; Robert Lee Dunn; J. B. Eaves; Colonel Edwin Emerson; W. T. Evans; H. R. Everall; O. Gerlach; J. Gordon Smith; Gribayedoff; R. J. W. Haines; Angus Hamilton; JAMES H. HARE; M. Hejkis; I. D. Hejk; S. Iwase; Captain Lionel James; Dr C. Kawachi; Walter Kirton; Lavrantieff; KARL LEWIS (photographed soldiers in Yokohama but probably did not go to the front); R. Little; JACK LONDON; Dr Merckel;

P. Phillips; HERBERT PONTING; M. de Prev-
ignaud; Raoul Recouly; JAMES RICALTON;
J. Rosenthal; T. Ruddiman Johnston; R. C. Ryan;
S. Smirnoff; Grant Wallace; T. C. Ward; Frederic Whiting; K. Yoshida; and A. Zavadsky.

140 One of these albums was described in the
Old Japan 21st Anniversary Catalogue No. 31,
September 2003. The photographs, which
measured 7¾ x 10 inches (200 x 250 mm),
consisted of views of Kobe, Osaka, Kyoto,
Okayama, Hiroshima, Miyajima, Yokohama,
Tokyo, and Nikko. There were also two portraits of geisha. One photograph depicted
the Kyoto studio of Kajima Seibei (Fig. 331).

141 Elmer Funkhouser, "'T.' Fuka-sawa Meiji Era
Photographer," *Daruma*, Vol. 3, No. 2, 1996, pp.
10–18. The Kajima image, Fig. 8, is a view of
Mount Fuji and the same image appears in
The Practical Photographer, Vol. 7, No. 81, Sep-
tember 1896, correctly attributed to Kajima.

APPENDICES

APPENDIX 1
Negretti and Zambra China/Japan Stereoviews

There has been great confusion concerning the
numbering sequence of Pierre Rossier's stereoviews
for Negretti and Zambra's *Views in China* and *Views
in Japan* series. The following lists, although not
quite complete, now clarify the position. Significant
help in their compilation was given by Rob Oechsle,
who supplied many of the missing numbers and
first speculated that the Japan section was likely to
have been part of a wider China/Japan offering. He
was also instrumental in discovering a previously
unidentified second Rossier series of Japan, also
published by Negretti and Zambra. Other collectors
who have helped in the compilation of these lists
include John Cameron, Arthur Hacker, Junichi
Himeno, Ken Jacobson, Gwyn Nicholls, Wolfgang
Wiggers, David Wood, and Clark Worswick.

A series of fifty *Views in China* was registered
for copyright protection on November 19th, 1859 at
Stationers' Hall, London. Just prior to that, Negretti
and Zambra issued a *Descriptive Catalogue of Stereoscopes and Stereoscopic Views*. A copy of the catalogue is in the British Library with an accession
stamp of September 27th, 1859. This catalogue lists
only thirty-nine of the set, which was mentioned as
being "still in progress." The catalogue reads: "India
and China. Messrs. Negretti and Zambra are publishing a series of highly interesting Views from
India and China. The following subjects have already
been issued."

What follows is a list of the first published commercial photographic views of China. One number
is still unknown and some carry the same number
but a different view. The reason for this is not clear,
but almost certainly represents the publisher's up-
dating of the set with newer or better views.

Views in China – First Series

1. General View of Hong Kong
2. View from Hong Kong Harbour
3. Panorama of Canton, taken from Magazine
   Hill, now the headquarters of the allied troops
4. Canton, General view of Magazine Hill
5. Canton, The Five-Storied Pagoda
6. Canton, The Landing Place, taken from the
   house of the commissariat
7. Canton, The Jetty
8. Canton, The Temple of the Five Genji
9. Canton, Panorama taken from the walls and
   looking outside the city
10. Canton, Panorama from the Temple of the Five
    Genji
11. Canton, Panorama of Canton taken from south-
    east to northwest
12. Canton, Panorama taken from the South Gate

13. Canton, Panorama overlooking Treasury Street
14. Canton, Panorama taken from the South Gate
    and looking to the north of the city
15. Canton, View taken from the walls on the west
    side
16. Canton, View of the Canton River, junks, and
    the Island of Hohnan
17. Canton, Southeast suburbs of the city of
    Canton
18. Canton, View taken from the South Gate
19. Canton, View from the West Gate
20. Canton, The South Gate
21. Canton, View of the West Gate, taken within
    the city walls
22. Canton, The South Gate
23. Canton, Joss House, perspective view
24. Canton, Joss House, front view
25. Canton, Chinese Joss
26. Canton, Small pagoda on the southeast of the
    city
27. Canton, Joss House
28. Canton, Street view, Treasury Street
29. Canton, The Nine-Storied Pagoda
30. Canton, The Nine-Storied Pagoda
31. Canton, The Examination Hall
32. Canton, The grounds of the Examination Hall
33. Canton, Entrance to the yamun of Pey Kwei,
    the Governor of Canton
34. Canton, View in the grounds of the Imperial
    College
35. Canton, Yamun of the Allied Commissioners
35. Canton, View in the grounds of the Imperial
    College
36. Canton, Entrance to the Imperial College
36. Canton, Entrance to the yamun of Pey Kwei,
    the Governor of Canton, Mandarin of the First
    Class
37. Canton, Group of palanquin bearers, resting
    opposite the parcel office at Canton
38. Canton, Portraits of Pey Kwei, the Governor of
    Canton … with Commissioner Parkes
39. Canton, Portrait of Tseang-Keun, Tartar
    general-in-chief of the Canton army of braves,
    Mandarin of the First Class or Red Button
40. Canton, Group of sailors in the garden of the
    Allied Commissioners' yamun
41. Pah tah lom boo, Tartar brigadier-general,
    Second Class Mandarin, with family
42. Canton, Group of a Chinese lady and atten-
    dants
43. Canton, Group of British Officers in the
    garden of the Allied Commissioners' yamun
    [Illustrated in Tilley (1861)] (Fig. 39)
44. Canton, Carved gates in the garden of the
    Allied Commissioners' yamun
45. Canton, View of the walls of Canton, White
    Cloud mountains in distance
46. ?
47. Canton, Farewell visit of General Sir Charles
    Straubenzie to the Chinese general-in-chief
48. Canton, Group of mandarins in the garden
    of the yamun
49. Canton, Entrance to the Temple of the Five
    Genji
50. Canton, General view in the grounds of the
    Temple of the Five Genii
51. Canton, General view of Magazine Hill from
    the Parade Ground, Canton
52. Canton, Triumphal arch by the yamun of the
    allied commissioners
53. Canton, Chinese marine store stall, and sugar
    cane dealer
54. Canton, Group of Coolies or Street Porters

In the November 1861 edition of *The Art Journal*
(p. 351), there is an article entitled "Negretti and
Zambra's Stereoscopic Views and Stereoscopes, &c."
The relevant extract reads: "At the head of the many
establishments that London contains, devoted especially to works of this class (i.e. stereographs) are
those of NEGRETTI & ZAMBRA, who have just completed what we may call a stereographic *cordon* in
and about London. This collection, in addition to the
productions of other publishers, contains, amongst
the publications of Negretti and Zambra themselves,
their extraordinary stereographs, one hundred and
eight in number, from China and Japan...."

The following list of Japan views (first series)
was released at this time as part of the 108. We have
already discussed in the section on Pierre Rossier
(page 41) the inexplicable delay in publishing these,

considering that a number of them could well have
been taken as early as June 1859. Nevertheless, the
number sequence provides compelling evidence
that they were never issued as a separate group,
but as part of a "China and Japan" collection. Again,
there are some unexplained number discrepancies,
but the overall intention behind the numbering
seems clear and a set of twenty-five Japan views
was issued at this time.

Views in Japan – First Series

55. Jeda, Entrance to the residence of the British
    Minister [Illustrated in George Smith, *Ten
    Weeks in Japan* (1861)] (Fig. 38)
56. Jeda, General view of the residence of the
    British Minister, Mr Alcock, at Jeda
57. Jeda, Group of Japanese officers with Mr
    Gower, attaché to the British Legation at Jeda
58. Jeda, Cemetery of princes and nobles at Jeda
58a. Jeda, Cemetery of the nobles and princes
    at Jeda [Illustrated in Terry Bennett, *Early
    Japanese Images* (1996); Henry Arthur Tilley,
    Japan, the Amoor, and the Pacific (1861); and
    T. C. Westfield, *The Japanese: Their Manners
    and Customs* (1862)]
59. Jeda, The Great Bell, Jeda
59. Odji, Houses by the sea in the Bay of Jeda Odji
59. Kanagawa, Port of Kanagawa with Japanese
    shipping
60. Jeda, Group of Japanese officers with Macdon-
    ald, Gower, and Fletcher, British Legation, Jeda
    [Illustrated in Bennett (1996) and Westfield
    (1862)] (Fig. 42)
61. Jeda, Group of Japanese and general construc-
    tion of a Japanese dwelling [Illustrated in
    Smith (1861) and Tilley (1861)] (Fig. 49)
62. Jeda, View taken from United States Legation
    at Jeda
63. Jeda, Small temple near the United States
    Legation at Jeda
64. Jeda, The Emperor's Temple [Illustrated in
    Bennett (1996), Tilley (1861), and Westfield
    (1862)] (Fig. 43)
65. Jeda, Panorama of Jeda [Illustrated in Tilley
    (1861)] (Fig. 36)
66. Jeda, Houses by the sea in the bay of Jeda
    [Illus-trated in Smith (1861)] (Fig. 46)
67. Jeda, General view of Jeda from the gardens
    of Yatoan (Fig. 47)
68. Jeda, Gardens of Yatoan in the vicinity of Jeda
69. Kanagawa, General view of Kanagawa
    [Illustrated in Tilley (1861)] (Fig. 39)
70. Kanagawa, Port of Kanagawa with Japanese
    shipping [Illustrated in Bennett (1996) and
    Westfield (1862)] (Fig. 41)
71. Kanagawa, View of the town and bay of
    Kanagawa [Illustrated in Bennett (1996) and
    Westfield (1862)]
72. Yakuama, General view of Yakuama (Fig. 40)
73. Yakuama, View in the vicinity of Yakuama
    [Illustrated in Tilley (1861)] (Fig. 48)
74. Kanagawa, Group of European lady and
    Japanese attendants at the vice-consulate at
    Kanagawa [Illustrated in Smith (1861) – with
    the lady removed!]
75. Yakuama, View of the new city of Yakuama,
    with European shipping in the bay
76. Japanese workmen in summer costume
77. Odji, View of the emperor's sporting quarters
    at Odji [Illustrated in Smith (1861) and Tilley
    (1861)]
78. Odji, Public grounds and restaurant
79. Japanese ladies in full dress – winter costume
    [Illustrated in Bennett (1996) and Westfield
    (1862)] (Fig. 45)
79. Jeda, Residence of the British Minister
    Mr Alcock at Jeda (Fig. 44)

What follows is the second series of China
views which, together with the preceding Japan and
China groups, make up the approximate 108 views
mentioned in *The Art Journal*. It may also be worth
mentioning that the first China series often shows
the initials "NZ" scratched into the negatives of the
stereoviews. The writer has not seen the same
initials appearing on any of the following China
views, nor for that matter on any of the Japan views.
Note that several numbers in the series are yet to
be determined.

The American researcher John Cameron has been studying early French glass stereos for many years and is currently preparing a book for publication. Cameron has a photocopy of an extremely rare November 1863 Negretti and Zambra catalogue entitled *Catalogue of all the Stereoscopic Views on Glass, Published up to the Present Time, with a List of the Various Stereoscopes Manufactured by Negretti and Zambra*. The catalogue was advertised in the November 21st, 1863 issue of *The Times*. This important catalogue shows that Negretti and Zambra offered forty-five of the first China series as glass stereos but the second China series does not appear to have been offered in this form. Of even more interest is the listing of a second Japan series on glass. Moreover, these forty views are completely different to the first series. These were offered for the first time in *The Times* advertisement referred to above:

JAPAN, 6s. – Most interesting SERIES of STEREOSCOPIC VIEWS on glass, illustrating the manners and customs of the Japanese, 6s. each. A catalogue of all the glass views published since first invented, four stamps. – Negretti and Zambra, No.1, Hattongarden; 59 Cornhill, 122, Regent St.; and 153, Fleet Street.

The 1863 catalogue listed the following views:

It seems almost certain that these views, presumably taken between 1860 and 1861, are a second Pierre Rossier Japan series. Stylistically, they are very similar to the first, and Rossier, who only returned to Europe in early 1862, was presumably still contracted to the firm up until then. We know that Rossier made several visits to Nagasaki, and it would be odd if he had not used his stereo camera. The first series contains no Nagasaki views and so the second series complements it in that respect.

It is strange that view number 40 is of the Taal Volcano at Manila. We know that Rossier took two photographs of this scene on behalf of Negretti and Zambra (see *OIP*), but it seems bizarre to include a view from the Philippines in amongst a Japan series! It is unlikely to have been an error, since the view is labeled "Manila." Nevertheless, its presence serves to strengthen the "Rossier" flavor of the whole group. We know that at some time in 1861 Rossier was photographing in Siam. Included in the 1863 catalogue are twenty-five views of Siam, and the two or three examples seen by the writer are strongly suggestive of Rossier's style.

Interestingly, Rossier's second Japan series was, like his first, produced on paper. But unlike the first series, the second series was also produced on glass. The overall number of Rossier's Japan photographs, including his non-stereo large-format work, is now known to exceed seventy.

Du Pin/Fauchery Japan Views – 1861

The 1863 catalogue also lists a series of China and Japan views for which Negretti and Zambra must have obtained publishing permission from the French stereo producers Ferrier, Soulier, & Levy. The series is a selection from the Du Pin/Fauchery 1860–1 China and Japan stereos described elsewhere in this book. The twenty-eight numbers published by Negretti and Zambra in respect of the 1861 Japan views are as follows:

Photographic Difficulties in 1860s Japan and China

1. Henry Woods

This important description, outlining the difficulties faced by photographers in Japan in the mid-1860s, is extracted from Sir Henry F. Woods' autobiography, *Spunyarn: Strands from a Sailor's Life* (1924, pp. 194–7). Further information on Woods' activities in Japan, and his association with Felix Beato, is given elsewhere in this book.

"Photography in the open was no easy matter in those days, and my friend Beat's [sic] success in that line was due to his wonderful skill in manipulating his plates. There was nothing but the wet process as yet to the fore. It was still in the full vigour of employment as the dry plate had not passed beyond a very elementary stage of experimental success, and the gelatine film had not even entered the realm of thought. The reader can imagine me marching off when I landed surrounded by my escort of six fine-looking, two-sworded gentry. I was carrying the camera, fixed upon its stand, ready for use at a moment's notice, with a coolie alongside of me carting along the portable dark chamber. This consisted of a large box with all the requisites, a folding table for it to stand upon, and a large square mantle of red cotton material to serve as a covering for the whole, and screen off all rays of light but those wanted for the production of the photograph. Two small panes of red-coloured glass were fitted into the sides of the covering to give a little more illumination than the cotton cloth allowed. Intense was the curiosity our appearance excited, and it wasn't long before we had a tail to our procession that developed into a big crowd by the time I commenced my preparations for my first picture.

The Globe Trotter of the present day, armed with a quick-firing Kodak, knows nothing of the troubles of the Old Timer of the wet process. The former has but to touch the button and 'we do the rest', as the advertisements say, whilst the latter had to carefully pour collodion over a glass plate to form a film, and then, at the right moment, dip it into the mercury bath. Then with it in the transport frame, I turned my attention to the camera, which I had previously fixed in position, and focussed, with one of the guards standing by to see that no one meddled with it. Another hasty look and all was in readiness. Unfortunately I had not thought it necessary to warn the eagerly gaping crowd not to move. With watch in one hand I removed the cap cover and instantly half a dozen heads were striving to see what was inside the curious-looking machine on three out-stretched legs. I felt a bit distressed over it, but I could not feel very angry, considering the bait I had offered to their ever-growing curiosity. I got the 'yakonins' to explain to them that they had spoilt the effect of my incantations, and that the next time I approached the wonderful object they were gazing upon, they must all keep perfectly quiet. I got them also to arrange that portion of the crowd near us into two lines on each side, far enough apart to be out of the field of vision. I prepared another plate, and all went well until I had taken my shot and removed the 'shutter frame'. I had just got into the operating tent and drawn the covering round when suddenly I found the whole thing toppling over. Fortunately I had not yet taken out the plate, and the photo was saved. I clutched at the mercury bath, and fortunately succeeded in saving about two-thirds of its contents, not sufficient to cover a whole plate, but still enough to carry on with, and succeeded in taking several rather good photos in my subsequent attempts. The accident had occurred through the pressure of the people behind the dark chamber in their anxiety to see what was going to happen with the hidden thing I had put into the camera and carried away again.

My next attempt was the forefront of a famous temple. The court-yard was full of people, as it was a special fete day. Warned by my previous experience, I took possession of the platform of a small shrine, with steps leading up to it, and placing my 'yakonins' about, so as to prevent all access to my operating position, I got my picture all right. I followed this plan on all subsequent occasions, and was well satisfied with the result of my day's work, although in addition to the little present I felt bound to give my escort I ruined the gold lace on my left sleeve by the nitrate of silver that fell upon it from the bath. These photographs of mine, I may mention, were the very first that were ever taken in Tokio, Yedo as the place was called whilst the capital of the Tycoon." [Woods was optimistic in asserting his photographs as being the first to be taken in Tokyo. Beato, Jocelyn, Parker, Rossier, Saunders, and Wilson were amongst those who had photographed there before him.]

2. Paul Champion

The following talk, given by the chemist and amateur photographer Paul Champion at the Assemblee Generale De La Societe on January 11th, 1867, first appeared in the *Bulletin De La Societe Francaise De Photographie* and was summarized, in English, in *The Photographic News* (February 8th, 1867, p. 66). It clearly shows the levels of knowledge and commitment needed by photographers of the Far East during the mid-1860s. Although his text contains some technical terms no longer in use, it nevertheless serves to reinforce the point that in the early days of photography, science and art walked hand in hand. Given that the successful gelatin dry plate that revolutionized the world of photography did not arrive in Japan until the early 1880s, it is of great interest to read of Champion's struggle with the experimental collodion dry plates of the mid-1860s.

"A lot of travelers carrying out photography in distant countries find they must put up with the inconvenience of high temperatures or intense cold. Under these circumstances, one should only try taking medium-sized images, due to the difficulties encountered in obtaining images of larger dimensions. Despite the advice that I received on this matter at the time of my departure from France to China I resolved, for several reasons, to especially make some plates of 27 x 33 cm. Today, I congratulate myself on this decision, which at the time, however, gave me a great deal of worries. Perhaps it might be interesting to point out to travelers some of the difficulties that I encountered during my stay in the Far East. I propose to do exactly that in a few moments, after presenting to the Society some of my images, a few of which are worthy of mention.

At the time of my departure, I had already meticulously studied the most popular photographic processes, including new attempts at making 'dry plates.' [These experiments predated the commercially successful gelatin dry-plate process of the late 1870s.] Being unaware of the conditions that I was going to encounter, I had prepared myself to be able to use any of those processes that might seem the most appropriate for the circumstances that would present themselves. I had, moreover, equipped myself with one-hundred glass dry plates, prepared with tannin according to the procedures described by Major Russell, having heard from some reliable sources (other travelers) that glass plates prepared in this way could travel a long time without changes to the emulsion or sensitivity. Later, I unfortunately failed to obtain good images with these dry plates, in spite of the precautions I had taken for their protection from the destructive effects of the air and sea.

It was in Ceylon, three weeks after my departure from France, that I made my first photographic attempts using the above-mentioned plates, despite the high temperature which is common on this island. I left for shore equipped with my apparatus: a camera body of Mr. Relandin's design and Mr. Dallmeyer's triplet achromatic lens. This camera, built by Relandin, and the lens mentioned, are those that I personally consider the most useful for a traveler who has to move around a lot and cover great distances on foot. Despite the camera's fragile appearance and minimal weight, it is sturdy and has dimensions which are only a little larger than the glass plates themselves. It doesn't take up much room in your luggage, which is important to take into account when traveling long distance. This ability to safely pack the camera helped me to withstand bad weather and traveling mishaps. As for the Dallmeyer lens, at the time, the added advantage for me consisted in the lenses' ability to magnify the image clearly and distinctly, while using a lens of small diameter. Moreover, they allow you to obtain at will, any image of landscape, or portraits of quite large dimensions, without making any change to the apparatus.

When I returned on board the ship, I wanted to develop my negatives. The development of the images could only be carried out using a slow and incomplete method. The process I used produced spots and stains all over the surface of the plate. In spite of taking considerable time, I could not get a better result. At Shanghai, a month later, the same thing happened when I opened other cases of protective tin containers holding these prepared glass plates. The protective tins had also been welded shut with utmost care by the same procedure that packaged the plates used in Ceylon. My relating these past problems is not intended to discourage the long-distance tourist who wants to try this particular, or any other experimental dry plate method. However, of all the attempts at the new dry plate processes which are used in photography, none has rendered greater service to this art than the use of tannin as a preservative substance in maintaining the plates' sensitivity. My intention here is only to point out the difficulties of conserving prepared glass plates by this process, especially in certain climates. Regardless, it is better in every respect to use the tannin, especially on long journeys. However, in passing, let us point out something else. In this situation, it is important to use enough distilled water in any process that requires it. This is the one liquid that we often have a lot of difficulty getting, even under the best of circumstances.

Today, the largest type of sailing ships which criss-cross the seas, have on board a distillation galley in which lost heat [from the kitchen or boilers] is used to distill sea water for the crew. However, even then there were times when it was impossible for me to obtain good quality distilled water intended for preparing the silver salt solution and sometimes the iron salts solution. This is because distilled water obtained under the sea-faring conditions just mentioned, always contain a small quantity of hydrochloric acid. Ocean water, as we know, contains magnesium chloride. During the distillation process, this decomposes into hydrochloric acid and magnesium. To prevent this problem, one has to add a small quantity of lime to the distillation apparatus. The lime combines with hydrochloric acid and removes it from the water, leaving us with the high quality water we want to obtain.

It is interesting to note that for several months of the year (especially during the wet seasons), the Chinese and the Japanese make special use of rain water which they collect with great care by use of jars placed on the ground around their dwellings. This water drains mostly off the glazed tile roofs and is noticeably pure. But when this water is used up, they must resort to natural [stream or well] water, which often contains great quantities of foreign matter. One can purify this water in a sufficient manner for domestic use by mixing in a weak solution of alum, of which the Chinese use a great deal. Water thus purified is first left to stand for several days. However, from the photographer's point of view, water purified in this way presents big problems: when one wants to prepare the silver salt solution, it changes itself into silver sulphate. The problems associated with this chemical change have already been pointed out several times in the *Bulletin of the French Photographic Society.* To partly prevent this problem, one can add a small quantity of of baryta to the water, which wholly precipitates the sulphuric acid.

After many attempts of using the various processes, I finally decided to photograph only by means of the wet plate process which, used conventionally, can still give good results. This is so even in the midst of the very high temperatures that you encounter in China and Japan during the summer, and the intense cold of North China during winter. When operating in the colder climates, gently heat the baths before their use. The large collection that I made during my stay in the Far East was entirely by means of the wet plate, and I hardly ever had to redo my negatives again.

The difficulties of finding good water by myself, especially when in the countryside, made me give up the idea of using pyrogallic acid for reinforcing the plates. I therefore only used ammoniacal sulphate of iron. In some cases, when it was not possible to get this agent in the necessary strength, after returning home I just reinforced gradually the negatives with bichloride of mercury with some alcohol added.

Concerning the materials used in photography, I must point out here the quick deterioration of the collodion under certain conditions. While in France, one can successfully sensitize and use it for several months. However, it is necessary in hot countries, such as those I visited, to only use the necessary quantity each time during the heat of the summer. When the temperature rises to 38 or 40 degrees Celsius in the shade, the sensitized collodion is only good for about 6 or 8 days. However, it is very important to use the products economically in countries where one cannot purchase other products right away, and especially where a liter of ether costs 40 to 50 francs. I do not need to say that in conditions such as that, the collodion must be very alcoholic. I might even add a small quantity of water. The formula I use is indicated under the name Bayard in the excellent work of M. M. Bauvereswil and Davanne. I used this before in France, and it contains a lot less iodine. Although this emulsion was more sensitive, it did not do everything that I expected of it. As the light was often so intense, it was much more difficult to arrive at the exact time of exposure for collodion when it had been endowed with too much sensitivity. It was during this trip to the Far East that I really appreciated the advantages of some processing trays and bowls made of well-varnished paper. They were convenient to use, and resistant to the changes in temperature, as well as travel mishaps. They weren't like the bowls made of gutta-percha that had the problem of becoming soft with the heat.

To sum up, the difficulties, although great, can be overcome – especially when one has some knowledge of chemistry. For my part, I consider the wet plate process the best way to go, even if I am the only man who thinks so. This method is still fine in most situations where it is interesting to liven up a countryside scene with people or animals. Anything you can include in the image to increase the general interest would be good. These things are all necessary to give a more precise idea of the customs and features of the different countries you visit.

I shall finish by making some observations on the Chinese people's fear of the camera. In many situations I wanted to photograph some groups of Chinese, who were so interesting in their various poses and costumes. But as soon as they saw me aim the lens towards them, they quickly ran away! They were all afraid of being put under some evil spell. The Chinese, in effect, are very superstitious, and are afraid of what they don't understand. If I had to go on another trip to China, I certainly would prepare a camera in such a way that one could not easily notice which way the lens was pointing. [See the story on page 248 and in endnote 122, page 303 concerning world traveler Walter Clutterbuck, who encountered the same problems and solved them with a camera constructed in prophetic response to Champion's desires expressed here – a camera, by the way, that was constructed in Champion's native France.] On several occasions, their ignorance on this issue prevented my getting some really interesting images. The difficulties that I met with in getting good views, often with efforts that called for obtaining unwilling models, were many. However, I often managed to overcome their superstitious terror by means of some money.

Thinking about my reputation as a photographer, I wanted to capture some kind of market scene that would show large numbers of Chinese people. Once having found that scene, however, I had to resort to a strange means of obtaining immobility, for I need-ed to have these large numbers of Chinese standing still. One day I accidentally discovered the way to do this. After preparing my glass plate and readying the camera, I stood for a few moments watching the bustling people and was becoming concerned, fear-ing that the crowd would leave. Then, I wildly shook my hat into the air and screamed. The astonished Chinese came back, and began to look at me. At the perfect moment I uncovered my lens, while continuing to wave my hat in the air with my other hand. Some seconds after, I returned to my tent and successfully developed one of the most interesting views I had made during my trip! The Chinese have now, however, begun to take an interest in photo-graphy. There are even some Chinese who, provided with instruments bought from Europeans, are already succeeding with satisfying results."

Photographic Copyright Regulations in Japan, 1887

The following regulations in the form of the Photo-graphic Copyright Ordinance took effect from Dec-ember 1887. They replaced the first copyright rules which had been operating as the Photography Ordi-nance since June 1876. The new rules appeared in *The Photographic News* on March 16th, 1888, copied from an earlier issue of the *Japan Daily Mail*.

Art. 1 Any representation of the human figure, of implementa, of views, or of any other object, taken by means of light and chemicals, shall be called "a photograph"; and the right of exclusively enjoying the profits arising out of the sale of photographs shall be called "the photograph copyright."

Art. 2 Copyright shall belong to the photographer who has taken the pictures, and, after his death, to his heir. But in the case of photographs in safe keep-ing for other persons, the photograph copyright shall belong to the person for whom the photographs are so held, and, after his death, to his heir. In the case of photographs held as above by a photographer, the copyright-holder may demand from the photograph-er any of the original plates still in existence.

Art. 3 Any person desiring to receive protection for photograph copyright shall apply, previous to the publication of the photograph, to the Department of State for Home Affairs for the registration of his copyright, at the same time sending to the said Department of State two specimens from each plate and any amount of money corresponding to a money value of six of the photographs. Photographs of human form shall be entitled to protection even before registration.

Art. 4 During the period of protection, the name of the copyright-holder, his address, and the date of registration shall be inscribed on the photographs for which the registration of copyright has been made. When these particulars are not set forth, the photographs shall lose the effect of registration.

Art. 5 In the Department of State for Home Affairs there shall be kept a photograph copyright registra-tion book, in which entries shall be made whenever application is made for registration; and a certificate of registration shall be issued to applicants for the same. What regards certificates of registration of photograph copyrights shall be similar to what regards certificates of registration of copyrights for literary works and of pictures.

Art. 6 The period of protection for photograph copy-right shall be ten years from the month in which the registration was effected.

Art. 7 A photograph copyright may be sold or transferred with or without conditions.

Art. 8 To take reproductions of a photograph, the copyright of which is protected, or to produce imita-tions by a method resembling photography, by which a large number of pictures can be taken by means of a mechanical or of a chemical process, is prohibit-ed. Photographers are also prohibited from taking without the consent of the copyright holder, or of his heir, extra copies of the photographs entrusted to their care.

Art. 9 Any person who shall have falsely alleged a registration of copyright without having gone through the process laid down in Article 3, shall be liable to a fine of not less than 2 yen and not more than 20 yen.

Art. 10 Any person who shall have violated Article 8 shall be regarded as a counterfeiter in accordance with the copyright regulations, and shall be liable to a fine of not less than 20 yen and not more than 200 yen. He shall also be obliged to pay an indem-nity for damages. The term of prescription for the obligation to pay such indemnity for damages shall be one year after the expiration of the period of the copyright of the original photograph.

Art. 11 The period for public prosecution in connec-tion with the present regulations shall be one year, and shall be computed from the time that the photo-graphs or the imitations, which shall have been recognized as unlawful, were produced. In case the photographs or the imitations have been sold, the computation shall commence from the time of the last sale thereof.

Art. 12 The provisions mentioned in the Criminal Code for the mitigation of penalties on account of voluntary confession, for the aggravation of penal-ties, on account of repetition, and for the concur-rence of several infractions committed by the same person, shall not be applied in the case of the viola-tion of any of the provisions of the present regula-tions.

The first photograph copyright regulations of 1876 only provided protection for five years from registration. (At this time photographers in Britain, for example, could rely upon the greater protection afforded them by the Fine Arts Copyright Act of 1862. This provided protection for the lifetime of the author plus seven years, whether or not the pho-tograph had been published, as long as it had been registered at Stationers' Hall in London.) Copyright-ing registration fees were high and it seems unlike-ly that many photographs received protection. Such registration was probably reserved for "special" images where the likelihood of future sales would justify the fees. We know that Usui Shusaburo copy-righted the portrait he took of General Grant in his Tokyo studio in 1879, and Esaki Reiji probably regis-tered his famous 1893 collage of 1700 babies. Regis-tration required the face of the photograph to show the photographer's name and address and the date of copyright application. Certainly this information is evident on the Esaki print, but other examples are rarely encountered. It is possible that such informa-tion was "cropped" from the print for aesthetic rea-sons, on request from the customer, before being pasted into souvenir albums. This is suggested in a letter written by Adolfo Farsari to his family (see page 223 above) where he makes clear that all of his photographs had the Farsari name printed at the bottom. However, if the photograph was to be placed in a "better-class" album, this signature was trimmed off. Perhaps, therefore, Farsari copyrighted some of his images – or even his entire portfolio.

It is clear, however, that the copying of photo-graphs by competing studios was quite common. Many examples of such "pirating" can be found in surviving souvenir albums. Such copying might occur because the protection period had ended, or simply because it was known that a particular image had not been copyrighted. It seems that there was a tacit agreement among photographers that such copying would not occur even where registration had not taken place. This can be understood from the report of the December 12th, 1889 meeting of the then recently formed Photographic Society of Japan, which appeared in the *Japan Weekly Mail* issue of the 21st. Objection had been taken to a certain proposed member on account of his having copied, without permission, and sold, the pictures of a member of the Society. An explanation which was satisfactory both to the objecting member and to the Society was given, but the following resolu-tion, proposed by Mr. E. R. Holmes, and seconded by Mr. Pallister, was unanimously passed: "That this Society discountenance, by all means in its power, the practice of copying the photographs of other artists for sale, and that, if the practice be continued, the Society take into consideration the desirability of making a by-law, whereby such practice shall *ipso facto* exclude from membership of the Society."

Uchida Kuichi died in 1875, one year before the first regulations came into effect. The appearance of his work in other photographers' portfolios suggests that such copying was not considered unethical because Uchida was no longer alive.

CHRONOLOGY

1839	Commercial photography becomes possible with the announcement of Daguerre's invention.
1844	The calotype is invented, allowing multiple prints.
1848	The first camera to come to Japan is import-ed through Deshima.
1849	The Satsuma clan purchase the camera and begin experiments.
1851	Archer's wet-plate process is announced.
1851–2	Distressed Japanese sailors taken to San Francisco become the first Japanese to be photographed.
1853	In April Commodore Perry arrives in Oki-nawa. In May or June Eliphalet Brown, Perry's official photographer, takes daguer-reotypes in Okinawa. In July Perry arrives in mainland Japan.
1854	Eliphalet Brown takes daguerreotypes in Japan in Frebruary or March. The Russian Lieutenant Aleksandr Mozhaiskii also takes daguerreotypes in Japan in April.
1855	Edward A. Edgerton takes daguerreotypes at Shimoda. Edward Kern may also have taken daguerreotypes of Japan.
1856	The Dutch physician Van den Broeck gives photography lessons to some Nagasaki students.
1857	Pompe van Meerdervoort continues Van den Broeck's lessons. In September Ichiki Shiro and Ujuku Hikoeman take a daguer-reotype of Shimazu Nariakira – the earliest surviving photograph of a Japanese by a Japanese. The "Norwegian" allegedly takes photographs outside the Nagasaki treaty limits.
1858	Jocelyn uses wet-plate photography in Japan and takes the oldest confirmed photographs in Edo.
1859	In June or earlier Russian naval officers take photographs at Nagasaki. In July Pierre Rossier photographs in Kanagawa, Yoko-hama, and Edo. Also in July the treaty ports of Yokohama, Nagasaki, and Hakodate are opened for foreign trade and residence.
1859–60	Pierre Rossier teaches students in Naga-saki.
1860	Orrin Freeman arrives in Yokohama (possibly end 1859) and opens Japan's first commercial studio. Duane B. Simmons's Kanagawa studio room is in operation by May at the latest, and is being used by Frank Hall and possibly others. Members of the Japanese embassy are photographed in America. In Japan the American John Wilson is appointed by the Prussian Embassy as official photographer. In May *The Times* of London advertises the sale of the first commercial photograph of Japan. In October Pierre Rossier takes photographs of Nagasaki Harbor for Consul Morrison. By October at the latest, Nakahama Manjiro is taking successful daguerreotypes in Edo and opens a commercial studio in the city around this time which he later sells.
1860–2	Frank Hall is an early amateur photogra-pher in Yokohama. Around this time Julia Brown becomes Japan's first female pho-

tographer and helps Shimooka Renjo.

1861 Antoine Fauchery and Colonel Du Pin arrive in Japan in January and either, or both, takes photographs using a stereo camera. Antoine Fauchery dies in Yokohama in April. Ukai Gyokusen purchases Orrin Freeman's equipment and opens a studio in Edo and becomes Japan's first professional photographer. Abel Gower takes photographs during an overland journey from Nagasaki to Edo in the month of June. John Wilson takes photographs in and around Edo, exchanges his camera equipment with Shimooka for a painted scroll, and leaves Japan in December. Around November Negretti and Zambra publish Pierre Rossier's stereos, the first commercial photographic views of Japan.

1862 By February Shimooka Renjo has opened his first Japanese studio in Yokohama. William Saunders arrives in Yokohama in August. In October Samuel R. Brown sends forty-three of his own photographs to his Church in America. Later that month Brown and Saunders are given permission to photograph in Edo. In Hong Kong Milton Miller photographs members of the first Japanese embassy to Europe. Ueno Hikoma opens his first studio in Nagasaki. Nadar photographs members of the Japanese embassy in Paris. Rossier returns to Europe.

1862–4 Antonius Bauduin, an amateur photographer, builds a studio next to his house on Deshima.

1863 In May William Saunders advertises the sale of tinted photographs in Shanghai. Charles Parker arrives in Yokohama by July at the latest. Felix Beato arrives in Yokohama, also by July at the latest.

1864 Nadar photographs members of the Japanese embassy in Paris. Shima Ryu takes a portrait of her husband, thereby producing the earliest known photograph taken by a Japanese woman. Felix Beato photographs the Shimonoseki campaign in September. French Lieutenant Jules Le Bas, attached to the French fleet, photographs in Yokohama and Shimonoseki.

1865 Uchida Kuichi opens his first studio in Kobe but later that year moves it to Osaka. During July Sir Henry Woods, a naval officer and amateur photographer, takes photographs in Edo using Felix Beato's borrowed equipment. Hori Masumi opens his first studio in Kyoto.

1864–6 Kizu Kokichi opens the first Hakodate studio.

1865–7 Shima Kakoku and his wife open a studio in Edo.

1866 Tomishige Rihei opens his first studio in Yamagawa. The French chemistry engineer Paul Champion takes photographs in Nagasaki and Yokohama.

1867 Frederick Sutton takes photographs at Okinawa and Kyushu. Orrin Freeman dies in Yokohama. Frederick Sutton photographs the last Shogun at Osaka. Kusakabe Kimbei accompanies Felix Beato on a trip to Shanghai. Tamamura Kozaburo is apprenticed to Kanamaru Genzo. Angus C. Fairweather, amateur, uses the experimental collodion dry-plate technology in Japan this year, or earlier.

1867–8 Charles Weed takes mammoth-plate views of Japan around this time.

1867–9 Tamato Kenzo opens a studio in Hakodate.

1868 Yokoyama Matsusaburo opens his first studio in Yokohama or Tokyo. Uchida Kuichi opens a studio in Yokohama. Ichida Sota opens his first studio in Kyoto.

1869 Uchida Kuichi opens a studio in Tokyo. Wilhelm Burger arrives in Nagasaki in September with the Austria-Hungary mission and is accompanied by Michael Moser. Futama Asama is apprenticed to Kitaniwa Tsukuba.

1870 *The Far East* begins publication in May. Michael Moser joins *The Far East* as photographer. Ichida Sota moves his studio and

operations to Kobe. In August E. Parant & Co. opens short-lived earliest known foreign commercial studio in Kobe.

1871 In August Baron Raimund von Stillfried opens his studio in Yokohama. Esaki Reiji opens his first studio in Shiba, Tokyo. Tamoto Kenzo and Ida Kokichi photograph parts of Hokkaido together. Takebayashi Seiichi's newly opened Hakodate studio is destroyed by fire. Kitaniwa Tsuba opens a studio at the Asakusa Flower Gardens, Tokyo. John Sandwith, an amateur, photographs the Hakone Mountains. Felix Beato, accompanied by H. Woollett, joins the American expedition to Korea and photographs the conflict. Auguste Gordes operates the first commercial foreign studio in Osaka. C. Parant leaves Gordes Brothers and opens his own studio in Osaka.

1872 In January Stillfried takes illicit photographs of the Emperor. In May Stillfried goes on a photographic tour to Kobe and Nagasaki. In October he is commissioned by the Japanese government to photograph in Hokkaido. Shimazu Tokoku transfers his studio operations from Yokohama to Tokyo. William Willmann joins Stillfried & Co. Uchida Kuichi takes the first official portraits of the Emperor and Empress. Kyoto is temporarily opened to foreigners during the exhibition and a number of photographers travel there and bring back photographs. Many photographers, including Usui Shusaburo, Felix Beato, and Michael Moser, photograph the opening of Japan's first railway.

1873 Stillfried exhibits a Japanese "tea-house" at the Vienna Exposition. In February Michael Moser leaves *The Far East* and travels to Vienna. In July *The Far East* publishes photos from Suzuki Shinichi's *shajo* series.

1874 In May Matsuzaki Shinji travels to and photographs in Taiwan. Kitaniwa establishes the first photographic magazine – the *Datsuei Yawa*. The Gordes brothers open a studio in Kobe. Many international astronomical teams descend on Nagasaki, one of the prime locations for observing the Transit of Venus. The United States party included S. R. Seibert as chief photographer, H. E. Lodge as first assistant, and F. H. Williams as second assistant. Some time in October or November Ueno Hikoma was taken on to assist as third assistant. The Transit was photographed in December. The American photographer D. R. Clark is attached to the Vladivostok station and also takes stereoviews in China and Japan.

1875 In March Stillfried is in China building his Chinese portfolio. In October Matsuzaki Shinji is commissioned to photograph the Ogasawara Islands. Usui Shusaburo is known to be operating a studio in Yokohama. Nakajima Matsuchi opens his first studio in Tokyo. Uchida Kuichi dies. William Willmann operates his own Yokohama studio for a few months.

1876 Hermann Andersen joins Stillfried to form Stillfried and Andersen. Moser accompanies a Japanese delegation to the Philadelphia Centennial Exhibition as interpreter and does not return to Japan. In April Stillfried is in China again, building his portfolio. In October David Welsh joins Stillfried and Andersen. Suzuki Shinichi II opens a studio in Nagoya. In December John Douglas is said to have given technical training to Usui Shusaburo. Takebayashi opens a studio in Sapporo.

1877 In January fire destroys Stillfried and Andersen's studio and stock, but the negatives are saved. Stillfried and Andersen purchase Felix Beato's business. In June Stillfried leaves for America and is away for twelve months. Nakajima Matsuchi wins the high class award at the first National Industrial Exhibition. Futami Asama opens his first studio in Tokyo. William Metcalf tours Japan and produces a fine stereo series –

A Summer in Japan. John Douglas joins Stillfried and Andersen this year or next. Ogawa Kazumasa opens his first studio in Tomioka, Gumma Prefecture.

1878 In March Matsuzaki Shinji sells photos of the 1877 National Industrial Exhibition. June sees the termination of the Stillfried and Andersen partnership. In November Stillfried is appointed by the Japanese government to teach various printing processes. In December the last issue of *The Far East* is published. Endo Rikuro opens a studio in Sendai. Ida Kokichi takes the first photographs of the Kuril Islands. Schleesselmann operates his own Yokohama studio for a few months in this year. Shima Shukichi opens a studio at Miyanoshita, next to the Fujiya Hotel.

1879 In April Stillfried resigns the government position and opens a Tokyo studio in contravention of his partnership dissolution agreement. In October Stillfried's brother Franz arrives in Japan. Baron Franz von Stillfried-Ratenicz opens a Yokohama studio called Baron Stillfried. In December David Welsh leaves Usui's studio and joins Franz von Stillfried but leaves the same month to rejoin Stillfried and Andersen. Dry plates are imported into Japan but are not immediately popular. Suzuki Shinichi II apprentices himself to Tabor in San Francisco, becoming the first Japanese photographer to study photography abroad.

1880 Kusakabe Kimbei opens his first studio in Yokohama. Maruki Riyo opens his first studio in Tokyo.

1881 Baron Raimund von Stillfried-Ratenicz leaves Japan.

1882 Tamamura Kozaburo is commissioned to produce tea and silk industry photographs for advertising purposes. Ogawa Kazumasa helps found the *Shashin Shimpo* and then leaves Japan in July to study photography in America. Francis Guillemard, amateur, is the first to use the new gelatin dry-plate process in Japan.

1883 Tamamura Kozaburo opens a Yokohama studio. Hermann Andersen leaves Japan. Esaki Reiji uses dry-plate photography.

1884 In January Ogawa Kazumasa returns from studying in America. Stillfried and Andersen are awarded the gold medal at the Calcutta International Exhibition. Cheong Tong sets up a Yokohama studio. Felix Beato leaves Japan.

1885 Ogawa Kazumasa opens a large studio in Tokyo. Adolfo Farsari sets up his first photo studio at the old Stillfried and Andersen address, No. 17 Bund, after buying up the company and stock. C. Sugawara sets up a studio at Usui Shusaburo's old Otemachi address.

1886 In February a fire at No. 17 Bund destroys all of Farsari's stock and negatives, including the old negatives taken by Felix Beato and Stillfried and Andersen.

1887 Farsari relocates to No. 16 Bund following Usui Shusaburo's return to his old studio in Otemachi.

1888 Ogawa Kazumasa accompanies Ernest Fenollosa on a tour of Nikko and photographs the region's art. Maruki Riyo is asked to photograph a drawing of Emperor Meiji, which is then circulated nationally as the new imperial likeness. James Ricalton makes his first visit to Japan this year, or possibly early next. Endo Rikuro photographs the eruption of Mount Bandai.

1889 Ogawa Kazumasa helps to relaunch the *Shashin Shimpo* and is founder-member of the Photographic Society of Japan. Ogawa also sets up his photo-engraving company Ogawa Shashin Seihanjo and launches the art magazine *Kokka*. Emma Lasenby Liberty takes photographs during a five-month tour.

1890 William Burton publishes an article in *The Photographic News* on Mizuno Hanbei's unique invention of gold and silver photographs on lacquer. William Burton and Tanaka Takeshi take a fourteen-plate panorama of Tokyo. A boom in glass lantern slides begins. In April Adolfo Farsari leaves Japan and returns to Italy. David Welsh operates a studio in Yokohama and is probably the only owner-managed Western studio in Japan

1891   John Milne, William Burton, Ogawa Kazumasa, Miyashita Kin, and others photograph the Gifu and Aichi earthquakes. Endo Rikuro photographs an expedition to the Kuril Islands. In July Ogawa Kazumasa exhibits 100 photographs of Tokyo geisha at the recently opened twelve-story Ryounkaku.

1892   E. Burton Holmes makes his first photographic tour of Japan. *Ayame-san* is published in Yokohama and the illustrations printed by Ogawa Kazumasa are the first to be produced using a true half-tone photo-mechanical process. John Milne and William Burton publish *The Great Earthquake in Japan*. Enami Tamotsu sets up a studio in Yokohama.

1893   William Burton organizes the Foreign Photography Exhibition, held at Ueno, Tokyo. Ogawa Kazumasa exhibits in, and attends the Chicago World Exposition.

1894   William Burton publishes articles on Ogawa Kazumasa and Kajima Seibei in *The Practical Photographer*. Okamoto Rokuhei is the sole agent for the sale of Kajima Seibei's photographs. Kamei Koreaki photographs the Sino-Japanese War.

1895   In February Kajima Seibei opens the Genrokukan. William Henry Jackson, on a world tour, photographs in Japan. Ogawa Kazumasa becomes the first Japanese to be elected as fellow of the Royal Photographic Society.

1896   Ogawa Sashichi opens a studio in Yokohama (possibly earlier). An important and extensive article on Japanese photographers and photography, edited by William Burton, appears in *The Practical Photographer*. Henry Strohmeyer tours Japan taking stereoviews. Tamamura Kozaburo receives an order from the United States for around a million hand-colored albumen-print photographs. Kajima Seibei is disinherited by his family and loses control of his business.

1897   Kajima Seibei photographs the Empress Dowager's funeral at night.

1898   In December Walter Clutterbuck takes photographs in Okinawa.

1899   E. Burton Holmes uses movie film in Kyoto for the first time in Japan's history. William Burton dies of fever in Tokyo. While on vacation, Baron Adolf de Meyer takes photographs in Japan.

1900   Picture postcards are introduced in October. James Ricalton photographs the Boxer Rebellion and takes pictures of Japanese troops. Ogawa Kazumasa photographs the Boxer Rebellion and Beijing.

1901   Benjamin Kilburn makes a stereoview series in Japan. Herbert Ponting makes his first photographic tour of Japan.

1902   Karl Lewis opens a studio in Yokohama.

1903   George Rose makes a photographic tour of Japan, or possibly in 1904. Adam Clark Vroman makes a photographic and collecting tour of Japan.

1904   Various photographers – James Ricalton, James Hare, Richard Barry, Jack London, etc. – cover the Russo-Japanese War.

1905   Otis Poole photographs the Japanese Alps. Frank Lloyd Wright, the American architect, photographs around Kyoto and Kobe.

1908   Arnold Genthe makes a photographic tour of Japan.

1909   Adam Clark Vroman makes a second photographic and art-buying tour of Japan.

1912   The Emperor Meiji dies.

PHOTOGRAPHIC TERMS AND GLOSSARY

Ambrotype A process whereby a very thin underexposed negative is placed in front of a dark background making the image look like a positive. The glass plate is produced using the wet-plate collodion process. The process was announced by the sculptor Frederick Scott Archer in 1851 and quickly became an inexpensive alternative to the daguerreotype, particularly when used in the portrait studio. Although ambrotypes slightly resemble daguerreotypes, the method of production was very different, and much cheaper. Ambrotypes required shorter exposure times, the image reversal seen with daguerreotypes could be avoided, and they could be viewed from any angle. As a result, daguerreotypes were almost completely displaced by 1860. Ambrotypes in the West peaked in popularity in the mid-1860s, but continued their popularity in Japan until around 1900. The American Orrin Freeman opened the first commercial photographic establishment in Japan when he moved his ambrotype portrait studio from Shanghai to Yokohama in late 1859 or early 1860.

Albumen paper A light-sensitive paper prepared with a coating of egg white and a salt (e.g. ammonium chloride) and sensitized by being treated with a solution of silver nitrate. This very popular form of printing paper, introduced in 1850, was used for the vast majority of nineteenth-century Japanese photographs.

Bakumatsu (or late Edo) The last years of the Tokugawa shogunate (1853–68).

Cabinet card A larger version of the *carte de visite*, the cabinet card's approximate mount measurements were 4$\frac{1}{4}$ x 6$\frac{1}{2}$ inches (108 x 165 mm). Introduced in 1866, the cabinet card gradually overtook the smaller *carte de visite* in popularity. Interest in this format peaked between 1875 and 1895, but by around 1910 it had all but disappeared. Baron Raimund von Stillfried-Ratenicz was an early exponent of this format in Japan and issued cabinet cards in the early 1870s.

Calotype Invented and patented by William Henry Fox Talbot in 1841, the calotype anticipated modern photographic needs by using a negative which enabled multiple positive prints to be made. The negative was a sheet of high-quality writing paper which had been made light-sensitive with chemicals.

Carte de visite A close-trimmed photograph, approximately 2$\frac{1}{4}$ x 3$\frac{1}{2}$ inches (58 x 89 mm), mounted on a slightly larger card that served as a popular form of visiting card in the 1860s. *Cartes de visite*, which started to appear from 1859, depicted mainly portraits, but also views and other subjects. The *carte de visite* retained its popularity until around 1880 in the West and the 1890s in Japan, after which interest began to fade until it had disappeared altogether by the 1920s. The *carte de visite* competed for popularity with the stereoview. Nevertheless, the two formats were largely complementary: stereoviews concentrated on views and *cartes de visite* on portraits. The first known Japan-related *cartes de visite* were those produced in the United States when a Japanese mission was there in 1860. In the mid-1860s, some Japanese studios were producing *cartes de visite*, notably the studios of Shimooka Renjo, Ueno Hikoma, and Uchida Kuichi. The earliest *cartes de visite* of Japan appear to have been taken by William Saunders during his photographic tour there in 1862, although Milton Miller may have taken some in 1861.

Collotype process A high-quality fine-grain printing process whereby gelatin is applied to a glass plate that is allowed to dry and is then exposed to a photographic image. The process was invented by Alphonse Poitevin in 1855 and was popularised in Japan in the 1890s by Ogawa Kazumasa, who produced many beautiful collotype works.

Composite souvenir album A souvenir album issued by a studio containing photographs of usually hand-colored views and costumes wholly or predominantly originating from other studios. Cheaper than studio souvenir albums, composites were usually compiled and sold by photo-dealers.

Daguerreotype The first successful commercial photographic process, invented by Louis J. M. Daguerre in 1839 and used by Eliphalet Brown Jr for the first known photographs of Japan in 1853. A daguerreotype is a direct positive that results from a sensitized copper plate exposed for approximately fifteen minutes. Depending on the skill of the photographer and the light conditions, exposure times of just a few seconds were sometimes achieved. The daguerreotype is a unique photograph since no negative is used. Although very sharp images were produced, they could only be viewed from a certain angle and the picture was reversed. By the time that the first successful daguerreotype was taken by a Japanese in 1857, the process was already being phased out in the West and seldom appeared after 1862. When Rossier arrived in Nagasaki in 1859, Japanese students of photography were still struggling to master the art and had already turned to wet-plate collodion. As a result, only sixteen daguerreotypes of Japanese interest have surfaced so far. See lists in *OJP*.

Dry-plate process From the early days of photography, there had been many attempts to develop dry-glass plates which could be coated with a sensitized emulsion before exposure. Significant progress was made in the 1860s, but the real breakthrough came in 1871 when Dr Richard Maddox discovered a way of using gelatin as a basis for the photographic plate. It was not until 1878, however, that the first commercially viable plates were manufactured. Dry plates could be developed much more quickly than any previous wet-plate technique and were easier to transport and store. Photographers required fewer chemicals and no longer needed to carry around a darktent. Shorter exposure times meant that it was easier to photograph movement.

Edo The old name for Tokyo, and sometimes rendered Yedo. The capital changed its name in 1868 but the old form was still in use for a few years.

Edo period 1600–1868. Late Edo (or Bakumatsu) is thought of as 1853–68.

Hand coloring The coloring of photographs with watercolors or oil. The process, introduced in Europe but never popular there, became an art form in Japan from the 1860s. William Saunders seems to have been the first to use it in China and Japan, but Felix Beato was the first to employ it consistently. The quality of the finished product depended upon the photographic paper used, the ability of the artist, and the time taken to complete the work. It is an underestimated art form.

Jeda/Jedda/Jedo The old name for Tokyo, and sometimes rendered Yedo.

Lantern slide The forerunner of the modern color transparency, lantern slides are positive photographic images on clear glass, produced from a negative and sandwiched in glass to protect the emulsion. The image was projected onto a screen by having light shone from behind via a projector. The standard British slide size is 3$\frac{1}{4}$ x 3$\frac{1}{4}$ inches (83 x 83 mm), while American and Continental slides are 3$\frac{1}{4}$ x 4 inches (83 x 102 mm). Many Japanese lantern slides were attractively hand colored. Although photographic lantern slides appeared from 1849, their halcyon days were between the 1870s and 1920s. Their role as the first mass-communication tool has, as with the stereoview, been underestimated. Although they lacked the three-dimensional reality of stereoviews, their large size when projected onto a screen, together with their vivid colors, insured their popularity. As Kempler states in "America 'Discovers' the World" (1991, p. 140), in the same time it took a stereoview to be viewed by one person, a lantern slide could be seen by an audience of a thousand or more. The lecture circuit then, as now, was big business and famous figures such as John Stoddard from the 1880s and Burton Holmes in the 1890s used lantern slides extensively to illustrate their popular travel lectures. Before the days of cinema and television, attendance at such events was very much seen as a fashionable form of entertainment, and an appealing night out. Burton Holmes gave more than 8000 lectures in his career. By the 1880s millions of Europeans and Americans would have attended these so-called magic lantern shows. Illustrated talks would have been given by photographers, travelers, missionaries, and teachers. Schools, in particular, used lanterns as effective educational devices. Lantern slides of Japan started appearing from the late 1860s. From 1890 there was an export-led boom in hand-colored lantern slides of Japanese scenes. These were very popular in the West and studios such as Kusakabe Kimbei, Nakajima Matsuchi, and Enami Tamotsu responded to the demand and produced exquisitely colored slides. Globetrotters passing through Yokohama would often arrange to have their own photographs converted over to slides and then hand colored.

Large-format print Refers, in this book, to any size print larger than a cabinet card.

Late Edo (or Bakumatsu) The last years of the Tokugawa shogunate (1853–68).

Mammoth plate A very large print measuring approximately 22 x 19 inches (56 x 46 cm) made from negatives of the same size. Cameras that were used for taking such photographs were large and cumbersome. Not surprisingly, such photographs are very rare.

Meiji period (or era) 1868–1912.

Meiji Restoration 1868.

Small-format print In this book, any size smaller than cabinet size.

Souvenir albums These were albums of various sizes containing photographs of what were called Japanese views and costumes (landscapes and portraits), usually hand colored. The wooden album covers were decorated with Japanese silk cloth or elaborate lacquer designs such as *shibiyama*. Produced for the export market, they were very popular with visiting tourists from the late 1860s to around 1920. The majority were produced by Yokohama photo studios and are sometimes therefore called Yokohama Albums – something of a misnomer.

Stereoview or stereograph A print consisting of two images of the same object taken from slightly different angles. The two images are mounted side by side on a stiff card and viewed through a stereoscope to produce a three-dimensional effect. The stereoscopic process was invented by Sir Charles Wheatstone in 1838. Used for entertainment, education, or both, the stereoview was hugely popular from the 1850s and continued until the 1920s. It was the longest lasting photographic format, but is all but forgotten these days.

Studio souvenir album A souvenir album issued by a studio where all or the vast majority of photographs were taken by the resident photographer(s).

Taisho period (or era) 1912–26.

Wet-plate or wet-collodion process A process invented by Frederick Scott Archer in 1851 in which a glass plate was coated with a special chemical mixture and exposed while still wet. Exposure could take up to a minute or more. The operation was messy and complex and required of the photographer both skill and manipulative dexterity.

Yedo or Edo The pre-1868 name for Tokyo.

Yokohama albums *See* Souvenir Albums.

BIBLIOGRAPHY

Alcock, Sir Rutherford, *The Capital of the Tycoon*, London: Longman, Green, 1863.

Angus, D. C., *Japan: The Eastern Wonderland*, London: Cassell & Co., 1904.

Arnold, H. J. P., *Herbert Ponting: Another World*, London: Sidgwick & Jackson Ltd, 1975.

_____, *Photographer of the World: The Biography of Herbert Ponting*, London: Hutchinson, 1969.

"The Athenaeum," *Fine Art Gossip*, No. 1805, May 31st, 1862, p. 729.

Australian Dictionary of Biography, Vol. 4, 1851–90, Melbourne University Press, 1972.

Babbitts, Judith, "'To See Is to Know': Stereographs Educate Americans about East Asia, 1890–1940," Ph.D. dissertation, Yale University, 1987.

Barry, Richard, "An Old Fashioned Traveler," *Personality*, February 1928.

_____, *Port Arthur: A Monster Heroism*, New York: Moffat, Yard & Co., 1905.

Beasley, W. G., *Japan Encounters the Barbarian: Japanese Travellers in America and Europe*, New Haven: Yale University Press, 1995.

Beaulieu, Annette Leduc, "Hugues Krafft (1853–1935): Ethnographer, Photographer and French Member of the Japan Society," *The Japan Society Proceedings*, No. 143, 2005, pp. 143–51.

Bennett, Alice, "Has Weapons, Trophies and Pictures of Far Off Lands," *Watertown Daily Times*, March 20th, 1927, p. 2.

Bennett, Terry, *Early Japanese Images*, Rutland: Charles E. Tuttle Co., 1996.

_____, "Early Japanese Images of Nineteenth-century Japan," *The Japan Society Proceedings*, No. 126, 1995, pp. 57–72.

_____, "The Early Photographers: Photographing Japan 1860s–1890s," *Japan Digest*, January 1991, pp. 57–62; April 1991, pp. 65–8; July 1991, pp. 59–62; October 1991, pp. 59–62.

_____, "Early Photographic Images of Japan," *The PhotoHistorian*, No. 112, 1996, pp. 16–23.

_____, "Herbert George Ponting, 1870–1935: Photographer, Explorer, Inventor," in Hugh Cortazzi (ed.), *Britain and Japan: Biographical Portraits*, Vol. 4, London: Japan Society Publications, 2002, pp. 303–11.

_____, *Japan and The Illustrated London News: Complete Record of Reported Events 1853–1899*, Folkestone: Global Oriental Limited, 2006.

_____, *Korea: Caught in Time*, Reading: Garnet Publishing Ltd, 1997.

_____, *Old Japanese Photographs: Collectors' Data Guide*, Purley, Surrey: Old Japan, 2006.

_____, "The Search for Rossier: Early Photographer of China and Japan," *The PhotoHistorian*, No. 147, 2004, pp. 9–13.

Bennett, Terry and Dobson, Sebastian, "The First British Photographer in Japan: William Nassau Jocelyn and the Elgin Mission of 1858," *The PhotoHistorian*, No. 120, 1998, pp. 7–16.

_____, "The Sentaro Daguerreotype: A New Episode in Japanese Photo-History Discovered," *The PhotoHistorian*, No. 116, 1997, pp. 7–13.

Bethel, Denise, "The J. B. Millet Company's Japan: Described and Illustrated by the Japanese," *Image*, Vol. 34, Nos. 1–2, 1991, pp. 3–22.

Bird, Isabella, *Unbeaten Tracks in Japan*, London: John Murray, 1880.

Bishop (née Bird), Isabella, *Views in the Far East, Photographed by Isabella L. Bishop F.R.G.S.*, collotyped by S. Kajima, Tokyo, ca. 1896.

Birk, Melanie (ed.), *Frank Lloyd Wright's Fifty Views of Japan: The 1905 Photo Album*, California: Pomegranate Artbooks, 1996.

Black, John Reddie, *Young Japan: Yokohama and Yedo 1858–79*, Tokyo: Oxford University Press, 1968.

Blum, Ron, *The Seige at Port Arthur: The Russo-Japanese War through the Stereoscope*, Adelaide: Self-published, 1987.

Boyd, T. and Izakura, N., *Portraits in Sepia*, Tokyo: Asahi Sonorama, 2000.

Braive, M. F., *The Photograph: A Social History*, London: Thames & Hudson, 1966.

Brinkley, Captain Francis, *Japan: Described and Illustrated by the Japanese*, Boston: J. B. Millet Co., 1897-8.

Brooke, George M., Jr, *John M. Brooke: Naval Scientist and Educator*, Charlottesville: University Press of Virginia, 1980.

[Burger, Wilhelm], *Bilder Aus Japan*, Wien: Druck V. M. Munk, 1871.

Burton, W. K., *Burton's Modern Photography*, London: Piper & Carter, 1885.

_____, "A Japanese Photographer," *Anthony's Photographic Bulletin*, March 22nd, 1890, pp. 181–5.

_____, "Japanese Photographers, No. 1–K. Ogawa," *The Practical Photographer*, June 1st, 1894.

_____, "Japanese Photographers, No. 2–Kajima Seibei," *The Practical Photographer*, August 1st, 1894, pp. 204–8.

_____, "Japanese Photographs in Gold," *The Photographic News*, November 14th, 1890, p. 890.

_____, "Photography for Amateurs in Japan," *The American Annual of Photography and Photographic Times Almanac*, New York: Scovill & Adams Co., 1895, pp. 29–40.

_____, "Photography in Japan," *British Journal of Photography*, Vol. 34, 1887.

_____, "Photography in Japan," *The Photographic News*, March 27th, 1891, p. 248.

_____, "Photo-mechanical Work in Japan," *The Photographic News*, February 22nd, 1895, pp. 117–19.

_____, *Practical Guide to Photography*, London: Marion & Co., 1892.

Caldwell, Genoa (ed.), *The Man Who Photographed the World: Burton Holmes Travelogues 1886-1938*, New York: Harry N. Abrams, Inc., 1977.

Carnes, C., *Jimmy Hare News Photographer: Half a Century with a Camera*, New York: The Macmillan Co., 1940.

Cary, Julia Metcalf, *William Henry Metcalf: A Biography by His Daughter*, New York: The Press of the Woolly Whale, 1937.

Chamberlain, B. H., "The Luchu Islands and Their Inhabitants," *The Geographical Journal*, Vol. 5, No. 4, 1895, p. 298.

Chamberlain, B. H. and Mason, W. B., *A Handbook for Travellers in Japan*, 3rd edn, London: John Murray, 1891, and New York: Charles Scribner's Sons, 1893; 4th edn, 1894; 5th edn, 1899; 6th edn, 1901; 7th edn, 1903; 8th edn, 1907; 9th edn, 1913.

Checkland, Olive, "W. K. Burton, 1856–99: 'Engineer Extraordinaire'," in Hugh Cortazzi (ed.), *Britain and Japan: Biographical Portraits*, Vol. 4, London: Japan Society Publications, 2002, pp. 174–86.

Chronicle and Directory for China, Japan and the Philippines, Hong Kong: Daily Press Office, 1864-92.

Clark, John, *Japanese Exchanges in Art 1850s–1930s*, Sydney: Power Publications, 2001.

Clark, John; Fraser, John; and Osman, Colin, "A Revised Chronology of Felice (Felix) Beato (1825/34?–1908?)," in John Clark, *Japanese Exchanges in Art 1850s–1930s*, Sydney: Power Publications, 2001, pp. 89–120.

Clutterbuck, W. J., *About Ceylon and Borneo*, London: Longmans, Green, & Co., 1891.

_____, "The Lu-Chu Islands," *Travel and Exploration*, Vol. 4, No. 20, 1910, pp. 81–90.

_____, *The Skipper in Arctic Seas*, London: Longmans, Green, & Co., ca. 1890.

Coates, P. D., *The China Consuls*, Hong Kong: Oxford University Press, 1988.

Cocking, Samuel, "1869–1909: Philosophies of an Early Rover to Japan's Shores," *Yokohama Semi-Centennial: 1859-1909*, Yokohama: Japan Gazette Press, 1909, pp. 38–40.

Cortazzi, Hugh, *Victorians in Japan: In and around the Treaty Ports*, London: Athlone Press, 1987.

Cortazzi, Hugh (ed.), *Britain and Japan: Biographical Portraits*, Vol. 4, London: Japan Society Publications, 2002.

Cortazzi, Hugh and Bennett, Terry, *Japan: Caught in Time*, Reading: Garnet Publishing Ltd, 1995.

Cortazzi, H. and Webb, G. (eds.), *Kipling's Japan: Collected Writings*, London: Athlone Press, 1988.

Cotteau, Edmond, *Une Touriste dans L'Extreme Orient japon chine, indo-chine et tonkin (4 Aout 1881–24 Janvier 1882)*, Paris: Librairie Hachette etc. Cie, 1884.

Couteur, Wilson Le, *To Nippon: The Land of the Rising Sun*, Sydney: John Andrews & Co., 1899.

Craig, John, S., *Craig's Daguerreian Registry, Vol. 3 Pioneers and Progress, Macdonald to Zuky*, Torrington, Connecticut: John S. Craig, 1996.

Croly, Herbert, *Willard Straight*, New York: The Macmillan Co., 1925.

Dal Pra, Elena, "A. Farsari: Un avventuriero fotografo," *Domina*, No. 33, January 1991.

Darrah, William C., *The World of Stereographs*, Gettysburg: William C. Darrah, 1977.

Darrah, W. C.; Treadwell, T. K.; and Sell, W., *Photographers of the World*, Portland, Oregon: National Stereoscopic Association, 2003.

Davis, Richard Harding, "Photography as a Profession," *British Journal of Photography*, March 4th, 1904, p. 192.

Del Mar, Walter, *Around the World through Japan*, London: Adam and Charles Black, 1903.

Dictionary of National Biography, London: Oxford University Press, 1975.

Dobson, Sebastian, "Felice Beato in Japan, 1863–1877," in N. C. Rousmaniere and Hirayama Mikiko (eds.), *Reflecting Truth: Japanese Photography in the Nineteenth Century*, Amsterdam: Hotei Publishing, 2004; first published as *Old Photography Study*, Sainsbury Institute for the Study of Japanese Arts and Cultures and Nagasaki University Library, 2003.

_____, "Frederick William Sutton, 1832–83: Photographer of the Last Shogun," in Hugh Cortazzi (ed.), *Britain and Japan: Biographical Portraits*, Vol. 4, London: Japan Society Publications, 2002, pp. 289–302.

Dobson, Sebastian and Bennett, Terry, "British Photographers in Japan: 1858–1898," in *The Theme and Spirit of Anglo-Japanese Relations: An Exhibition of Photographs*, exhibition catalogue, London: The Japan Society, 1998, pp. 3–19.

Dower, John D., *A Century of Japanese Photography*, London: Hutchinson, 1981.

Du Pin, Le Colonel D'Etat, Major, *Le Japon: Mœurs. Coutumes. Description. Geographie. Rapports avec les Europeens*, Paris: Arthus Bertrand, 1868.

Earle, E. W, "The Orient Viewed," *California Museum of Photography Bulletin*, Vol. 3, No. 3, 1984.

Early Works of Photography, exhibition catalogue, Tokyo Metropolitan Museum of Photography, 1992.

Earns, L. and Burke-Gaffney, B., *Across the Gulf of Time: The International Cemeteries of Nagasaki*, Nagasaki: Nagasaki Bunkensha, 1991.

Erickson, Bruce, T., "Eliphalet M. Brown, Jr: An Early Expedition Photographer," in Peter E. Palmquist (ed.), *The Daguerreian Annual, 1990*, official yearbook, Eureka, California: The Daguerreian Society, 1990, pp. 145–56.

Esaki Reiji, "Professional Photography in Japan: From Its Introduction to the Present Day," *The Practical Photographer*, Vol. 7, No. 81, 1896, pp. 226–9.

Estebe, Claude, "Ueno Hikoma (1838–1904): Un pionnier de la photographie japonaise," MA dissertation, Departement Coree-Japan Section japonais, Institut National des Langues et Civilisations Orientales, 1998.

Falconer, John, *A Vision of the Past: A History of Early Photography in Singapore and Malaya: The Photographs of G. R. Lambert & Co., 1880–1910*, Singapore, Times Editions, 1987.

[The] Far East, May 1870–August 1875, 7 vols., Tokyo: Yushodo Booksellers Ltd; reprint, 1965.

Fauchery, A., *Lettres d'un Mineur en Australie*, Paris: Poulet Malassis & de Broise, 1857; English edition published as *Letters from a Miner in Australia* (trans. A. R. Chisholm), Melbourne: Georgian House, 1965.

Freiburg State Archives, Staatsarchiv Freiburg, Zeughausstrasse 17, 1700 Freiburg, Switzerland.

Funkhouser, Elmer, "Japan: Described and Illustrated by the Japanese," *Arts of Asia*, Vol. 29. No. 2, 1999, pp. 133–8.

_____, "'T.' Fukasawa: Meiji Era Photographer," *Daruma*, Vol. 3, No. 2, 1996, pp. 10–18.

Gartlan, Luke, "Changing Views," in N. C. Rousmaniere and Hirayama Mikiko (eds.), *Reflecting Truth: Japanese Photography in the Nineteenth Century*, Amsterdam: Hotei Publishing, 2004, pp. 40–65; first published as *Old Photography Study*, Sainsbury Institute for the Study of Japanese Arts and Cultures and Nagasaki University Library, 2003, pp. 16–31.

_____, "A Chronology of Baron Raimund von Stillfried-Ratenicz (1839–1911)," in John Clark, *Japanese Exchanges in Art 1850s–1930s*, Sydney:

Power Publications, 2001, pp. 121–88.

Genthe, A., *As I Remember*, New York: Reynal & Hitchcock, 1936.

Giron, Paule, "Le descendant des marquis de Gordes est Japonais," *Historia*, No. 441, 1983, pp. 65–8.

Gordon Smith, Richard, *Ancient Tales and Folklore of Japan*, London: A. & C. Black, 1908.

Goto Kazuo (ed.), *Hugues Krafft: Bonjuru Japon, Furansu seinen ga kasha shita 1882-nen* (Hugues Krafft: Frenchman Who Took Photographs in 1882 Japan), Tokyo: Asahi Shimbunsha, 1998.

Goto Kazuo and Matsumoto Itsuya (eds.), *Yomigaeru Bakumatsu: Raiden Daigaku shashin korekushon yori* (The Bakumatsu Era Resurrected: Images from the Leiden University Photography Collection), Tokyo: Asahi Shimbunsha, 1986.

Gould, L. L. and Greffe, R., *Photojournalist: The Career of Jimmy Hare*, Austin: University of Texas Press, 1977.

Griffis, William Elliot, Collection, Rutgers University Libraries, New Brunswick, New Jersey.

Griffis, William Elliot, *A Maker of the New Orient*, New York: Fleming H. Revell Co., 1902.

_____, *The Mikado's Empire*, New York: Harper & Brothers, 1876.

Gubbins, J. H., *The Progress of Japan (1853–1871)*, Oxford: Clarendon Press, 1911.

Guide Book of Yedo: The Tokio Guide, by a Resident, Yokohama: F. R. Wetmore & Co., 1874.

Guillemard, F. H. H., *The Cruise of the Marchesa to Kamschatka and New Guinea: With Notices of Formosa, Liu-Kiu and Various Islands of the Malay Archipelago*, London: John Murray, 1886.

_____, "The Years That the Locusts Have Eaten," unpublished memoirs, ca. 1930, Cambridge University Library (Syn.4.92.142-148).

Habersham, A. W., *The North Pacific Surveying and Exploring Expedition; or, My Last Cruise. Where We Went and What We Saw*, Philadelphia: J. B. Lippincott & Co., 1858.

Hacker, Arthur, "Eastern Exposure," *Hong Kong Tatler*, June 1999, pp. 95–9.

Hall, R. (ed.), *1904 Korea through Australian Eyes*, Seoul: Kyobo Book Centre, 2004.

Hammersmith, Jack L., *Spoilsmen in a "Flowery Fairyland": The Development of the US Legation in Japan, 1859–1906*, Kent, Ohio: Kent State University Press, 1998.

Hare, J. H. (ed.), *A Photographic Record of the Russo-Japanese War*, New York: P. F. Collier & Son, 1905.

Harris, David, *Of Battle and Beauty: Felice Beato's Photographs of China*, Santa Barbara: Santa Barbara Museum of Art, 1999.

Hawks, Francis L., *Narrative of the Expedition of an American Squadron to the China Seas and Japan: Performed in the Years 1852, 1853, and 1854*, Washington: A. O. P. Nicholson, 1856.

Heffernan, William J., *Edward M. Kern: The Travels of an Artist-Explorer*, Bakersfield, California: Kern County Historical Society, 1953.

Henry Smith Munroe Papers, Box 3, Connecticut Historical Society, Hartford, Connecticut.

Herbert-Gustar, A. L. and Nott, P. A., *John Milne: Father of Modern Seismology*, Tenterden: Paul Norbury Publications Ltd., 1980.

Hess, Larry L., "H. H. Bennett of Wisconsin," *Stereo World*, Vol. 18, No. 5, 1991, pp. 4–17.

Himeno Junichi, "Encounters with Foreign Photographers: The Introduction and Spread of Photography in Kyushu," in *Old Photography Study*, Sainsbury Institute for the Study of Japanese Arts and Cultures and Nagasaki University Library, March 2003, pp. 38–46.

Hine, Robert V., *Edward Kern and American Expansion*, New Haven: Yale University Press, 1962.

_____, *In the Shadow of Fremont: Edward Kern and the Art of American Exploration, 1845–1860*, Norman: University of Oklahoma Press, 1982.

Hoare, James, "British Journalists in Meiji Japan," in Ian Nish (ed.), *Britain and Japan: Biographical Portraits*, Vol. 1, Folkestone: Japan Library, 1994, pp. 20–32.

_____, *Japan's Treaty Ports and Foreign Settlements: The Uninvited Guests 1858–1899*, Sandgate: Japan Library, 1994.

Holmes, Burton E., *Burton Holmes Travelogues*, Vol. 10, New York: The McClure Company, 1910.

_____, *A Trip around the World through the Telebinocular in 3-D Pictures*, Meadowville: Keystone View Co., 1942.

Holmes, Oliver Wendell, *Soundings from the Atlantic*, London: Sampson Low, 1864.

Humphrey, S. D., *American Hand Book of the Daguerreotype: Giving the Most Approved and Convenient Methods for Preparing the Chemicals, and the Combinations Used in the Art*, 5th edn, New York: S. D. Humphrey, 1858.

Ichikawa Nizo (Ninsan), *Toto Ryogoku yagenbori Shashinshi Ukai Gyokusen shoki* (A Brief Record of the Photographer of Ryogoku Yagen-bori, Tokyo – Ukai Gyokusen), *Rissho University Cultural Bulletin*, No. 22, March 1989.

Ion, A. H., "Mountain High and Valley Low: Walter Weston (1861–1940) and Japan," in H. Cortazzi and G. Daniels (eds.), *Britain and Japan, 1859–1991: Themes and Personalities*, London: Routledge, 1991, pp. 94–106.

Iioka Sennosuke, "Ko Uchida Kuichi Tanreki" (A Brief History of the Late Uchida Kuichi), ca. 1876, Uchida family archives.

Ishiguro Keisho, "Bakumatsu shashinshi Satton woo u" (Bakumatsu Photographs by Sutton), in *Bakumatsu-Meiji no omoshiro shashin* (Interesting Photographs from the Bakumatsu and Meiji Eras), Tokyo: Corona Books, 1996, pp. 23–37.

Ishiguro Keisho (ed.), *Dai-Nippon zenkoku meisho ichiran: Itaria koshi hizo no Meiji shashincho* (A Catalogue of Famous Places throughout Greater Japan: An Italian Minister's Treasured Meiji Photograph Album), Tokyo: Heibonsha, 2001.

Itier, Jules, *Journal d'un voyage en Chine, 1843, 1844, 1845, 1846*, Paris: Dauvin & Fontaine, 1848.

Izawa Shuji, "Sketches of the Lives of a Few of the Leading Professional Photographers in Japan," *The Practical Photographer*, Vol. 7, No. 81, 1896, pp. 230–5.

James, H. A., *The Price Guide to Photographic Cards*, London: Bishopsgate Press, 1982.

"[The] Japanese Dry Plate Factory," *The Photographic Dealer*, March 1910, p. 108.

Jephson, R. M. and Elmhirst, E. P., *Our Life in Japan*, London: Chapman & Hall, 1869.

Jocelyn, William Nassau, to Robert, Earl of Roden, leafs 75 and 113 in the volume of letters written during Jocelyn's attachment to Lord Elgin's Mission in China and Japan, 1858–9, Yokohama Archives of History, Yokohama, Japan.

Jones-Parry, Captain S. H., *My Journey round the World*, London: Hurst & Blackett, 1881.

Kato Yuzo (ed.), *Yokohama Past and Present*, Yokohama: Yokohama City University, 1990.

Keeling, W. E. L., *Tourists' Guide to Yokohama, Tokio, etc.*, Tokio: A. Farsari, 1880.

Keene, Donald, "Portraits of the Emperor Meiji," *Impressions*, No. 21, 1999, pp. 17–29.

Kempler, Susan, "America 'Discovers' the World: James Ricalton's 'Travels on Next to Nothing,' 1844–1929," Ph.D. dissertation, Rutgers the State University of New Jersey, New Brunswick, 1991.

Kinoshita Naoyuki, "The Early Years of Japanese Photography," in Anne Wilkes Tucker et al., *The History of Japanese Photography*, New Haven: Yale University Press, 2003, pp. 14–99.

_____, "Shima Kakoku (1827–70)," in *The Advent of Photography in Japan*, exhibition catalogue, Tokyo: Tokyo Metropolitan Museum of Photography, 1997, pp. 178–81.

Koizumi Kinshi (ed.), *Nihon Rekishi Jinbutsu Jiten* (Biographical Dictionary of Japanese History), Tokyo: Asahi Shinbunsha, 1994.

Koyama Noburo, "The Guillemard Collection (Early Photographs of Japan) at Cambridge University Library," paper presented at the 14th Annual Conference of the European Association of Japanese Resource Specialists (EAJRS), Valenciennes, France, September 2003.

_____, *Kenburijji Daigaku hizo Meiji koshashin: Makezago no Nihonryoko* (Early Photographs of the Meiji Era at the University of Cambridge: The Journey of the Marchesa in Japan), Tokyo: Heibonsha, 2005.

Krafft, Hugues, *Souvenirs de notre tour du monde*, Paris: Hachette, 1885.

Kumamoto Prefectural Museum of Art, *Tomishige Shashinjo no 130 nen: bakumatsu kara gendai* (130 Years of the Tomishige Studio: From the Bakumatsu to the Present), exhibition catalogue, 1993.

Laidlaw, Christine Wallace (ed.), *Charles Appleton Longfellow: Twenty Months in Japan, 1871–1873*,

Cambridge, Massachusetts: Friends of the Long-fellow House, 1998.

Lambert, C., *The Voyage of the "Wanderer,"* London: Macmillan and Co., 1883.

Lane-Poole, S. and Dickins, F. V., *The Life of Sir Harry Parkes*, London: Macmillan & Co., 1894.

Lees, J. A. and Clutterbuck, W. J., *B.C. 1887: A Ramble in British Columbia*, London: Longmans, Green, & Co., 1892.

_____, *Three in Norway*, Oslo: Nor-Media A/S, 1984; first published 1882.

Lensen, George Alexander, *Report from Hokkaido: The Remains of Russian Culture in Northern Japan*, Hakodate: Municipal Library of Hakodate, 1954; reprinted Westport, Connecticut: Greenwood Press, 1973.

Lia, Beretta, "Adolfo Farsari: An Italian Photographer in Meiji Japan," *Transactions of the Asiatic Society of Japan*, Vol. 11, 1996, pp. 33–48.

Liberty, E. L., *Japan: A Pictorial Record*, London: Adam & Charles Black, 1891.

Linortner, Johann, "Michael Moser: Ein Altausseer als Fotograf in Japan," *Da Schau her. Beiträge aus dem Kulturleben des Bezirkes Liezen*, Liezen: Arbeitskreis für Heimatpflege, Vol. 8, No. 4, 1987, pp. 13–17.

Livingston, Jane, *Odyssey: The Art of Photography at National Geographic*, Charlottesville, Virginia: Thomasson-Grant, Inc., 1988.

Lloyd, A., *Every Day Japan*, London: Cassell & Co., 1909.

Lucas, C. J. (ed.), *James Ricalton's Photographs of China during the Boxer Rebellion: His Illustrated Travelogue of 1900*, Lewiston: The Edwin Mellen Press, 1990.

Mahood, R., *Photographer of the Southwest: Adam Clark Vroman 1856-1916*, Los Angeles: Ward Ritchie Press, 1961.

Manthorpe, Victoria (ed.), *The Japan Diaries of Richard Gordon Smith*, Harmondsworth: Penguin, 1986.

Matsumoto Itsuya, *Bakumatsu Hyoryu*, Tokyo: Nigen to Rekishi sha, 1993.

Matsunobu Yasuke and Yokohama Kaiko Shiryokan, *Meiji no Nihon*, Yokohama: Yurindo K. K., 1990.

McCabe, Patricia, *Gaijin Bochi: The Foreigners' Cemetery Yokohama, Japan*, Putney: British Association for Cemeteries in South Asia, 1994.

McShane, Linda, *When I Wanted the Sun to Shine*, Littleton, New Hampshire: Linda McShane, 1993.

Milne, J. and Burton, W. K., *The Great Earthquake in Japan 1891*, Yokohama: Lane, Crawford & Co., 1892.

_____, *The Volcanoes of Japan, Part 1 Fujisan*, Yokohama, ca. 1892.

Mitsui Keishi, "The Relationship between Two Portraits of Yokoi Shonan," in Tokyo Metropolitan Museum of Photography (eds.), *Samurai Nihon No Dandizumu*, Tokyo: Nigensha, 2003.

Moeshart, H. J., *Arts En Koopman in Japan 1859-1874*, Amsterdam: De Bataafsche Leeuw, 2001.

_____, "Nihon Shashinshi ni okeru Gaikokujin no Yakuwari" (The Dutch and the Introduction of Photography in Japan), in Goto Kazuo and Matsumoto Itsuya (eds.), *Yomigaeru Bakumatsu: Raiden Daigaku shashin korekushon yori* (The Bakumatsu Era Resurrected: Images from the Leiden University Photography Collection), Tokyo: Asahi Shimbunsha, 1986, pp. 221–8.

Morison, Samuel Eliot, *"Old Bruin": Commodore Matthew Galbraith Perry*, Boston: Little, Brown & Co., 1967.

Motoyasu Hiroshi, "Ono Benkichi and Photography in the Kaga Domain," in *The Advent of Photography in Japan*, exhibition catalogue, Tokyo Metropolitan Museum of Photography, 1997, pp. 169–72.

Murphy, Kathryn Ricalton, "The Life of James Ricalton," unpublished MSS by Ricalton's daughter; quoted in Helen B. Bates, *Maplewood Past and Present: A Miscellany*, Princeton: Princeton University Press, 1948, p. 75.

Nagasaki Kiyouyuchi Gaikokujin Meiroku, Vol. 1, Nagasaki: Nagasaki Kenritsu Toshokan, 2004.

Nigano Shigeichi, Iizawa Kotaro, and Kinoshita Naoyuki (eds.), *Nihon no shashinka 2: Tamoto Kenzo to Meiji no shashinka tachi* (Photographers of Japan, Part 2: Tamoto Kenzo and the Photographers of the Meiji era), Tokyo: Iwanami Shoten, 1999.

Nishina Matsuke, "Shashin-jutsu no kaiso wa betsu ni ita: Edo de saisho ni shashin-kan o hiraita Ukai Gyokusen" (The Founder of Photography in Japan Was Somebody Else: Ukai Gyokusen, the Man Who Opened the First Photographic Studio in Edo), *Photo Art*, September 1969.

_____, "Ukai Gyokusen and Utagawa Kuniyoshi," *Kikan Ukiyo-e*, Nos. 146 & 147, 1969.

Nordenskiold, Adolf Erik (trans. Alexander Leslie), *The Voyage of the Vega round Asia and Europe, with a Historical Review of Previous Journeys along the North Coast of the Old World*, London: Macmillan & Co., 1885.

Norton, Russell, "Preliminary Checklist of French Stereo Card Photographers and Publishers," *The Photographic Collector*, Vol. 5, No. 3, 1985, pp. 278–96.

Notehelfer, F. G. (ed.), *Japan through American Eyes: The Journal of Francis Hall, Kanagawa and Yokohama 1859-1866*, Princeton: Princeton University Press, 1992.

O'Conner, R., *Jack London: A Biography*, London: Victor Gollancz Ltd, 1965.

Oechsle, Rob, *Aoi Me Ga Mita Dai Ryukyu* (Old Okinawa Seen through Blue Eyes), Naha City: Nirai Sha, 1987.

Ogawa Dosokai (ed.), *Sogyo Kinen Sanju Nenshi* (Thirty Years' Celebration of Photography Business), Tokyo: Ogawa Shashin Seibansho, 1913.

Ogawa K., *Fuji San*, Tokyo: Ogawa Shashin Seihanjo, 1912.

Ogawa Kazumasa, *Shinkoku Pekin kojo shashincho* (Photographs of Palace Buildings of Peking), Tokyo: K. Ogawa, 1906.

Oliphant, Laurence, *Narrative of the Earl of Elgin's Mission to China and Japan in the Years 1857, '58, '59*, Edinburgh: William Blackwood & Sons, 1859.

Ono, P. and Wright, E. A., "Tourist Photographs of the 1930s: The Work of 'T. Enami'," *Daruma*, Vol. 4, No. 3, 1997, pp. 38–44.

Ozawa Takesi, *Bakumatsu Shashin no Jidai* (The Era of Bakumatsu Photography), Tokyo: Chikuma Shobo, 1994.

_____, "The History of Early Photography in Japan," *History of Photography*, Vol. 5, No. 4, 1981, pp. 285–303.

_____, *Shashin de Miru Bakumatsu Meiji* (The Bakumatsu and Meiji Eras as Seen in Early Photographs), Tokyo: Sekai Bunkasha, 1990.

Palmer, Frederick, "About 'Jimmy' Hare," *Collier's Weekly*, February 25th, 1905, p. 18.

Palmquist, Peter E., "California's Peripatetic Photographer Charles Leander Weed," *California History*, Vol. 58, No. 3, 1979, pp. 195–219.

_____, *Lawrence & Houseworth/Thomas Houseworth & Co.: A Unique View of the West 1860-1886*, Columbus, Ohio: National Stereoscopic Association, 1980.

Palmquist, P. E. and Kailbourn, T. R., *Pioneer Photographers of the Far West: A Biographical Dictionary, 1840-1865*, Stanford: Stanford University Press, 2000.

Parker, Calvin F., *The Japanese Sam Patch*, Notre Dame: Cross Cultural Publications, 2001.

_____, *Jonathan Goble of Japan: Marine, Missionary, Maverick*, Lanham: University Press of America, 1990.

Paske-Smith, M., *Western Barbarians in Japan and Formosa*, New York: Arno Press, 1968.

Paullin, Charles O., *American Voyages to the Orient 1690-1865*, Annapolis, Maryland: United States Naval Institute, 1971.

Pedlar, Neil, "Appendix 11: Freemasons of Yokohama 1866-1896," in *An Indexed List of British Marriages Solemnized during Extraterritoriality 1860-1899 in Japan*, Newquay: Four Turnings Publications, 1993.

_____, *The Imported Pioneers*, Folkestone: Japan Library, 1990.

Phillips, David, C., "Art for Industry's Sake: Halftone Technology, Mass Photography and the Social Transformation of American Print Culture, 1880–1920," Ph.D. dissertation, Yale University, 1996.

Pineau, Roger, *The Japan Expedition 1852-1854: The Personal Journal of Commodore Matthew C. Perry*, Washington: Smithsonian Institution Press, 1968.

Pitkin, Thomas C., manuscript papers, Washington, DC: Library of Congress, Pitkin, folder 2, frag. 14.

Plummer, Katherine, *The Shogun's Reluctant Ambassadors: Sea Drifters*, Tokyo: Lotus Press, 1984.

Ponting, H. G., *Fuji San*, Tokyo: K. Ogawa, 1905.

_____, *In Lotus Land Japan*, London: Macmillan & Co., 1910.

_____, *Japanese Studies*, Yokohama: Kelly & Walsh Ltd, 1906.

Poole, O. M., *The Death of Old Yokohama in the Great Japanese Earthquake of 1923*, London: George Allen & Unwin Ltd, 1968.

_____, *The Tokaido*, New York: The Lotus Press, 1892.

Raemy, Alfred, *Livre D'or du Canton de Freibug: Nomenclature des Bourgeois de la Ville de Freiburg des Anciennes Familles Patriciennes et des Notablities et Celebrites du Canton*, Freiburg: Bonny, 1898.

Rea, Mary Alice, private journal, 1881, Yokohama Archives of History Museum.

Ribaud, M. Michel, *Japonais et Ainos Dans Le Yeso (Kokkaido) Un Ete au Japon Boreal*, Paris: Delhomne et Briguet, 1897.

[Ricalton, J.], *China through the Stereoscope*, New York: Underwood & Underwood, 1901.

Ricalton, J., *India through the Stereoscope*, New York: Underwood & Underwood, 1907.

_____, "My Travels on Next to Nothing," *Outing*, No. 10, April–October 1887.

_____, "Strange Sleeping Places in 500,000 Miles of Travel," *South Orange Record*, April 1st, 1921.

Rogers, G. W., "Early Recollections of Yokohama," *Japan Weekly Mail*, December 5th, 1903, pp. 629–32.

Romer, Grant, "Near the Temple at Yokushen," *Image*, Vol. 29, No. 2, 1986, pp. 1–11.

Rosenberg, Gert, "Michael Moser: Photographer (1853–1912)," *Camera Austria*, No. 17, 1985, p. 33.

_____, *Wilhelm Burger: Ein Welt-und Forschungsreisender mit der Kamera, 1844-1920*, Wien and Munchen: Christian Brandstatter, 1984.

Rosin, Henry, "Etudes sur les debuts de la photographie japonaise au 19e siecle," *Bulletin de l'Association franco-japonaise*, No. 16, April 1987, pp. 33–9.

Saito Takio, *Bakumatsu Meiji: Yokohama Shashinkan Monogatari*, Tokyo: Yoshikawa Kobunshakan, 2004.

_____, "The First Photography in Yokohama and William Saunders," *The PhotoHistorian*, No. 86, 1989, pp. 62–3.

_____, *Saishoku arubamu – Meiji no Nihon –Yokohama shashin no sekai*, Yokohama: Yurindo, 1990.

_____, "Shimooka Renjo (1823-1914)," in *The Advent of Photography in Japan*, exhibition catalogue, Tokyo: Tokyo Metropolitan Museum of Photography, 1997, pp. 173–7.

_____ (ed.), *Bakumatsu, Meiji Zainichi Gaikokujin Kikan Meikan 1861-1912* (Foreign Residents' Directory of the Bakumatsu and Meiji Periods 1861-1912), Tokyo: Yumani Shoboh, 1996–7.

Sandwith, J. H., *A Trip into the Interior of Japan, Being the Journal of J. H. Sandwith, Lieutenant, Royal Marines, from the 20th August to the 20th September, 1871*, 2nd edn, Yokohama: Japan Gazette, 1872.

Sasaki Shigeichi, *The Illustrated Japan Directory*, Yokohama: S. Sasaki, 1886.

Satow, E. M. and Hawes, A. G. S., *A Handbook for Travellers in Central and Northern Japan*, 2nd edn, London: John Murray, 1884; first published Yokohama: Kelly & Co., 1881.

"74 nen-mae noshitsuban: Ukai-o no shashin-zuka kara no hakkutsu" (Wet Plates from 74 Years Ago: Excavation of Mr Ukai's Monument to Photography), *Sun Photo Journal*, October 20th, 1956.

Sharf, F. A., "A Traveler's Paradise," in E. K. Usui and M. Polizzotti (eds.), *Art and Artifice: Japanese Photographers of the Meiji Era*, Boston: Museum of Fine Arts, Boston, 2004, pp. 7–14.

Singer, Noel F., "Felice Beato's Burmese Days," *Arts of Asia*, Vol. 28, No. 5, 1998, pp. 96–107.

Smith, Albert, *To China and Back*, Hong Kong: Hong Kong University Press, 1974.

Smith, George, *Ten Weeks in Japan*, London: Longman, Green, & Co., 1861.

Stafford Ransome, J., *Japan in Transition*, London: Harper & Brothers, 1899.

Stapp, Will (contrib.), *Early Works of Photography*, exhibition catalogue, Tokyo Metropolitan Museum of Photography, 1992.

Stoddard, J. L., *John L. Stoddard's Lectures*, Chicago: Geo. L. Shuman & Co., 1911; first published 1897.

Suchomel, F. and Suchomelova, M., *Journal of a Voyage: The Erwin Dubsky Collection: Photographs from Japan in the 1870s*, Brno, Czech Republic: The Moravian Gallery in Brno, 2006.

Sutton, F. W., *First Reading for Lantern Exhibitions of Travels in the Eastern Island World, China, Loo-Choo, and Japan: Readings and Photographs by F. W. Sutton, R.N.*, London: W. F. Stanley, ca. 1882.

Tajima Shi'ichi (ed.), *Selected Relics of Japanese Art, Volumes I–XX (Shimbi Taikan)*, Kyoto: Nippon Bukkyo Shimbi Kyokwai, 1899–1908.

Taylor, Bayard, *A Visit to India, China, and Japan in the Year 1853*, New York: G. P. Putnam's Sons, 1855.

Taylor, D. Crane, *John L. Stoddard: Traveller, Lecturer, Litterateur*, New York: P. J. Kenedy & Sons, 1935.

Terry, T. P., *Terry's Japanese Empire*, Boston and New York: Houghton Mifflin Company, 1914.

Thiriez, Regine, *Barbarian Lens*, The Netherlands: Gordon & Breach Publishers, 1998.

Tilley, Henry Arthur, *Japan, the Amoor, and the Pacific*, London: Smith, Elder & Co., 1861.

Todd, Mabel Loomis, *Corona and Coronet*, Boston: Houghton, Mifflin & Co., 1898.

_____, "In Aino-Land," *The Century*, July 1898.

Tomita Gentaro, *Stranger's Handbook of the Japanese Language*, 2nd edn, Yokohama: Kelly & Walsh, 1893.

Trachtenbergh, Alan, *Reading Photographs: Images as History, Mathew Brady to Walker Evans*, New York: Hill & Wang, 1989.

Trautman, Frederic, *With Perry to Japan: A Memoir by William Heine*, Honolulu: University of Hawaii Press, 1990.

Treadwell, T. K., *The Stereoviews of H. H. Bennett*, Texas: The Institute for Photographic Research, 2002.

Treadwell, T. K. and Treadwell, J., *Catalog of Current Original Stereoscopic Views Published by the New Photographic Company*, Texas: The Institute for Photographic Research, 2003.

Tucker, Anne Wilkes et al., *The History of Japanese Photography*, New Haven: Yale University Press, 2003.

Ueno Hikoma and Horie Kuwajiro, *Shamitsu-kyoku hikkei* (Manual of Chemistry), Nagasaki, 1862.

Ueno Ichiro et al., *Shashin no Kaiso: Ueno Hikoma. Shashin ni Miru Bakumatsu Meiji* (Memoirs of Photography: Ueno Hikoma. Bakumatsu and Meiji as Seen through His Photographs), Tokyo: Sangyo Noritsu Tanki Daigaku Shuppanbu, 1975.

Umemoto Sadao and Kobayashi Shujiro, *Nihon Shashin Kai no Bukko Korosho Kenshoruku* (Late Meritorious Photographers in the World of Japanese Photography), Tokyo: Nihon Shashin Kyokai, 1952.

Van Zandt, Howard, F., *Pioneer American Merchants in Japan*, Tokyo: Lotus Press Ltd, 1981.

Waldron, Theodore (ed.), *Letters and Journals of James, Eighth Earl of Elgin*, London: John Murray, 1872.

Waldsmith, John, *Stereo Views: An Illustrated History and Price Guide*, Iola: Krause Publications, 2002.

Warriner, Emily, V., *Voyager to Destiny*, Indianapolis: The Bobbs-Merrill Company, Inc., 1956.

Webb, William and Weinstein, Robert, *Dwellers at the Source: Southwestern Indian Photographs of A. C. Vroman, 1895–1904*, Albuquerque: University of New Mexico Press, 1992.

Weppner, Margaretha, *The North Star and the Southern Cross: Being the Personal Experiences, Impressions and Observations of Margaretha Weppner, in a Two Years' Journey round the World*, New York: Margaretha Weppner, 1876.

Westfield, T. C., *The Japanese: Their Manners and Customs*, London: Photographic News Office, 1862.

Weston, W., *Mountaineering and Exploration in the Japanese Alps*, London: John Murray, 1896.

_____, *The Playground of the Far East*, London: John Murray, 1918.

White, H. C., *The Twentieth Century Way*, North Bennington, Vermont: H. C. White Co., 1908.

White, Stephen, "The Far East," *Image*, Vol. 34, Nos. 1–2, 1991, pp. 39–47.

Williams, Harold, S., manuscript collection, National Library of Australia, Canberra.

Wing, Paul, *Stereoscopes: The First One Hundred Years*, Nashua, New Hampshire: Transition Publishing, 1996.

Woods, Sir Henry F., *Spunyarn: Strands from a Sailor's Life*, London: Hutchinson & Co., 1924.

Worswick, Clark, "The Disappearance of Uchida, Kyuichi and the Discovery of Nineteenth-century Asian Photography," *Image*, Vol. 36, Nos. 1–2, 1993, pp. 17–31.

_____, *Imperial China: Photographs 1850–1912*, New York: Pennwick Publishing, 1978.

_____, *Japan Photographs 1854–1905*, London: Hamish Hamilton, 1980.

_____, "Notes on Japanese Collections of Photographs," *Worswick Collection of Japanese Photographs*, Tokyo: Pacific Press Service, 1988, pp. 1–3.

Worswick Collection, held at the Tokyo offices of Pacific Press Service.

Yamaguchi Saiichiro, "Shashin Jireki" (The Story of Photography), in *Shashin Shinpo*, Tokyo: Haku-bundo Shoten, Nos. 46–48, 1893.

Yokoe Fuminori, "The Arrival of Photography in Japan," in *The Advent of Photography in Japan*, exhibition catalogue, Tokyo: Tokyo Metropolitan Museum of Photography, 1997, pp. 166–8.

_____, "Yokoyama Matsusaburo (1838–84)," in *The Advent of Photography in Japan*, exhibition catalogue, Tokyo: Tokyo Metropolitan Museum of Photography, 1997, pp. 182–3.

Yokohama Kaiko Shiryokan, *Saishoku Arubamu: Meiji no Nihon-Yokohama Sashin no Sekai* (Hand-colored Albums: Meiji Era Japan, and the World of Yokohama Photographs), Yokohama: Yurindo, 1990.

Yokohama Kaiko Shiryokan (ed.), *Bakumatsu Nihon no Fukei to Hitobi: Ferikusu Beato Shashin-shu* (The Scenery and People of the Bakumatsu Era: The Photographs of Felix Beato), Yokohama: Heibunsha, 1987.

Yokota Yoichi (ed.), *Meiji no Yokohama/Tokyo* (Meiji Era Yokohama and Tokyo), Yokohama: Meiji no Yokohama/Tokyo o Kanko Suru Kai, 1989.

Index of Commercial and Amateur Photographers in Japan, 1853–1912

This list refers only to those photographers and studios mentioned in this book. It does not attempt to cover the many Japanese portrait studios whose numbers grew from the early 1860s onwards. They can be found in the publication *Portraits in Sepia* (2000) by Boyd and Izakura. Pages numbers for the main entry of each photographer/studio are given in brackets.

AKITSU CO. (THE) (p. 245) Traded in Yokohama as the Fine Art Depot and Manufacturing Association between 1892 and 1896. It offered a range of art objects, including bronzes, ivory and wood carvings, Satsuma porcelain, and photographs. There is an apparent connection with Kusakabe who is listed as the manager in 1893. The company also boasted of a portfolio of more than 2000 photographs of views and costumes of Japan, matching the number that Kusakabe himself was advertising at this time.

ANDERSEN, Hermann (p. 153) Appeared on the Yokohama scene in 1874 as a clerk/book-keeper and was the German half of the Stillfried and Andersen partnership which he had joined by 1876. It is possible he was an amateur photographer at this time but almost nothing is known about his life. Following an acrimonious split with Stillfried in 1878, Andersen took a more active role in photography as proprietor of Stillfried and Andersen. He left Japan in 1883. His work is yet to be identified.

ANDREW, William Parke (p. 118) English photographer in partnership with Charles Parker from September 1863 to July 1865. It is not known if he was previously an amateur or commercial photog-

rapher. He announced his own Yokohama studio in an October 1865 newspaper advertisement. The studio was very short-lived.

AZUKIZAWA Ryoichi (p. 217) Taught by Yoko-yama Matsusaburo in the 1870s, he opened a Tokyo studio in the early 1880s. He described himself as a "Patent Oil-Painter on Photograph and Lithograph, and Common Oil-Painter and Photographer." He had devised a special photographic oil-painting process for which he was granted a fifteen-year patent in 1885.

BARON STILLFRIED (p. 154) Trading name for Baron Franz von Stillfried-Ratenicz' Yokohama studio 1879–83.

BARRY, Richard (p. 291) American photo-journalist who covered the 1904–5 Russo-Japanese War. He took photographs on behalf of the stereoview publishers T. W. Ingersoll.

BAUDUIN, Albert Johannes (1829–90) **(p. 118)** Younger brother to Antonius and also an enthusiastic photographer. He arrived in Japan in 1859 as a merchant and became Dutch Consul at Nagasaki in 1863.

BAUDUIN, Antonius Franciscus (1820–85) **(p. 118)** Dutch physician who succeeded Pompe van Meerdervoort in 1862 as the chief medical officer attached to the Yoseiji Hospital in Nagasaki until 1864. He was an enthusiastic amateur photographer who took many photographs in and around Nagasaki.

BEATO, Felix (1834/5–ca. 1907) **(p. 86)** The most famous Western photographer to have worked in Japan, being equally talented in landscape and portraiture. He arrived around June 1863 and operated a Yokohama studio until 1877 when it was sold to Stillfried and Andersen. He was of Italian ancestry but was probably born in Corfu and subsequently became a British citizen. He left Japan penniless in 1884 and subsequently settled in Burma. The place and date of his death remain unknown. He is thought by many to be the best Western photographer to work in Japan during the Bakumatsu and early Meiji eras.

BELCHER, H. W. (p. 256) Amateur photographer and mountaineer who took photographs of alpine Japan whilst climbing with Walter Weston in 1891.

BIGOT, Georges (1860–1927) **(p. 229)** French artist and cartoonist who resided in Japan 1883–9. He was an accomplished photographer who, like many artists, used his camera to assist in his artistic endeavors.

BIRD (née Bishop), Isabella (1831–1904) **(p. 227)** Writer, traveler, explorer and amateur photographer. Bird visited Japan four times between 1878 and 1896.

BLACK, John Reddie (1826–80) **(p. 146)** Journalist, publisher, singer, and photographer. Black came to Japan in 1864 and in 1870 started publishing *The Far East*, a fortnightly magazine with original photographs as illustrations. Although he relied upon the staff photographer Michael Moser and external contributors, Black periodically supplemented their work with his own photographs. In September 1876 he set up The Far East Art Agency which sold works of art and photographs, presumably taken from negatives used in *The Far East*.

BOLAK (p. 292) Unknown photographer who photographed the Ainu and the Japanese silkworm industry around 1910. That year *The Illustrated London News* published a selection of his work.

BOTTLEWALLA, H. E. (p. 291) Kobe-based merchant and amateur photographer (1899–1905). He produced his own presentation souvenir album, "Scenic Japan, An Album of Photographs of the Chief Places of Interest."

BROEK, Jan Karel Van den (1814–65) **(p. 36)** Dutch physician at Deshima 1853–7 who gave photography lessons in Nagasaki in 1856 and whose students included Furukawa Shumpei and Yoshio Keisai.

BROUWER, L. (p. 259) Unknown amateur (?) Yokohama photographer who arrived in Japan in

1891 and in 1894 advertised "my large and fine collection of views of Japan, China, Corea and Java, coloured and uncoloured ... also stereoscopic views and magic lantern slides."

BROWN, Eliphalet, M., Jr. (1816–86) **(p. 27)** Accomplished American daguerreotypist, lithographer, and artist. He was appointed official photographer to Perry's 1852–4 Japan Expedition. He took daguerreotypes on Okinawa in May or June 1853, and mainland Japan from February 1854. Only six of some 400 reported daguerreotypes have so far been destroyed. Some were destroyed in an 1865 Philadelphia fire. He has the distinction of taking the earliest surviving photographs in Japan. He gave up commercial photography after the expedition and embarked on a naval career until his retirement in 1875.

BROWN, Julia Maria (1840–1919) **(p. 56)** Eldest daughter of the American missionary Samuel Brown who probably learnt photography in 1860 from her friend Francis Hall. She appears to be the first recorded female photographer in Japan. She gave some assistance to Shimooka Renjo.

BROWN, Samuel Robbins (1810–80) **(p. 54)** American missionary who arrived in Japan in November 1859. The father of Julia Brown, probably the first female photographer in Japan. He taught himself photography between 1860 and 1861 and gave lessons to Shimooka Renjo. In October 1862 he sent forty-three photographs of Japanese scenery back to his Church in America. In the same month he accompanied the US Minister Pruyn to Edo and took photographs.

BURGER, Wilhelm Joseph (1844–1920) **(p. 109)** Exceptionally talented Austrian commercial photographer appointed as the official photographer to the Austria-Hungary Mission which arrived in Nagasaki in September 1869 and Yokohama in October. The mission left in November but Burger stayed until March 1870. He secured a stunning series of landscapes and genre subjects and also photographed Japanese works of art.

BURNSIDE-JOHNSON Miss C. (p. 292) Unknown amateur who took photographs of the Ainu in Hokkaido around 1904.

BURTON, Professor William Kinninmond (1856–99) **(p. 252)** Scottish by birth, Burton came to Japan in 1887 as an engineer. By then he was already well known as a prolific writer and expert on photography. Through friendships with Ogawa Kazumasa, Kajima Seibei, and others, Burton was able to assist in the development of Japanese photography and oversee the introduction of many new photography techniques. In 1889 he founded the Nihon Shashin Kyokai (Photographic Society of Japan) and in 1893 organized Japan's first International Photographic Exhibition. This event first introduced art photography to the country. He personally photographed the aftermath of the 1891 Gifu earthquake and co-authored a book of the event with seismologist John Milne.

CHAMPION, Paul (1838–?) **(p. 121)** Distinguished French chemist and gifted amateur who also edited the *Bulletin De La Société Française De Photographie*. He was sent to China and Japan in 1865–6 by La société française de l'acclimatation for zoological specimens. Champion also brought back many stereoviews and large-format photographs.

CHEONG Tong (p. 229) Yokohama-based Chinese photographer whose studio was open for one year in 1884 but was not a success. Whether Cheong was related to the only other Yokohama Chinese photographer, Cheong Hung, is not known.

CHONG Hung (p. 164) Chinese photographer who ran a Yokohama studio from 1875 to 1885. His name was also rendered as Cheong or Chiong.

CLARK, E. WARREN (p. 164) American missionary and amateur photographer in Japan 1871–5. In 1872 he gave the Emperor and Empress a magic lantern slide show at the Imperial Palace.

CLARK, D. R. (p. 162) American photographer who passed through Japan in 1874 on his way to Vladivostok as senior photographer for the expedition which was recording the Transit of Venus. He

produced a small series of stereoviews containing Japanese scenes.

CLUTTERBUCK, Walter John (1853–1937) **(p. 248)** English aristocrat, travel writer, and talented pictorialist photographer. He photographed in Okinawa from December 1898 to January 1899 following a photographic tour of mainland Japan.

COCHRANE, Julian (p. 291) American photojournalist who covered the 1904–5 Russo-Japanese War. He took photographs on behalf of the stereoview publishers Keystone Company.

COCKING, Samuel (p. 162) Australian amateur and long-term Yokohama resident and merchant. He was a founding member of the Nihon Shashin Kyokai (Photographic Society of Japan). In 1877 he had a successful business importing photographic equipment. He was also the first to import the Kodak camera in 1890–1.

COLLINS, Charles Miller (1820–1909) **(p. 126)** Amateur photographer and fleet engineer in the Royal Navy who used his stereo camera to take views in Yokohama in 1862.

COUTEUR, Wilson Le (1853–1925) **(p. 257)** Australian amateur photographer and writer who visited and photographed in Japan during 1899.

CRANE, William Almeida (1833–1903) **(p. 120)** English accountant and amateur photographer who entered into partnership with Charles Parker on November 1st, 1865 as Parker, Crane & Co. This lasted one or two months only and by June 1866 Crane was advertising his own Yokohama studio. His advertisements continued until December after which Crane was no longer involved with commercial photographic activities.

DOUGLAS, John (p. 160) An American who worked for Stillfried and Andersen from 1878 to 1883 and then left to open his own Yokohama studio. Shortly after opening, it was destroyed in a fire and Douglas left Japan.

E. PARANT & CO. (p. 160) A very short-lived Kobe studio in 1870, almost certainly operated by the Frenchman C. Parant. It is the earliest known Western studio in Kobe.

EDGERTON, Edward A. (ca. 1827–?) **(p. 34)** American lawyer turned daguerreotypist. He resided at Shimoda from March to June 1855 and took daguerreotypes. He is the likely photographer of the 1855 daguerreotype of the American gravestones in the cemetery at Shimoda. He operated a commercial studio in Singapore from 1858 to ca. 1860. Subsequently, he operated a studio in Gowanda, New York, ca. 1870s. He may have been the first photographer in East Asia to offer hand-colored photographs since he was advertising in Singapore in February 1858 for a colorist.

ENAMI Tamotsu (p. 232) Assumed to be the same person as Enami Nobukuni. He is a major Japanese photographer who trained under Ogawa Kazumasa before setting up his Yokohama studio in 1892 which may have operated until the 1940s. He was a dynamic individual who had branches in the Philippines and Hong Kong, and a portfolio encompassing those territories as well as Japan, Singapore, and China. Enami sold souvenir albums, individual photographs of all sizes, and had a major share of the stereoview and lantern slides market. He was Japan's most talented stereo-photographer. His work was published internationally.

ENDO Rikuro (p. 192) Operated a studio in Sendai from 1878. He photographed the eruption of nearby Mount Bandai in 1888. In 1891 he was the official photographer on an expedition to the Kuril Islands. In 1902 he moved to Taiwan and opened a studio there.

ESAKI Reiji (1845–1910) **(p. 165)** Major Japanese photographer who apprenticed for a short time in 1870 to Shimooka Renjo. After opening his first studio in Tokyo in 1871, his business developed steadily and he was able to move to a grand studio in 1889. Esaki is credited with being the first Japanese to employ dry-plate technology and he used this when photographing the funeral procession of Iwakura Tomomi in 1883. The following year he became the first to capture a lunar eclipse in Japan.

FAIRWEATHER, Angus C. (p. 124) English amateur photographer who took views and portraits in Japan during the 1860s using the collodion dry-plate process.

FARSARI, Adolfo (1841–98) **(p. 219)** One of the most colorful photographers of nineteenth-century Japan. He opened his first studio in Yokohama in 1885 by acquiring the stock, negatives, and goodwill of the Japan Photographic Association (Stillfried and Andersen). This was a time of fierce price competition and Farsari bucked the trend by charging more but focusing on quality. At the peak of his popularity, when he was providing very serious competition to Kusakabe and Tamamura in the sale of souvenir albums, he left Japan in 1890 and returned to Italy.

FAUCHERY, Antoine Julien (1823–61) **(p. 104)** Commercial French photographer who arrived in Nagasaki from Shanghai, unwell, in January 1861. He moved on to Yokohama and died there in April. It is not known whether his illness enabled him to photograph in Japan.

FINE ART DEPOT AND MANUFACTURING ASSOCIATION (p. 245) *See* Akitsu Co.

FISLER, L. F. (p. 164) Photographer based in Shanghai who was a serious rival to William Saunders in the 1870s. An 1877 advertisement mentioned he had Japanese views and portraits for sale which he had personally taken.

FLOYD, William Pryor (p. 162) Fine British commercial photographer who operated a studio in Hong Kong from 1867. He also occasionally photographed the local Japanese community.

FREEMAN, Orrin Erastus (1830–66) **(p. 58)** Early American pioneer who opened the first commercial photo studio in Japan following a move to Yokohama from Shanghai in late 1859 or early 1860. He taught the first Japanese professional photographer, Ukai Gyokusen, and sold him his ambrotype equipment and used the proceeds to develop an extremely successful general store business. He died unexpectedly in Yokohama in 1866.

FUKASAWA Tadashi (p. 295) Kobe-based dealer in composite souvenir albums and general curios 1901–8. Whether Fukasawa operated a portrait studio is not known. He was possibly connected with Okamoto Rokuhei since Fukasawa's studio used the same stag's head trademark logo.

FUKUSUISHA (p. 217) Studio name used by Mizuno Hanbei which appeared in 1892–3 advertisements.

FURUKAWA Shumpei (p. 36) Samurai of Fukuoka domain who studied photography under Jan Karel Van den Broek at Nagasaki in 1856.

FUTAMI Asama (1852–1908) **(p. 192)** Apprenticed to Kitaniwa Tsukuba for four years from 1869 and thereafter worked with Stillfried until 1876. He opened his own studio in Tokyo in 1877 and in that year photographed the peak and crater of Mount Fuji.

GENROKUKAN (p. 240) The name of Kajima Seibei's ambitious Tokyo-based photographic business, "The Most Complete Photographic Establishment in the Orient," which opened in February 1895. It quickly ran up heavy losses and was forced to close. From March 1896 Kajima may no longer have been involved. It is not clear what happened to the business or whether it was connected to the Genroku-kwan. *See* Genroku-kwan; Kajima Seibei; Okamoto Rokuhei; Tokyo Genrokukan.

GENROKU-KWAN (p. 245) The studio name for Okamaoto Rokuhei's Tokyo-based business which ran from ca. 1901 until at least 1913. *See* Okamoto Rokuhei.

GENROKU-KWAN (Koda & Co.) (p. 295) Photographic studio and dealers in composite souvenir albums which operated in Yokohama during the year 1902. This must have been an unsuccessful attempt to expand, through Koda & Co., the Tokyo-based Genroku-kwan operation.

GENTHE, Arnold (1869–1942) **(p. 274)** One of the leading commercial photographers in America, with studios in San Francisco and New York. He initially attained fame as a portrait photographer in San Francisco, where he also photographed the Chinese in the city and the aftermath of the 1906 earthquake. An interest in oriental art took him to Japan in 1908, where he spent six months touring the country and taking photographs.

GODDARD, John (ca. 1824–1903) **(p. 161)** British photographer employed by Felix Beato as an assistant from 1869 to 1873.

GORDES, Auguste (ca. 1846–94) **(p. 142)** French commercial photographer who came to Japan in around 1870. He opened a studio in Osaka in 1871, the first foreign studio in that city. By 1875 the studio had moved to Kobe. During 1877–9 he appears to have worked in Vladivostok, probably with his brother Henri. The brothers ran a photo studio in Nagasaki from 1880 until 1888. Auguste was buried with his brother in Nagasaki in 1894. How the brothers split their photographic activities is not known and further research is required.

GORDES BROTHERS (p. 142) French photo studio that operated in Japan between the years 1871 (or earlier) and 1888, the longest running Western studio in nineteenth-century Japan.

GORDES, Henri Eugene Marie (ca. 1842–89) **(p. 142)** French commercial photographer and merchant who, together with his brother Auguste, managed the longest running foreign studio in Japan from ca. 1871 to 1888. Henri was in Nagasaki by 1862 and was employed for a time by Glover & Co. He set up his own merchanting firm, Henri Gordes & Co., in 1867. The same year he visited Kobe and taught photography to Hiramura Tokubei. In 1868 he taught Hanabuchi Tamesuke and Wakabayashi Koka; 1869, Moriwawa Shinshichi; 1871, Tomita Juhan (Shigenori). However, it is not until 1872 that the *Japan Directory* for that year lists the Gordes Brothers and gives their occupation as photographers, based in Osaka – the first Western studio in that city. By 1875 the studio has moved to Kobe. It seems possible that Henri ran a branch studio in Nagasaki. From 1877 to 1879 it is likely that he lived in Vladivostok with his brother. By 1880 both are listed as running a studio in Nagasaki which continued until 1888. Henri died in Nagasaki in 1889.

GORDON SMITH, Richard (1858–1918) **(p. 292)** Wealthy English amateur photographer, traveler, and big-game hunter. He arrived in Japan in 1898 and settled in Kobe. He spent several years in the country and took numerous photos.

GOSHKEVICH, Iosif Antonovich (1814–75) **(p. 117)** Russian Consul at Hakodate (1859–65) and amateur photographer who taught Kizu Kokichi, Yokoyama Matsusaburo, and Yanagawa Shunzo.

GOWER, Abel Anthony James (ca. 1836–ca. 98) **(p. 116)** British career diplomat and enthusiastic amateur photographer who arrived in Japan in June 1859 and is credited with an early view of Nagasaki. He accompanied Minister Alcock in 1861 on an overland journey from Nagasaki to Edo and took some photographs en route.

GRATAMA, Dr Koenraad Wolter (1831–88) **(p. 118)** He was Antonius Bauduin's successor in 1864 and was also keen on photography. He was based in Japan from 1866 to 1871.

GUILLEMARD, Francis Henry Hill (1852–1933) **(p. 224)** A wealthy English travel writer, naturalist, and amateur photographer who took the earliest recorded dry-plate photographs in Japan in June 1882. Guillemard left England in April 1882 on the schooner yacht *Marchesa* and embarked on a two-year world cruise. Whilst in Japan he employed the services of Usui Shusaburo and his brother.

GULICK, Orramel Hinckley (1830–1923) **(p. 125)** American missionary and amateur who took photographs in Edo in October 1862, having been invited by the US Minister Pruyn. The party also included William Saunders and Samuel Robbins Brown.

HALL, Francis (1822–1902) **(p. 57)** American journalist, merchant, and amateur photographer who lived in Japan from 1859 to 1866. He was close friends with D. B. Simmons and S. R. Brown. He photographed enthusiastically between May 1860 and April 1862, initially using Simmons' photographic room. Only one surviving photograph has been identified.

HAMILTON, H. J. (p. 256) Amateur photographer and mountaineer who took photographs of alpine Japan whilst climbing with Walter Weston in 1894.

HARE, James Henry (1856–1946) **(p. 286)** Celebrated British photo-journalist and war photographer. In 1904 he covered the 1904–5 Russo-Japanese War in Korea and Manchuria. He retired in 1922.

HIMEN, J. (p. 260) Listed in the 1895 and 1896 *Japan Directory* as managing the Yokohama-based Japan Photographic Co. Whether this was a studio or photographic supplies outlet is not clear.

HOLLAND, Lieutenant Swinton C. (1843–1922) **(p. 161)** British naval officer and amateur photographer who took photographs in Wakayama in 1870. In 1871 Holland traveled to Hokkaido and photographed the Ainu and local scenery.

HOLMES, Elias Burton (1870–1958) **(p. 258)** Holmes followed in the footsteps of his fellow American and mentor John Stoddard, and became a famous travel lecturer. Holmes took many of his own photographs which were converted onto hand-colored lantern slides. His first visit to Japan was in 1892, and he met John Stoddard on the voyage out. In Kyoto in 1899 Holmes was the first to use a movie camera in Japan.

HORI Masumi (Yohei) (1826–80) **(p. 126)** Opened an early studio in Kyoto in 1865 which remained under family control until 1942.

HORIE Kuwajiro (p. 41) Learnt wet-plate photography in Nagasaki from Pierre Rossier some time between 1859 and 1860. In 1860 Horie and fellow student Ueno Hikoma were provided with money by Lord Todo of the Tsu domain to purchase a camera and continue experiments at the *daimyo*'s estate in Edo. He co-wrote *Shamitsu-kyoku hikkei* (Manual of Chemistry) with Ueno in 1862.

ICHIDA Sota (1843–96) **(p. 184)** Opened a studio in Kyoto in 1868 but relocated to Kobe in 1870. Ichida's studio was dominant in Kobe well into the 1920s. Ichida himself retired in 1887 and handed over to his son.

ICHIKI Shiro (1828–1903) **(p. 35)** Satsuma retainer ordered by Lord Shimazu to study photography in 1851. With Ujuku Hikoemon he took a daguerreotype of Lord Shimazu on September 17th, 1857, the oldest surviving photograph taken by a Japanese.

IDA Kokichi (1846–1911) **(p. 192)** Born in Hakodate, Ida apprenticed to Tamoto Kenzo and helped him to photograph Hokkaido in 1871. He was the first to photograph in the northernmost Kuril Islands in 1878 and opened his own studio in Hakodate in 1884. In 1897 he became the first to open a studio on the remote island of Sakhalin, where he stayed until the start of the Russo-Japanese War in 1904.

JACKSON, William Henry (1843–1942) **(p. 260)** Famous American landscape photographer who visited and photographed in Japan in 1895.

JAPAN PHOTOGRAPHIC ASSOCIATION (1874–84) **(p. 141)** The legal vehicle which contained Raimund von Stillfried's and later Hermann Andersen's various business interests.

JAPAN PHOTOGRAPHIC CO. (p. 260) Listed in Yokohama 1895–6. Whether this was a studio or photographic supplies outlet is not clear. *See* J. Himen.

JOCELYN, William Nassau (1832–92) **(p. 38)** British amateur attached to Lord Elgin's 1857–9 diplomatic mission to China and Japan as assistant secretary and photographer. He photographed the Japanese commissioners at Edo in August 1858. Jocelyn's are the oldest surviving photographs of Edo and thought to be the earliest use of wet-plate collodion photography in Japan.

KAJIMA Seibei (1866–1924) **(p. 238)** Wealthy heir to the family saké business. He used his wealth to finance his passion for photography and promote photography's development in Japan, and was a founder member of the Photographic Society of Japan. He was a talented photographer who toured Japan and produced a massive portfolio of views and portraits. He was constantly experimenting with different techniques. He helped finance Ogawa Kazumasa's venture into photo-engraving and collotype printing. By 1894 he had the title of "King of Amateur Photographers." He opened a major studio and photographic store in Tokyo in 1895 called Genrokukan. He had been neglecting the family business, and when the new enterprise started accumulating large losses relations between him and his family broke down. In March 1896 he lost control of the saké business, was disinherited, and forced to leave his wife. Kajima continued his photo activities for a while before turning to a career as a performing musician. He seems to have died in poverty and obscurity.

KAMEI Koreaki (1861–96) **(p. 244)** Count Kamei was the son of a court noble and studied art and photography in Germany. When the 1894–5 Sino-Japanese War broke out, he organized at his own expense a private photographic unit to cover the conflict and took more than 300 photographs.

KAMEYA Teijiro (p. 128) Became the adopted son of Kameya Toyo in 1871 and was immediately involved in the Nagasaki studio there. Around 1880 he became manager of the branch studio in Korea.

KAMEYA Tokujiro (1825–84) **(p. 128)** Early important but unsung Nagasaki commercial photographer whose studio may even have predated Ueno Hikoma's. He taught at the Dutch medical school and in turn instructed Tomishige Rihei. He opened Kyoto's first studio in 1862. He returned to Nagasaki in 1868 and opened a studio. Subsequently, he opened branches in Vladivostok and Korea.

KAMEYA Toyo (1852–85) **(p. 128)** Assisted her father Tokujiro in the Nagasaki studio, thereby becoming one of Japan's first female photographers.

KANAMARU Genzo (1832–?) **(p. 192)** Early pioneer about whom little is known other than that his studio was in Tokyo and Tamamura Kozaburo was an apprentice until 1874. Kanamaru's work can occasionally be found in the smaller-sized accordion-style souvenir albums from the 1870s.

KAWAMOTO Komin (p. 35) Satsuma retainer ordered by Lord Shimazu to study photography in 1851. He published an instruction manual on the daguerreotype in 1854.

KERN, Edward Meyer (1823–63) **(p. 29)** An American employed from 1853 to 1860 as an artist, daguerreotypist, and taxidermist on Commodore Ringgold's North Pacific Exploring Expedition. He made several visits to Japan and possibly used his camera on Okinawa in November 1854. He is the likely photographer of the 1855 daguerreotype of Shimoda cemetery. He stayed at Yokohama between August 1859 and February 1860 but his activities are unknown. Kern had the knowledge, equipment, and opportunities to take photographs in Japan, but none have been discovered.

KERR, Lord Walter Talbot (1839–1927) **(p. 125)** English naval officer, aristocrat, and amateur photographer who photographed in Japan in the 1860s.

KILBURN, Benjamin West (1827–1909) **(p. 293)** American commercial photographer and stereoview publisher who issued a 1901 series on Japan labeled "Photographed and Published by B. W. Kilburn." However, there is no evidence Kilburn traveled to Japan. He also issued a 1905 series on the Russo-Japanese War, photographed from the Russian side of the conflict.

KITANIWA Tsukuba (1842–87) **(p. 195)** Considered to be in the first rank of Tokyo photographers in the 1870s. He was apprenticed to Yokoyama Matsusaburo in 1868 and then studied under Ukai Gyokusen and Shimooka Renjo. He opened his first studio in 1871 in Tokyo and a second in the same city shortly afterwards. At around this time he received lessons from Stillfried in fixing and lighting techniques. In 1874 he established *Datsuei yawa* (Tales of Photography), the first photographic magazine. In 1875, following the untimely death of Uchida Kuichi, he somehow acquired a major portion of the estate, including the late photographer's main residence. From there he operated a studio which he named Kyu Uchida-sha (former Uchida studio). He seems to have suspended all photographic activities in 1885.

KIZU Kokichi (1830–95) **(p. 126)** A Hakodate-based tailor who gave up his profession after being taught photography by the Russian Consul Goshkevich. He opened a studio in Hakodate in ca. 1864, becoming Hokkaido's first professional photographer.

KRAFFT, Hugues (1853–1935) **(p. 227)** Wealthy French tourist and amateur photographer who spent five months in Japan during an 1881–3 world tour and took back to France more than 250 dry-plate negatives. Until the recent discovery of the work by Guillemard, he is thought to have been the first to use dry plates in Japan in August 1882.

KREITMANN, Lieutenant Louis (p. 162) French military engineer and amateur photographer who traveled throughout Japan from October 1875 until May 1878 taking photographs. His personal album was recently donated to the Edo-Tokyo Historical Museum.

KUMAGAI Shin (p. 195) Commercial photographer who accompanied Matsuzaki Shinji on the 1874 expedition to Taiwan and was killed there by a stray bullet.

KUSAKABE Kimbei (1841–1932) **(p. 203)** Not much is known of Kusakabe's early life. He was born into a family of textile merchants but left home at eighteen to move to Yokohama to further his ambition of becoming an artist. At some time in the early 1860s he joined Beato as a photo-colorist. Soon he was a fully fledged assistant and accompanied Beato on a trip to Shanghai in 1867. In the 1870s he joined Stillfried but in what capacity is not known. He also seems at this time to be in business selling his own silk paintings. In 1880 he opened his own Yokohama studio and, like his great rival Tamamura, targeted the foreign community selling souvenir albums. By 1892 he was advertising a portfolio of some 2000 images and by 1901 his studio was the largest in Japan. Kusakabe retired in 1914 and spent his later years painting. He was an exceptional artist and photographer.

LASENBY LIBERTY, Emma (ca. 1845–1920) **(p. 227)** Amateur female photographer who, in 1889, spent four months traveling around Japan with her husband Arthur, the founder of Liberty's in Regent Street, London. She took over 1000 photographs.

LE BAS, Jules Apollinaire Felix (1834–75) **(p. 121)** French naval lieutenant and amateur on board the warship la Semiramis during the hostilities at Shimonoseki in 1864 between the Choshu clan and the Western powers. He was charged with making a pictorial record of the campaign.

LEWIS, Karl (1865–1942) **(p. 276)** American photographer who arrived in 1901 and set up his Yokohama studio the following year – at a time when picture postcards were taking off – and Lewis dealt in them as much as he did photographs. He advertised himself as "The only Western Photographer in Japan." In 1910 he started stocking Eastman cameras and supplies. His studio closed in 1917. His was the last Western commercial studio of the Meiji era.

LONDON, Jack (1876–1916) **(p. 288)** Celebrated American author who spent a short time as a war correspondent and photographed the 1904–5 Russo-Japanese War.

MAEDA Genzo (p. 41) Samurai of the Fukuokoa clan who studied photography under Pompe van Meerdervoort in Nagasaki. On instructions from Matsumoto Ryojun, he assisted Pierre Rossier in Nagasaki (probably in 1859) for one month and learnt much about wet-plate techniques. Subsequently, he was appointed photographic artist to the *daimyo* of Fukuoka.

MARUKI Riyo (1850–1923) **(p. 217)** One of Japan's finest portrait photographers whose Tokyo studio was sought out by Japanese and foreigners alike.

William Burton, in a June 1894 article, wrote that his portrait work was exceptional and that only Esaki and Suzuki (Shinichi II) could be considered as worthy competitors. Maruki opened his first studio in Tokyo in 1880. In 1915 he received his greatest honor when chosen, along with Ogawa Kazumasa, to photograph the Emperor Taisho. His business continued up until the early 1920s.

MATSUKI Koan (p. 35) (later changed name to Terashima Munenori) (1833–93) Satsuma retainer ordered by Lord Shimazu to study photography in 1851 and who later became a noted Japanese diplomat.

MATSUMOTO Ryojun (1832–1907) **(p. 36)** Employed as a supervisor in Pompe van Meerdervoort's medical school and acquired proficiency in photography. He became chief physician to the Shogun.

MATSUZAKI Shinji (p. 195) Operated a studio in Tokyo in the 1860s. In 1874 he traveled with a military expedition to Taiwan as official photographer. In 1875 he accompanied Meiji government officials as the official photographer to the Ogasawara Islands. In 1886 Matsuzaki published the first Japanese manual on studio portrait photography, *Shashin Hitsuyo Shakyaku no Kokoroe*.

McLELLEN, J. W. (p. 292) Unknown photographer who had a photograph of a Japanese shrine published in a 1904 edition of *The Graphic*.

METCALF, William H. (1821–92) **(p. 158)** American amateur photographer who spent six months in Japan in 1877 and produced an attractive series of twenty-six stereoviews entitled "A Summer in Japan."

MEYER, Baron Adolf de (1868–1949) **(p. 260)** Famous American pictorialist photographer, said to be the founder of fashion photography and referred to as the "Debussy of Photography." He took pictures in Japan in 1899 whilst on honeymoon with his wife.

MILLER, Milton (p. 112) Important and highly talented American photographer based in Hong Kong who photographed a series of Japanese stereoviews for E. & H. Anthony in the early 1860s. He also photographed at Hong Kong members of the 1862 Japanese Mission to Europe.

MILNE, John (1850–1913) **(p. 256)** Famous English seismologist and Professor of Geology and Mining at the Imperial College of Engineering in Tokyo 1876–95. A keen amateur photographer, Milne took many photographs, including some early images of the Ainu.

MITTMER, R. J. H. (p. 292) Unknown photographer who had a photograph of Japanese laborers published in a 1904 edition of *The Graphic*.

MIYASHITA Kin (p. 192) Nagoya's best-known early photographer. He studied photography under Yokoyama Matsusaburo in Tokyo. Miyashita's studio opened some time in the 1870s and was still in operation in 1912. Miyashita is known for photographing the aftermath of the 1891 Gifu earthquake.

MIZUNO Hanbei (p. 217) Invented gold- and silver-lacquered photographs and introduced them to the market in 1890. He initially operated a studio in the 1880s in Shizuoka but then moved to Yokohama and opened there in around 1890. An 1892 advertisement gives the studio name as Fukusuisha.

MORITA Reizo (1830–89) **(p. 128)** Opened a studio in Kobe in 1869. Japanese scholars disagree on whether he assisted Uchida Kuichi in Osaka in 1865.

MOSER, Michael (1853–1912) **(p. 150)** An Austrian who came to Japan in 1869 with the Austria-Hungary trade and diplomatic mission as a teenage assistant to Wilhelm Burger. He stayed on in Japan and joined the *The Far East* magazine as staff photographer in 1870. He traveled throughout Japan with two assistants, photographing wherever he went. In 1873 he left the magazine to travel to his homeland as the interpreter to the Japanese delegation to the 1873 International Exhibition in Vienna. Moser returned to Japan and was employed as a "photographer in Government service." He left Japan in 1876 as the interpreter to the Japanese delegation to the Centennial Exhibition in Philadelphia. There

he became ill and decided to return to Austria where he recovered and opened his own studio.

MUSUMI T. (p. 295) Kobe-based photographic dealer in composite souvenir albums (1906–8).

NAKAHAMA Manjiro (1827–98) **(p. 129)** Famous Japanese castaway who was shipwrecked in 1841 and taken to America. He returned to Japan in 1851 after many adventures. Manjiro accompanied the 1860 Japanese Embassy to America and brought back a daguerreotype camera and mastered daguerreotype photography by October 1860 at the latest. He temporarily opened a commercial studio in Edo some time between 1860 and 1862 before selling the business to a friend. More research is required to establish whether his studio predated Ukai Gyokusen's. His contribution as a pioneer should also be studied.

NAKAJIMA Matsuchi (1851–1938) **(p. 182)** Nakajima had a very high reputation during the 1880s and 1890s, and in 1889 was one of the founding members of the Nihon Shashin Kyokai (Photographic Society of Japan). He was particularly famous for his lantern slides which were exquisitely hand colored by his wife Sonoko, a very talented artist.

NARUI Raisuke (1858–1902) **(p. 217)** An exceptionally fine and successful Kyoto-based portrait photographer who was patronised by the town's top geisha, *maiko, kabuki* actors and socialites during the 1880s and 1890s.

NIVEN, Reverend G. C. (p. 292) British missionary and amateur photographer based in Gifu. His photograph of Mount Asama was published by the *The Illustrated London News* in 1907.

NORWEGIAN (The) (p. 36) Claimed to have photographed around the Nagasaki region in the summer of 1857 before it was legally permissible to do so. His story, outlined in *The Photographic News*, October 1859–February 1860, is likely a hoax.

OGAWA Kazumasa (1860–1929) **(p. 210)** Pivotal figure in early Japanese photography. He adapted cutting-edge Western technology in photo-printing processes to produce numerous half-tone and collotype publications which transformed the market which had previously concentrated on the more expensive souvenir albums. Ogawa's publications were also instrumental in introducing Japanese art and culture to a mass international audience. He built one of the most successful photographic businesses in late Meiji Japan. He opened a portrait studio in Tomioka, Gumma Prefecture, in 1877.

OGAWA Sashichi (?–1909) **(p. 241)** Yokohama photographer not apparently related to Ogawa Kazumasa. He married Kusakabe Kimbei's daughter and received much support from his father-in-law. He started off as an agent for Kajima Seibei's work. It is possible to find Kajima and Kusakabe's work in Ogawa's souvenir albums. The main competitors were Tamamura and Enami. He was active also in lantern slides and gold- and silver-lacquer photography. He started a studio in 1895. After his early death in 1909, the studio continued in his name, although under new ownership, until at least 1920.

OKAMOTO Rokuhei (p. 245) Commercial photographer and dealer who played an important role in distributing composite souvenir albums to Western audiences in the late Meiji era from his Tokyo studio. He was the sole agent for Kajima Seibei's work in 1894 and continued to distribute his work for a number of years even after Kajima had granted agencies to other studios. By 1901 he was proprietor of a Tokyo studio named Genroku-kwan which is remarkably similar to Kajima's Genrokukan. It is possible that Okamoto acquired a number of Kajima's negatives when the latter's business folded. The studio continued until at least 1913.

ONO Benkichi (1801–70) **(p. 126)** Amateur and scientific writer who studied Western medicine, science, and weaponry. He was an early experimenter with photography in the 1850s. Ongoing research into his life may reveal a significant contribution to the field and precipitate a reassessment of his work.

PARANT, C. (p. 160) French photographer who was almost certainly the operator of E. Parant & Co., the earliest known Western studio in Kobe which opened for just a few weeks in 1870. After closing the studio he joined Auguste Gordes in nearby Osaka, but by May 1871 had left and set up a rival studio in the same city. This was not successful and Parant moved on and worked with Stillfried for a year or so.

PARKER, Charles (p. 102) British photographer who moved to Yokohama from Hong Kong around May 1863 and opened a studio which lasted until the end of 1865. His first studio advertisement in July 1863 offered "Panoramas of the Settlement of Yokohama and the neighbourhood. Views showing the Cemetery, Hatoba and Main Street." By May 1864 he had taken on William Parke Andrew as a partner in C. Parker & Co. and this partnership lasted until July 1865. In November 1865 Parker Crane & Co. was formed when William Crane was taken on, but that partnership was also short-lived, as by the beginning of 1866 Parker had disappeared from the scene.

PARKER, CRANE & Co. (p. 104) Yokohama-based studio which operated for just a few weeks in 1865. The partners were Charles Parker and William Crane.

PEARSON, Hugo Lewis (1843–1912) (p. 125) English naval officer and amateur who photographed in 1860s Japan.

POMPE VAN MEERDERVOORT, Jonkheer, J. L. C. (1829–1908) (p. 36) Successor to Jan Karel Van den Broek as Dutch physician at Deshima from 1857 to 1862. His photography lessons were more successful than Van den Broek's and by December 1859 Pompe was able to take photographs, albeit with some difficulty. He taught Maeda Genzo, amongst others.

PONTING, Herbert George (1870–1935) (p. 265) English commercial photographer, author, and inventor famous for stunning large-format photographs of the ill-fated 1910 Antarctic Expedition and also of Mount Fuji. Ponting was also one of the world's finest stereo-photographers. He took up photography seriously in 1900 and almost immediately won a number of competition prizes. His career progression was meteoric and in 1902 he was photographing Japan and the Far East on behalf of the American journal *Leslie's Weekly* and the stereoview publishing company Universal Photo Art Co. Many similar assignments followed over the next ten years and he made five visits to Japan from 1901 to 1906.

POOLE, Otis Augustus (1840–1904) (p. 273) American tea trader who moved to Yokohama in 1888. He was an an amateur photographer who inspired his son Otis Manchester to take up the art. Both father and son had a number of their photographs published.

POOLE, Otis Manchester (1880–1978) (p. 271) American amateur photographer who moved to Yokohama with his family in 1888 and remained in Japan until 1925. In 1895 he joined the Yokohama office of the British merchant house of Dodwell, Carlill & Co. He stayed with the firm until his retirement in 1948. Poole was a talented photographer, a skill he learned from his father, Otis Augustus. Several writers, including Walter Weston and Burton Holmes, used Poole's photographs (and also his father's) in their books and articles. His negatives were lost in the 1923 earthquake.

RAU, William Herman (1855–1920) (p. 290) Well-known Philadelphia photographer whose stereographs, lantern slides, and larger-format photographs are in many museum collections and photographic archives. Despite the fact that some published photographs of Japan carry his credit, there is no evidence he ever visited the country.

RIBAUD, Michel M. (p. 260) French missionary and amateur photographer who photographed the Ainu and Hokkaido in 1892.

RICALTON, James (1844–1929) (p. 279) American commercial photographer, war correspondent, travel writer, photo-journalist, naturalist, and school-teacher who used his various cameras in most countries around the world. Between 1879 and 1914 he traveled over 500,000 miles (800,000 km) and took 100,000 photographs and 30 miles (48 km)

of motion picture film. "... the greatest traveller the world has ever known, living or dead, and the most daring photographer." Ricalton's first visit to Japan was either late 1888 or early 1889. He was one of the key photographers in the 1904–5 Russo-Japanese War and was later decorated by the Japanese imperial government for his bravery on the battlefield. Ricalton took arguably the most famous picture of the war – the actual flight of a mortar being fired from a siege-gun.

ROSE, George (1861–1942) (p. 292) Australian commercial stereo-photographer who photographed Japan in 1904 and published a series of fine stereo-views.

ROSSIER, Pierre Joseph (1829–?) (p. 41) A major figure in Japanese photo-history, Rossier was a Swiss commercial photographer employed by the London photographic firm Negretti and Zambra to secure stereoviews in the Far East. He arrived in Japan in June 1859, taking the first large-format commercial photographs of the country, the first of which was published in May 1860. In October 1860 he did the first large-format landscape photography in Japan, taking a panorama of Nagasaki Harbor. He visited Japan several times during 1859–61 and secured around seventy photographs in all. Some time between 1859 and 1860 he taught wet-plate photography at Nagasaki to Ueno Hikoma, Horie Kuwajiro, Maeda Genzo, and others.

RYOUN-DO (p. 295) Kobe-based photographic studio positioned close to the famous Nunobiki waterfall (1906–8). It is likely to have been a photographic dealership which issued composite rather than studio souvenir albums.

SACHTLER, August (p. 126) Singapore commercial photographer who operated in the colony during the 1860s. He photographed in Japan in 1860 on behalf of the Prussian Mission.

SANDWITH, Lieutenant John Henry (1846–95) (p. 161) British amateur photographer stationed at Yokohama with the Royal Marines in the early 1870s. He published an account of an 1871 trip to the Hakone Mountains and illustrated it with his photographs.

SAUNDERS, William Thomas (1832–92) (p. 98) Very fine British photographer based in Shanghai who photographed in Japan between August and November 1862 and on several subsequent occasions. In 1862 he was able to secure views in Edo, thanks to US Minister Pruyn, and a six-plate panorama of Yokohama. He appears in 1863 to have been the first photographer in East Asia to advertise hand-colored photographs. He took views of Kobe and Osaka in 1868 and studio portraits in Kobe in 1871.

SCHLEESSELMANN, A. (p. 159) Photographer who operated a short-lived portrait studio in Yokohama in 1878.

SETSU Shinichi (1844–1909) (p. 129) Opened a studio in Nagasaki in 1869 after a six months' apprenticeship with Shimizu Tokuku in Yokohama. His studio continued until at least 1903.

SHIMA Kakoku (1827–70) (p. 129) Itinerant artist who married Ryu (1823–1900), also an artist, in 1855. It is not clear how or when the couple learnt photography but an 1864 wet-plate portrait of Shima taken by Ryu exists – the earliest known photograph taken by a Japanese woman. The couple may have operated a studio in Edo from around 1865 to 1867. When Shima died in 1870, Ryu returned to her native town of Kiryu and opened her own photo studio.

SHIMA Shukichi (1850–1917) (p. 195) Established a studio in Miyanoshita in 1878 in the same year as the famous Fujiya Hotel opened its doors. The studio was a short walk from the hotel and both are still in existence today.

SHIMAZU Nariakira (1809–58) (p. 24) Powerful Satsuma *daimyo* who purchased daguerreotype equipment in 1849 and started experiments. In 1851 he ordered his retainers Kawamoto Komin, Matsuki Koan, Ichiki Shiro, and Ujuku Hikoemon to study and learn the art of photography at the Satsuma mansion in Edo (Tokyo).

SHIMIZU Tokoku (1841–1907) (p. 192) Shimazu opened his first studio in 1868 in Yokohama but then moved to Tokyo in 1872. During the first decade of the Meiji era, Shimizu was considered one of the very best portrait photographers in Japan. The rich and famous flocked to his Tokyo studio.

SHIMOOKA Renjo (1823–1914) (p. 69) Born into a samurai family in Shimoda. Whilst studying to become an artist, he discovered photography and later became Japan's most famous photographer. He moved to Yokohama in 1859 or 1860 and there met John Wilson. He purchased Wilson's camera and equipment in 1861. Supplementary lessons were received from Samuel and Julia Brown, and possibly others. Shimooka himself taught Yokoyama Matsusaburo, Usui Shusaburo, Esaki Reiji, and Suzuki Shinichi I and II, amongst others. He established his first studio in Yokohama in 1862. Diversification into other businesses was not successful. He retired from active photography in the 1870s and devoted more time to his first love of painting.

SHIN-E-DO (p. 295) Photographic studio based in Kobe from ca. 1894 to 1901, which dealt in composite souvenir albums.

SIMMONS, Duane B. (ca. 1832–89) (p. 54) American medical missionary who arrived in Japan with Samuel R. Brown in November 1859. He had responsibility for the camera equipment provided by the Dutch Reform Church and may therefore have been an amateur enthusiast. A photographic room was built at his residence – a temple in Kanagawa – and this was functioning by May 1860 at the latest.

STILLFRIED AND ANDERSEN (1875–84) (p. 139) The partnership name for Raimund von Stillfried and Hermann Andersen which was still used after the former left in 1878.

STILLFRIED & CO. (1871–3) (p. 134) Raimund von Stillfried's first studio name.

STILLFRIED-RATENICZ, Baron Franz von (1837–1916) (p. 154) Elder brother to Raimund (see below), he established a Yokohama studio in 1879, trading as Baron Stillfried. The name caused great confusion with residents and visitors. Franz probably bought the Stillfried and Andersen business in 1883 or 1884 before selling it to Adolfo Farsari.

STILLFRIED-RATENICZ, Baron Raimund von (1839–1911) (p. 133) Austrian aristocrat, painter, entrepreneur, world traveler, soldier, and diplomat, and a colorful and major Western figure in Japanese photo-history. He opened a Yokohama studio in August 1871, trading as Messrs. Stillfried & Co. By the beginning of 1876 Stillfried and Andersen was formed. In January 1877 Felix Beato's business was purchased. An acrimonious dissolution of the partnership took place in June 1878.

STODDARD, John Lawson (1850–1931) (p. 257) American traveler, public lecturer, stereo-photographer, and author who visited most countries throughout the world and whose career as a travel lecturer, where he used lantern slides to illustrate his journeys, spanned the years 1879–97. Stoddard made the first of several visits to Japan in 1892.

STROHMEYER, Henry (p. 246) Fine American stereo-photographer and stereoview publisher who visited Japan in the spring of 1896 and took around 200–300 negatives. A selection of seventy-two was published by Strohmeyer & Wyman as a boxed set but distributed by Underwood & Underwood.

SUDZUKI Toocoku (p. 217) His Yokohama portrait studio was advertised in 1880 and continued until 1906.

SUGAWARA C. (p. 217) Known from an 1885 advertisement in the *Japan Directory* which listed his portrait studio in Usui Shusaburo's vacated Yokohama premises at Otemachi. Apparently he was unsuccessful because Usui reoccupied the studio the following year.

SUTTON, Frederick William (1832–83) (p. 106) Talented British amateur photographer and naval engineer who photographed in Okinawa, Kyushu, and Shikoku in 1866. He photographed the Shogun at Osaka in 1867 and the same year secured what appear to be the first published photographs of the Ainu. In 1868, just hours before his execution, Sutton photographed Saegusa Shigeru who had failed in his attempt to assassinate the British Minister Sir Harry Parkes.

SUZUKI Shinichi I (1835–1919) **(p. 165)** Apprenticed to Shimooka Renjo in 1866 before opening his own Yokohama studio in 1873. Suzuki operated a portrait studio and also sold souvenir albums. He pioneered a technique for printing photographs onto porcelain. In 1872–3 Suzuki was commissioned by J. R. Black to produce a fine series of genre scenes which authentically documented the life and customs of rural communities. Suzuki retired in 1892 and his son Izaburo took over the studio.

SUZUKI Shinichi II (1855–1912) **(p. 172)** In 1870 he became an apprentice to Shimooka Renjo and was with him for seven years. There he met fellow apprentice Suzuki Shinichi I who later became his father-in-law. In 1876 he left Shimooka and opened his first studio in Nagoya. In order to improve his technique, he decided to study in America and left Japan in 1879. In 1888 Suzuki was able to photograph the Emperor and Empress. At the height of his fame, he lost everything in a shipping business speculation.

TAKAGI Teijiro (p. 294) Kobe-based photographer who was a prolific producer of hand-colored lantern slides and collotype albums in the late Meiji era and beyond. He was the manager of Tamamura Kozaburo's Kobe branch in 1903, and the owner the following year. He continued to trade under the Tamamura name until 1914 and then switched to T. Takagi. The studio continued until at least 1929. Although Takagi operated as Tamamura's agent for a number of years, the studio's output was increasingly dominated by Takagi's own fine work. He produced over twenty-five different titles of hand-colored collotype photo books of Japanese life and customs. Takagi was also a major rival of Enami's in the manufacture of hand-colored lantern slides.

TAKEBAYASHI Seiichi (1842–1908) **(p. 195)** He apparently opened a studio in Hakodate in 1871, which almost immediately was destroyed by fire. In 1872 he acted as Stillfried's assistant for some fifty days when the Austrian was photographing in Hokkaido. He opened a studio in Sapporo in 1876, but shifted the main focus of his activities to Tokyo where he set up his main studio in Kojimachi in November 1884.

TAMAMURA Kozaburo (1856–19?) **(p. 198)** In 1867 he began a seven-year apprenticeship with the Edo photographer Kanamaru Genzo. He then left in 1874 to establish own studio, also in Tokyo, and then moved his operations to Yokohama in 1883. In 1896 he was at the peak of his fame when he received an order from the Boston publishing house J. B. Millet for more than one million photographs. He also received other lucrative commissions, including international orders for educational lantern slides. His work won many domestic and international awards. Tamamura's photographic enterprise was a huge commercial success.

TAMATO Kenzo (1832–1912) **(p. 126)** Studied Western sciences at Nagasaki from the age of twenty-three and in 1859 moved to Hakodate. There he assisted Dr Zalesky, a Russian amateur photographer, who worked at the consulate. Tamato became increasingly interested in photography and in 1866 collaborated with Kizu Kokichi in photographing the construction of Fukuyama Castle. He opened his own studio in Hakodate some time between 1867 and 1869 and is particularly famous for documenting, in 1871, the rapid development of Hokkaido as a settlement area.

TAMEMASA Torazo (1871–?) **(p. 245)** Successful dealer in composite souvenir albums and general fancy goods. He also ran a portrait studio. The main business operated in Nagasaki from the early 1890s and a branch was opened in Kobe from ca. 1899. His business was in operation until at least 1913.

TERASHIMA Munenori *See Matsuki Koan.*

TOKYO GENROKUKAN (p. 241) Short-lived Kyoto photo studio run by Kajima Seibei in ca. 1896.

TOKYO PHOTOGRAPHIC CO. (THE) (p. 319) Tokyo-based photographic supplies retailer which advertised in 1900.

TOMISHIGE Rihei (1837–1922) **(p. 84)** Major figure in Kyushu photo-history and one of the pioneers in Japan of the wet-plate process. His landscape work is of the highest quality. He was apprenticed in 1862 to the Nagasaki photographer Kameya Tokujiro and later continued his studies under Ueno Hikoma with whom he developed a life-long friendship. He opened his own studio in 1866 in his home town of Yanagawa but it was not successful. During the years 1868 and 1869 he again apprenticed to Kameya and in 1870 or 1871 opened a studio in Kumamoto where he received a military commission to photograph the castle. Both studio and castle were destroyed in the 1877 Satsuma Rebellion. His studio was rebuilt and continues to this day.

UCHIDA Kuichi (ca. 1844–75) **(p. 76)** Japan's greatest landscape photographer. He was taught by Pompe van Meerdervoort at the Dutch Medical School at Nagasaki. He then set up a successful photographic equipment import business in 1863 before moving to Kobe in 1865 where he opened a studio with Ueno Sachima, a younger brother of Ueno Hikoma. The same year he opened a studio in Osaka. Uchida opened in Yokohama in 1868 with a Tokyo branch the following year. His reputation was sealed when he was asked to photograph the Royal Family in 1872. That same year he accompanied the Emperor on visits to central Japan and Kyushu as official photographer. He died suddenly aged thirty-two just as his international reputation was growing.

UENO Hikoma (1838–1904) **(p. 73)** Famous early pioneer who operated one of the first and most successful studios in Japan. He was taught by Pompe van Meerdervoort at the Dutch Medical School in Nagasaki from around 1858. His progress accelerated when Pierre Rossier showed a number of the school's students the practicalities of the wet-plate process in 1859 or 1860. In 1860 Ueno and fellow student Horie Kuwajiro were provided with money by Lord Todo of the Tsu domain to purchase a camera and continue experiments at the *daimyo*'s estate in Edo. There he co-wrote *Shamitsu-kyoku hikkei* (Manual of Chemistry) with Horie in 1862. Returning the same year to Nagasaki, he decided to open his own photographic studio. Gradually the studio's fame grew and for the next forty years his business prospered.

UJUKU Hikoemon (p. 35) Satsuma retainer ordered by Lord Shimazu to study photography in 1851. With Ichiki Shiro he took a daguerreotype of Lord Shimazu on September 17th, 1857, the oldest surviving photograph taken by a Japanese.

UKAI Gyokusen (1807–87) **(p. 60)** Japan's first professional photographer who opened an ambrotype portrait studio in Edo in 1860 or 1861 – earlier than Shimooka Renjo or Ueno Hikoma. His equipment and lessons were purchased from Orrin Freeman. Four years before his death, Ukai buried several hundred glass negatives in the Yanaka Cemetery, Tokyo, beneath a monument. His studio was initially very successful and he photographed over 200 members of the aristocracy. He closed it in 1867.

USUI Shusaburo (p. 174) Major photographer who operated a successful studio in Yokohama from the late 1860s until 1889 aimed specifically at foreign residents and visitors. He discounted prices aggressively but managed to maintain high artistic standards. Usui also had a studio in Tokyo, and in 1879 was able to photograph Ulysses S. Grant. In July 1882 Usui may have became the first Japanese to successfully take a dry-plate photograph whilst he and his brother escorted Francis Guillemard on two photographic tours of the country. In 1885 Usui opened another studio called the Yokohama Photographic Co. but this was discontinued the following year. Usui continued to advertise until 1889, after which he disappeared from the scene.

VAUGHAN, John Alfred (p. 259) British naval officer and amateur photographer who photographed the arrival in Korea of the Japanese Army during the 1894–5 Sino-Japanese War.

VROMAN, Adam Clark (1856–1916) **(p. 291)** Renowned American photographer of the American Southwest frontier who toured Japan in 1903 and 1909 photographing and collecting Japanese art.

WEED, Charles Leander (1824–1903) **(p. 115)** Now recognized as one of the finest American landscape photographers of the nineteenth century. He visited Japan in 1867–8 and took a series of stereoviews and large-format photographs. He is almost certainly the first to take mammoth-plate photographs in Japan.

WELSH, David (p. 156) A peripatetic Britisher who settled in Japan in around 1870 and worked with at least three different photo studios before setting up his own studio in 1890. The studio was short-lived and closed by 1892 at the latest, but for that period Welsh was probably running the only owner-managed foreign studio in Japan.

WESTON, Walter (1861–1940) **(p. 256)** English missionary, alpinist, and amateur photographer known as the "Father of Japanese Mountaineering," who had three periods of residency in Japan, the first being in 1888. Weston took some of the finest photographs of alpine Japan and published a selection in his *Mountaineering and Exploration in the Japanese Alps* (1896).

WILLMANN, William (p. 158) In 1871 the Austrian Willmann joined the newly formed Stillfried & Co. as an assistant. Some time in 1873–4 he briefly set up his own Yokohama studio, W. Willmann's Photographic Establishment. It is doubtful the studio was a success as he left Japan in 1875.

WILSON, John (ca. 1816–?) **(p. 62)** American photographer who took early photographs in Edo (1860) in his capacity as photographer to the Prussian Embassy to Japan. He probably photographed the body of the unfortunate Henry Heusken who was assassinated in January 1861. He sold his photo equipment to Shimooka Renjo the same year. Together with other artists, Shimooka Renjo was commissioned to produce a giant scroll containing paintings of Wilson's photographs. Wilson was unsuccessful in selling this in America and Europe.

WOODS, Sir Henry F. (1842–1929) **(p. 125)** English naval officer and amateur who borrowed a camera from Beato to take photographs in Edo in 1865 whilst accompanying the British Minister Sir Harry Parkes.

WOOLLETT, H. (p. 162) Photographic assistant to Felix Beato (1871–7). He accompanied Beato to Korea in 1871. Later he managed Beato's establishment.

WRIGHT, Frank Lloyd (1867–1959) **(p. 290)** Famous American architect who designed Tokyo's Imperial Hotel. Wright was proficient in photography and used his camera as an aid to his work. He arrived in Japan as a tourist in 1905 and took photographs of the Kyoto and Kobe areas.

YAMABE Zenjiro (p. 244) Successful Yokohama studio which operated 1898–1913 offering a wide range of services and goods. A particular speciality was the production of "photographic paintings." It is not known whether Yamabe created his own portfolio of souvenir photographs or acted as a dealer and distributor for other studios.

YAMAMOTO (p. 186) Almost nothing is known about this Yokohama studio which was a prolific producer of souvenir albums in the 1870s. Most of Yamamoto's work is centered on striking studio shots of beautiful geisha or of artisans practicing their trades. His studio must have suddenly ceased trading for some reason since his work subsequently appears amongst the 1880s portfolios of other photographers such as Tamamura Kozaburo and Kusakabe Kimbei.

YOKOHAMA PHOTOGRAPHIC ART STUDIO (THE) (p. 319) Known only from a ca. 1910 postcard which illustrates the store in Motomachi-Dori, Yokohama.

YOKOHAMA PHOTOGRAPHIC CO. (p. 156) Usui Shusaburo's trading company name from 1885–6.

YOKOHAMA PHOTOGRAPHIC CO. (THE) (p. 319)
This company appears in the 1892 *Japan Directory* at No. 80 – Baron Franz Stillfried's old haunt. Presumably it is not to be confused with Usui's company – the Yokohama Photographic Company. There is no indication as to who the operator/owner is and it disappears after this listing.

YOKOYAMA Matsusaburo (1838–84) **(p. 82)**
Major Japanese photographer whose early interest

was in painting but who became intrigued by daguerreotype work performed in his home town of Hakodate by Eliphalet Brown in 1854, followed shortly by the Russian Mozhaiskii. He opened his first studio in 1868 in either Tokyo or Yokohama. He photographed Edo Castle in 1871 and Japanese art works for the Vienna Exposition in 1873. He became Japan's first serious stereo-photographer.

YOSHIO Keisai (1822–94) **(p. 36)** Student of

Western medicine at Nagasaki where he was taught photography in 1856 by Jan Karel Van den Broek. He encouraged his nephew, Uchida Kuichi, to study photography.

ZALESKY, Dr (p. 118) Russian naval medical officer and amateur photographer attached to the consulate in Hakodate from 1859. He taught photography to his assistant Tamato Kenzo. He seems to have left Japan in 1865.

ACKNOWLEDGMENTS

Writing any book on photography puts the author in the unenviable position of needing to secure a sufficient number of representative and interesting illustrations, more so if his subject deals with rare, if not unique, images. I am therefore deeply grateful to those individuals who have generously allowed me to reproduce photographs from their collections or in other ways helped to make images available. In this respect, I would like to especially thank Clare Agate, John Benjafield, Robert Blum, Gerard Bourgarel, Torin Boyd, Mr and Mrs J. Brooke-Smith, Bill Burgess, Dr Joseph Dubois, Sylvie Henguely, Itoh Isako, Izakura Naomi, Ken Jacobson, Serge Kakou, Robert Kirshenbaum, Koyama Noburu, Carolyn Longworth, Dr Herman Moeshart, Alfred Moser, Fred Notehelfer, Rob Oechsle, Ozawa Takesi, Dr Peter Pantzer, Jillian and Richard A. Poole, Tony Poole, Elena Dal Pra, Hanc de Roo, Saito Takio, Hans Schreiber, Fred Sharf, Shimazu Kimiyasu, Charles A. L. Swenson, Takahashi Norihide, Ueno Ichiro, Clark Worswick, Madeline Yale, and Yano Hiroshi. The other illustrations have been obtained from the institutions named elsewhere, and from my own collection.

For information and advice, I would also like to thank Clark Worswick, whose pioneering work on Asian photo-history has always been an inspiration to me; Joseph Dubois has done more than anybody to advance the identification process of Japanese photo studios, and I was able to gain much information from our discussions and from his vast collection of souvenir albums; Rob Oechsle's encyclopedic knowledge of Japanese stereoviews is unequaled, and his decision to include the results of thirty years of study in the form of the landmark stereo index provided in my book, *Old Japanese Photographs: Collectors' Data Guide* (2006), will, I am sure, be appreciated by many photo-historians and collectors; Torin Boyd, Brian Burke-Gaffney, Claude Estebe, Himeno Junichi, and Izakura Naomi, all went out of their way to provide help in searching for difficult-to-find pieces of data. Other help was provided by Lambert Van Der Aalsvoort, George Baxley, John Benjafield,

Charles Blackburn, Robert Blum, Gerard Bourgarel, Bill Burgess, Alex Byrne, William Collyer, Hugh Cortazzi, Philippe Dallais, Lane Earns, Luke Gartlan, Jim Hoare, Sylvie Henguely, Ken Jacobson, Steven Joseph, Serge Kakou, Gerard Levy, Herman Moeshart, Alfred Moser, Morishige Kazuo, Koyama Noburu, Fred Notehelfer, Christian Polak, Elena Dal Pra, Saito Takio, Fred Sharf, Charles A. L. Swenson, Uchida Shin, Ueno Ichiro, and Eric Bos Waaldijk.

Although an extensive bibliography is provided on pages 311–14 above, there were some books and writings published within the last few years to which I found myself constantly referring. Of these, I would single out T. Boyd and N. Izakura's *Portraits in Sepia* (2000), John Clark's *Japanese Exchanges in Art 1850s–1930s* (2001), Luke Gartlan's "A Chronology of Baron Raimund von Stillfried-Ratenicz" (2001), Himeno Junichi's "Encounters with Foreign Photographers" (2003), Ozawa Takesi's *Bakumatsu Shashin no Jidai* (1994), Saito Takio's *Bakumatsu Meiji: Yokohama Shashinkan Monogatari* (2004), and Anne Wilkes Tucker et al.'s *The History of Japanese Photography* (2003).

The *Japan Directories* from 1861 to 1912, and especially the 1996–7 reprint edited by Saito Takio (*Bakumatsu, Meiji Zainichi Gaikokujin Kikan Meikan*), were indispensable, as were the contemporary *China Directories*. The scattered, remaining copies of the early English-language newspapers of Japan, China, and Hong Kong also provided vital information. Aside from my visits to many archives in Japan, the United States and Europe, it is worth mentioning that the exponential growth of readily available genealogical data on the Internet (including old newspapers, periodicals, and directories) has proved to be of immense value, especially when attempting to track down information on Western photographers.

Lastly, I would like to thank my wife Kishiko and my daughters Emma, Sarah, and Carla for their understanding and support during a project which I optimistically promised would take a few months but which actually took three years.